Evreinov
The Theatre of
Paradox and Transformation

Theater and Dramatic Studies, No. 19

Bernard Beckerman, Series Editor
Brander Matthews Professor of Dramatic Literature
Columbia University in the City of New York

Other Titles in This Series

No. 14	*Stanislavski's Encounter with Shakespeare: The Evolution of a Method*	Joyce Vining Morgan
No. 15	*The Art of the Actor-Manager: Wilson Barrett and the Victorian Theatre*	James Thomas
No. 16	*Male-Female Comedy Teams in American Vaudeville, 1865–1932*	Shirley Staples
No. 17	*Distance in the Theatre: The Aesthetics of Audience Response*	Daphna Ben Chaim
No. 18	*French Theatre Experiment Since 1968*	Lenora Champagne
No. 20	*William Poel's Hamlets: The Director as Critic*	Rinda F. Lundstrom
No. 21	*Gertrude Stein's Theatre of the Absolute*	Betsy Alayne Ryan
No. 22	*Boulevard Theater and Revolution in Eighteenth-Century Paris*	Michèle Root-Bernstein
No. 23	*A Critical Examination of Theatrical Designs of Charles Ricketts*	Eric Binnie
No. 24	*Theatre in Revolt: Revolutionary Aesthetics in the American Theatre*	Ira Levine

1. Portrait of N. N. Evreinov by Grigorij Šil'tjan (c. 1932). Reprinted by permission from Christopher Collins, trans. and ed., *Life as Theater: Five Modern Plays by Nikolai Evreinov* (Ann Arbor: Ardis, 1973)

Evreinov
The Theatre of Paradox and Transformation

by
Spencer Golub

UMI RESEARCH PRESS
Ann Arbor, Michigan

Copyright © 1984, 1977
Spencer Golub
All rights reserved

Produced and distributed by
UMI Research Press
an imprint of
University Microfilms International
Ann Arbor, Michigan 48106

Library of Congress Cataloging in Publication Data

Golub, Spencer.
  Evreinov: the theatre of paradox and transformation.

  (Theater and dramatic studies ; no. 19)
  Revision of thesis (Ph.D.)–University of Kansas, 1977.
  Bibliography: p.
  Includes index.
  1. Evreinov, N. N. (Nikolaĭ Nikolaevich), 1879-1953.
2. Theater–Soviet Union–20th century–History. I. Title.
II. Series.

PN2728.E8G6 1984   891.72'3   84-80
ISBN 0-8357-1540-X

For my parents

Contents

List of Illustrations   *xi*

Preface   *xvii*

1 Introduction: Harlequinade   *1*
   St. Petersburg between the Revolutions
   Evreinov's Commedia of the Soul

2 The Original and the Portraitists   *17*
   The Original
   The Portraitists

3 Monodrama   *35*
   Prototypes
   "Death dances..."

4 The Theatre in Life   *53*
   Theatricality
   Theatre as Crime and Punishment
   The Chief Thing

5 The Ancient Theatre   *107*
   The Medieval Cycle
   The Reconstructive Method
   The Spanish Cycle
   The Legacy of the Past

6 The Crooked Mirror Theatre   *145*
   The Theatre of Small Forms
   The Reformed Crooked Mirror

Evreinov on Wit and Humor
The Waning Years
Mozart and Salieri, Again

7 The Storming of the Winter Palace and After   *191*

8 Conclusion: Evreinov at the Vanishing Point   *209*

Appendix A: Theatres of Pre-Revolutionary St. Petersburg   *221*

Appendix B: Cast Lists of Productions at the Ancient Theatre   *223*

Appendix C: Premieres at the Crooked Mirror Theatre 1910–1917
 (During Evreinov's Tenure as Artistic Director)   *227*

Appendix D: Productions Staged by N. N. Evreinov at the
 Crooked Mirror Theatre   *237*

Notes   *241*

Bibliography   *275*

Index   *299*

List of Illustrations

1. Portrait of N. N. Evreinov by Grigorij Šil'tjan (c. 1932). Reprinted by permission from Christopher Collins, trans. and ed., *Life as Theater: Five Modern Plays by Nikolai Evreinov* (Ann Arbor: Ardis, 1973)   *iv*

2. Portrait of Evreinov by Salevij Sorin (1913)   *78*

3. *The Chief Thing* translated into various languages, overseen by Evreinov-Harlequin   *79*

4. Portrait of Evreinov by Prince A. K. Šervadšidze   *80*

5. Baron Nikolaj V. Driezen   *81*

6. A. N. Benois: The act curtain at the Ancient Theatre   *82*

7. N. K. Rerix: Scenic rendering for *The Three Magi*   *82*

8. A scene from *The Three Magi*   *83*

9. A scene from *Le Miracle de Theofile*   *84*

10. V. A. Ščuko: Scenic rendering for *Present-day Brothers*   *85*

11. Costumes, props, and scenic pieces from *Le Jeu de Robin et Marion*   *86*

12. Marion (M. A. Rigler) and the Knight (P. È. Nelobin), *Le Jeu de Robin et Marion*   *87*

13. An announcement of the Ancient Theatre's first season   *88*

14. K. M. Miklaševskij as the Nephew in *An Amusing Farce about a Cuckhold's Hat*   89

15. N. K. Rerix: Scenic rendering for *Fuente Ovejuna*   90

16, 17. Two scenes from *Fuente Ovejuna*   91

18. I. Ja. Bilibin: Costume rendering from *Fuente Ovejuna* (The Commander)   92

19. A. K. Šervadšidze: Scenic rendering for *Marta la Piadosa*   93

20. N. K. Kalmakov: Scenic rendering for *El Gran Ducque da Moscovia*   94

21, 22. N. K. Kalmakov: Two costume renderings from *El Gran Ducque da Moscovia* (Tsar Ivan the Terrible and his wife)   95, 96

23. I. Ja. Bilibin: Costume rendering from *El Purgatorio de San Patricio* (An angel)   97

24. Z. V. Xolmskaja   98

25. A. R. Kugel'   98

26. L. A. Fenin as Strafokamil. [Inset]: The cast of *Vampuka, African Bride*   99

27. [(upper)] L. I. Lukin as Lodyrè; [(lower)] the emblem of the Crooked Mirror Theatre   100

28. N. N. Evreinov (1909)   101

29. The White platform   102

30. The Red platform   102

31. The Red platform with connecting bridge   103

32. The bridge   103

33. The general plan of *The Storming of the Winter Palace*   104

34. Jurij Annenkov's sketch of *The Storming of the Winter Palace*   *105*

35. Portrait of Evreinov by Jurij Annenkov (1921)   *106*

KHLESTAKOV. I know all the pretty actresses. You see, I have written a few little things for the stage, too. I am often in literary circles...on friendly terms with Pushkin. I used often to say to him, "Well, Pushkin, old man, how are things going?" "So-so, old man," he would answer, "only so-so,"... He is quite a character.

ANNA. So you write too? How delightful it must be to be an author! No doubt you have things in the magazines?

KHLESTAKOV. Yes, I send things to the magazines, too. I am the author of lots of works, really: *The Marriage of Figaro, Robert the Devil, Norma.* I can't remember the titles of all of them. And it was all a mere chance—I had no intention of writing, but the Director of Theaters said to me, "Come, old boy, write something for us!" Well, I thought, why not? And on the spot, in one evening I think it was, I wrote the whole thing, to the surprise of everybody. I have a wonderfully ready wit. Everything that has been published under the name of Baron Brambeus, *The Frigate Hope,* and *The Moscow Telegraph*...I wrote them all.[1]

Preface

Director, dramatist, theorist, historian, musician, composer, would-be philosopher and full-time provocateur, Nikolaj Nikolaevič Evreinov (1879-1953) was among the most versatile, significant, and, even if not to all tastes, the most profound of theatrical innovators of the Silver Age of Russian culture (c.1894-1917) and Russian theatre's golden age (c.1898-1939). Soviet theatre critics and historians dismiss Evreinov as a light-minded aesthete and apolitical formalist. His emigration to Paris in 1925, where he lived with his wife until his death in 1953, did little to illuminate for western critics the importance of this strangely paradoxical figure. His plays seemed to have developed from Pirandellian conventions, his directorial approaches, less familiar in the West than his plays, from Gordon Craig and Vsevolod Mejerxol'd, and his aesthetics from Oscar Wilde. The confused chronology, which made Evreinov seem beholden to artists whom he, in many ways, anticipated, persisted until history had passed him by.

It is not difficult to understand why Evreinov has proven to be so troublesome. A theatricalist like Mejerxol'd but with a Stanislavskijan sense of verisimilitude in art, Evreinov prided himself on being nobody's disciple, a self-proclaimed original and "aristocrat of the theatre," an anti-Stanislavskijan and an anti-Mejerxol'dian, an aesthete and a popularizer whose work ranged from the quasi-scientific to the whimsical and grotesque. Evreinov revealed little of his true personality, choosing instead to hide behind a created persona. His substantial writings dealt more with philosophy than craft, addressing what he felt to be the major ideas confronting theatre and society. He left no cohesive body of ideas regarding acting and directing, like those that have solidified the reputations of so many of his contemporaries. His highly subjective approach to art has made both his value and intentions seem suspect.

Evreinov's work embraced the twin poles between which the history of the modern theatre unfolds and is defined—theatre as illusion (lies like truth) and theatre as event (a present-tense reality transcending the boundaries of art). Leaning more often toward the latter, Evreinov's was ultimately a visionary theatre, always the most difficult to understand and to accept.

It was with these difficulties in mind and in the interest of clarifying the Evreinovian paradox without disarming it that this study was undertaken. In recent years there has been something of a thaw, which is not to say a complete resuscitation, of Evreinov in the Soviet Union. It was through this thin and perhaps temporary crack in the ice that I slipped in order to conduct my research. I became one of the first Western scholars to gain relatively free access to the archival holdings on Evreinov, which include memoirs, personal correspondence, notes and rough drafts of his various theatrical and historical works.

The resulting study aims at finding a workable structure in which to place the myriad of projects, manifestos and often conflicting impressions that make up Evreinov's highly active career in the Russian theatre. For the most part, I have chosen not to be anecdotal concerning Evreinov's daily life but to focus instead on his created life, to treat Evreinov the theatrical phenomenon, the persona, which is how he presented himself to the world. This is not, of course, an original approach, but it is, in Evreinov's case, an especially appropriate one since he created the means by which to examine him so—the theories of monodrama and the theatre in life.

In 1925, perhaps the first true Evreinov scholar, Boris Vasil'evič Kazanskij, likewise chose to study Evreinov the "theoretical personality" rather than pursue a historical-biographical approach. Kazanskij's argument, that historical biography is in large part a matter of chance (and genetics), while theory is a matter of logical, systematic and conscious development and so preferable as a structuring principle for critical study, is debatable. One always hesitates to approach a subject in a certain way because the subject wanted and planned it so, but Evreinov has left us little choice. His personal biography is so private and his created life so public that one invariably opts for the latter, thus studying Evreinov as he intended, through idea and performance. Judgments upon what Evreinov's ideas meant to him as a man rather than simply as a member of the St. Petersburg, Russian and world artistic communities, must be hazarded with some caution and yet some speed before Evreinov again performs his disappearing act. Actually Evreinov only seems to want to program our response to him. In fact, he is inviting us to create a fantasy on the theme of Evreinov as he has—an "Evreinov" at the vanishing point. It is a grave responsibility and not always a pleasurable one, given the scholar-critic's conditioned need for validation. By refusing his critical audience validation via himself, Evreinov compels it to share his dilemma, to enter into his condition, to become an actor in *his* theatre.

My decision to deal only with Evreinov's work in Russia, while allowing the material to coalesce naturally around certain of his major theoretical ideas, necessitated certain omissions. These include a discussion of several of Evreinov's later plays, most notably the latter two-thirds of his theatre-in-life trilogy—*The Ship of the Righteous* (*Korabl' pravednyx*, 1924) and *The Theatre of Eternal War* (*Teatr večnoj vojny*, 1928)—both of which belong more properly to his émigré career. (The first and most important part of this trilogy, *The Chief Thing*, is discussed at some length in this study as the most complete dramatic expression of his pre-emigration theoretical thinking.) Likewise, Evreinov's directorial work in exile, primarily in Paris, while substantial in terms of the sheer number of productions mounted, does not add appreciably to the thematic core being developed in this study. Evreinov's reputation in France seems today to remain undiminished, and his entire post-Russian theatre career continues to be studied in the West to great advantage.

I have, however, treated in some detail the two major pre-Revolutionary Russian theatres in which Evreinov served as chief artistic director and attempted to transform his theories into practice. Evreinov's work at the Ancient and Crooked Mirror Theatres reveals different sides of his personality. In themselves, these theatres are significant cultural indicators of their time. Conversely, I felt that Evreinov's work at the Dramatic Theatre of V. F. Komissarževskaja and the Merry Theatre for Grown-up Children, although interesting as formative influences, was too short-lived and too partially realized to necessitate extensive discussion.

Finally, I did not feel that a first study of Evreinov was the proper place for extensive comparative analysis with similarly disposed artists. While I have sketched in the broad outlines of some shared concerns with the likes of Jarry, Pirandello and Artaud, I felt that the detailed treatment of such suggestive themes should properly await a fuller understanding of the much-neglected Evreinov in his own right.

Concerning the transliterations, I have opted for the international scholarly system used by linguists and literary scholars specializing in Russian and Slavic studies. This requires the reader to adjust to the use of diacritical marks and to what to him may be unfamiliar and possibly awkward spellings of familiar names—e.g., Stanislavskij instead of Stanislavsky, and Mejerxol'd rather than Meyerhold—but in the long run the accuracy of this system as it relates to the original Russian makes its usage necessary and worthwhile.

I am, of course, indebted to a good many people and institutions for their help in planning and completing this book. I here wish to acknowledge from the University of Kansas: Professor William Kuhlke, for patiently and enthusiastically sharing with me his considerable Russian theatre experience and critical acumen; Professors Robert Findlay and Ronald Willis, for knowledgeable editorial advice; Professor Gerald Mikkelson, for help with translation problems. I am grateful also to: Elizabeth Tokoi of the Helsinki University Library for bibliographical assistance; Soviet theatre scholars Jurij Konstantinovič Gerasimov and Sergej L'vovič Simbal for insights on Evreinov and pre-revolutionary St. Petersburg and for directing me to valuable sources; A. G. Avvakumov and S. A. Raxmanova for firsthand information on the Crooked Mirror Theatre; the staff of the Leningrad State Theatrical Museum for the use of their archival sources; my friends at the All-Russian Theatre Society in Moscow for assistance in making contacts and securing materials; the staff of the A. A. Baxrušin State Central Theatrical Museum for allowing me to examine their holdings; the United States Office of Education (Fulbright-Hays Committee) and the International Research and Exchanges Board for the fellowship monies and entree which made research in the Soviet Union possible; Gerard Abensour, editor of *Revue des Études Slaves,* Professor Harry B. Weber and Peter von Wahlde, editor and publisher, respectively, of the forthcoming edition of *The Modern Encyclopedia of Russian and Soviet Literatures,* and Professor Ron Engle, editor of *Theatre History Studies* for publishing excerpts from this study; Professor Christopher Moody of the University of Witwatersrand, Union of South Africa, for expert counsel and extensive source referral; Professor Laurence Senelick of Tufts University for encouragement and help in updating the bibliography; my wife Jeanie, for typing and editorial assistance, understanding and forbearance; and most especially, the late Anna Kašina-Evreinova, for tireless advocacy, for sharing with me very special memories and personal materials, as well as for encouraging me to tell Evreinov's story fairly as I perceived it.

1

Introduction: Harlequinade

St. Petersburg between the Revolutions

> We are all here carousers and harlots
> What a dismal and unhappy crowd!
> On the walls the birds and the flowers
> Seem to yearn and strain for a cloud.
>
> You are smoking away on a black pipe
> With the hovering smoke strange and dim
> And I wear a skirt that is narrow
> To make me seem even more slim
>
> The windows are covered completely
> What's outside—frost or storm? Tell me that.
> Your eyes seem to have the appearance
> Of the eyes of a cautious cat.
>
> Oh, my heart is so sad in its anguish!
> Am I here waiting for the death bell?
> And that woman right there who is dancing
> Is certainly going to hell.
>
> —Anna Axmatova, 1 January 1913[1]

Pre-Revolutionary St. Petersburg was alive with the spirit of masquerade. Poets, painters, dramatists and directors walked the streets and sat for portraits dressed in outlandish attire, either *commedia*-based or of their own device. Makeup was applied to faces and radishes and wooden spoons to buttonholes by futurist artists, recalling Oscar Wilde's informal Society of the Green Carnation, which proclaimed artificiality a more honest condition than naturalness and naturalness nothing more than a particularly irritating pose.[2]

The influences of the German romantic, E. T. A. Hoffmann, the Italian commedia dell'arte and its revivifier, the eighteenth century Venetian fabulist, Carlo Gozzi, could be seen everywhere in the various arts and all of the artistic accessories to life: in the group of Russian writers who called themselves the Serapion Brothers after E. T. A. Hoffmann's circle of friends whose annual meetings on St. Serapion's Day (1816–20) gave them their name; in the multitude of journal covers, theatrical posters, handbills and advertisements which depicted commedia figures; in the leisure time haunts of Petersburg artists such as the Comedians' Halt (*Prival komediantov*) with its Hall of Gozzi and Hoffmann and an atmosphere described by one eyewitness as "Old Venice viewed through the prism of Harlequin"; and in the preponderence of harlequinades and masquerade balls.[3]

Director Vsevolod Mejerxol'd, who was twice painted in the costume of Pierrot and whose ubiquity was captured in the professional alias he borrowed from E. T. A. Hoffmann (*"Doctor Dapertutto"* or "Doctor Everywhere"), was especially fond of masquerades. One such occasion, the intriguingly entitled *"Evening of the Paper Ladies" (Večer bumažnyx dam)*, marked the opening of Mejerxol'd's third production of poet-dramatist Aleksandr Blok's *The Fairground Booth (Balagančik),* which was modelled after the commedia with an ironic contemporary edge. The cream of Petersburg's artistic society attended the post-premiere affair and staged their own kind of performance, wearing black half-masks and hats and clothing made from colored crepe paper.[4] The transience of this often frenetic gaiety was not lost on the more perceptive of the revelers. They knew that in the wave of a fan, they and the fantasy that sheltered them could all disappear.

The masquerade was a kind of feast in time of plague, an attempt to dispel at least temporarily the apocalyptic sense of doom which hung over St. Petersburg between the revolutions of 1905 and 1917. Russian society was undergoing at this time a major identity crisis. The country had suffered through a humiliating war with Japan and an abortive revolution; a world war was imminent, with the bloodiest revolution in history to follow. In the chaos of such tumultuous events, Russian society had temporarily lost its moorings.

The searching and often flailing motions of society at large were reflected most intensely in the arts, where realism and rational positivist philosophy were replaced by a myriad of so-called irrational trends—symbolism, impressionism, cubism, futurism, Neo-Raphaelism, acmeism, surrealism and others not so clearly labelled. An outbreak of hypnotist-charlatans revealed the mystical solutions people were willing to pursue in the name of truth.[5]

With the breakdown of social institutions and the class structure of the tsarist regime, the charismatic individual became highly visible, and a strong cult of personality developed. Commedia dell'arte's playful yet serious secular faith in man's ability to penetrate into essences and unmask their mysterious power was highly attractive to the artist and intellectual of the day. But then so too was commedia's image of man the "king of shreds and patches" controlled by his own vices—if not the puppet of fate, then surely the victim of his own excessive nature. There was tragedy and farce to be found here, metaphors and archetypes, inspired improvisation and improvised salvation. In 1912 Mejerxol'd proclaimed the theoretical principles of the fairground booth. Echoing the words of Ernst von Wolzogen, founder of the German theatre of small forms, he called for "depth and extract, brevity and contrast!" It was a vision of nicely balanced tensions in which "the pale, lanky Pierrot," representing "the eternal tragedy of mutely suffering mankind," is overtaken by the merry Harlequin, and "harsh satire replaces the sentimental ballad."[6] Pierrot's passive suffering seemed on equal occasion to be as romantic as Harlequin's brash, active stance and unalloyed faith in self. The two masks fought each other for the imagination of artists and intellectuals much as they had for centuries battled for the heart of their muse, the inconstant Columbine.

These were mortal tales wearing immortal masks, perfect for a time in which feverish social interaction could not completely dispel what the influential theatre critic, journal editor and theatre of small forms producer, Aleksandr Kugel', referred to as a vapor of antisocial feeling in the air. Society in its political, institutionalized forms was deemed corrupt and so social feeling was replaced by egoism as theory and modus operandi.[7]

Writing on Evreinov, critic Boris Kazanskij, said of this period:

> Art became exclusive and its power absolute, being cited as responsible for all natural phenomena and historical events. Everything in life came to be regarded as a work of art, invested with an artistic point of view. Aesthetics absorbed man's consciousness. It substituted itself for all man's philosophy, became his most sacred truth, his new evangelical morality, his new "book of life."[8]

Egoism and individualism, along with strong currents of cultural retrospectivism, aristocratism, aestheticism, subjectivism and the idea of art as the transformer of life were bequeathed to the Russian artist, and to Petersburg cultural society in particular, by the group which became known as the "World of Art" (*Mir iskusstva*). This former "society for self-education," founded in 1890 by the artist Aleksandr N. Benois (1870–1960) and some like-minded upper-class gymnasium friends and acquaintances—Val'mer F. Nuvel', Lev Rosenberg (better known as Leon S. Bakst), Grigorij Kalin, Nikolaj K. Rerix, Konstantin A. Somov, Nikolaj Skalon, Evgenij E. Lansere (Benois's nephew), A. P. Novrok (pseudonym Silen),

Sergej P. Djagilev, and Dmitrij V. Filosofov (Djagilev's cousin) — became intoxicated with Huysmans, Baudelaire, Verlaine, Heine, Beardsley, the Marquis de Sade and numerous other of the so-called decadent Western European writers and artists who had been banned in Russia by the government censor.[9] Under the refined leadership of Sergej Djagilev (1872-1929), the World of Art transformed interest and appreciation into self-generated activity, first in the form of exhibitions of art from abroad (1897-1903); next as a high-quality cosmopolitan journal. *The World of Art (Mir iskusstva,* 1898-1904), which was similar in look and tone to the Berlin modernist journals *Pan* and *Insel* and London's *The Yellow Book* and *The Savoy;* and finally in musical performances (beginning in 1907) and dance, culminating in Djagilev's "Ballets Russes."[10] The World of Art wanted to create a cultural window on the West to serve the god Apollo by devoting itself to creative work "of the greatest Parnassian heights," to educate the Russian reader and theatregoer in the power and value of sheer physical beauty as an aesthetic and moral force. Finally, it hoped to forge a regenerated Russian art which could in turn be exported to the West.[11]

The World of Art group transformed the subjectivism and exoticism promulgated by German romanticism, French and Belgian symbolism, atheism, amoralism, Nietzscheism and the like into a new breed of Russian individualsim. Art became again an elevated, mysterious phenomenon of regal grandeur with man as its center and raison d'être.

Djagilev viewed all history as an expression of personality, a process whose development is immanent, and not dependent on any objective conditions. "If the beauty of the world is a manifestation of divine will," he reasoned, "then of course, man is the highest emblem of the divine spirit." This in turn led to a belief in the primacy of subjectivism in art and World of Art painter Konstantin Somov's proclamation: "The whole world revolves around my 'I,' and I don't have a concern which stretches beyond the limits of this 'I.'".

Two former staff writers for the journal, *World of Art,* Valerij Brjusov and Andrej Belyj, became important spokesmen for the Russian symbolist movement in which subjectivism again played a prominent role. The artist, Brjusov maintained, should "shake off the fetters of reason," leaving himself open to irrational and subconscious influences in his art and thus becoming better able to express, via intuition, the essence of himself. Brjusov believed that any enjoyment we derive from a work of art comes from the possibility of communicating with the artist's soul.[12] The poet should "hypnotize the reader" into forging this most meaningful of relationships.

"The entire world is within me," proclaimed the Russian symbolist, and yet the thrust of the movement was less "art for art's sake" than art as transforming force. Life, Brjusov believed, is the only ground in which anything can grow. "Art in the name of aimless beauty is dead art." Brjusov issued a charge which a number of the self-dramatizing artists of his generation answered: "Let him [the artist] create not his books, but his life."[13]

Although enamored from the start of what it felt to be history's three great civilizations, Ancient Egypt and Greece and medieval Europe, the cultural retrospectivism of the World of Art group came to focus intently on masterfully painting two models from another age: Versailles as a dramatic spectacle conceived by the director Louis XIV, representing "the self-consciousness of humanity" and "aristocratism," regality divorced from politics; and St. Petersburg itself, the result of a protean act of willfull self-creation by the Great Designer-Director Petr I., who came to represent the artist himself. The city stood as a towering tribute to the transformative power of man, symbolizing mystical beauty and grandeur and the triumph of art and artifice. It seemed appropriate that this same St. Petersburg was now the stage on which these great themes were being replayed. St. Petersburg was, after all, nicknamed "the Venice of the North," both for its waterways and for the Gozzi-like air of fantasy that pervaded it. The traditional home of literary fever dreams, it was in modern times watched over by its creator, Petr, himself a larger-than-life fiction come to life, and immortalized by Russia's own fabulist, Aleksandr Puškin, in "The Bronze Horseman." As Finnish legend has it:

> The town of St. Petersburg...must have been constucted as a whole in the airy blue and afterwards lowered by mysterious forces upon the banks of the river Neva, and that is why the houses of the young city never sank, one after the other into the marshy ground.[14]

Itself a great experiment, Petersburg seemed the perfect place to improvise an imaginative life of mystical power.

The impetus behind cultural retrospectivism, as with the other major trends of the period, was to discover essences. We must, these artists argued, pass through the historical to the contemporary, just as the symbolists sought passage through the phenomenal to the noumenal. Out of this impulse grew such groups and enterprises as "The Commission for Old Petersburg" (*Komissija starogo Peterburga*), "The Museum of Old Petersburg" (*Muzej starogo Peterburga*), Sergej Makovskij's journals *Bygone Years* (*Starye gody*, 1907-17) and *Russian Icons* (*Russkie ikony*), and most significantly in terms of reconstituting ancient and classic art as living theatrical art, The Ancient Theatre (*Starinnyj teatr*) of Nikolaj Evreinov and Baron Nikolaj Driezen which employed World of Art artists as theatrical designers.[15]

A group of young history professors at Petersburg University—D. K. Petrov, I. A. Šljapin and V. V. Siposkij, among others—supported the experiments of directors such as Evreinov and Mejerxol'd in the area of theatrical reconstructivism.[16] From among this group, Vladimir Solov'ev authored a series of commedia-style scenarios and appreciative essays on commedia character types, stage techniques and theatricality which helped lead to Mejerxol'd's initial fascination with the commedia form.[17]

This most theatrical of times resembled an ongoing dialogue. Russian artists, like certain of their commedia models, possessed a great "talent for talking" which they indulged freely.[18] Ideas were exchanged and tried on like costumes in the public market place. Everywhere there were public discussions, "disputes" (debates), symposia, lectures, demonstrations, literary and musical evenings, artistic journals, critical anthologies. . . and theatres, thirty-one theatres in Petersburg alone between 1905 and 1917.[19] The proliferation of theatres developed as a result of three main conditions: (1) the growth of a wider, more variegated, more self-aware and more demanding theatregoing public, (2) a shift in power from the few imperial theatres to more numerous private theatres, and (3) the increased significance of educating the public and finding theatrical forms new to artists and audiences alike.[20]

The "crisis in the theatre," which these conditions intensified paralleled artistic upheavals then current in Western Europe. August Strindberg stated that "theatre will soon be abolished like an extinct form," while Gordon Craig dreamed of the "*Übermarionette*" and Georg Fuchs called for the re-theatricalization of the theatre.[21] In Russia, this crisis was variously blamed on the dramatists, actors, audiences and the nature of theatre itself, on the misguided illusionism of naturalism at one extreme and the excessive formalism of stylization on the other.

Although certain groups, such as the two branches of the symbolist movement, were centered in either St. Petersburg or Moscow, most Russian artists of this period travelled between the two cities fairly frequently to work, to observe the work of others and to cross-fertilize. It was believed that out of this glorious confusion of energies and ideals, some artist, a Galahad pure of soul and chastened for the quest, would discover the key to Truth, Beauty and the Life of the Future.

Books and journals played their part, serving as convenient forums for debate and speculation. Among the most important publications, *The Scales* (*Vesy,* 1903-9), was a stronghold of Russian symbolism, as was Moscow's *The Golden Fleece* (*Zolotoe runo,* 1906-9), whose editor, N. P. Rjabušinskij, published the poetry and fiction of Leonid Andreev, Konstantin Bal'mont, Aleksandr Blok, Ivan Bunin, Vjačeslav Ivanov, Aleksej Remizov, Vladimir Solov'ev and Fedor Sologub, among others.

The journal also featured the work of virtually the entire World of Art group of painters and was itself modelled after that group's publication in its use of high-quality paper, graphics and design. Of the remaining modernist journals, *Apollo (Apollon),* which published its first number on 15 October 1909, and continued in operation until 1917, listed among its contributors such theatre luminaries as Baron N. V. Driezen, N. N. Evreinov, V. È. Mejerxol'd, V. I. Nemirovič-Dančenko, K. S. Stanislavskij and Gordon Craig.

Included among the major publishing houses were Moscow's "Scorpion" (*Skorpion*) and "Musaget."[22] A singular contribution was made by yet another important publisher, Petersburg's "Dogrose" (*Šipovnik*) with the appearance of the influential anthology, *Theatre: A Book on the New Theatre* (*Teatr, kniga o novom teatre,* 1908). Included in this landmark work were articles by Anatolij Lunačarskij, E. Aničkov, A. Gornfeld, Aleksandr Benois, Vsevolod Mejerxol'd, Fedor Sologub, Georgij Čulkov, S. Rafalovič, Valerij Brjusov and Andrej Belyj.[23]

Aimed at solving the crisis in the theatre and establishing a higher ideal for dramatic art, the authors represented in *A Book on the New Theatre* disagreed on a great deal. However, they all viewed theatre as first and foremost a means of communication and thus as an event to be co-created and co-experienced by stage and audience. Symbolist writer and classical scholar, Vjačeslav Ivanov, in this and independent theoretical works of sometimes convoluted brilliance, argued for returning the theatre to the sort of dynamic actor-audience relationship that it enjoyed in ancient Greece, a theatre of myth-creation (*mifotvorčestvo*) and communal action (*sobornoe dejstvo*).[24] His search for an inner or more real reality (*realiora*) necessitated a return to sources in order to rediscover essences and owed much to Nietzsche's theory of the birth of tragedy. Andrej Belyj questioned the possibility of successfully pursuing such a course given Russian society's lack of cohesiveness and ritualistic base. To him the current crisis could be blamed on the failure of dramatists to unite stage and audience via their work.[25] Mejerxol'd, who at this stage in his career still believed that literature created the theatre, modestly offered the director as a bridge uniting the souls of author and actor.[26]

Fedor Sologub's "Theatre of One Will" (*Teatr odnoj voli*) seemed to borrow from both camps and to offer the most specific and concrete, albeit extreme, remedy. Envisioning the spectator as a participant in the mystery, the secret ritual of theatre, Sologub sought to reaffirm the author by neutralizing the actor as a creative force. He proposed a theatrical presentation without footlights, curtain or scenery in which the author or a professional reader would sit at a table to one side of the theatre and recite the entire play including stage directions. This idea of offering the audience a professed single perspective from which to view the action was pursued by other Russian artists, most notably Evreinov, in his less mystical and more director-oriented theory of monodrama.[27]

Underlying the entire antirealist position was the concept of *uslovnost'* or conscious, conventional theatricality (some would say "stylization"), originally articulated by Valerij Brjusov in his seminal article, "Unnecessary Truth" (*Nenužnaja pravda,* published in *The World of Art,* 1902, no. 4). Here, Brjusov stated the obvious but necessary truth that the stage does not naturally lend itself to realism since it is "in and of itself *uslovnaja.*" Theatre artists, he said, must make peace with this fact and exploit it to the utmost.[28]

Integral to the concept of *uslovnost'* was the notion of conditionality as expressed in critic Anatolij Nelidov's statement that "since art is a product of the spiritual life of mankind, truths in art can only be *uslovnye* and not absolute."[29] Critic-historian Boris Alpers wrote off the whole naturalistic bourgeois pre-Revolutionary theatre as a theatre of "dream" in which "the spectator *subjected* his will to illusion" and thus "sacrificed his objectivity."[30] The brilliantly idiosyncratic and versatile poet-dramatist Mixail Kuzmin cogently stated that naturalism in art is destructive and nearly impossible since the laws of art and life are almost contradictory.[31]

"This mania for *uslovnost'* " was answered in 1909 by a group of Moscow professors and men of letters in the aptly-named anthology, *The Crisis in the Theatre.* The same year saw the publication of other individual and collective position papers on the state of the art, including *The Fall of the Theatre (Padenie teatra)* and *The Theatre of Quest (Teatr iskanii).*[32] The next major offensive was mounted three years later with the March 1912 publication of critic Julij Ajxenval'd's article "Rejecting the Theatre" (*Otricanie teatra*) in the journal *Studio (Studija).* Ajxenval'd boldly proclaimed that at this point in history the theatre is not in a crisis but at an end. Theatre, he argued, had no value except as dramatic literature, no justifiable aesthetic of its own, and made the mistake of combining arts that were better left to their separate realms. The entire *uslovnyj* theatre movement, "the theatrical theatre" or "theatre for theatre's sake," he maintained, is nothing more than a defensive reaction designed to disguise this fact. Such a movement represents "the fetishism of pure form—formalism." True creative art is never collective. Art demands solitude, so why bother with the theatre when you can contemplate the dramatic text alone?[33]

The vast majority of the theatre's critics came to its defense in the face of Ajxenval'd's attacks. They saw now that the theatre had to get better not only in the pursuit of the ideal but so as to withstand the very real presence of critics such as Ajxenval'd who saw little value in it.

Russian theatre artists looked hopefully to the West, as had the World of Art, in search of clues and cures, and in some cases the West came to Russia. Max Reinhardt brought his 1910 production of *Oedipus Rex,* originally staged at Berlin's Circus Schumann, to St. Petersburg in the spring of 1911 with Alexander Moissy in the title role. The production, which found a modern equivalent for the grandeur and communality of the ancient Greek amphitheatre, impressed the more innovative Russian artists. Eleanora Duse (1907–8), Sarah Bernhardt (1908) and the Japanese actress Ganako (fall, 1909) also made appearances, but no single artist made a more dramatic impression on the Russian cognoscenti than the dancer Isadora Duncan.[34]

Critic and biographer of Mejerxol'd, Nikolaj Volkov, said of Duncan's first St. Petersburg appearance (13 December 1904) that it opened a new page in the history of contemporary art. Dancing to "serious music" in her bare feet, dressed in a light, semitransparent tunic and bathed in lilac-tinged light before a Grecian landscape of marble columns, black cypresses and light blue sky, Duncan's performance was for her a *"succès de scandale"* and for many of the artists in attendance a revelation.[35] She seemed a siren or perhaps a goddess sent from ancient Greece to summon the theatre back to its former glory. She held aloft a torch brought from Mount Olympus with which to rekindle the dying flame of modern art. The young Nikolaj Evreinov stated that Duncan's dances produced in him one of the most profound impressions of his life by showing him the simplicity and inevitability of "real, honest art."[36]

Duncan's "free dance" or "natural" *plastique* was soon followed into Russia by the system known as eurhythmics, or rhythmic gymnastics, first demonstrated in Russia by its creator, Emile Jaques Dalcroze, at Petersburg's Imperial Mixajlovskij Theatre on 20 January 1912. Two years earlier, Prince Sergej Volkonskij had discussed Dalcroze's system in his lecture, "On Man and Rhythm." Volkonskij claimed that whereas Duncan's system had a subjective base, Dalcroze's was objective. Whereas Duncan expressed her self, her mood, Dalcroze expressed the rhythm and soul of the music painted by the body.

Duncan's approach was offered in a number of schools which sprang up around Petersburg immediately following her first appearance. She became, too, a frequent target for criticism and parody. Dalcroze's eurhythmics were taught both in private schools and as part of the high school curriculum.[37] More importantly, both approaches shifted the emphasis back to the individual performer at a time when those like the blackly fatalist Sologub were plotting his demise.

In 1909, Edward Gordon Craig's influence began to manifest itself in Russia with the appearance of his article, *"Etwas über der Regisseur und die Büchner-Ausstattung,"* and Mejerxol'd's article, "Edward Gordon

Craig," in *The Journal of the Literary Artistic Society* (No. 9). The year 1912 saw the appearance of the first Russian translation of Craig's *On the Art of the Theatre* and Craig's work with Stanislavskij on *Hamlet* at the Moscow Art Theatre.[38]

Craig's theories and techniques paralleled much of what was then current in Russia: his monodramatic approach to staging (*Hamlet*); his ambivalent regard for the actor, simultaneously a god, a potential symbol of "noble artificiality" and "deathlike silence" or an egoist wallowing in his own humanity; his disgust with realism, which he called "a vulgar means of expression bestowed upon the blind"; and his own tendency to posture and declaim in print.[39]

Mejerxol'd, who had in his 1909 article on Craig rejected the Englishman's direct influence upon the Russian theatrical revolution, nevertheless shared Craig's belief in the necessity of the actor's transcending himself in order to operate on the level of symbol. Mejerxol'd's experiments with rhythmic movement—from his early work with the actor-carbotin or strolling player-singer-dancer-juggler of the *balagan* and the commedia dell'arte to his *biomechanical* phase in the twenties which stressed reflex action and the proletarian actor—embodied many of the period's ambivalent attitudes toward man the creator-performer of his own life. Mejerxol'd's concern with the marionetteness, regimented *plastique* and sculptural qualities of the actor, like Craig's *Übermarionettes* and actor-eating sets, demanded of man the performer that he rediscover his eloquence, resilience, stature and divinity so as to recreate an art that could once again be called universal.[40]

Aleksandr Kugel', whose pen name *Homo Novus* ("New Man") attested to his optimism for the future, was perhaps the actor's greatest champion at this time. The actor, he said, gave the theatre its right to be. He not only translates the play into the language of the theatre, he humanizes it. Along with Volkonskij, Dalcroze's popularizer in Russia, Kugel' argued that the actor's art is unique in that it is indivisible, a perfect union of creator, material and object. Man, they and others began to say, *is* in essence the art of the theatre.[41]

In 1917 came the Revolution and with it the death of contrasts and contradictions, artistic posturings and romantic role-playing. Life now belonged to those who could be decisive. Confusion was deadly, a prolonged suicide.

Gone was the light-mindedness (*legkomyslennost'*), the optimistic impracticality of spirit, born of extreme subjectivism, aestheticism and aristocratism, which caused many innovators of the period to undertake challenges that reason argued against. The opinionated but not generally light-minded Kugel' wrote its eulogy:

> Light-mindedness helps us to live. Without it there would be no optimism, no cheerfulness of the spirit and no will to life.... Humanity without light-mindedness would be a tragedy, a catastrophe, death. Without profundity one can not only make do but even continue to live pleasantly.... [But] if there were no light-mindedness...no momentary possession...humanity would fall into an eternal sleep, frozen stiff in cold, continual meditation.[42]

Kugel' recorded these thoughts in 1926, one year following the emigration from Russia of a man who was their exemplar. In fact the Russian career of Nikolaj Evreinov, a onetime co-worker of Kugel''s, embodied nearly all the major concerns and tendencies of the period between the revolutions: masquerade and marionettes; identity crisis and egoism; individualism and subjectivism; aestheticism and retrospectivism. A great actor who viewed the whole world as *his balagan,* he warred against conventional definitions of the theatre and of the roles of actor and audience. Accused throughout his career of being light-minded, he was serious to the point of self-consciousness in pursuing his life's goal — to transform himself into a work of art. Evreinov's role-playing and paradoxical personality struck some as foolish and others as pretentious. Nothing, however, weakened Evreinov's resolve to transform himself into what he most wanted to be, and he most wanted to be Harlequin.

Evreinov's Commedia of the Soul

> *I'm such a man! I never look at anyone---I tell them all: I know who I am, I know. I'm everywhere.*
> —Xlestakov[43]

Nikolaj Evreinov was powerfully drawn to the actor-based, inner-directed commedia dell'arte, taking from it some of the inspiration for his theory of monodrama in which the individual, the actor, transforms his world as it is manifested onstage via scenery, lighting and props, from his highly personal perspective. Commedia, the drama of mortality (being) and transformation (becoming) was for him a true "theatre of the soul" (a variant translation for the title of his most famous monodrama). He saw in commedia's reliance upon masks, conventions and *plastique,* a dramatization of the human condition — man pushing up against his finiteness, his mortality and the limitations he imposes upon himself when he fails to adequately imagine his world or lapses into the obsessive behavior patterns which deaden life. Evreinov perceived the possibility of commedia dell'arte's conventional devices, propelled by the spirit of anarchic play, yielding new revelations to man about the self, allowing him to trade in self-consciousness for self-awareness.

The struggle between freedom and restraint with the possibility of achieving freedom *through* restraint was to Evreinov the greatest of human dramas and the ultimate heroic act. Life may be a bittersweet affair, a carnival with its calliope music winding down, but man can break free of the clockwork mechanism if he has the will—the will to theatricalize.

Evreinov was concerned with discovering the point at which personality hardens into persona or mask. The action of most of his thirty plays and of his life was, like commedia, a public struggle between the mask and the face, naturalness and artifice, a glimpse of theatre at play with its own conventions, a spectacle of paradox, antithesis, duality. Archetypes are, of course, the repositories of myth and legend, and Evreinov sought to make himself into one, by appearing in his own name as a character in his theoretical works and biographical monographs on other artists, and in the guise of Harlequin in his many plays with theatrical settings and motifs. His characters, like those in commedia, are more essences, primary colors, agents (in this case of the author), than self-perpetuating entities.

The seriousness of Evreinov's intentions was balanced in tone and profoundly intensified in meaning and significance by his sense of playfulness, gamesmanship and love for puzzle structures. He spoofed himself and the theatre at every turn, playing off the purity or ideality of a concept against the reality of life and human nature. This is nowhere better illustrated than in his treatment of the love theme which is so important in commedia—the ideal of love becoming confused with the social game of love (the "love comedy" of courtship) and with self-love, which Evreinov treated under the various guises of *monodrama,* "theatre for oneself" and "erotic theatre for oneself." Evreinov derived a great deal of inspiration, technique and vision from the commedia dell'arte, but he also put a good deal back into the form. Here are some examples of ideas and devices which Evreinov adopted and transformed:

Direct audience address and a play-within-a-play format, leading to direct audience involvement, leading to and from a "theatre as event" persepctive. The immediacy of commedia dell'arte's improvisatory nature and public square mentality manifests itself in both Evreinov's dramaturgy and in his directing. All of his major dramatic works "play the audience," via direct address, the self-conscious reversal of expectations, the violation of the fourth wall and their self-referential theatricalizing. Several of his plays, including his major full-length work, *The Chief Thing* (*Samoe glavnoe,* 1920), and his early experiment in monodrama, *The Presentation of Love* (*Predstavlenie ljubvi,* 1910) follow play-within-a-play formats.

In directing as in playwriting Evreinov was always seeking to fully engage the spectator in the onstage action, to so identify the spectator with the protagonist that *he becomes* the protagonist and the border separating actor from spectator and theatre from life breaks apart. This was to Evreinov the natural state of things from which so-called realistic art had mistakenly led man and to which he must return in order to make himself and his culture well and whole again. At the Ancient Theatre Evreinov employed an onstage audience, costumed and well-schooled in the manners, modes and mores of the Middle Ages and the Spanish Golden Age in order to reconcile the perspective of the contemporary audience member with the mental set of the historical period being depicted.

This idea of "reconstructing the spectator," as part of the overall "artistic reconstruction" of historical events, transcended antiquarian interest and strictly theatrical concerns. In the most famous of Soviet mass spectacles, *The Storming of the Winter Palace* (*Vzjatie Zimnego dvorca*, 1920) Evreinov assembled some one hundred thousand spectators and performers, including actors, workers, dancers, circus performers and whole sectors of the Red army and Baltic Fleet to re-enact an event of great socio-political consequence which in its original occurrence actually involved many of the same participants.

The Origins of Theatricality—Masks, Rites and Rituals. In arguing theatre's primacy in life as a pre-aesthetic instinct, Evreinov made careful studies of primitive man and ancient cultures. He was particularly interested in the idea of theatricality as it manifested itself in secular and religious rites and rituals and in the use of the mask as a theatrical property of shamanistic power. Evreinov was as interested in the process whereby human behavior became ritualized and theatrical elements self-consciously conventionalized as he was in the earlier stages of man's history when theatre, like religion, effected an awesome and spontaneous sense of shared mystery and communion in its audience.

Evreinov's Faustian thirst for knowledge and Promethean ego, his overinsistence on the originality of his intellect, his scholarly pursuits and quasi-scholarly stances, his perception of the history of human achievement as the justification of his theories and ideas, seem at first glance to be at odds with his claim that "least of all would I like to be considered a serious man."[44] Conversely, his work in the areas of parody and entertainment, harlequinade, buffonade, theatrical pantomime and his wearing of the Harlequin motley as a personal badge of honor seem inconsistent with his claim to be a major theatre philosopher. The paradox only becomes intellectually palatable when one realizes that the mercurial ego Evreinov so often displayed was being modelled, as it were, to set a fashion. He hoped that through his example, mankind could perceive a more active, more optimistic role for itself in the future. Man would not simply become the grim "master of his own fate," but the lead actor in and director of his life as theatrical spectacle. Evreinov, like so many other theatricalist artists of his day, saw in commedia dell'arte the paradigm for a revivified theatricalist art. But as the leading purveyor of the theatre-in-life philosophy, Evreinov saw in it also a dramatization of the human condition and a possible clue to making this condition more bearable — a sort of commedia of the soul.

Evreinov's optimistic view of mankind was toughened by an ironic sense of detachment. It was this personal quality as much as anything that led Evreinov to don the mask of Harlequin when many other artists of his day, found themselves attracted to the romantic suffering of Pierrot. Evreinov eschewed the romantic fatalism of this mask which read the greatest joys of life and love through a congealed attitude of all-suffering sensitivity and self-love.

Ironic detachment is, of course, the strong suit of Harlequin, whose childlike ego does not stare reflectively at itself but rather engages the world actively so as to change it, even though in his heart he knows that the human condition ultimately cannot be changed. Just as irony sharpened the cutting edge of Evreinov's vision while dulling the naked force of ego, so did whimsy serve a dual purpose — disarming his audience, defusing pain, evoking laughter and, when necessary, earning sufferance — while keeping his own innate sorrow at bay and a heartfelt romantic idealism hidden safely away from public ridicule and personal apprehension.

Harlequin is a truly universal figure — everywhere a guest but nowhere at home, ever ready and willing to change because even as he connects to life at different junctures, he is ultimately in no way tied. This too is a hallmark of and perhaps a prerequisite for ironic detachment. Evreinov suffered and benefited from a similar sense of displacement. This may account in part for his obsessive efforts to capture the living presence of time and place in his work, whether it be religious ecstasy enacted on a medieval town square at the Ancient Theatre or the quasi-religious revolutionary fervor that spilled out before the Winter Palace in 1917 and again in Evreinov's mass spectacle of 1920.

And so Evreinov's mask fell into place with the weight of an inevitability — Harlequin, the alchemist, changing base matter into spirit, a seeker of forms unmasking essence, a process embodied in his own alchemical personality. The harlequinade which he played was *The Philosopher's Stone,* wherein the hero strives to discover the single key which will lead man to true and eternal happiness.

Evreinov, the self-created original, was much more a product of his time and its preoccupations than he cared to admit. But he was by no means alone in this. What emerges from the great variety and sheer number of high-toned artistic profiles of this particular time and place is something like a consensus. These self-proclaimed Harlequins and Pierrots, Dapertuttos and certainly Xlestakovs, all claiming originality for their proposed remedies and propounded beliefs, were perhaps too caught up in the turn-of-the-century fever and the thrill of strangeness via juxtaposition and hyperbole that romanticism brings to life to realize the sense of community, the shared vision that connected them. For a brief moment in time, they were living the ideal that they so fervently hoped to achieve. However, the great romance of life is in the quest and not in the attainment. They buffered themselves with their eccentricities, their stylistic flourishes, their self-conscious masquerades and self-advertisements, from clearly sighting the future and the possible realization of their worst fears and of their most fervently hoped for dreams, which might be worse still. Their declaration that life is a tragic *balagan* with themselves noble if ultimately doomed maskers seems not ridiculous, which would to them be damnation indeed, only intensely human and filled with the paradox of life. Thus it was with Evreinov, only more so.

2

The Original and the Portraitists

The Original

> Two or three special movements were commonly associated with Harlequin. The first was his way of entering the stage, with a sense of quick urgency, his legs held almost unbent and given a kind of strutting effect. In this was created an impression of self-confidence, perhaps of impertinence, certainly of his own awareness of the humor of his role....[1]

Aleksandr A. Mgebrov, an actor at the Dramatic Theatre of V. F. Komisarževskaja and later at the Ancient Theatre, records his first impression of Nikolaj Evreinov:

> I recall that on one occasion I was sitting in a cinema and behind me sat a young man with two pretty girls. His face stood out among hundreds of others. I was greatly struck by it. It was not a face, but a portrait — an ancient portrait from the Middle Ages. The white oval forehead was fringed by locks of not very long but slightly unruly hair, trimmed round the ears as in pre-Raphaelite portraits. From the two delicate arches of the brows which looked as if they had been drawn, extended the lines of an almost classical nose. The feminine and at the same time sensuous lips were parted in a captivating smile, revealing beautiful, firm white teeth. In the long pale oval of the face were set large blue eyes, shining with laughter. If one adds the characteristic set of the head, the slightly sloping shoulders, the fine, elegant hands and almost feminine gentleness, the portrait of Evreinov is complete as I saw him for the first time, not knowing who he was. I looked at him for a long time and listened to his loud bursts of laughter.[2]

It was 1910. Evreinov was thirty-one years old and had already begun to work his charms and extend his influence over the cultural life of St. Petersburg. Evreinov loved to pose, and painters, photographers and critics alike tried manfully to render him accurately so as to capture his essence. Idolaters and detractors of Evreinov (there were few, if any, indifferent observers) were certainly at no loss for words with which to describe him, and their efforts are instructive in the range of seemingly contradictory possibilities which they suggest.

Evreinov was labeled a dilettante, an original, uniquely talented, pretentious, a character, harlequin, decadent, conjurer, dandy, eccentric, a Xlestakov and a reactionary, antidemocratic aesthete; charming, tasteful, witty, courageous, persuasive, vague, banal, paradoxical, flashy, deceitful, passionate, vain, condescending, coquettish, foppish, insincere, very Russian, very European, self-dramatizing, egotistic, light-minded, premeditated, bombastic, an individualist and a fanatic. He was likened to the Bolognese pedant of the commedia dell'arte and said by his critics to have assigned himself the role of the Mephistopheles of the twentieth century.[3] And yet one critic could be moved to say that "everyone today has affected manners and wants to flaunt his education, but Evreinov is simple, straightforward and does not deceive anyone."[4] Xlestakov indeed.

An admittedly self-advertising personality and an oft-described "Narcissus in love with himself" who carried on his love affair in public, the private (one hesitates to say "real") Evreinov remained in hiding.[5] So carefully did he erect a persona for himself and so single-mindedly did he play his chosen role that Evreinov attained more notoriety than he did genuine respect and appreciation for his artistic accomplishments and the serious goals toward which his self-dramatization was directed.

Nikolaj Nikolaevič Evreinov was representative of the paradoxical temper of "the epoch of beautiful romanticism" which preceded the Russian Revolution of 1917.[6] The second of four children of Boyar stock, he was born on 13 February 1879, in Moscow, where his family had taken up temporary residence.[7] Evreinov's father was a well-to-do engineer who had graduated with distinction from the Russian Institute of Railroads and whose job necessitated frequent relocations. The family moved to Derpt from Moscow and from there to Ekaterinoslav in the 1880s and Pskov in the early 1890s.

Evreinov was always closest to his mother, Valentina Petrovna de Grandmaison, the granddaughter of a Frenchman who had emigrated to Russia during the French Revolution. A talented pianist and amateur singer, she encouraged her son's readily discernible musical talent, his love of theatre and his will to perform. Evreinov played the violin, cello, okarina, cornet-à-pistons, piccolo, and flute for his family at home concerts while growing up. At the age of five his mother took him to see his first theatrical production, the operetta *Girofle-Girofla*. There followed many such excursions to plays and concerts.

In the winter of 1884 Nikolaj and his brother Volodja built a theatre in their home. Evreinov would shout whenever his little sister climbed over the footlights from the audience to reach her brother on-stage, thus destroying the illusion of another world. In this way Evreinov discovered for himself the concept of "the fourth wall," an idea for which he had little use in his adult years. What he did preserve from his childhood was an awareness of how completely a child can absorb himself in play. Evreinov as an adult theorist repeatedly pointed to the child's ability to create theatre with the simplest of properties or no properties at all and with only an imaginary audience in attendance. He called this "the theatre of five fingers," because five fingers is all a child needs in order to create it.[8]

As a child Evreinov was interested in puppets, particularly the Russian *balagan* character Petruška. He tells of bothering his parents incessantly until they bought him all of the available Petruška puppets. He and his brother would hoard materials from around the house that they needed for their presentations. Parents and guests alike were compelled to watch and applaud ten times over while Petruška was dragged off to the underworld. Evreinov later wrote that the marionette "returns us to childhood, which I believe mankind abandoned only to consciously return to in the future."[9]

At the age of seven, Evreinov wrote his first parody (a genre that became a cornerstone of his professional work), based on an official dinner his father had arranged for a minister. Young Evreinov continued to write parodies, using as targets his teachers at the gymnasium in Pskov. In this he resembled another lover of puppets and parody, Alfred Jarry. Evreinov's imagination ran apace with his willful behavior, and he was very nearly expelled from school. At the age of ten he wrote his first novel under the influence of his then-favorite author, the adventure writer Mayne Read (1818–1883). In 1892, Evreinov contracted scarlet fever. The resulting period of confinement is credited by his biographer Vasilij Kamenskij, with helping make Evreinov into a magnificent dreamer capable of living "the free life of a free man." In the summer of 1892, Evreinov appeared as a clown under the pseudonym "Boklaro" in a travelling circus near Pskov.

With the arrival of autumn, Evreinov was again off to school, this time to the Imperial School of Jurisprudence in Petersburg where he was admitted because of his privileged status as a son of the gentry and where it was hoped his tendency toward disobedience would be curbed. The school's rigorous curriculum placed great emphasis on the arts and culture as well as law. Among the school's graduates were the composer Čajkovskij and the artist Serov.

While on vacation in Pskov during the summer of 1893, Evreinov made his first public appearance in a play under the pseudonym "Gorkin." Returning to school that autumn, he read about Stanley's adventures in Africa and began to dream about that faraway, miraculous place. Evreinov later travelled to Africa and, upon his return in 1913, posed for a photograph clothed in African garb, staring wistfully at a wooden bird.

Following his family's move to Moscow in 1894 and their taking a *dacha* in Puškino, Evreinov spent his summer holidays (1895–96) performing as a conjurer and travelling about the Moscow suburbs of Sokolniki and Perlovka playing the mandolin and singing serenades in the costume of Pierrot. Pierrot was but a youthful flirtation. Harlequin would become an enduring adult relationship.

Back at the School of Jurisprudence, Evreinov played an active part in the dramatic circle. Here he performed the roles of Franz Moor in Schiller's *The Robbers,* Glumov in Ostrovskij's *Enough Stupidity in Every Wise Man,* and the Son in *The Whirlpool (Omut)* by Vladykin. He excelled in comic roles, especially old men.[10] He directed many of these performances as well. Evreinov wrote his first play, *The Rehearsal (Repeticija),* for this group and composed his first serious musical work at the school. It was a harlequinade-opera-bouffe entitled *The Power of Goblets (Sila čar).*

It was during this period, while on summer vacation from the School of Jurisprudence, that Evreinov saw Leonid Vitalievič Sobinov play Harlequin in an opera by Leoncavallo. Sobinov's performance as Harlelquin later inspired Evreinov to a significant degree to write the one-act harlequinnade *A Merry Death (Veselaja smert',* 1908), the pantomime with a "heroic" Harlequin, and the theatrical pantomime *A Columbine of Today (Kolombina segodnja,* 1915).[11] Evreinov no doubt had Sobinov in mind when he adopted Harlequin, the wise child, as his own persona and as a symbol for his vision of theatre as a world of transformation and imaginative play.

In 1900, under the influence of his history teacher, G. I. Senigov, Evreinov wrote a long four-act drama entitled *Idols, Pagan Gods (Bolvany, kumirskie bogi),* his first play to be published and a forerunner of the large-cast historical dramas he later wrote for the Ancient Theatre in Petersburg.[12]

From 1901 to 1905 Evreinov studied philosophy under the tutelage of Arsenij Vvedenskij. Evreinov had always been and always would be drawn to philosophical questions. At fifteen he was an atheist. At eighteen he began studying Nietzsche, who greatly influenced his thinking on the nature and origins of theatre and on questions of morality. At twenty, following the death of a friend, he began studying the gospels, which remained a lifelong interest, often manifesting itself in his dramatic and theoretical writings. Evreinov's interest in formal religion was as a seeker into the mystery of origins, the ecstasy of religious mystery and the hypnotic power of religious ritual, to which he likened the magic of true theatrical art.[13]

Evreinov graduated from the Imperial School of Jurisprudence in 1901 with a silver medal of merit. His thesis on the history of corporal punishment in Russia was published in 1924. In 1901 he entered the civil service in the office of the Ministry of Roads and Communications in St. Petersburg, where he earned his living until 1910. One of his co-workers there was Mixail Lunačarskij, whose brother Anatolij would become the first People's Commissar of Enlightenment following the 1917 Revolution. Another colleague, the artist Mstislav Dobužinskij, would later design sets for Evreinov at the Ancient Theatre.

At this time the relationship between Evreinov's parents, which had been strained since the birth of their last child, Natalja, in the early 1890s, fell apart in a manner as dramatic and ironic as Evreinov's writing for the theatre. Evreinov's father was having an affair with his children's governess, a fact which came to light when he wrote letters to both his wife and his lover while in Rome. He accidentally put the letter to his wife in the envelope addressed to his lover and vice-versa. The wife decided to use this opportunity to ruin her husband's career and reputation. She took the letter that had been intended for the mistress to the Minister of Communications, who felt compelled to relieve her husband of his position. Evreinov's mother refused to give his father a divorce so that he could marry his mistress, although he lived with her until his death in 1921.

In the family rift that ensued, Evreinov stayed with his mother and broke entirely with his father. His father cut off all financial support to his eldest son, and so Nikolaj had to work and apply for state aid in order to support himself. Evreinov was deeply affected by this turn of events. His comfortable existence had suddenly been disrupted. He kept wondering how his life would have been different had this never happened, an idea which was probably the motivating force behind the creation of *Stepik and Manjuročka* (*Stepik i Manjuročka*, 1905). The play, which concerns an old married couple and their young daughter, examines marital infidelity and incompatibility, a theme echoed in Evreinov's fascination with the eternal romantic triangle of the *commedia dell'arte*—Harlequin, Columbine and Pierrot.[14] Evreinov himself did not marry until the age of forty-two (22 July 1921), and then to a woman twenty years his junior whom he perhaps thought he could influence or control. Anna Evreinov claims that she married her husband in order to "save" him from his mother, who had earlier ruined his father. This is probably more than idle mother-in-law talk and is an interesting observation, given Evreinov's closeness to and, to some extent, identification with his mother. Evreinov, who saw life as an eternal war, an image drawn from the animal kingdom (and one which shows up in the third part of his theatre-in-life dramatic trilogy—*The Theatre of Eternal War*) was not much given to marriage, as the women who pursued him throughout his life discovered to their dismay and consternation.[15]

In the fall of 1901 Evreinov enrolled at the St. Petersburg Conservatoire. Here he studied for four years under Nikolaj Rimskij-Korsakov and Aleksandr Glazunov, taking a course in theory of composition from the former (as had poet Mixail Kuzmin) which included harmony, counterpoint and fugue. Evreinov discontinued his musical studies because of a lack of perfect pitch and his dislike for the strict regimen which a professional musician's life demands. However, his training helped develop in him the strong musical and rhythmic sense that came to characterize his work as director and dramatist. He also composed music for productions at the Ancient and Crooked Mirror Theatres and elsewhere. Paradoxically, Evreinov later said that he regretted having spent so much time studying music.

While he continued to work at his civil service job, Evreinov's plays were being published and performed. In 1902 Evreinov wrote the three-act symbolist-influenced play *The Foundation of Happiness (Fundament sčast'ja)*, a forerunner of his monodramas. It was staged in late January 1905 at St. Petersburg's New Theatre with L. B. Javorskaja in a major role and was, as Evreinov attests, a *"succès de scandale."* It was later produced at the Aleksandrinskij Theatre. On 22 December 1905, *Stepik and Manjuročka* was performed for the first time at the Aleksandrinskij Theatre and was published simultaneously in the second edition of the journal *Theatre and Art (Teatr i iskusstvo)*. On 16 December 1906, *The Beautiful Despot (Krasivyj despot)* premiered at the Literary Artistic Society and played in the same month at the Malyj Theatre in Petersburg. It was later published in an edition by Aleksej Suvorin as well as in the journal *Theatre and Art*. *War (Vojna)* was staged by Javorskaja in Tbilisi and elsewhere in 1906. Evreinov's one-act play *Grandmother (Babuška)*, subtitled "Scenes from a Life," was published as a supplement to *New Time (Novoe vremja)* and performed on 27 January 1907. Written for the actress Strel'skaja, who was celebrating her fiftieth anniversary in the Russian theatre, the play included some of the actress's own words and events from her life. Evreinov's dramatic paradox, *Such a Woman (Takaja ženščina)*, subtitled "The Last Act of a Drama," was published in *Theatre and Art* and performed at the Malyj Theatre in Petersburg on 2 September 1908. In this same period Evreinov adapted Aristophanes' *Plutus* for the modern theatre.[16] The first volume of Evreinov's collected dramatic works appeared in 1908 with volumes two and three appearing in Russia in 1914 and 1923 respectively.

Of the early plays, *The Beautiful Despot*, about a "retrospective dreamer" who, like Evreinov, wants to escape the vulgar present for the beautiful past, is interesting as a precursor of Pirandello's *Enrico IV*. But despite obvious similarities in theme (reality versus illusion, truth versus falsehood, mask versus face, theatre versus life), situation (theatre as locale and metaphor for role-playing in life), in methodology (the play-within-a-play format, violation of the "fourth wall," use of the curtain as an actor in the play, shifting character identities) and in underlying philosophy (theatre as event, life as theatre), significant temperamental and cultural differences too complex to discuss here distinguish the work of the two men. Each artist owed much to philospher Henri Bergson's theory of "creative evolution," whereby man seeks to free himself from the pettiness and egoism of mundane reality so as to transform himself progressively toward spiritual perfection and ultimate happiness. Certainly Pirandello recognized similarities between his work and Evreinov's. In 1924 Pirandello selected Evreinov's *The Chief Thing* as the sole non-Italian offering of his theatre's premiere season in Rome.[17]

In autumn of 1908 Vera Komissarževskaja chose the still relatively unknown Evreinov to replace the already established Vsevolod Mejerxol'd as artistic director of her theatre in St. Petersburg. It was Evreinov's first major directorial appointment. In this same year Evreinov made his first significant contribution in the area of dramatic theory. He called it *monodrama*. At this juncture the real life of Nikolaj Evreinov is partially eclipsed by his self-created and performed biography.

The Portraitists

> *He [Man] feels himself to be godlike and strides with the same elation and ecstasy as the gods he has seen in his dreams. No longer the* artist, *he has himself become a* work of art....
> —Friedrich Nietzsche on the Dionysian rite[18]

Virtually everything that Evreinov wrote—plays, theory, criticism, even history and biography—represented but another chapter in the continuing monodrama of Nikolaj Evreinov. Nowhere is this process better illustrated than in the series of nine monographs he wrote about artist-contemporaries whom he admired.[19]

Of these subjects, Aubrey Beardsley (1872-1898), the great British decadent artist whose drawings graced the pages of *The Yellow Book* and the works of Oscar Wilde, appealed to Evreinov the aesthete and the sensualist.[20] The prevalence of women as goddesses and of hermaphrodites in Beardsley's work found a sympathetic audience in Evreinov, who himself harbored an ambivalent attitude toward Woman as half-devil and half-goddess. Evreinov called Beardsley a fetishist, identifying him with the hero of Beardsley's own novella *Under the Hill,* who "looked at a woman from foot to head instead of the reverse." Evreinov was fascinated and to an extent identified with this artist who, like his hero, was a composite of vices and eccentricities. Like Evreinov, Beardsley was a highly cultured man whose musical training in youth translated into his work as musicality. Evreinov claimed that Beardsley turned from music to drawing because he sought *plastic* rather than *abstract* form. Perhaps he linked Beardsley's attitudes with his own regrets of his early formal study of music. As an artist Beardsley confronted the erotic nature of man and was a perpetrator of what Evreinov called "talented scandal." This talented scandal, argued Evreinov, saves us from deadening routine and engages the free creative will of mankind, whose last vestiges are to be found in childhood and primitive cultures.

Evreinov pursued his own penchant for "talented scandal" in his 1908 production of Oscar Wilde's *Salomé* at the Dramatic Theatre of V. F. Komissarževskaja (with a set design by the painter Kalmakov), which was banned on 28 October, the day following its dress rehearsal. The synod called the production, which played under the title *The Tsar's Daughter,* an "unheard-of blasphemy," although evidence indicates that it was not at all obscene. The banning was a great blow to Evreinov and Komissarževskaja personally and a serious financial setback for the latter's theatre.[21]

All of Evreinov's heroes from Napoleon to Oscar Wilde displayed this propensity for "talented scandal," both in their art and in their lives. Evreinov believed that we remember the actions in life of eccentric historical personages more vividly than we do their accomplishments in whatever their field of endeavor. The true artist creates his life. Beardsley exemplified this. A true eccentric—"capricious," "willful," and "faultfinding" from an early age—he unfortunately ventured too far into dandyism, which caused him, in Evreinov's estimation, to dissipate his life prematurely.[22]

Evreinov had nothing but praise for the "ultra-subjectivism" of Beardsley's art. But like most great artists, his work was misunderstood in its day. The public could not see that Beardsley, whom Evreinov at one point identifies with Harlequin, was laughing "in the face of his own fate." They saw only dissoluteness in his work, the "pranks" of the trickster-artist but not the vision of the "genial seer." "In a word," wrote Evreinov, "the majority acted like a majority with all its distinguishing characteristics." Evreinov was here speaking as much for himself as for Beardsley. An integral part of his philosophy was the concept of "aristocratism." He regarded himself and his supporters as "aristocrats of the theatre," that is, the theatre of life.

Above all, said Evreinov, we are indebted to Beardsley for "the justification of vice through beauty; the ornamentation of sin beyond aesthetic recognition; the transformation of the Black God into the White God who represents the highest magic of art. In this is displayed the great charm of frankness."[23] And here stated with a degree of consciousness befitting him is also Evreinov's own major achievement which his feigned candor and performed egoism so skillfully concealed.

This talent for "artistic scandal" was exercised with perhaps even greater intensity by the subject of another Evreinov monograph, Belgian artist Felician Rops (1833–1898).[24] Various aspects of Rops's life, like Beardsley's, coincided with Evreinov's, a fact which naturally appealed to the latter. Each had a sober, business-minded father and a passionate mother of an artistic bent to whom he was closer. Rops studied law as did Evreinov. Although both men were strongly influenced by women in their youth, Evreinov believed that Rops was susceptible to women's charms at too early an age, precipitating in him a process of degeneration, reminiscent of Beardsley's slide into dandyism. Both Evreinov and Rops were men of striking physical appearance, the former's Renaissance-angelic and the latter's "a cross between Mephistopheles and Apollo."

But most of all, the two men shared much in the way of ideas and temperament. Evreinov suggested that Rops's temperament was largely determined by his mixture of Hungarian and Spanish blood. Evreinov's wife, Anna A. Kašina-Evreinova, suggested that her husband's "flamboyant and artistic nature" is attributable to his Gallic blood which he inherited from his mother.[25]

Rops's illustrations for other people's work tended to offer an independent narration on the artist, much as Evreinov's monographs on artists such as Rops constituted chapters in his own created life's story. Evreinov defended Rops, and thereby himself, arguing both for the integrity of this pursuit and the aestheticism of its treatment as a value unto itself.

Both Rops and Evreinov were fascinated by the mystical and the erotic, two tendencies that combined to produce in them a very strong desire to explore the forbidden. The symbol of and inspiration for these forbidden desires was Woman with whom both men were obsessed.

Rops believed that the spirit of the Devil lived in Woman. This image recurs throughout his work as it does in Evreinov's. It is as if Harlequin, who also has been equated with the Devil, were using his magic slapstick to work his transformative powers on the proceedings.

The artist's muse was a naked maiden, half-Flemish and half-Parisian, throwing open her cloak to reveal her stockings "coquettishly held up by beautiful garters." Rops's picture of his muse bears the inscription: "I want to look for timeless joy...even if the world reacts with terror at my ecstasy in its coarseness, not recognizing what I want to say." Huysmans later took these words for his epigraph to *À rebours*.[26]

Because, said Evreinov, Rops undressed women, looking for a sign of the Devil, he never drew a nude woman, only a naked one. This was a significant point for Evreinov, who had already differentiated between the concepts of nakedness and nudity in an article entitled "The Scenic Value of Nudity."[27] Nakedness, Evreinov maintained, is related to the "problem of sexuality" and nudity to the "problem of pure aesthetics." While every nude woman is also naked, it is by no means true that a naked woman is always nude. Nudity requires "sharpness of outline, a discriminating look in the eyes, chasteness of pose and gesture, the absence of underscoring (i.e., in an exploitative manner) and innocence of action."[28]

Nudity was for Evreinov a means and symbol of revelation. Through the body (the phenomenal) can be perceived the soul (the noumenal). Evreinov wrote in his memoirs, "We grasp the internal via the external. This is the implicit message in every art. Our body is too valuable a conduit to our soul to renounce out of the sanctimonious hypocrisy of bourgeois morality."[29]

Rops needed the naked body, not the nude. He strove to depict "the hideousness of the naked body." At the same time, unlike other artists who sought to capture the beauty of the female form, Rops tried to reveal its "otherworldly essence." He undressed women "beyond nakedness" in order to reveal to men the secret power of Woman. His use of gloves, boots, and hats made the women he drew seem more naked, and his black-and-white drawings provided a greater stimulus to the viewer's imagination than would have brightly colored ones.

In the final analysis, according to Evreinov, Rops came to realize that he had not mastered his subject; it had mastered him. Woman was not his plaything, he was hers, and both he and Woman were the playthings of the Devil.[30] Evreinov found himself in somewhat of a predicament. His own attitude toward women was extremely ambivalent, embodying the fin-de-siècle decadent theme of the harlot-saint. He loved them in a passionate, erotic sense and yet saw them as seductive destroyers. One need only recall his fascination with Columbine, the archetypal symbol of female coquettishness, and Salome, who lured men to their deaths with her dance of the seven veils. This image of Woman the Destroyer was repeated in many of Evreinov's plays, including: Columbine in *A Merry Death;* the Songstress in *In the Stage-Wings of the Soul;* the Barefoot Dancer in *The Chief Thing;* the Seductive Maiden in *The Theatre of Eternal War;* the title character in *Such a Woman (Takaja ženščina,* 1907, originally titled *A Catarrh of the Soul)* who kills her man out of boredom; the female plantation owner with her male slaves in *The Unalterable Betrayal (Neizmennaja izmena,* 1914); "She" in *The Presentation of Love;* and Death in the person of the Dark Lady in *The Foundation of Happiness.* Central to all of these plays is the betrayal of love by Woman, which is a basic theme in the scenarios of the commedia dell'arte.

At the same time, Evreinov had before his eyes a model of erotic womanhood in the most positive sense, combining poetry with sensuality. This was Isadora Duncan, the original "barefoot dancer." Evreinov viewed Isadora Duncan as representing the purity of Woman and of Art. On first seeing Duncan, Evreinov recalled that he thought he saw a Greek goddess enter the stage. This was consistent with the second half of Evreinov's vision of Woman as a spiritual being capable of communing with that higher plane of reality to which Vjačeslav Ivanov had referred. Evreinov's descriptions of actress Vera Komissarževskaja suggest that she was also for him one of these spiritual women but perhaps without Duncan's potentially destructive sensuality. Evreinov presented such an idealized image of Woman in his play *The Ship of the Righteous* (1924) in the person of "the One Called Dream."[31]

"Forget about Rops," wrote Evreinov, "and your vision of Woman is altogether different, positive."[32] But Evreinov's own divided vision of woman could not be so easily reconciled. He loved women, he said, because he loved puzzles and because Woman has a thousand masks. As he lay upon his deathbed, Death appeared to Evreinov in the image of a woman.[33]

Evreinov claimed that hardly a single intimacy of Rops's "criminally normal" private life or personality is illuminated by his work, a claim which likewise could be made of Evreinov. Rops, like Evreinov, expressed private dissatisfaction with the century of positivism into which he was born, however, and yearned for the "now extinct passions of the Middle Ages." Both men wanted to live in dreams, and through their art (and in Evreinov's theatricalization of his life), they succeeded partially in doing so.[34]

Unlike the generation of Russian artists who looked to the past for inspiration in their work, Evreinov sought to return to the past out of a sense of personal need and belonging. Evreinov was interested in more than simply restaging old plays in naturalistic detail. He wanted to re-create the theatrical event, all the particulars of the theatrical milieu of a particular day and age. That is, he sought to re-create the sense of *being there*.

Behind the mask called "Nikolaj Evreinov" there was a man in search of his true identity, who seemed to gravitate toward artists like himself in search of his own true essence. There was, in this quest, the ever present danger that Harlequin could eventually transform himself into nothingness.

Evreinov ran the banner of subjectivism into the camp of another artist in his monograph on the Russian painter Mixail V. Nesterov (1862-1942).[35] Evreinov refers to the "Nesterov landscape," the "Nesterov mood," the "Nesterov woman," the "Nesterov face," and says how wonderful it must be for the artist "not only to enrich the world of our images but further to instill his subjective differentiation in a definite series of images so immediate that we all recognize the artists by his work...." The artist who, by means of his "creative I," can reveal "the objects of the real world which we do not see, do not think about, and do not feel in any way other than as objects, must either be a genius or at least a man of genius, i.e., brilliant."[36]

Aside from the subjective attitude which Evreinov maintained was embodied in Nesterov's work, this painter of religious subjects would seem to be a strange choice for the man who selected artists he could treat "monodramatically." Indeed, Evreinov states that he once "felt himself to be a sinner who could not ascend into the Nesterov heavens," until he came to realize that even an atheist is religious in a small corner of his soul and so can attempt to approach such a subject. As he liked to remind his friends and acquaintances as well as himself on occasion, the atheist Evreinov was a religious man after his own fashion.[37]

Evreinov was not an atheist in his wife's estimation. Although he did not subscribe to any of the professed faiths, he did believe in the forces of good and evil, surely in God and possibly in the Devil. Yet he believed in the necessity of man to control his own fate.[38] Atheism was, one suspects, a badge which Evreinov wore rather proudly, a sign of the times and of his own provocative personality.

Evreinov did not, in any case, approach Nesterov as a "religious" painter in the formal sense of the word. What appealed to him was the mystical, symbolist qualities of Nesterov's paintings and perhaps even more than this, their Russianness.[39] Nesterov's view of art closely resembled that of Lev Tolstoj, who said that art should be a means of conveying feelings with religious consciousness. Nesterov makes us feel through his work that "before us is by no means a religious man in a general sense, but an orthodox (i.e., Russian Orthodox) religious man, a genuine Russian artist, a Russian thinker, a Russian man, and a mystic."

Another disaffected member of the century of positivism, Nesterov created portraits of holy Russia and not the secular image into which it had been transformed by the Revolution. In his affinity for Nesterov, Evreinov's own nostalgia for the pre-Revolutionary days is evident. His mourning the passing of the "Nesterov landscape" is a cry for his own paradise lost, a homeland as with many other Russian artists that was more a dreamscape than a reality in the first place.

Aside from the nostalgia that Nesterov's paintings evoked in him, there were particular qualities which appealed to Evreinov. The "childlike clarity of the forms" to which Evreinov responded in Nesterov's springtime landscapes resembled the spirit, vision, and forms manifested in his own work at the Merry Theatre for Grown-up Children, the Ancient Theatre, and the Crooked Mirror Theatre. The Ancient Theatre in particular took a primitivistic approach to the design and staging of plays. This was in keeping with the spirit, religion, and theatrical conventions of the times being represented (the Middle Ages and the sixteenth through seventeenth centuries in Spain). The Merry Theatre for Grown-up Children and the Crooked Mirror Theatre had at their core the soul of childhood play, although at the Crooked Mirror naive staging methods belied sophisticated artistic sensibilities.

It is not at all surprising that the man who adopted the mask of Harlequin as his persona could relate to the gentle, childlike quality of Nesterov's paintings. Evreinov recalled how Nesterov once showed him a painting of his on which were written the evangelical words: "Until you become like a child, you will not enter into the kingdom of heaven." This more than anything may explain why the sinner Evreinov could "ascend into the Nesterov heavens."

Nesterov used the methods of realistic painting to achieve irrational, unreal effects of spiritual significance. "In these 'fairy tale' forms of religious painting," Evreinov reflected, "we are returned to the blissful times and genuine mystical experiences of childhood." There seem to be mythic overtones to Nesterov's work, the sense that throught the hypnotic power of art, we can be led back to childhood, to origins and essences. This belief in the power of art was part of the symbolist legacy inherited by Evreinov and molded into his own personal vision.

In discussing the effect produced upon the viewer by Nesterov's painting, Evreinov again equated the power of art with dream-induced hypnosis, which can "convert even an atheist."[40] Art, and theatre in particular, was for Evreinov a kind of magic. The connection between art and magic had been perceived earlier by Oscar Wilde and the French decadent poets. In Evreinov's day Konstantin Bal'mont proclaimed "poetry as magic." Although Evreinov's detractors regarded his brand of magic as mere sleight of hand, he had something a good deal more serious in mind.[41]

Evreinov said of Nesterov that "his focus is not on God but on man. He loves man and believes in his salvation." So it was with Evreinov. Theatre's magic was for him its power to transform. Transformation could eventually cure man and society at large. Oscar Wilde had said that man is saved by the therapeutic, "beautiful lie" that is art. Evreinov believed quite literally that theatre could cure sickness. He wrote:

> It is the magic of the theatre, and nothing else, that gives you a new consciousness, a new scale of feelings, a new interest in life and a new will to live. And in this will to live, as we know, lies the secret of our victory over many bodily ills.[42]

In order to cure man, however, art must pervade life. Oscar Wilde wrote:

> If it is to have any therapeutic effect on individuals and nations it [art] must be closely related to common experience, for all the objects we use have their own part in the pattern of our lives and should therefore come as clearly within the province of art as paintings and statues. For he who does not love art in all things does not love it at all, and he who does not need it in all things does not need it at all.[43]

This could be an apologia for Evreinov's central theory of the theatre in life. It is also a restatement of the theme of Evreinov's major dramatic work, *The Chief Thing*. Evreinov saw in Nesterov's paintings the development of a single idea "almost to the extent that it seems one painting follows the other."[44] Evreinov does not actually mention which idea he has in mind, but this is of little consequence. What is important is the process, the sense of an idea being explored, defined and redefined throughout the artist's life and work. This is precisely what Evreinov did in his work, be it original or interpretive, practical or theoretical. Indeed, in his monograph on Evreinov, B. V. Kazanskij insists that it is only from this point of view that Evreinov's "method of theatre" is explicable. One must study not only Evreinov's theories, Kazanskij claims, but his "active slogans which powerfully dictate a new direction and even a new 'life' for the theatre, and also Evreinov, himself, as a theatrical phenomenon." Henri Bergson, a major influence on Evreinov's work, once said "his entire life's work, his ever expanding philosophy, was an attempt to express the simple concrete truths which he felt intuitively."[45] Evreinov's complex artistic masquerade may ultimately have been created to mask just such a simple truth, experienced intuitively and a bit guiltily but steadfastly held nonetheless.

One more example from Evreinov's monograph writing will suffice. In 1922 Evreinov sprang what was perhaps his most self-conscious, idiosyncratic written conceit on the unwary public. It was entitled *The Original on the Portraitists (Original o portretistax)* and exemplified Evreinov's life as monodrama. Evreinov claimed with a touch of false humility that this book was written only for and at the prompting of his friends. Let them take full responsibility for it, he said, "I wash my hands of the whole thing."

The question the book ostensibly seeks to answer is the same which Evreinov examined in his treatment of the futurist poet Vasilij Kamenskij in *The Theatricalization of Life,* namely: "Why do other artists find me [Evreinov] so attractive?"[46] Evreinov's hypothesis in *The Original on the Portraitists* is that it is not he the artists find attractive, but themselves.

Evreinov refers to each of these portraits of him as a "soul's photograph" (*duševnyj snimok*). He cites Gogol''s narrative tale "The Portrait," Oscar Wilde's *The Picture of Dorian Gray,* Edgar Allan Poe's short story

"The Oval Portrait," and the Polish writer Andzrej Strug's novel *The Portrait* to support his belief that in general the soul of the portraitist is transferred to the portrait on which he is working, even though some other person is the subject.[47]

It soon becomes apparent that Evreinov has an ulterior motive in writing the book. He seeks not only to reveal the portraitist in the portraits which they painted of him but, *via his written descriptions of the portraitists,* to create a self-portrait. This is more than simple revenge. It is the premeditated crime of which Evreinov accused the portraitists but of which they were never guilty in the first place. It is Evreinov who has perpetrated the ruse, and by cataloging the qualities which he ascribes to the portraits and the portraitists, we can at last attempt to complete that self-drawn picture of the original which has been the subject of this chapter.

Evreinov examines portraits of himself by Repin, Dobužinskij, Sorin, Majakovskij, Annenkov, Miss, Kul'bin, Bobyšov, Mak, Šervadšidze, Burljuk and others. Not surprisingly, he felt an ideological kinship with most of these artists and enjoyed close personal and working relationships with some.

Il'ja Repin was Evreinov's summer neighbor in Kuokkala, Finland. But Evreinov rejected Repin's portrait of him on several grounds. First, it depicted him as being too serious. This from a man whose light-minded posturing was designed to disguise or set off his at times embarrassed intellectualism. Second, it makes him seem ponderous. However, it certainly could not do so more than the scholarly advertisements and undigested data that litter Evreinov's work. Third is what Evreinov sees as being the gracelessness of the man here painted. How presumptuous of the artist to suggest that Evreinov, the self-proclaimed Harlequin, could be stiff-legged and artificial. But then the very knowing artifice of Evreinov's performance, the consciousness of process, is very much the point. Fourth, this Evreinov seems proud and self-important. But again he means to be, in the very hope of eliciting a response. He wants to be criticized for thinking himself above the masses so that he can interest them in exploring the whole notion of aristocratism.

Finally, Evreinov protests, there is nothing here which shows him to be light-minded, youthful or even effeminate in his appearance. He seems rather to be strong, mature, and masculine. Paradoxically, Evreinov here turns real compliments into criticism (whereas before he feigned insult at self-generated critical responses) and then rejects this criticism, because it is inconsistent with his role as the childlike Harlequin. The subtlety of Evreinov's literary game of image manipulation is concealed beneath his typically self-conscious, clumsy, declamatory, theatrical style of expression.

M. B. Dobužinskij was a designer for Evreinov at the Ancient Theatre in St. Petersburg. Evreinov describes him as having had "an aristocratic, lordly, somewhat haughty air." This, Evreinov says, along with the jaded, dissipated look of the overripe aesthete, was reflected in the artist's portrait of him. However, by rejecting the qualities which Dobužinskij projected upon him in a book offering a mirror image of the truth, Evreinov actually confirms them. As final proof of this, Evreinov labels Dobužinskij "a retrospective dreamer" (a term borrowed from Sergej Makovskij), inferring that this quality likewise has been transmitted to "Evreinov's" portrait. Could Evreinov seriously refute this characterization of himself? His work as cofounder and director of the Ancient Theatre and his personal correspondence makes it seem impossible.

Evreinov's ability to bend the truth, which he would say is relative, in any case, derived in large part from another quality he ascribed to Dobužinskij — a sense of irony. He regarded Dobužinskij's portrait of him as an exercise in self-caricature. So may we regard Evreinov's treatment of the portraitists.

S. A. Sorin, who like Dobužinskij belonged to the World of Art group, was spiritually akin to Evreinov. Sorin painted a highly angelic-looking, Italianate portrait of Evreinov as a Renaissance youth (see fig. 2). It again conveys the image of Evreinov as the affected aesthete, a characterization Evreinov naturally ascribes instead to Sorin himself. Evreinov credits Sorin with having a quiet, cultured manner. The critics, Evreinov relates, argued over the extent of Sorin's talent, but Evreinov loves him for, of all things, his sincerity.[48] Evreinov is again offering his own defense.

N. I. Kul'bin was, in Evreinov's words, "the chief of the Russian futurists." Evreinov's friend and co-worker, Kul'bin did the illustrations for *The Theatre as Such* and *The Theatre for Oneself* (parts 1 and 3). Evreinov wrote a monograph entitled *Kul'bin* (1912) which was highly complimentary of the artist. Evreinov admired Kul'bin, because he, like Kamenskij, had "theatricalized" his life, injected it with a sense of "theatrical hyperbole." Evreinov suggests that there was a cross-fertilization of identities between them, a "spiritual marriage" based upon the concept of theatricality.

The two were further linked by their belief in the primacy of subjectivity in art. In his article "Free Art as the Basis of Life" (*Svobodnoe iskusstvo kak osnova žizni*) in the anthology *The Studio of the Impressionists (Studija impressionistov),* Kul'bin wrote that the theory of artistic creation "appears to me to consist of three parts: the psychology of the artist, of the picture, and of the spectator." Evreinov added that for Kul'bin, as for himself, the artist comes first. In his article "He who

Disturbs the Water" (*Tot komu nado vozmuščat' vodu*) in *Kul'bin,* Sergej Gorodeckij characterized the world depicted by Kul'bin as "a field of battle between Subject and Object." It follows, Evreinov contends, that Kul'bin's portrait of him should be highly subjective. Evreinov writes:

> It is he [Kul'bin], he himself in the role of Evreinov. It is he craning his neck and inspirationally called to something "on high!" It is over his forehead that the alluring legs of Harlequin twitch and dance! It is he, he himself, who is "acting like a madman" — he himself who is half-fool and half-saint, astounding indefatigable, unyielding!... It is his theatre, his, his, his![49]

After discussing the creative efforts of Burljuk, Majakovskij, and Miss, Evreinov brings the various portraits of himself to life in a discussion format. Each claims to be the real "Evreinov," but speaks with the voice of the portraitist, and each tries in comic fashion to act in a manner which it thinks befits Evreinov. As the discussion concludes, an unidentified voice is heard. It names all the "Evreinovs" imposters, paralleling the very charge brought by the critics against the "real" Evreinov (who has by now become increasingly more spectral) in each of the roles he played in life: Evreinov-theorist, Evreinov-historian, Evreinov-dramatist, Evreinov-director. Harlequin again displays the capacity to laugh at himself. However, in so doing, Evreinov's agile Harlequin mind has turned the laughter against his critics.[50]

The Chinese puzzle structure of this book is symbolic of the self-conscious, third person manner in which Evreinov viewed himself. One of the book's photographs succinctly illustrates this. It shows Il'ja Repin painting Evreinov's portrait. The artist and subject are visible but the portrait is not. Thus could Evreinov not only pick up this photograph and see himself in the process of being transformed into a work of art, he could help render the unseen portrait by setting this photograph among his own carefully "painted" words.[51] The effect, to borrow Robert Alter's description of a moment from *Don Quixote,* is:

> that of a mirror within a painting reflecting the subject of the painting, or the deployment of still photographs within a film: through a sudden glimpse of multiple possibilities of representation we are brought up short and thus moved to ponder the nature of representation and the presence of the artful representer.

Not only is the mirror a pervasive metaphor in Evreinov's work, but the theatre is by its very nature as seeing-place, with its stage the reverse image of the audience perspective, the perfect setting for this metaphor. Evreinov was a great admirer of Don Quixote, with whom he shared an overwhelming impulse toward a metatheatrical mode of existence. At the same time,

Evreinov shared with Cervantes a penchant for dramatic sleight of hand and interpolated narrative. We might then dub Evreinov, who impersonates both Cervantes the creator and Quixote the creation, with an appropriate title—the Knight of the Crooked Mirror, calling everyone to the theatre in life with a series of well-rehearsed and well-played fanfares.

Luigi Pirandello, with whose dramaturgy Evreinov's work has often been compared, wrote:

> When a man lives, he does not see himself. Well, put a mirror before him and make him see himself in the act of living. Either he is astonished at his own appearance, or else he turns away his eyes so as not to see himself, or else in disgust he spits at his image, or, again, clenches his fist to break it. In a word, there arises a crisis...[52]

Pirandello did not here take into account another crisis upon which he built his plays—the confusion of subject with object, of the original with a clever artist's copy. Throughout his career, Evreinov delighted in singing the refrain, "I am not that man!" The picture which emerges of him, his *duševnyj snimok,* is consequently drawn from absence and is so riddled with doubt, contradiction, and compounded reflections as to suggest nothing so much as a seductive, bottomless, "moving void," Jan Kott's capsule description of Xlestakov.[53] Evreinov, the alleged narcissist, was seduced by the very blankness he saw in his crooked mirror.

3

Monodrama

> *I am Harlequin and as Harlequin I shall die.*
> —Evreinov[1]

Prototypes

Monodrama was an almost forgotten form when Evreinov appropriated the name but changed the meaning to fit the mood of pre-Revolutionary Russian society and his own particular frame of mind. In the nineteenth century the term had been used to denote a dramatic medley composed of a series of scenes from famous tragedies, presented by a single actor and designed to show off the performer's abilities. It described a form, an arrangement of dramatic pieces, no more.[2] Evreinov internalized the idea of monodrama. Although it retained its character as a means of display dependent more on form than content, he brought to it psychological and even philosophical implications which the original concept never could suggest. The theory of monodrama legitimized, indeed extolled the idea of subjectivism in the theatre. Evreinov's concept of monodrama reflected the new consciousness of the theatre of his time, which could no longer return to the naive realism of the Moscow Art Theatre nor to a dogmatic form and so looked for a path in the direction of relativism.[3] For Evreinov personally monodrama was just one of several attempts to apply to his art the principles of behavior he applied to his life. In his anxious hands monodrama became as dogmatic as the forms he was seeking to avoid.

Evreinov introduced his theory of monodrama in a public lecture delivered at the Literary-Artistic Circle in Moscow, on 16 December 1908.[4] In what he called his "apology for theatricality," Evreinov argued that theatre was theatre, and not meant to be used as a school, temple, podium or mirror reflecting reality, as his contemporaries had maintained. That theatre has lost its sense of identity, its theatricality, can be attributed to an unhealthy reliance on literature and worn-out convention. It is not enough to do away with the footlights and Stanislavskij's mythical "fourth wall." The theatre must destroy the footlights that continue to burn in the mind of the spectator, preventing him from entering completely into the drama onstage.

Evreinov believed that the spectator will relate only to that stage action which he can call *his* drama, which he can co-experience with the character in the play as if *he*, the spectator, were playing the role. The conventional play dissipates the spectator's concentration by asking him to divide his attention among a number of different characters and to adopt, to a limited extent, their points of view. The result is that the spectator, whose attention has been spread too thin, becomes a passive observer.

In monodrama, we are given a single hero with whom to identify, and he is reinforced by all of the events and other characters onstage. The spectator can readily absorb the unified view being presented, namely the world as refracted through the prism of the hero's consciousness. The spectator is meant to co-experience each new sensation, each new perception with the hero. The hero's drunkenness is suggested to the spectator by projecting circles of green light onstage, his dizziness by causing the scenery to sway, and so on to express his various states of mind. Stage properties are to be treated as if they were circulating in the hero's blood and so may change size, color, and shape. All of this is necessary, in Evreinov's opinion, because we listen more with our eyes than with our ears. He believed, as did many of the theatrical innovators who were his contemporaries, that words constitute an insufficient mode of expression in the theatre.

Critical reaction to Evreinov's theory was immediate and vociferous, attacking its vagueness and vagaries. Most of the criticism focused on monodrama's central concept, co-experiencing. It was the opinion of some that such an arrangement between character and spectator would destroy the latter's aesthetic distance. Evreinov countered that only through monodrama could the spectator experience a moment of true "aesthetic significance," a complete impression, rather than the fragmented one that standard drama provides.

Some critics argued that co-experiencing could have ludicrous and unfortunate results. We know that if the hero goes to sleep or is depressed, the stage may be plunged into darkness. But what happens to the spectator if the hero is hit over the head with a stick? If this question seems facetious, it does nevertheless draw attention to the fact that Evreinov never made it clear just how far he wanted his concept of co-experiencing to go, and how it would be effected beyond the several instances which he cited.

It was said, too, that Evreinov's eagerness to mingle stage and audience abnegated the responsibility for creation to the spectator. Evreinov answered that monodramas were to be fully scripted, carefully staged and scrupulously rehearsed performances in which the audience would play an important but limited role. It seems ironic that the perceptions of the audience, the nominal co-creator of the theatrical event, were more carefully manipulated in monodrama than in a standard stage piece. Ultimately, increased audience involvement is not really synonymous with audience freedom or creativity.

Another criticism of monodrama as a theoretical concept was that it forces us to sacrifice our objectivity regarding the hero. Whereas in a traditionally structured play we learn much about the hero from what others say, in monodrama these other characters are all shaped by the hero's imagination and perceptions.[5] Who, then is to tell us about him? Evreinov replied that in any play, we are essentially seeing the character from a single, subjective point of view, the author's. He cited as examples, Puškin's *Tales of Belkin,* Robert Browning's *The Ring and the Book,* and Griboedov's *Woe from Wit.* All of the characters in Griboedov's play, with the exception of Čackij, who represents the author, are filtered through the creative "I" of the author/hero and made to seem as grotesque to us as they do to him.[6] So why not accept this as a condition of art in general and allow the artist free rein to explore the power of this impulse in conscious agreement with his audience?

Evreinov was further accused of trying to ease the audience and the actor out of the theatre, a charge to which innovative artists of the day were extremely sensitive, because it was made so frequently. But this was not Evreinov's intention. What Evreinov wanted was to break down the concept of audience as an entity, separate from the dramatic action. For him, theatre flowed into life and life into theatre, with each of us serving both as actor and audience member. But this concept was not yet fully developed in Evreinov's mind, and monodrama, which was a step in the development of his theatre-in-life philosophy, was treated according to its own merits and demerits.

Evreinov built up gradually to the scripting of a full-fledged monodrama, experimenting first with isolating relevant techniques as a director and dramatist. For example, his primitivistic production of Schiller's *The Maid of Orleans* (1908) was designed to present Joan of Arc (played by the actor Glagolin) from a particular point of view, namely as she was conceived by the medieval mentality. The childlike style of design and acting foreshadowed Evreinov's later work at the Ancient Theatre, and his abolition of the footlights preceded Reinhardt's production of *Oedipus Rex* by two years.

In his production of D'Annunzio's *Francesca da Rimini* (1908) at the Dramatic Theatre of Vera Komissarževskaja, Evreinov sought to create a picturesque and evocative rendering of the mood of the thirteenth century, while capturing also the absolute values and naive perspective of its people. To accomplish this, Evreinov divided a bare platform stage diagonally into areas of darkness and light. On the dark side Evreinov concentrated all of the negative elements in the play and on the light side all of the positive.[7] Costumes and lighting were designed so as to make even death and terror appear beautiful. The actors in the crowd scenes were divided according to their vocal pitch and utilized as a sort of chorus. This increased the auditory beauty and removed the production from the domain of realism. The result was a highly stylized production which, although not historically accurate in every detail, conveyed what Evreinov felt to be the essence of the spiritual life of that century. It is significant that some critics made reference to the cold, dispassionate quality of the actors' play.[8] This was one of the accusations hurled at monodrama when it surfaced one year later as a formal theory.

Evreinov's three-act "black comedy," *The Foundation of Happiness* (1902) introduces in dramatic form Evreinov's preoccupation with death and the means at man's disposal for defeating it.[9] Evreinov presents death in the person of the Dark Lady, a symbolist specter representing his archetypal woman—wet nurse, lover and executioner, giving life and taking it away, bearing the scent of sexuality and mortality.

The play's protagonist, Černuškin the coffin-maker, has callously calculated the value of a corpse as being greater than that of a living body. His insensitivity is used ironically since the coffin-maker serves as a spokesman for Evreinov's relative outlook on life. One person's happiness, he says, depends upon another's unhappiness, and everything in the world is determined by your point of view.

The Dark Lady appears to Černuškin on two occasions, once when he is drunk and later when he is sleeping. The stage is completely dark. "The silence unnoticeably gives way to the sound of muffled voices, street noise, a funeral knell, footsteps, the slamming of doors." Then the stage is bathed in sunlight. Černuškin stands behind a writing desk, and before him stand several customers. He conducts business as usual until a policeman appears and hands him a summons to report to the police station. It seems that three coffins Černuškin built have fallen apart. A moment later three workers appear demanding a raise. The stage darkens. Someone shouts "Fire!" The stage is bathed in red light. After much smoke, noise and confusion, the fire is put out.

The Dark Lady reappears. Lifting her veil of mourning, the stage is again plunged into darkness as her words echo forth:

> I am death! (Loud laughter of inhuman voices. Clear bluish light. Before Černuškin, in place of his former vision, there stands a tall, pale lady dressed in fantastic black attire

with a glittering royal crown on her head, curls black as pitch framing a supernaturally exquisite face with huge, lustrous eyes, a thin nose, and deathly blue lips. On her back are majestically-spread black wings. The gestures of her boney white hands with blue finger nails are full of assurance and beauty.) Death! (A second burst of ghoulish laughter.) Death!!! (A third burst of laughter more violent than the first two. Clear bluish light changes into shimmering bluish-green half-light.)

The Dark Lady approaches Černuškin. He gives a shout, and she disappears. It seems that it was all a dream. And yet a moment later Černuškin falls down dead, apparently of a heart attack. His last words are "God works in mysterious ways," the same hollow line he habitually repeated to each of his customers.[10]

This heavy-handed play, laden with chiaroscuro effects and symbolist devices, images and themes, showcases Evreinov's early tendencies toward fatalism and romantic excess, and toward philosophizing at the expense of dramatizing, which the full-fledged monodramatic form would help him to check with succinctness and humor. Already apparent in this play, however, are a number of ideas and perspectives Evreinov would utilize to greater advantage in the near future: (1) the Demonic Woman, (2) unorthodox subject matter presented in strange occupations, settings and circumstances, (3) a sense of ironic detachment regarding life and death, together with the disclaimer that nothing should be taken seriously, (4) a preponderance of scenic effects, especially lighting, to suggest the state of mind of the protagonist (there is even a lace curtain drawn across the proscenium to suggest Černuškin's dream state), and (5) the search for happiness through a consistent philosophy of life.

Evreinov's first full-scale monodrama, *The Presentation of Love (Predstavlenie ljubvi)*, with an accompanying introduction, was published in the almanac *The Studio of the Impressionists (Studija impressionistov,* 1910) and echoed nearly all of the major points in Evreinov's *Introduction to Monodrama*. In his introduction to the play, Evreinov was careful to point out that the play preceded the theory; indeed, the theory developed as a *consequence* of the play. Evreinov felt it necessary to emphasize this in order to forestall accusations that the play was cooked up according to a recipe. Others, he said, had appropriated the name "monodrama" for plays they had written without fully understanding the implications of this approach. Evreinov claimed that "monodrama"—which he here defined as "a theory of architectonic drama with a subjective-impressionistic base"— had been employed by others only for the purpose of seeming modish. *The Presentation of Love,* he insisted, was the first true example of monodrama.[11] Evreinov added that in presenting monodrama as the most perfect form of drama, he was by no means excluding other forms of dramatic presentation.[12]

The Presentation of Love premiered not in Russia but in Vienna and later in Budapest. It is an ironic play beginning with the title, borrowed from Schopenhauer's concept of the world as presentation, a key influence on Evreinov's idea of theatrical role-playing in life.[13]

Utilizing the play-within-a-play structure that would become a staple of his dramatic writing, Evreinov illustrates how the fire of a young man's love and young love and idealism transforms the world. He then contrasts this monodramatic perspective with the more sober and realistic view of the same character grown old.

The play begins and ends with the protagonist, known unromantically and generically (typical of Evreinov) as the Catarrhal Subject (C.S.), in his old age meditating and discussing on a bench by the sea with his cohort, the similarly named Hemorroidal Type (H.T.).

In the midst of his conversation with H. T., C. S. breaks into a scene of remembrance which will become the play we see or read. It is a scene from his youth in which C. S. is "I," a cheerful twenty-year-old man. "I" runs on stage with his friends, following a little ball which is rolling away. C. S., who like us is observing the scene from the outside, offers some narration: "My appearance transforms the entire scene. The sky becomes deep blue, clear. The sea livens up and becomes extraordinarily beautiful. Exceptionally brilliant sunlight illuminates the dark pine trees, etc." We quickly note that when a character is no longer of immediate concern to "I," he or she disappears.

"I" tells a fairy tale to Ženja, a child (the prototype for Evreinov's theatre of imaginative play and transformation), about a princess whose father and mother, the Sun and Moon, sent her to earth to cheer up the inhabitants with her miraculous beauty. This foreshadows Evreinov's quintessential theatre-in-life play *The Chief Thing* in which brothers and sisters of mercy, the children of one Doctor Fregoli (and by inference of Christ and of God), are sent to a drab boarding house to raise the spirits of its inhabitants by administering the curative power of the "beautiful lie" which is theatre.

"I" keeps getting lost in thought as he tells the story, creating the impression that it is autobiographical. Whenever he becomes lost in thought, his friend Ženja disappears. "I" does not notice this, and when he covers his eyes there is darkness.

An interesting feature of this play is that all of the stage directions for "I" are written in the first person as if he were to read them aloud. The stage directions for "She" are written in the third person. This produces a narrative effect, the sense of having an additional angle of perception on the action. In the introduction Evreinov advises the reader of his play that the stage directions indicate only the major transformations of the world surrounding "I." The remaining transformations should be provided by the reader in accordance with the motion of the play.

"I" describes the princess in ideal terms, and once described, she appears. When "My Rival" appears for the first time, the stage grows dark. He is a military officer of colossal height, almost a giant. His attire is dark and his face red with a black moustache and a huge lower lip. He has a well-muscled body, a "brutal and indescribably banal face, a hoarse, raucous, disgusting voice. He smokes a large cigarette which makes him look like a steam engine." When he leaves, all again becomes clear and bright. When "I" closes his eyes after receiving a kiss from She, "there is a heavenly-pink light like the kind you see when you close your eyes from happiness after looking into the bright, midday sun."[14]

As the tale progresses, "I" is transformed into the Prince and "She" into the Princess. The latter is also identified with the sea which the Catarrhal Subject, who is imagining/remembering the story, observes through binoculars and discourses upon. He says that you cannot help loving the sea, because it is always moving and changing. Yet, the C.S. feels compelled to justify the sea from several different points of view: (1) the *aesthetic* (its ever-changing character); (2) the *medical* (the sea refreshes us, although if we are not careful it can give us colds); (3) the *gastronomical* (we get fish from the sea); and (4) the *erotic* (he never explains). In doing this, the C.S. is justifying his youthful ideals and his past love. Not incidentally, these were precisely the ways in which Evreinov justified theatre, as his writings, laden with descriptive adjectives and adverbs drawn from these categories, attest. "It is a sin," the C.S. says, "to be a naturalist. When the nymphs are bathing in the sea who can be a naturalist?"[15] So asked Evreinov of the realistic-naturalistic theatre to which he offered the haute cuisine of theatricality.

At the same time, these justifications represent the various functions artists and theorists of the period ascribed to theatre to validate and, in some cases, idealize its existence: temple of art, political forum, medical arena, school, tribunal, pulpit, and the like. These attempts to define the theatre in turn elicited Evreinov's response. Although Evreinov rejected the popular notion of theatre as mirror accurately reflecting reality, he did in his monodramas and parodies embrace the concept of theatre for oneself as a *crooked* mirror distorting reality. The sea in *Presentation,* reflected upon and reflecting back ones subjective reality, is one of many symbols in Evreinov's work of the crooked mirror. The relationship between the perceiver and the sea represents then a kind of theatre of the crooked mirror.

In this play, nature in general reflects the protagonist's mental and emotional states. Trees droop and the sky darkens to dramatize how we turn the world gray in our moments of grief. We cannot bear the world to be indifferent to us, to be unresponsive to our suffering. Again, we hear Evreinov's voice craving response at any expense while at the same time mocking his own self-absorption by wittily (although it reads sentimentally) painting the world gray with his grief.

"I"'s story ends abruptly in disillusionment, since, as he says, "a real fairy tale cannot last long." He has, in a sense, been victimized by his dreams, but he and Evreinov tell us, it is better to have felt something than to have felt nothing at all. This, from the poet of intensified subjectivism and theatrical hyperbole, rings true, although equally true and necessary is "I"'s eventual working through his adolescent angst to a more balanced and realistic older self, the storyteller C.S.

Each of us, Evreinov believed, is like a mirror held before the face of the Almighty. The extent to which we purge ourselves will determine how clear a reflected image of the Deity we will become. This idea of working through the self to the more hallowed reaches of the soul beyond, which defines Evreinov's view of his own role-playing and that of theatre, finds its most direct expression in his most unique and successful experiment in monodrama, *In the Stage-Wings of the Soul* (*V kulisax duši,* 1911). Evreinov called this the most original play in the history of world theatre. Even discounting his usual flair for hyperbole, it would be difficult to imagine a more unusual play than this, set inside a man's body and depicting his giant internal organs onstage. The directorate of the Crooked Mirror Theatre, to whom Evreinov submitted the play at the end of the 1911-12 season, was not sure that the public would understand a play the directorate itself had difficulty visualizing. The play was judged to be "wild," "extravagant," and unstageable. It proved to be an overwhelming success, surpassing even Evreinov expectations.[16]

In his efforts to convince the directorate that the play should be staged, Evreinov had already devised a detailed model from original sketches. The actual set, designed by M. P. Bobyšov, featured a gigantic spinal column upstage. A large heart, lungs and other organs moved rhythmically in time to the music. Evreinov records that when the curtain went up revealing the set, a lady in the audience fainted and had to be carried out of the auditorium.[17]

The play appeared on a bill of "tragi-farces," a suitable name for Evreinov's dramaturgical fare in general. One critic likened its mixture of tragedy and comedy to blending wine with poison.[18] *In the Stage-Wings of the Soul* was the perfect theatrical vehicle for Evreinov's theory. Its simple, melodramatic tale of a man who abandons his wife and child for a café singer, only to be left by her and so driven to suicide, is infused with irony and has all the hallmarks of the monodramatic form. The cast of characters includes the hero's three Selves — the rational, the emotional and the eternal — as well as the subjective images of the Songstress and the Wife which they summon up.

The rational and emotional Selves are in constant conflict, co-existing in an adversary relationship, while the eternal Self remains aloof. Naturally, the rational Self demands that the man return to his wife and child, while the emotional Self urges him to forsake his boring existence and run away with the Songstress. The emotional Self depicts the Songstress as a gay and seductive young woman who sings in French and dances, while the man's heart beats joyfully in time. The rational Self counters with a grotesque caricature of the Songstress, forty years old with ingrown toenails, corns on her feet, a wig, falsies and false teeth. She gums her words and "prances about with all the grace of some old nag being sent off to the glue factory."[19]

As a pleasant alternative, the rational Self offers an image of the man's wife as an ideal mother, rocking her baby in her arms and singing a gentle lullaby. But the emotional Self calls this a "crude idealization" and presents his image of the Wife as "a sharp-tongued petty bourgeoise with a slovenly chignon and dressed in a shabby dressing gown covered with coffee stains." This less than ideal image proceeds to berate the man as a drunken atheist who loves to philosophize but is really stupid as a log.[20]

The wife's image of her husband suggests Evreinov himself, the atheist, the philosopher and, at times, the excessive drinker. For one of their wedding anniversaries, Evreinov drew a picture of himself kneeling at an altar on which stood a giant bottle of liquor, renouncing his weakness forever in favor of his wife's love.[21]

Evreinov, like the unseen hero of his play, was infatuated with a female *artiste* who could very well have been the inspiration for the Songstress, namely Isadora Duncan. The Songstress, representing female demonism, is a close relative of Salome and Columbine in Evreinov's work. Evreinov's use of generic character names suggests a direct line of descent from the character masks, the tragicomic essences of the commedia dell'arte. The split between sainted wife and evil temptress represents only one of the many dualities or paradoxes upon which Evreinov built his theatrical world. In the end, as with Rops, one senses that Evreinov, the would-be Harlequin, was really a Pierrot victimized by Columbine and the earthy reality she embodies.[22]

The "grotesque caricatures" and "crude idealizations" offered by the Selves are equally true and untrue. In an imperfect world everything is relative. Unable to reconcile his internal conflict, the man shoots himself through the heart, an event symbolized by red ribbons emerging through a large, gaping hole in the onstage organ. As the man dies, darkness descends and the Conductor enters with a lighted lantern. The two combatant Selves having been silenced, the eternal Self is now awakened from his sleep and instructed by the Conductor to change here for "Newville." Man is ready for the next step in his transformation, moving toward that time when he will become, according to Evreinov, an image of the Deity in his transparent mask and be happy.[23]

In this play, Evreinov is again arguing for the relativity of truth and in his characteristically ironic way is offering a defense of the primacy of subjectivism, even as he dramatizes its dangers. The play's ending suggests the need to transcend this phenomenal realm for the noumenal as part of Bergson's process of "creative evolution."

However, when the sleeping eternal Self is awakened by the Conductor and moved on to Newville, he is escaping not only a woman who does not understand him and a life that trivializes his dreams but a theatre, embodied in the highly subjective images of wife and mistress, that encourages false values and stagnation. In a world that perceives beauty in "painted sluts" (the Wife's name for the Songstress) on the one hand and the desire to seek beauty and to impart philosophical importance to it as a sort of drunken aesthetic rationale (the Wife's accusation directed at the author/protagonist) on the other, man's spiritual self might just as well sleep until a man of vision appears to show him the way to something better. This godlike figure, this conductor with a lighted lantern and a pathway to the future, is a symbol for the visionary theatre and, if you will, for Evreinov himself.

The play's title, *In the Stage-Wings of the Soul,* relates to Evreinov's message that the real action is not happening here, that is, in the wings, but beyond, on the stage, in a truer reality than the material world can offer. Man, in general, like the actor in the theatre, is always waiting to "go on," whether it is to the stage or to the next stage in his life. We have not yet apprehended the true nature of the soul because we are still mired in the self, but we are en route. Evreinov ingeniously employs the narcissistic theatrical form of the monodrama to make his case that we must work through the self to apprehend where the soul and with it human happiness on its truest, most meaningful level resides. In that the self is the means through which we experience life most directly, we must be allowed to experience it fully and openly without guilt or denial of the sort we see manifested in *Stage-Wings.* Evreinov's own life served as a model for what he preached.

In the Stage-Wings of the Soul reflects the subtle ends to which a paradigm as broadly based as the commedia dell'arte could be applied. It features a prologue (which Kugel', the theatre's coproducer, claims to have written), delivered to the audience in the best theatricalist tradition by an

Il-Dottore type of professor who pompously discourses on current psychophysiological research into the divisible nature of the soul. This scientific justification of art, the calling in of an outside specialist who knows nothing about the nature and function of art (and in this case little more of science) as well as the habit of artists to wrap themselves in an ill-fitting mantle of learning beyond their expertise, is meant to satirize Stanislavskij and his fascination with the writings of Wilhelm Wundt, Sigmund Freud, Johann Gottlieb Fichte and Théodule Armand Ribot, all of whom are mentioned here by name.

Evreinov is also here spoofing his own attempts at achieving intellectual parity for himself and his theatrical concerns by raiding the scholarly coffers of more traditionally academic disciplines. His productions at the Ancient Theatre were preceded by lectures delivered by noted scholars which not only oriented the audience but lent credibility to the productions they were about to see.

As in commedia, the eternal Self in *Stage-Wings* wears a black half-mask, while the remaining Selves are dressed and made up in mask-like, emblematic fashion. More importantly, all three Selves represent agents or essences rather than full-bodied characters. The set in which the greatly magnified internal organs of the unseen man move rhythmically to suit the shifting moods of the action and keep time with the music, creates a comical impression. The two Selves throttle each other in the tradition of the commedia and the puppet theatre, and when the hapless protagonist dies, it is by a self-inflicted gunshot wound to the heart—where once his strings were plucked by emotion and which now gives up red ribbons instead of blood.

In the bulk of Evreinov's dramatic work, as in the classic commedia scenarios on which it is based, it is the treacherous heart that does the hero in. Harlequin, in Evreinov's most famous harlequinade, the one-act *A Merry Death* (*Veselija smert'*, written 1908, premiere 1909), suffers a mild heart attack while doing the Dance of Love (a euphemism for sex) with Columbine and what will be a fatal attack while singing a song. The strings of his lute break like the strings of his heart.

Stage-Wings, a seemingly overripe aesthetic statement spoofing then current scientific developments even as it satirized man's more irrational melodramatic tendencies, embodies the sense of romanticism dying into science that one gets in all of Evreinov's work, a tragicomic paradoxical tone like that of a harlequinade. Like Evreinov's other theories and their artistic manifestations, monodrama was concerned with the drama of being and the search for the ultimate truths of the human condition. Like Sartre after him, Evreinov located the metaphorical hell of other people within the soul, where a man's several selves *are* those other people, engaging in an often vituperative dialectical combat for the right to determine his choices.

Monodrama as a form was ultimately outstripped by the cinema (especially the German expressionist cinema) which it anticipated.[24] However, monodrama soon appeared to Evreinov to be the key to parody and the grotesque, which he developed most fully at the Crooked Mirror Theatre and at the Merry Theatre for Grown-up Children.[25] As a concept, monodrama led logically into his theories of the theatre in life and the theatre for oneself. But as a practical device, a self-contained method of staging, monodrama was a cul-de-sac. It was not, as Aleksandr Bakšij suggested, solely "a specimen of drawing-room philosophy," but neither did it ever really transcend the realm of ideas and establish itself in the realm of stage technique.[26]

Monodrama was perhaps the most brazen example of Evreinov's drawing attention to his "creative I" as the structuring and transforming factor in the theatre of life. As such it serves as a useful construct to apply toward an understanding of the whole Evreinov phenomenon. But as a self-contained subgenre, monodrama suffered, appropriately enough, the fate of Narcissus. It faded away in enraptured contemplation of itself.

However, aside from the continued importance of the "monodramatic" perspective in Evreinov's later work as director and dramatist and the evolution of this idea into his later theories, the form itself has implications for us today. Among its contributions to the modern theatre can be listed the following: (1) the idea of the play's protagonist being split into several selves impersonated by different actors, the concept of a divided self serving as a statement in itself on the condition of modern man; (2) ultra-subjectivism—the tale told from the protagonist's point of view, literally from the inside; (3) this ultra-subjectivism reflected in the transformation of scenic elements; and (4) the physicalization of the abstract mental process of a human being and the resultant demystification of that process: we are machines that function or malfunction depending upon the input from our systems and how well our systems manage to process it.

There is an inherent tension in *Stage-Wings* between this idea and the acute egoism that seems to inform this subjective point of view. Man is the center of the universe and yet he is as a physical being only a bit player in his own life's drama. Evreinov managed to deflate, in characteristically ironic fasion, the Freud-soaked consciousness of Stanislavskij, who saw man as a complex spiritual being.[27] The purposely clichéd romantic plot likewise parodied Stanislavskij's well-known sentimentalism. The very idea of going inside the protagonist's heart and mind made the Stanislavskijan school of psychological realism seem absurd. The scent of absurdism that arose from this rather unusual theatrical stew still effectively titillates our senses today.

Noting the "curious resemblance" between *Endgame* and *In the Stage-Wings of the Soul,* Martin Esslin suggests that Samuel Beckett's play may well be a monodrama "depicting the dissolution of a personality in the hour of death." Albert Camus, one of the prophets of the absurdist theatre, said in his famous manifesto that

> a world that can be explained by reasoning, however faulty, is a familiar world. But in a universe that is suddenly deprived of illusions and of light, man feels a stranger.... This divorce between man and his life, the actor and his setting, truly constitutes the feeling of Absurdity.[28]

The hero of Evreinov's play may represent one of the first casualties of the modern condition.

"Death dances..."

Evreinov's work is unique in that it embodies both the symbolist and realist positions that were current in his day—the possibility of transcendence through transformation and its impossibility. This accounts in part for the tension one experiences between tragic and comic elements in his plays.

But in order to consider transcendence, Evreinov had first to get past the idea of death, something the romantic artists of the last century were unwilling or unable to do. Evreinov, too, was obsessed with mortality—his own and the theatre's—but was neither seduced nor defeated by it. He prized those cultures—the Middle Ages in particular—whose proximity to death, a cautionary sense of death in life, and a compensatory faith in life beyond death, made them inherently theatrical. He recommended that people "try on deaths" as Sarah Bernhardt had lying in her coffin at night, so as to conquer the fear that kept them all from living life to the fullest. And when death comes, he said, laugh and you will have defeated it, for "a Buffoon who does not cease to be a Buffoon before the face of death is a hero, nay a super-hero...."[29]

While the protagonist of *Stage-Wings* is decidedly unheroic, falling upon Death impetuously as if upon his sword, Harlequin in *A Merry Death* approaches Death heroically and fully conscious, laughing "in the face of his own fate," as Evreinov had said of Aubrey Beardsley. He is as conspicuous by his presence as his counterpart in *Stage-Wings* is by his absence, but then Harlequin represents what Evreinov wanted the theatre and mankind to be, while the other represents only what they are.

In *Stage-Wings* and even more so in *A Merry Death,* Evreinov illustrates how the essence of time itself—duration—is masked by its quantitative form — sequence, the ticking of the clock. When Evreinov calls for the action of *Stage-Wings* to transpire "within the space of thirty seconds," he is referring to the time that dictates the inner life of the soul and not to real time or even stage time. As in Maeterlinck's *The Intruder,* Evreinov treats the approach of Death (in *Stage-Wings* and *A Merry Death*) as the distillation into a brief moment, the life of man, that is, his attitudes and what he stands for, who he is. His outer life plays at the speed of farce while his inner life pretends to the grave strains of tragedy.

A Merry Death begins with Pierrot "playing the audience" as befits a theatricalist playwright like Evreinov. Pierrot tells us that the reason people come to the theatre is not to discover meaning or masterful dialogue but "simply to find out how it all turns out in the end."[30] Causality, or the sequence of events toward a resolution, has been served notice. Evreinov frustrates audience expectations from the outset, that is, he "plays the audience." The play's title itself pulls us in two opposite directions, and Pierrot meaningfully suggests that nothing, not even he, is as simple as it seems. Evreinov does this to prepare us for the more significant frustration inherent in the play's theme — the condition whereby man strives against the borders of reality and of the self in an effort to transcend to the realm of the spirit.

When the curtain opens, we find that the set is flat and symmetrical, as we have come to expect from commedia and farce in general. A bed centerstage is framed on either side by a lute and an oversized thermometer. But on the bed lies an unfamiliar sight, not the eternally youthful Harlequin but a gray-haired Harlequin, asleep with flies buzzing around his head. And above his head is a giant clock. Time is clearly of the essence, an impression that is soon reinforced by Pierrot who tells us that Harlequin is dying.

Turning back the clock in a bid to stay the arrival of Death, Pierrot moans "Poor, poor Harle—" at which point a sudden fall changes his tune to "Poor Pierrot," a deftly theatrical comment by Evreinov on the egoism that underlies the mask's pallid romanticism — Narcissus in whiteface.[31] This small detail of observed behavior also pinpoints the tragicomic axis on which the play and Evreinov's theatrical vision in general turns.

Having first turned back the clock to delay the coming of Death, Pierrot now, in a fit of pique and envy, sets the clock ahead to hasten Death's arrival. The two hours' time with which Pierrot plays in either direction might well represent the normal two hours' traffic upon the stage of the realistic theatre. By having Pierrot play with the clock so as to make two hours pass in a single moment, Evreinov plays time much as he plays the audience.

Like Bergson, Evreinov believed that it is stasis, lack of movement through time, that produces conventions, habit, hardening into forms, into masks, into death. It is this inclination toward stasis that results in mechanical, puppetlike behavior, making man a laughable object and we the audience, losing feeling for what is no longer a person but now a thing, able to laugh. But unlike the symbolists, man for Evreinov need not be the puppet of fate. He is given a choice. "Man must conquer his love of geometry. He must see the essence and secret of the world in the movement of life rather than in the inertia of things." Time must be appreciated not in terms of sequence but in terms of duration, the quality of experienced time in the human soul. Duration, evolution, the *élan vital,* the will to transformation toward perfection, "the continual elaboration of the absolutely new," man's constant re-creation of himself—these related ideas accumulate in Evreinov's work (much as time does in Bergson's definition of duration) and resolve themselves into the theory of theatre in life, where every moment is theatricalized so as to realize its fullness.[32] The manner in which one confronts death says much about how one has lived his life. The Doctor who comes to treat Harlequin in *A Merry Death* with his large red nose, enormous glasses, oversized syringe under his arm and his pink pills— the famous quack from Bologna—is powerless to cure his patient or to be cured of his own fear of death. He represents that side of humanity which is death's clown, trembling wastefully through life, never having lived for fear of dying. Having worried away his life, this type of man (the norm) approaches death full of regrets, protestations, false promises, disbelief and oaths (or, like Pierrot, he tries to turn back the hands of the clock in the vain and naive hope that he can stop time). Harlequin, the vital man, is quite the opposite. He has "preserved enough good spirits to welcome death," because he has lived wisely, that is to say, he has lived.

As Harlequin and the Doctor haggle over the latter's fee for services not rendered, the former exclaims, "What is your art worth if it can't save me from death?"[33] He asks the question not only of a particular man but of a certain type of man and the way of life he represents. And since these are theatrical creatures, Harlequin, Evreinov's symbol of the vital theatre, is likewise asking the question of the doctor as a symbol of the deadly theatre: "What is your art worth if it can't save me from death?" This question will be asked again by Evreinov in *The Chief Thing,* subtitled *A Comedy for Some and a Drama for Others,* via the use of *Quo Vadis?* as a play-within-a-play. The Latin title asks the question, Whither goest thou?, a question Evreinov addresses to art in general and theatre in particular. The provincial theatre production of *Quo Vadis?* which we see being rehearsed represents theatre at its deadliest, just as the theatre-in-life mission of mercy being enacted by these same actors—assuming upbeat "real life" roles to cheer up some hard cases in a nearby boarding house—is meant to exemplify how a new, vital theatre can offer salvation to actors and audiences alike.

Harlequin leaves Death only his outer shell. The Doctor and Pierrot have only their outer shells to give. Deathly-pale Pierrot, who lives in fear of life and as a slave to convention, forever acting the role of jealous husband, is destined to lose Columbine over and over again. Sinking into a pool of complaints, he blames the world and bemoans his fate, until like Narcissus he becomes enamored of the pale image reflected in the pool — he learns to love his suffering.

Harlequin has set a table for Death, in the same spirit as Don Juan, another noted death-defier. She appears, "a bright, white skeleton dressed in a billowy transparent dress *similar to Columbine's;* there's some sort of triangle on the skull." Harlequin invites his guest to join him in the traditional Dance of Death — "the dance like they had in the good old days when people still knew how to die, not like today. And Death herself was a source of amusement..." "Harlequin these days," says Harlequin, "is nearly extinct!"

As Harlequin awaits his fate, "Pleasant violin music is heard, appetizingly mingled with the sharp sounds of a xylophone and castanets. Death dances..."[34] The rhythmic pulse of the dance can be heard throughout Evreinov's work as a theatre artist, sometimes distinctly and sometimes subtly as if at the edge of consciousness. It is in his monodramas, his harlequinades, his theatrical pantomimes and in his medieval mystery plays. It is at the conclusion of *The Chief Thing* where the forced merriment of a masquerade ball is revealed in the mechanical rhythms of a bravura waltz. Evreinov's belief in the mystical significance of the dance provided him with the will to explore this domain so frequently. His musical training in composition under Aleksandr Glazunov and Nikolaj Rimskij-Korsakov and his artistically talented inner ear gave him the means by which to set the dance in the drama so effectively. The idea that music and dance and especially their shared element, rhythm, were the basis of all art was, of course, widely held at this time. Russian artists such as Bakst, Mejerxol'd and Sologub, among others, addressed this issue frequently in their work.

A Merry Death climaxes in much the same way with Harlequin's bodily shell falling at Death's feet moments after the Harlequin theme is heard "somewhere far off." As the clock strikes twelve, Pierrot approaches the audience to make a curtain speech in which he disclaims all understanding of and responsibility for what has transpired onstage. Furthermore, he bemoans, à la Gogol''s narrators (see "The Nose"), having subjected them to "a work so lacking in seriousness." He can do no more since, as he tells us, he is "not a free agent." Indeed, his inability to deal meaningfully with time, his inability to change, to be anything other than "the stupid, cowardly Pierrot," his preoccupation with sequence rather than duration has doomed him to remain an inexpressive mask. Pierrot's struggle with what he perceives as his creator's (i.e., Evreinov's) demands effectively dramatizes the human condition that is the spiritual core of the play. Evreinov would have us believe that Pierrot has the human potential to wrest his fate away from the author but cannot yet find within him the greatness of soul that would enable him to play the hero's role.

But even as we are ready to dismiss Pierrot, he is not yet ready to dismiss us. "Lower the curtain! The farce is over!" he shouts, echoing Rabelais on his deathbed. The curtain falls, but Pierrot remains in front of it to urge the audience to refrain from hissing or applauding the play since what they have witnessed is a mere fiction. "Harlequin," he tells us, "has no doubt already risen from his deathbed and is now preening himself for the curtain call."[35] This is more than a bit of last-minute whimsy. For we realize if no one has died, then no one has been saved, no one has transcended. If actors and characters are not free agents—the other half of Evreinov's paradoxical argument says that they might or could be—then perhaps spectators and readers are not free agents either. The play and the employment of Harlequin and Pierrot as polar opposites have embraced both the possibility and the impossibility of meaningful human choice, the kind of paradox that fires the ironist's heart and fueled Evreinov's vision.

In Evreinov the dance of death is the penultimate action of the drama. The curtain makes the final statement. It falls with the impact of a question mark, punctuating without resolving an issue which by its very nature cannot be resolved. On one side of the curtain—the thin veil separating theatre from life—a character mask is frustrating our conditioned responses and sending us away to ponder; meanwhile, on the other side, a character mask, now once again become an actor, is picking himself up and dusting himself off. And like us, he is going home to a life filled with the possibility of victory and defeat.

4

The Theatre in Life

Theatricality

> We were born in twilight. Little by little the masquerade clothing was pulled off from life, the high buskins were thrown off, the laughing masks were torn away.... Reason, science...the satiety of the people, toil-hardened hands—what was left to us except for this? We were born with a concern for our daily bread and for truth and justice—but with the complete atrophy of the feeling of theatricality, the instinct for the transformation of life, the will to the creation of the fantastic. And so it happened as it was bound to happen: the more people came to neglect theatricality, the more they turned from art to life, the more tedious it became to live. We lost our taste for life. Without seasoning, without the salt of theatricality, life was a dish we would only eat by compulsion.[1]

Evreinov, the "retrospective dreamer," was among those artistic souls who found Russia at the turn of the century to be a rather boring, unimaginative, and tasteless place. He was too young to be a part of the wave of Russian romanticism represented by the World of Art, but he was deeply affected by the tendencies and general outlook that movement embodied. Like the Russian symbolists who preceded him and the second generation whose work ran somewhat parallel with his own, Evreinov was searching not simply for a "philosophy of art" but for a "guiding principle" on which to build a way of life.

The "guiding principle" Evreinov fastened upon was *theatricality*. He developed this idea in his major theoretical works, *The Theatre as Such* (*Teatr kak takovoj*, 1912) and especially his trilogy, *The Theatre for Oneself* (*Teatr dlja sebja*, 1915-1917). Each of these books was the printed equivalent of a theatrical presentation. *The Theatre as Such* begins with a loud trumpet blast ("TRA-TA TA!") which is meant to summon the reader to "the presentation of his own life." It is also a call to arms, since Evreinov perceived life as a continuous battle in which theatricality can help insure our salvation. It is by wearing the theatrical motley of the fool rather than by girding oneself in the armorlike conventions of society that one can persevere. Man must learn to play, to transform himself like a child or an animal in order to outwit life.[2]

Evreinov believed that there is in man a pre-potent, pre-aesthetic will to play, to transform himself and the world at large, to create theatre. "The instinct of theatricalization which I claim the honor to have discovered," wrote Evreinov, "may best be described as the desire to be 'different,' to do something that is 'different,' to imagine oneself in surroundings that are 'different' from the commonplace surroundings of our everyday life." In *The Theatre for Oneself* (*part 1*) Evreinov wrote that the chief imperative of the human soul is "Do not be yourself!" When Peer Gynt finally finds himself at the end of his long journey, there is nothing left for him to do but die.[3]

This basic drive can be observed most clearly in children and primitive savages, a fact arguing for its pre-aestheticism. Evreinov wrote: "The art of the theatre is pre-aesthetic and not aesthetic for the simple reason that *transformation,* which is after all the essence of all theatrical art, is more primitive and more easily attainable than *formation,* which is the essence of the fine arts."

The savage's tatooing and adornment of his body and his tendency to ritualize every important event in his life have philosophical implications as understood by Evreinov. He cited A. Zasodinskij (*The Legacy of Centuries*) and Cherbuliez, who argued in *L'Art et la nature* that primitive man in Africa and America, while unfamiliar with the plough, made use of the tambourine and the reed pipe and engaged in dramatic dances. Théodule Ribot, Theophile Gautier, Charles Darwin, and Herbert Spencer provide further evidence that primitive man placed greater importance on decorating (theatricalizing) himself than on safeguarding immediate well-being, that is, his material comfort. Clothing itself developed as a result of man's instinct to theatricalize himself, evolving out of skin decorations.

By transforming his life, Evreinov contends, man becomes its master and makes it meaningful to him: "Who gave the parrot its plumage? Nature. But man, this proud, strong, handsome being does not depend on nature...."[4] or as B. V. Kazanskij explains:

> Theatricality is an attempt by man to reconstruct his life according to a personal plan.... From the day of his birth man wants not only to live but *to be or seem to be something,* to create from the new material of life, a form of life, a personal role....[5]

Evreinov liked to quote a story told by Oscar Wilde of a man who wandered away from his village every morning. He would return in the evening with wonderful stories for the townspeople. In the forest he saw a faun playing on a reed pipe, and around him danced small elves. Then, coming to the sea, the man saw three sirens frolicking in the waves. The people loved these stories. But one time the man came to the sea and indeed saw three sirens frolicking in the waves. He ventured further and saw a faun playing on a reed pipe. Around him danced small elves. When the man returned to his village that night, the people asked him what he had seen, to which he replied, "I did not see anything."[6]

Where does the theatrical instinct come from, and when did it first appear? Evreinov theorized that the awakening of man's will to theatre coincided with his apprehension of his own dualistic nature—body versus soul. Primitive man falls asleep and dreams. In his mind is enacted a scenario which he accepts as being true (that is, he thinks that the events in his dream actually transpired) until it is disproved by comparison with reality. Thus, the wife who was killed in his dream is found still alive when the man awakens. Primitive man begins to realize that in addition to the conscious, waking "I" there is a second "I." In the dream he saw both what he wished for and feared. It is the soul that staged this mythical life, the dream, the spiritual "I" as opposed to the physical "I." Eventually, primitive man comes to realize that if he has the capacity to stage such wonderful plays while asleep, he should also be able to do so when awake. Having reached this awareness, man becomes the conscious theatricalizer of his own life.[7]

Given that the theatrical instinct is basic to all human endeavor, Evreinov reasoned:

> Psychologically speaking, there is but a step from the "masquerading" of the primitive man in his everyday life to theatre in the narrow, technical sense of the word. Indeed, is it not natural for man who adorns his colorless existence by organizing shows under such pretexts as marriage, death, administration of justice, etc., to organize them also without pretexts, that is to say, to stage shows for their own sake? Hence the institution of professional players, of actors....[8]

Evreinov's first full-length discussion of the nature of theatre and its relation to aesthetics in *The Theatre as Such* met with widespread criticism. Evreinov believed that by naming theatre a pre-aesthetic phenomenon, he could free it from the slavery to aestheticism that interfered with the free expression of our will to transform. Julij Ajxenval'd, who was at this time (1913) calling for the end of theatre and arguing that the aesthetics of theatre cannot be justified, attacked Evreinov for what he felt was a veiled attempt to get theatre off the hook.

Ajxenval'd said that by placing theatre in the category of "pre-aestheticism," Evreinov was supporting his (Ajxenval'd's) claim that "theatre is not art but something else, perhaps more perverted...." Evreinov, wrote Ajxenval'd, rejected the idea of theatre as a synthesis of all the arts by saying that it should be theatre and nothing else. Furthermore, Evreinov continually failed to distinguish adequately between theatre and art in general. Ajxenval'd said the fact that theatre is not art, but springs from different origins, is for Evreinov a source of strength, but for him the source of its destruction. Transformation, which is at the heart of Evreinov's theory, is not, according to Ajxenval'd, a sustaining instinct but rather a transient appearance. If transformation, the will to theatre, were truly instinctive, Ajxenval'd concluded, the present weakening of theatricality would not have come about.

Ajxenval'd turned to Oscar Wilde to refute what he thought to be Evreinov's position that art is greater, something more than life. Wilde's *Picture of Dorian Gray* teaches us that man should not and cannot entirely transform life into art. Evreinov addresses life as "Her Majesty," but subordinates it to theatricality. He expresses his desire to be her tailor, but, says Ajxenval'd, life is fine as it is and does not need to be dressed up in Evreinov's motley fashions.[9]

Evreinov inherited and modified Wilde's ideas, inscribing on the cornerstone of his own philosophical edifice the words: "Life should imitate theatre, should find in it fresh new sensations, and not the reverse." Both Wilde and Evreinov subscribed to Franz Grillparzer's motto, "Art is to reality as wine is to the grape."[10] Life is the pliant raw material from which the artist creates. Nature and "being," that is human existence, are only the shadow of "real being" made manifest in the creative will and fantasy of man. However, Wilde propagandized for the power of artistic lies over life. Beauty is the basis of everything, and life must be experienced as a work of art. Evreinov, on the other hand, believed that human striving is a personal act of will which is not in the service of anything, not even art. It is already an end in itself, a self-contained creative effort of anarchic will, not subordinate to any law, not even the law of beauty. On the contrary it even takes pleasure in the breach of all laws. Thus, Evreinov freed life from the cult of art to which Wilde had enslaved it. Evreinov is in turn freed from the onus of "art for art's sake" with which he was branded, along with the epithet, "the Russian Oscar Wilde."

Still, what do you do with a man who could proclaim as Evreinov did that "beauty is such a tasty sauce, you could eat your own father if he were garnished with it"? Evreinov's fondness for culinary imagery, aside from exhibiting his sensuous nature, is also a reminder (as if Wilde had not been reminder enough) that to wear a green carnation is sometimes the best disguise.[12]

Whether Evreinov was sincere in labelling theatre pre-aesthetic or was simply attempting to agitate the aesthetic conventions and staid thinking in which theatre had become bound is a moot point. The fact is that Evreinov succeeded in forcing people to react to his claims and in so doing to reexamine their own conceptions of theatre. Influenced by his reading of *The Theatre as Such,* Leonid Andreev wrote in 1913 that audiences were disappearing from the theatres "because theatre is being dispersed into life itself."[13]

Evreinov had in mind the dismantling of the old mental set regarding theatre and the erection of a new one which would recognize theatre as an all-pervasive, all-powerful determinant in the behavior of men and societies. For the moment, said Evreinov, it is enough to accept this argument. Drawing upon this knowledge, directions for the theatre of the future can be mapped out later.

Evreinov moved one step nearer this enigmatic future with the three-part *The Theatre for Oneself,* which at once focused and extended the argument begun in *The Theatre as Such.* The form and style of both works were, as the critics noted, quite similar.[14] Each was intended to be experienced by the reader as theatre in printed form. Many critics reacted negatively to their carnival tone as well as to their air of self-importance. They said that Evreinov managed to be both pretentious and didactic, light-minded and alogical. Julij Ajxenval'd complained that Evreinov defined theatre in such broad terms and brought together such a multitude of diverse facts that he destroyed any logical framework with an extreme liberalism approaching intellectual anarchy. Such runaway logic, said Ajxenval'd, "carries the concept of theatre into an abyss of indefiniteness and contentless haze."[15]

Although some critics objected to what they saw as the author's foppery, coquetry and insufferable self-regard, others like Aleksandr Benois more accurately identified Evreinov's posturing as that of the irrepressible Harlequin whose childishness disarms all accusations and reasonable arguments. All of Evreinov's mannerisms could then be indulged and even appreciated as part of a theatrical game using language as a mere prop. Rather than reprimand Evreinov for being what he has always claimed to be, a harlequin, one would do better to sit back and enjoy the show—if only half as much as its author is enjoying his own ease and his reader's discomfort.[16]

To return to what was perhaps his favorite sense—taste—Evreinov offered this tidbit for critical consumption:

> Just as in the field of the subtlest gastronomy the connoisseur is satisfied only with the cuisine prepared by his own personal cook, so in the realm of theatricality "the theatre for oneself" is the last refuge of the refined soul.[17]

If his earlier attempt to separate theatre from aesthetics caused controversy, Evreinov's call for an aristocratic theatre for oneself precipitated even more clamor and confusion. Was Evreinov actually suggesting that public performances be abandoned entirely in favor of private shows in which actor, dramatist, and audience would be one and the same? Was his call for a theatre of real gourmets with refined artistic palates designed to eliminate the vast majority of actors, writers, and audience members from the province of theatre? Such were the accusations.

The theatre flowered, according to Evreinov, when it was in the hands of aristocrats. He cites ancient Greece and Rome, as well as Spain, France, England, Germany, and Russia at various stages in their histories as examples. He even went so far as to claim aristocratic influence in the development of the commedia dell'arte, citing his colleague at the Ancient theatre, K. M. Miklaševskij as a source. Goethe was a proponent of the aristocratic theatre. Shakespeare likewise espoused aristocratic feelings, and reflected his position, Evreinov contended, in the contemptuous attitude toward the masses embodied in his plays (e.g., yesterday Julius Caesar, today Brutus, tomorrow Marc Antony) as well as in his respect for royalty.

Only blood aristocrats, Evreinov argued, dare to be, can afford to be, irrational. "Plebeians" are rooted in mundane reality, rationalism and the concrete truths yielded by science. The aristocrat can give himself up to dreams and the ideal world wherein true theatre resides. The plebeian brings the theatre down from its elevated place by propagandizing for his vulgar tastes and concerns, whereas the aristocrat is focused always on a point beyond. The plebeian foments his revolutions only in the political and economic arenas while in the realm of art he remains a conservative. The plebeian, who likes saying that he is courageous and original, loves only quasi-innovation. He lacks the originality of the aristocrat who carries within him the legacy of a theatrical way of life. The blood aristocrat, as Evreinov well knew, was afforded a good deal as his birthright. However, Evreinov believed that all men possess the transformational instinct, the birthright of imaginative play. It is only through compromise, faintheartedness, and the like that man squanders this most valuable natural asset.

At the heart of Evreinov's concept of the aristocrat was the desire, in the face of sharp criticism, to distinguish the true essence of the theatrical phenomenon—theatricality—from the atheatrical commercial enterprises and ossified institutions that passed for theatre. Only in this way, he felt, could he successfully defend theatre. It is to this impulse that we may in part attribute Evreinov's attacks upon MXAT, which he considered "representative of our contemporary mercantile theatre." This could not have sat well with Stanislavskij, who traded the role of Lopaxin in *The Cherry Orchard* which Čexov had written expressly for him for that of Gaev so as not to remind either the audience or himself of his merchant origins.

Evreinov's notion of aristocratism also helps to explain what seems at first to be a rather peculiar argument of his against professionalism in general. Evreinov sang the praises of the committed amateur who created theatre for love and not for profit. In that he acts only to express himself, the amateur, unlike the professional, will not compromise. This is as it should be, said Evreinov, because art will tolerate no compromise.[18] This argument, like so many others espoused by Evreinov, was a veiled apology for himself, a maverick theatre professional operating largely outside of the official theatrical establishment as represented by MXAT and the Imperial Theatres. Evreinov's call for amateurism in the theatre was not, however, a defense of dilettantism, a charge he personally had to parry on several fronts, as historian, social scientist, and philosopher.

In the theatre for oneself each person becomes the hero of his own life, just as a child is the hero of the games he plays. Evreinov pointed out that even Nietzsche, the "Antichrist," agreed with Christ that man must be taught the necessity of becoming a child again. (See Evreinov on Nesterov.) No one teaches a child to play: "Every newborn child is entrusted by nature with the duty of creating its own world."[19]

Yet despite man's movement away from child's play as he grows older, he never forgets entirely. The psychologist N. Tigler pointed out, says Evreinov, that what an adult remembers about his childhood is not real objects and events but those related to play. Thus, he will remember a doll's funeral but not a real funeral. Wilhelm Wundt, the founder of experimental psychology, wrote in *Fantasy as the Basis of Art* that in general each man lives more in an imaginary world than in the real one.[20]

The actor in the theatre for oneself was the Evreinovian theatrical equivalent of Nietzsche's superman. Nietzsche said that people are often only actors playing themselves. Morality and the growth of culture are based upon service to this ideal. The man we call great is merely acting out his own ideal. Rather than looking outside or above for a savior, man must search within himself. In the rediscovery and revitalization of the theatre lies the salvation of man.

Theatre as Crime and Punishment

All creative work was for Evreinov an inherent function of personality.[21] The theatre for oneself is a manifestation of man's need to express himself. Juvenile delinquents are, he said, in many cases, only expressing their will to the theatre, acting out the exciting roles they would like to play in life.

Naturally, the license to play in whatever form and to any degree one chooses can and does lead to excess. Literature offers us Don Quixote and Robinson Crusoe as examples of the "excessive theatre for oneself." Evreinov was especially fascinated with Don Quixote, whose very being represented a protest against the domination of man by mundane reality. Don Quixote is an example of what Lionel Abel would later define as "metatheatre." He is a self-sustaining character searching for self-expression and personal identity. In order to be self-sustaining, a character must convince us not so much of his actual existence as of the possibility of his existence. He must reflect basic human needs, desires, and fantasies. Don Quixote is you and I at war with our mundane existence, a knight whose strength and nobility derives from the fact that he goes mad not from some set of circumstances, but for no reason at all. Like Pirandello's Enrico IV, he turns back the clock. With this act begins the mystical monodrama in which everything emanates from the individual and exists for the individual.[22] These practitioners of the excessive theatre for oneself are, like children and savages, true aristocrats in Evreinov's scheme of things. It is not coincidental that Robinson Crusoe must return to primitive beginnings in order to learn how to re-create the world and become a true aristocrat.

Evreinov spoke in terms of an "erotic theatre for oneself" as one manifestation of the excessive school of play. By "erotic," Evreinov was referring to sex play, especially the courting ritual manifested harmlessly in such festive pastimes as ballroom dancing but taking a more dangerous turn in sadomasochistic rituals. Significantly, Evreinov made the "love comedy" Krafft-Ebing's term for the discreet behavior of the female and the quasi-conquest by the male in courtship, the core of nearly all his dramatic works, using as his paradigm the romantic triangle of Harlequin, Columbine and Pierrot.

The concepts of "erotic" and "excessive" theatre for oneself were to some extent overlapping. Evreinov gave as an example the subtlest form of both — autoeroticism, narcissism born of extreme subjectivism. One can, in a sense, see this condition embodied in Evreinov's theory of monodrama, although this concept was somewhat saved by its creator's sense of irony.

In a full-length work entitled *The Secret of Rasputin* (*Tajna Rasputina,* 1924) Evreinov explained and justified the mad monk's behavior as a monodrama from the excessive theatre for oneself. Rasputin was, for Evreinov, a man who played the role of God, an actor in the theatre of life, a fakir, a hypnotist and a magician in whom the religious and the erotic were intermingled. Although Rasputin was not a true miracle worker, he convinced others of his power by the hypnotic force of his personality. He self-consciously created a persona, a mask, which was a condensation, intensification and magnification of his essence as a person. In the end he lost control and became the mask.

Evreinov was fascinated with the image of the false Christ. He was fond of juxtaposing the images of Harlequin the trickster and Christ the

Savior, a tendency which culminated in his play *The Chief Thing*. The man who would be God or Christ is attempting to play the ultimate role, that of the Great Director of the Theatre of Life. For him there are no rules. All boundaries may be transgressed. His actions fall outside the realm of conventional morality. The historical figures Evreinov cited as representative of the excessive theatre for oneself all shared Rasputin's audacious desire to assume this ultimate role at whatever the cost to themselves and others. The list includes Ramses II, Pericles, Cleopatra, Alexander the Great, Julius Caesar, Nero, Savonarola, Martin Luther, Ludwig II, the Marquise de Pompadour, Catherine the Great and Evreinov's greatest historical hero, Napoleon. Thus, argues Evreinov, Ludwig was not mad but rather the victim of theatrical hyperbole.[23]

Evreinov quoted at length from Dostoevskij in support of his concept of excessive theatre for oneself. Both in *Crime and Punishment* in the person of Raskolnikov, the failed Napoleon, and in *Notes from Underground,* Dostoevskij, said Evreinov, offered arguments for the theatre for oneself, identifying the will to the theatre with the will to crime and transgression. He said we assume that if man could identify where his real interests lay, he would act in accordance with them, and being enlightened he would realize that "he would have no choice but to act good." However, there is, says Dostoevskij, overwhelming evidence to the contrary. "Man prefers to act in the way he feels like acting." All he needs is "independent will at all costs and whatever the consequences."[24] "Namely in this," Evreinov asserts, "in the screwing up of one's eyes against advantage, against the 'guaranteed arguments of reason and arithmetic,' is concealed the will to the theatre, *absolutely criminal...*" Evreinov continues in ecstatic, declamatory language that recalls his *Introduction to Monodrama:*

> Here norms and rules no longer exist like sticks in the wheel of our fantasy! Here one can no longer ascertain what is forbidden, illicit or, unlawful! This is the realm of our "transforming I," a minute ago a prisoner...now authoritatively turning the merest "nothing" into "everything," and this "everything" is superior to all else because it is *my* "everything," with *my* boundaries, *my* spirit, *my* Logos!

Theatre for oneself, Evreinov proudly declares, is "criminal to the core."[25]

Evreinov pursued the theatre-as-crime analogy in a series of lectures he delivered in Petrograd, Kiev, Odessa, and other cities under the collective title of *The Theatre and the Scaffold (Teatr i ešafot).*[26] The dual character of the theatre—as the site of both crime and punishment—was here symbolized by the scaffold, the historical place of execution. Evreinov used the scaffold as a metaphor for the theatre, although he acknowledged certain differences between them. Whereas the scaffold is a place for actual punishment, the theatre presents only the symbolic spectacle of punishment. The two "performers" on the scaffold, the executioner and his victim, are in the theatre both embodied in the actor. He is both the instrument of punishment and the goat of remission through which the sins of man and society at large are absolved. In his roles as priest and sacrifice, the actor bears both the power and the responsibility in the ritual. Entering into the theatre is like entering into purgatory where anything and everything is permitted, where man confronts his age-old secret passions and fears. Theatre as the scaffold is the central apparatus for the transformation of the elemental, blind, and destructive energies of man.[27]

In tragedy as it is enacted on the stage, fate is man's executioner. This, suggests Evreinov, is a reflection of man's situation in life. However, in theatre and in life, knowing the ending in advance does not lessen our interest in seeing the scenario unfold.

The real and symbolic representations of life and death on stage and scaffold, respectively, actively engage our sense of cruelty, our fascination with the piquant, the fatal, the obscene and the sensual, especially our scenic imagination. All the time we watch a bull being taunted and slaughtered, a man being executed, a puppet or commedia character being beaten with a stick, a Grand Guignol blood bath, or the farcical slip of a circus clown on a banana peel, we justify the thrill we feel with the thought that we are being morally edified, emotionally purged and spiritually uplifted. And so the designated places for torture and execution in primitive and medieval cultures East and West doubled as the sites where more genteelly palatable theatrical offerings were presented, and the crowd's blood lust was satiated while its conscience was assuaged.[28]

Evreinov's partial list of literary sources that are most obviously linked to the traditional function of the scaffold includes: Schiller, Lope de Vega, Calderón de la Barca, Shakespeare (especially the history plays), Byron, Victorien Sardou, Alexandre Dumas-*père,* as well as Aeschylus's *Prometheus Bound;* Goethe's *Faust, Part I, Götz von Berlichingen* and *Egmont;* Victor Hugo's *Marie Tudor* and *Le Roi s'amuse;* Büchner's *Danton's Death;* the biblical themes of the blinding of Samson and Salome's demanding the head of John the Baptist; tragedies taken from Roman history; all plays based on the life of Caligula; plays on the theme of religious persecution; plays involving the execution of kings; and plays concerning the epoch of Ivan the Terrible.[29]

In his book *Azazel and Dionysos* (*Azazel i Dionis,* 1924), Evreinov theorizes that the majority of heroes in the plays of Aeschylus, Sophocles and Euripides are poetically idealized "scapegoats." These include in Aeschylus, Prometheus, Iphigenia, Cassandra and Agamemnon; in Sophocles, Oedipus, Eteocles and Antigone; and in Euripides, Alcestis, Polixena, Medea's children, Hippolytus and Pentheus. Each scapegoat is sacrificed more for the sins of his progenitors than for his own personal, willful transgressions.

Evreinov's concept of the scapegoat derived from what he believed to be the Semitic origins of ancient tragedy. He claimed that all of the elements belonging to the ritual of Dionysos can be found in the Hebrew holiday of Yom Kippur, "the Day of Atonement." Dionysos was himself of Semitic origin, Evreinov argued, and Azazel is another name for the Hebrew god Ashim who is identified with the goat.

There is likewise a connection between Prometheus, the scapegoat on the mountain, and the Hebrew scapegoat on a mountain in the desert. Evreinov maintained that the scapegoat must be removed from the general populace. He cites Oedipus, who is made to wander without a home for his sins, and who eventually dies in a deserted place. Only a special person can know the secret of the death of the scapegoat. Adam and Eve were the first scapegoats. We have inherited their sin, much as the characters in Greek tragedy have inherited those of their ancestors. The holiday of Yom Kippur is reserved for the cleansing of the soul. This leads to the resurrection of man and nature.

Evreinov was fascinated with the role of the goat in ancient rituals as a symbol of both sin and repentance. The goat is the sacred animal of the underworld, and the goat's head, an offering to the Devil. But the goat is also a symbol of fertility. So it is with the theatre. Evreinov quoted Tertullian as having said that "demons inspired the creation of the theatre."[30] However, as Evreinov explains in *The Theatre and the Scaffold,* the theatre is a forum not only for sin, or transgression, but repentance, that is cure in the form of catharsis. The dual nature of the goat as a symbol for the theatre was transformed by Evreinov into the mask of Harlequin, who likewise embodies both good and evil. Evreinov concretized this vision of the theatre in the person of the Harlequin-Christ in his most famous play, *The Chief Thing.*

Before alighting from the scaffold, however, I should say a word about the relationship of Evreinov's ideas to those of Antonin Artaud, a connection which has already no doubt formed in the reader's mind. Evreinov's *The Theatre and the Scaffold* (1918-24) predates Artaud's similar-sounding concept of the "theatre of cruelty" by a decade. Artaud's essays and manifestos in which he formulated this idea date from the period 1931 through 1935 and were only collected and published in *The Theatre and Its Double* in 1938. Interestingly, both men lived and worked in France for some time, Evreinov from 1925 to 1953, Artaud until his death in 1948. However, the two, at least according to Evreinov's widow, never met and no causal linkage between their theories can be determined. Had they met, Evreinov no doubt would have regarded the paranoid-schizophrenic Artaud as an excellent example of his excessive theatre for oneself.

Evreinov and Artaud do meet, however, on the plane of suggestion and metaphor where visionaries disgruntled with and betrayed by life dream of the future. Here, like Beckett's immortal tandem, Evreinov's good doctor-father figure (Vladimir) and Artaud's patient-victim-child (Estragon) seem to share a mystical bond. Artaud, lost inside his disordered self, and Evreinov, manipulating a projected persona abstracted from the self, forge an uneasy relationship with theatre and life which they personalize as metaphors for these selves. Both seek salvation, but only Evreinov keeps one eye on the sleeping eternal Self. Artaud, like one of Evreinov's great-hearted, injudicious characters, is consumed by emotion and self-destructs. Artaud attacks the nerves, Evreinov seduces the mind. Evreinov invites conflict and Artaud chaos. Artaud finds for a time a partial mirroring of his disordered consciousness in surrealism, while Evreinov spots a somewhat familiar reflection of his aesthetic self-consciousness in symbolism.

The always hazy road leading to the discovery of the philosopher's stone is paved for both men by similar preoccupations, which include: ritual, alchemy, hypnosis, catharsis, doubleness, scapegoat-priests, origins and essences, mythic substrata, matter-spirit and mind-body dichotomies, profound ambivalences (toward women, death, sexuality) and purposeful ambiguities, dreams of communion and transformation. Artaud offers the heat of fire, feast and famine, shock-therapy to burn away the surface of reality which he has neither the time nor the disposition to contemplate. Evreinov polishes the surface of reality and shines in its reflected light, acting the aesthete-poseur, the aristocrat with a refined palate. He nonetheless continues his secret quest for illumination, Truth and salvation in the service of which this highly polished surface-reality is employed. Artaud locates his expressive power in signs; Evreinov discovers his in the suggestive shadows projected by words and cognition. Taken individually, each artist is a valuable conduit into the world of modern art. Cross-referenced, they suggest a great many of the artistic, anthropological and socio-psychological concerns of this century.

The Chief Thing

The cover of the first published edition in Russian of *The Chief Thing* (1921) depicts Harlequin crucified on a wooden cross. The black half-mask has fallen from his face and there seems to be a smile on his lips. A tambourine hangs from around the wrist of his left hand, which is nailed to the cross. The word *TEATR* appears on a background of Harlequin's traditional diamond motley. A lone blossom sprouts at the foot of the cross, along with a small flowerless plant. Droplets of blood fall from Harlequin's nailed feet and hands. He wears a cap and make-up on his cheek. Small bells hang from the waist of his diamond-patterned costume. There is a halo above his head.

Evreinov's original title for his play was *The Harlequin-Christ (Xristos-Arlekin)*. Although an atheist, Evreinov could certainly appreciate the story of Christ, the son of God, as the parable of a man, Jesus Christ, who found God in himself.

Soviet theatre historian David Zolotnickij states that Jurij Annenkov's cover illustration for the play represents Harlequin crucified on the cross of his art. However, this gives Evreinov and Annenkov too little credit as ironists who could not have missed the richness of so profound a jest. Several years later, one of Evreinov's harshest critics, Georgij Kryžickij, published a book entitled *Christ or Harlequin? (Xristos ili Arlekin?,* 1924) which could well have served as a useful background treatise for Evreinov's strangely dualistic vision. Kryžickij chronicled the historical conflict between the theatre and the church, proclaiming the first actor to have been the Devil, who impersonated a serpent in the Garden of Eden. He belonged, deadpans Kryžickij, to the school of transformation *(perevoploščenie)* rather than to the school of emotional experiencing *(pereživanie)* advocated by Stanislavskij.

Kryžickij traces the origin of the word *harlequin* and its association with the Devil from Dante's reference to a *helequin* in describing one of the levels of Hell in *The Inferno*. Following a similar line of reasoning, Soviet theatre scholar Jurij Gerasimov suggests that Harlequin represents a force of evil, the devil or his agent, in Evreinov's work rather than the image of the child with which he is often identified. Of course, Harlequin is the wise child, capable of engaging the world in nonstop imaginative play. It seems, however, that while he functions as a trickster in Evreinov's work and certainly represents the author's private demon, Harlequin is nevertheless intended to represent a benign force to the world at large.

This last observation distinguishes Evreinov from yet another Frenchman whose life and art otherwise reveal remarkable similarities. The title of Alfred Jarry's *Caesar Antichrist (César Antechrist,* 1895) suggests the proximity of his concerns to those of Evreinov and yet indicates too a sort of reverse-angle perspective on these matters. Like Evreinov, Jarry's childhood fascination with commedia dell'arte, puppet theatre and parodistic forms translated into an adult creative life which utilized the residual grotesque imagery and unfettered instinctive play of childhood. Like Evreinov, Jarry's life was a peculiar mixture of prolonged jest and transgression, crooked-mirror humor and quasi-symbolist mission. Jarry, the perpetrator of "talented scandal," an aristocrat in the theatre for oneself, sought like Evreinov that "moment of authentic enactment" which would reconcile him to life. His search led him to structure a theatre-as-event, life-as-theatre reality, to approach imagination pseudoscientifically, to push reason to the limit with his "science of imaginary solutions" and of "laws governing exceptions," "Pataphysics."

Jarry's feeling for abstraction, his fascination with character as mask-persona, the theatrical conventions of past epochs (he satirized the naturalistic conventions of the present) and demonism (Père Ubu as a petty demon by way of the medieval vice figure) further link him in spirit and interest to Evreinov. However, ultimately Ubu's "physick-stick," his perversion of the shamanistic power of the philosopher's stone, differs markedly from the slapstick of Evreinov's Harlequin. Although not even the latter could promise salvation as we will soon see, Evreinov would not yield to the seductive power of chaos and negativism. Evreinov yearned for simpler times and more primitive states of being such as childhood as the means through which to relocate the essential Self, which is the passageway to Truth. For the most part, he refrained from taking on the demeanor of the willful child whose casual cruelty becomes for the adult a vengeful cry shouted into the void of a dark and hostile universe. It was not for him "The Savage God," the Antichrist. Jarry was not so fortunate. Neither his wit nor his better, visionary self, Doctor Faustroll, could save him from the harsh master he had created for himself.[31]

Evreinov was, however, too knowledgeable in the ways of life and man to give himself over to naive and sentimental belief. If he had been otherwise, *The Chief Thing* would have been the parable of comfort and saving grace that its biblical underpinnings might lead one to expect. As it turned out, its peculiarly modern geometric structuring of perspectives and tonalities makes it too complexly self-analytical to serve as an article of simple faith.

The play's subtitle, *A Comedy for Some and a Drama for Others in Four Acts,* points toward a multiplicity of possible and actual sources. One senses in this the casual flip-flop of logic and illogic, reason and feeling, form and content, served up to perfection by Oscar Wilde in his *The Importance of Being Earnest* (1895), which its author identified as "a trivial comedy for serious people." Then too, there is a scent of the medieval Feast of Fools and Boy Bishop's inversion of status one finds in Shakespeare's *Twelfth Night, or, What You Will.* Evreinov entertained a medieval bias and such reversals will abound in his play. One can never overlook commedia dell'arte, spinning on its tragicomic axis, as the paradigm for Evreinov's calculated trifling with serious concerns. Finally, Horace Walpole's often-quoted remark that "the world is a comedy to those that think, a tragedy to those that feel," comes to mind and leads immediately to two related questions: Is Evreinov's art created at the bidding of his emotional or rational Self? Which Self was his mask and which his face? An examination of *The Chief Thing* will go further toward bringing these matters into focus.

The embodiment of Evreinov's paradoxical vision, the Harlequin-Christ, appears in *The Chief Thing* in the person of the Paraclete, whose coming is proclaimed in John 15:26.

> But when the Paraclete is come, whom I will send unto you from the Father, even the spirit of Truth, which proceedeth from the Father, he shall testify of me.

In his list of characters Evreinov tells us that Paraclete means "counselor, helper, consoler." Paraclete was also the name of the abbey founded in Champagne by Abelard in the twelfth century and later turned over to a sisterhood of which Heloise became the first priestess. So too, Paraclete is "an ecclesiastical paraphrase for the Holy Ghost."[32] This reference to the Holy Trinity is the first of many manifestations in the play of the magical number three.

The actions of Paraclete, the Harlequin-Christ, will elucidate Evreinov's vision of the theatre's role as a curative force in society. Its power to cure derives in large part from its ability to transform. Paraclete himself undergoes several transformations in appearance and personality in the play. He appears first as an old lady Fortuneteller, a caricatured figure, seated amidst obviously cheap theatrical properties, lovingly described by Evreinov the theatre director-magician. Significantly, this "lady" seer wears glasses, indicating that she has trouble seeing.[33] Evreinov will use a series of clichés and caricatures in this play, as he did with the "crude idealizations" and "grotesque caricatures" in *Stage-Wings,* as well as the element of simple disguise to play upon the easy solutions and naive expectations engendered by the contemporary theatre in its audience. In this way Evreinov can better contrast cheap theatrical tricks with the real magic of theatricality. Evreinov had himself often been accused of perpetrating the former.

Into the Fortuneteller's home come several customers in search of happiness. This profound quest, the central issue of the play, is introduced by Evreinov with characteristic irony in a series of two-character scenes reminiscent of the puppet stage.[34] Each character is clearly typed physically as well as by generic name. First to arrive is the Lady with the Small Dog (a possible Čexov reference) in search of her husband, a trigamist. This is the second manifestation in the play of the number three, suggesting that a pattern may be developing.

The Fortuneteller is next approached by the Retired Civil Servant who pleads with her to save his son, whose mind is set upon suicide. She is, after all, a wonderful hypnotist and so might persuade him via the power of illusion. Evreinov, as we have already seen, viewed all art and especially theatre as a form of hypnosis, or magic.

The Barefoot Dancer, another in the line of Evreinov's seductive women cast from the mold of Salome and Isadora Duncan, comes to call on the Fortuneteller. She, too, is unhappy, suspecting that her actor-husband with whom she performs has lost interest in her. As her life is going bad, so is her art. She once believed that the theatre was a temple, a Stanislavskijan perspective which, Evreinov implies here and has stated elsewhere on occasion, can never bring the transcendence we seek. But the Fortuneteller has hinted to her of an interesting proposal, a surprise that is to take place today at the theatre. This proposal will in time break down the hackneyed idea the Barefoot Dancer and the other performers have of the theatre. Although they do not yet realize it, the actors of this rather motley troupe have been chosen for a higher purpose — to enter into the theatre of life.

Next appears the Romantic Lead, who turns out to be the detective hired by the Lady with the Small Dog to shadow her philandering husband. The poorly disguised detective is an equally bad actor, and the philanderer, we are told, is "something like" a theatrical producer. The bogus romance of the actor contrasts sharply with the frustrated idealism and inherent spirituality of his wife, Evreinov's proverbial Barefoot Dancer.

Finally, the Fortuneteller is visited by the Retired Civil Servant's suicidal son, the student Fedja who has unwillingly accompanied the Boarding house Landlady, Mar'ja Jakovlevna, and her daughter Lidočka, "the best typist in town," but a rather plain, love-starved girl.[35]

Just as representatives from the theatre and life have come together in her apartment for advice, so the solution to all these ills will be in a merger between the two worlds. This is the surprise, "the interesting proposal" the Fortuneteller has in store for the characters. But first, she has one more surprise for us, the audience. The Director of the Provincial Theatre comes to call upon her but asks to see a Doctor Fregoli.[36] Before our very eyes, the old hag Lady Fortuneteller is transformed into Doctor Fregoli, "an elegant, handsome, fifty-year-old gentleman, with slightly gray, short hair." He has "an inspired face" with "clever, kind penetrating eyes" and "a trace of irony" on his lips. He projects charm and a strong will. When the Director asks in amazement how he can practice such deceit, Fregoli replies, "All of mankind, if one may believe the psychologists, instinctively prefers a pleasant deception to an unpleasant truth." He is about to prove the truth of this assertion by his theatre-in-life experiment.

The question the Director asks Fregoli at the end of act 1, "But what is truth?", segues directly into the question posed in the title of the play being rehearsed as the curtain rises on act 2 — *Quo Vadis?* or Whither goest thou? The rehearsal scene is written by Evreinov in the best Crooked Mirror tradition.[37] The actors are all carelessly made up and flagrantly miscast and misdirected. An accomplished director, Evreinov is able to deploy a crowd of actors in such a way as to suggest a general lack of mass, weight and depth — an underpopulated stage. In the same way, bare platforms and saw horses with "two tall fantastic harps," a Pan's flute and piano offer a poor impersonation of a Neronian feast. We are a long way from the magic of the Ancient Theatre and deliberately so.

Evreinov mocks contemporary theatre directors in his treatment of the company's Regisseur whose wrongheaded result-oriented instructions to the actors includes "more Christian martyrdom." In Evreinov's play, Nero, the Antichrist, is to Paraclete, the Harlequin-Christ, as the tired, bogus theatre of illusion is to the vital and profound theatre in life. The performers keep confusing art with life, mixing up their characters' lines with their personal opinions. The comic undercuts the actor's artificial "living on the stage" with his natural drunkenness. Here Evreinov is spoofing Stanislavskij by illustrating how systems of acting kill the natural ability of people to act.[38]

Fregoli has all this time been observing the company from the house, much to their embarrassment. Just as the real stage curtain became the curtain of the fictive rehearsal, so now the auditorium in which the real audience sits is commandeered as well. We are the "strangers in the house" at whom the Comic shouts, "Ladies and gentlemen, you're not wanted here...Leave!"[39] Evreinov's playful use of direct audience address, employed earlier in such plays as *A Merry Death,* illustrates the skillful way in which he adapted commedia conventions to modern thought.

Fregoli now offers his and Evreinov's "modest proposal":

> Along with the official theatre of illusion, I argue that we need an unofficial theatre, a sort of market place for illusions, a theatre in even greater need of reform, for it is Life itself! Life, where illusion is no less necessary than happiness, we must at least give them the illusion of happiness. That is the main thing.... With all my heart I believe in the actor's calling, the actor who steps off these boards into the pitch darkness of Life armed only with his art! For it is my sincere belief that the world will be transformed through the actor, through the actor's magic art.

Evreinov took this rather romantic, one might even say naive, belief quite seriously. Fregoli's answer to the Comic's question is this proposal offered "as a joke or in all seriousness," echoes Evreinov's subtitle to the play: "You may take it anyway you please!" In this way Evreinov satirizes his own serious intentions in writing the play.

As to the rewards of such a theatre, Fregoli replies:

> The part creates a man's character at times, just as the man, in performing, creates the part's character. *Transformation* through *transfiguration*. Changing for the better—isn't that sufficient reward?[40]

This restates one of Evreinov's major themes—man consciously transforms himself on the road to true happiness, with each change rooting out some of the evil within him, thus making him a clearer reflection of the Deity. Evreinov, the critics argued, only indicated general directions about the nature of these transformations without setting a definite course. But as always Evreinov is here speaking in parables and paradigms as befits a visionary or a Harlequin-Christ.

The actors and Fregoli depart for their new theatre, the boarding house of Mar'ja Jakovlevna Petrova. The actors who remain easily switch to the roles that have been vacated by those who have departed. They require only a change of costume, since they are not bound by a sense of inner belief to any of the roles in the play. The rehearsal continues, but at one actress's request—"There're some more people out there again" (i.e., the audience)—the Regisseur orders the curtain lowered. And so ends act 2.

Acts 3 and 4 take place in the boarding house. The set includes a series of nine doors leading to the boarders' rooms, which at least on the surface suggests that a farce is to be played. Each of the actors has been assigned a particular individual to cheer up: the Romantic Lead has been assigned to the Typist, the Barefoot Dancer to the Student, the Comic to the Retired Civil Servant and Aglaja Karpovna, a dour teacher of young ladies' deportment. Sidestepping sentiment, Evreinov has the actors in their private moments regard their charges quite dispassionately and their roles as nothing more than assigned jobs. Reality and illusion have begun to be mixed in the confusion of roles. The Comic, who is playing the role of a doctor, has actually begun to write prescriptions for the spinster Aglaja Karpovna. However, he now finds it difficult to play the role of comedian and must rely on a jokebook for his humor.

Evreinov's dialogue in this play is littered with scholarly references to such figures as the German romantics Novalis (1772-1801) and Johann Ludwig Tieck (1773-1853), the Viennese philosopher Otto Weininger (1880-1903) and the German idealist philosopher Nicolai Hartmann (1882-1950). These references bring onto the stage a number of Evreinov's recurring themes, including the transformation of the world through imagination, the celebration of death as the passage into a higher life, and the necessary fusion of art and life (Novalis); the grotesque and puppetlike man controlled by a capricious or spiteful fate (Tieck); the masculine-feminine duality of all living beings with the masculine tending to be productive and moral, the feminine destructive and amoral (Weininger); and the heroic act of living a human life in a meaningless world (Hartmann).

A charming courtship scene follows in which the conversation proceeds furtively by means of a typewriter, with commas changing to periods and finally to ellipses in an effort to indicate emotions so profound as to be inexpressible.

The act ends with a recording of Jaques's "all the world's a stage" speech from *As You Like It* being preempted by another recording, this one of the Faust-Margarita duet from Arrigo Boito's opera *Mefistofele* (1868) (the Devil as actor) which begins with the line, "There is a beautiful far distant land...." Fantasy has replaced reality as we are led into the carnival setting of act 4.

Act 4 takes place in the same boarding house on the last day of Shrovetide, the three days before Ash Wednesday, which is the first day of Lent. It is a time for feasting and rejoicing as well as confession and absolution.

A poster of Pierrot being attacked by little devils has been hung above the center door; one depicting a tender Columbine-Harlequin scene is visible above the ottoman. The face of the Carnival Prince laughs above the entryway door. There is a red heart under a black mask above door number three, the room occupied by Mar'ja Jakovlevna, the landlady, and her daughter, Lidočka, the lovesick typist. The face of the Bolognese doctor peers out from above door number four, Aglaja Karpovna's room. The entire stage is bathed in a not very bright pink light, producing "a confusing impression."[41] The effect of watching the characters move through these doors, in and out of this pink light, is to reinforce the sense of reality flowing into fantasy and life into theatre, and back again, that pervades the play.

Fregoli informed the Director at the end of act 1 that the last day of the holiday would mark the termination of his contract. It is clear that this ball is to be in some way climactic, a masquerade in which the truth will be revealed. This is a favorite image of Evreinov's, symbolizing his preoccupation with forms unmasking essence, whether those forms are masks or nude bodies. References to Aleksandr Ostrovskij's *Diary of a Scoundrel* and Aleksandr Griboedov's *Woe from Wit,* each of which climaxes with an unmasking of the truth, makes Evreinov's intentions clear.

We learn that the Romantic Lead will appear at the masquerade as Pierrot and Fregoli, now known as Schmidt, the record or fantasy-seller, as Harlequin to the Barefoot Dancer's Columbine. There is to be another masker as well. An anonymous letter informed the Romantic Lead that the trigamist discussed in act 1 will make an appearance disguised as a monk.

In the meantime Aglaja Karpovna has discovered that the Comic's affection for her was feigned and is deeply shaken. Moments later a shroud topped by a skull mask appears out of the door to Aglaja Karpovna's room. This was the costume that had been reserved for the old lady. When the Comic touches it there appears to be no one inside it. He screams, the lights go out, and the phantom disappears. When the light in the room comes back on, it is no longer flickering, and the setting appears somehow to have become more realistic. The stage is filled with a crowd of masqueraders, among whom can be seen the *Quo Vadis?* costumes from act 2. All join in a merry polonaise. The festivities are abruptly interrupted by the entrance of the Comic and the Student from the old lady's room. She has poisoned herself. Her suicide note reads (contrary to expectations): "I blame *everyone* for my death!"

An embarrassed silence follows as all but the Barefoot Dancer-Columbine exit to the old lady's room. In the hallway a mysterious monk in Capuchin habit appears with a cowl pulled around his face. The Monk's face, unseen by the audience, is visible to the Dancer, who exclaims: "Good heavens!... You were supposed to be Harlequin." He asks to be left alone and is a moment later joined by three "Black Dominoes," one with a little dog on an elegant leash, revealing the owner's identity.

The Monk, who addresses the three women as his wives, is the final incarnation in the play of Paraclete, the Harlequin-Christ. Paradoxically, this representative of the Holy Trinity is a trigamist. He is bitterly attacked by the Lady with the Small Dog but defended by the Fallen Woman, the second wife, whose name is Maria, suggesting Mary Magdalene. Her defense rests on the argument that the husband succeeded in giving each of the wives what she needed most — strength to the first wife, the Lady with the Small Dog; happiness to the second wife, a deaf mute; and self-respect to the third wife, the Fallen Woman. It is she who leads the others away with the words: "Let's not hinder him!... There are many of us and only one of him!"

Meanwhile, the others have succeeded in reviving Aglaja Karpovna. In this moment the actors and the other boarders have become true Christians after the model of Paraclete (Christ) by assuming responsibility for their fellow man and trying to ease his suffering. The Provincial Theatre Director arrives in the costume of a Roman Senator, and the Regisseur, dressed as the poet Lucan (costumes from the *Quo Vadis?* production). They have come to witness the last act of the comedy produced on the stage of life. The Monk is satisfied with how things have progressed, because, as he tells the Director (and here he is certainly speaking for Evreinov): "Hegel holds that when it comes to *idea,* the only important thing is the process, that the 'result' is only a lifeless corpse, forsaken by the living soul by the tendency."[42] Life is motion. Stasis is death. A very long continuum including Hegel, Bergson, Evreinov and Pirandello manifests itself here.

Evreinov illustrates this point in dramatic fashion. The play is abruptly brought to a halt, although not to an end. Masks are thrown off to reveal the eternal masks beneath, those of the commedia dell'arte. The Monk informs Pierrot-the-Romantic-Lead that "I'm the very one you've been looking for throughout the four acts of this play" (i.e., the trigamist). "You're Pierrot," the Monk exclaims, "and you've been made a fool of.... That's your fate, you know, if you're Pierrot" But Pierrot-the Romantic Lead counters, "If I'm Pierrot, then only Harlequin can make a fool of me! "He stands before you!" shouts the Monk, throwing off his habit to reveal "a harlequin in a shiny, blindingly bright costume."

Leaping onto the prompter's box, as if onto the dead carcass of the realistic-naturalistic theatre, Harlequin extolls the notion of the theatre in life and asks the audience whether they have understood the chief thing in the play. Harlequin proceeds to list different ways in which the play could be ended, but the Director assures him that "the main [chief] thing is to finish the play on time." "No," says the Regisseur, "the main [chief] thing is to have a smash ending for the play." So the Regisseur pulls some sparklers from a box and shouts: "Let's everybody dance!... More life!... Audacity!... Merriment!... Youthfulness!... Curtain!... (with an indulgent smile Harlequin uses a sparkler to illuminate the deliberately artificial merriment of the actors as they waltz to a dance band playing a bravura waltz.)"[43] The ending represents the false smile which for Evreinov is the realistic theatre, while "the chief thing" hovers above the proceedings like a still-unanswered question.

The Chief Thing premiered on 20 February 1921, at the Theatre of Free Comedy *(Teatr Volnoj komedii)* under the direction of Nikolaj V. Petrov (who also played Paraclete) with sets by Evreinov's frequent associate Jurij P. Annenkov. Although the play stimulated much interest among the critics and the public, it met with opposition in official circles.[44] Director of the Theatrical Section of the Ministry of Public Instruction, M. F. Andreeva, used it to prove Evreinov's aversion to the Revolution.[45] The evidence was not difficult to find. In act 2 Fregoli argues for the theatre in life by pointing out the inability of the contemporary realistic-naturalistic theatre and social institutions to meet the needs of the people. After first praising socialism, despite its "illegal origin," as the "new director" that could sweep away outmoded traditions, he continues:

> But there are millions of people on this earth deprived not only of material needs but also of personal joys, owing to impoverishment of the body or spirit, millions of our fellow men for whom the equality of Socialism isn't enough.

In Evreinov's estimation, no political or economic system could fulfill the spiritual needs of the people. Only the theatre was capable of doing this, not just as the most important of the arts but as the most potent force in life. The hope of the future lay in actors and actresses of mercy who could administer the cure to the scarred and impoverished soul of contemporary man.

Some critics regarded *The Chief Thing* as a serious philosophical and even metaphysical work. Others called it nonsensical. Still others, like Adrian Piotrovskij, thought it unduly negative, representing what he called "the apogee of catastrophic contradiction," a typically Soviet response to an essentially pre-Revolutionary Russian spirit. The Soviets in general considered the play irrelevant and closed it one season into its original run (it was later revived). Vsevolod Čadovec summed up the feelings of a good many critics about this highly paradoxical play. He began by calling *The Chief Thing* "the most significant, most provocative play of the last twenty years." He then added that he was not sure whether Evreinov was here "blazing a new path to the sun" or was instead offering only "a will-o'-the-wisp." Within this wide range of possibilities, he said, lies "the chief thing." The play fared much better abroad, where it was produced in twenty-seven languages in twenty-five countries, most notably by New York's Theatre Guild and by Luigi Pirandello and Charles Dullin in Rome and Paris, respectively. A French-Italian company made *The Chief Thing* into a film (1941–42) directed by Marcel L'Herbier with a cast including Micheline Presle, Jacquelin Delubac, Sylvie, Michel Simon, Alerme, Marcel Valleé, Louis Jourdan, and Ramon Navarro.

The Chief Thing is dedicated to the memory of Evreinov's "teacher," Julia Ivanovna Davydova (née Gravel) whose approaching death was made less fearful by her pupil's performance of feigned optimism and outward calm. This, said Evreinov, was the very definition of theatre for oneself.[46]

In responding to the play, the critics could not help but ask whether the actors were really to leave the stage and enter into life armed with the saving power of fantasy and performance. N. Nilli had called for just that in his article, "On the Theatre of the Future" (*O teatre buduščego,* 1919). He wrote that the actor must love life and people and that his life must be higher than art. Nilli called this the new art of life.

As preparation for the theatre of the future, Nilli foresaw a group of actors performing a single play and each actor a single role for an entire season. At the conclusion of the season, the actor would take this role into life and play it among the people, modifying the role according to his observations of the people. This idea combined Nilli's two major goals for the theatre—to create adventure and love for man.[47]

Most critics, however, were more interested in the structure and tone of Evreinov's play than in its message, which seemed to them rather naive. They were divided on whether Evreinov's use of vaudeville turns did the play more harm than good. The play was said to resemble "a cinematic crazy quilt, gaily and multicolored, without a beginning or an end." Others referred to it as an "expressionist experiment." Indeed, Sergej Sudejkin's set design for the 1926 Theatre Guild production, which resembled a geometric nightmare, suggests that this was a valid comparison.

Some labelled the play a mystery, an observation that opens up a provocative perspective on Evreinov's work,[48] from which Masonic imagery and philosophy may be suggested as a possible key to the play. Evreinov was a Freemason of the highest order, although he may not have become one until after his emigration in 1925, five years after this play was written. Anna Evreinova places her husband's acceptance into a masonic order between 1927 and 1928 and claims he saw in it only temples, rituals and ceremonies, systems of signs and symbols, that is, another form of play. Soviet theatre scholar Jurij Gerasimov, on the other hand, suggests that Evreinov may have become a Freemason shortly after the revolution of 1905 as did many other Petersburg artists.[49] It seems as likely, however, that Evreinov was not simply following fashion or even his own theoretical design but instead was in need of faith, which he pursued in various forms throughout his life. Furthermore, the elements that coalesced in his "conversion" to Freemasonry were long operative in his work.

The symbol of Freemasonry is a man laying bricks, embodying the idea that man is the master of his own fate. The phrase "know thyself" appears throughout Masonic literature. The Masons believe that knowledge inevitably leads to virtue. All sin and error result from insufficient comprehension of oneself, of nature and of God. Knowledge of self is a prerequisite for understanding God and nature. The person who knows himself is constantly striving for self-improvement. Knowledge is revealed to him by "degrees" through obedience to those who know more than he. Paraclete could represent this being of superior wisdom who has been sent to earth "from the Father" with "the spirit of Truth." He is referred to in the play as a priest and an apostle.

Evreinov expressed the idea that man perfects himself gradually, by gaining knowledge of himself, which is equated with virtue, and rooting out evil, which is synonymous with ignorance. He subscribed to the Masonic idea that as man became more virtuous, he could begin to penetrate into the secrets of the universe. Like the Masons, Evreinov turned to ancient cultures in search of this secret knowledge. The Masons employed such arcane sources as ancient Egyptian mysteries (Evreinov travelled to Egypt in 1914), medieval alchemy (Evreinov's interest in the Middle Ages was manifested in his work at the Ancient Theatre), and the Jewish cabala (Evreinov studied Hebrew culture and religion).[50] Evreinov's theoretical system, like that of alchemy, sought to transform base matter into gold, a metaphor for infusing the mortal body with an immortal soul. In alchemy this was sometimes represented by a father ingesting his son to whom he later gives birth.

The Masons sought to restore the time when "the book of nature was open to man's understanding, and he could understand all of its mysteries with his reason." They hoped to regain the paradise man had lost in the Fall. The Masonic lodge was itself referred to as a "restored paradise." Here the candidate participates in a series of initiation rituals in which he undergoes a symbolic death and rebirth. Skulls and skeletons are displayed in these rituals. In act 4 of *The Chief Thing* Aglaja Karpovna appears at the symbolically decorated masquerade ball in just such a skeleton costume. She, too, "dies" and is "reborn" through the ministries of her fellow man. Of course, the old lady is not the hero of the play, and so her symbolic rebirth should not be overemphasized. But Evreinov had addressed himself to what the Masons called "the love for death" in the section of *The Theatre for Oneself (part 3)* entitled "Trying on Deaths," to which we have already referred. The similarities between Evreinov's ideas and the Masonic belief in the regenerative power of death are substantial. Following a reference to the ancient Egyptians, Evreinov quoted from chapter 18 of *Venidades:* "Thou shalt call an atravan [a priest, a hermit], a man who wakes all night striving to attain sacred wisdom, *who stands fearless and joyous on the bridge of death* and to whom the holy, the magnificent paradise is open." Evreinov stated that there is no death, only illness and recovery, and recommends creating the conditions of death in play fashion. Evreinov was being facetious in suggesting, "If your physician raises no objections, 'open your veins' for a little while." However, he did seriously believe that by "dying" in a play manner, as did Sarah Bernhardt by sleeping in a coffin, "You will return to life with a regenerated soul: familiar things and men will appear to you in a bright, pure and attractive light."[51]

Another coincidence can be found between Masonic symbolism and the terminology employed by Evreinov. Masonic symbolism revolves around architecture and specifically, the Temple. God is referred to as "the Grand Architect of the Universe" and "the Builder of the Universe." Evreinov referred to his God as Theatrarch, "the Great Director of the Theatre of Life."

Similarities can be discovered in the other systems of imagery employed by the Masons, as well. In the fourth system, God or Christ is depicted as an alchemist, one of Evreinov's favorite images for the Harlequin-Christ, the great transformer. Another system associates the triangle and the pyramid with strength and employs them as symbols of perfection. Death appears to Harlequin in Evreinov's play "A Merry Death" in the form of a bright white skeleton with a triangle on her skull. A numerical system of Masonic imagery associates the number three with perfection. In *The Chief Thing* Paraclete, the agent of Truth, is a trigamist. At the heart of the Masonic system is the idea that as a person advances in knowledge, he learns to control his passions through reason, and so becomes more virtuous. In Evreinov's monodrama *In the Stage-Wings of the Soul* (in which the self is divided into *three* parts or entities) the main character allows emotion to triumph over reason with fatal results. Finally, in the second system of Masonic imagery the truth-seeker is represented as a traveller embarked on a long journey.[52] *The Chief Thing* is yet another installment and perhaps the single clearest representation of Evreinov's personal journey in search of "the philosopher's stone" of happiness.

The Chief Thing is a flawed, highly idiosyncratic and yet, in some ways, ingenious play. It is the work on which Evreinov's claim to being an important dramatist rests. The play is great more in what it attempts to do than in what it accomplishes. Evreinov has come closer to striking a successful balance between his natural impulses to proselytize and to entertain in this than in his other plays. His sense of purpose as a theatrical visionary does not so far outstrip his sense of theatricality as to make of the play a mere teaching device or, as in the case of his monodramas, to imprison it in its own artifice.

This play contains some of Evreinov's best dramatic writing. But *The Chief Thing* would be Evreinov's most important dramatic work even if it were not his best. The importance of Evreinov's individual dramaturgical works can only be fully appreciated in conjunction with his dramatic theories. *The Chief Thing* is the most complete embodiment in dramatic form of Evreinov's major theory of the theatre in life. It also occupies a significant place in the monodrama of Nikolaj Evreinov. He has reconciled the trickster and the saint in the person of the Harlequin-Christ. He has defined the nature and function of the theatre in terms of his own persona. In so doing, he has named both Theatre and Nikolaj Evreinov, the personification of Theatre, the saviors of mankind.

2. Portrait of Evreinov by Salevij Sorin (1913)

3. *The Chief Thing* translated into various languages, overseen by Evreinov-Harlequin

4. Portrait of Evreinov by Prince A. K. Šervadšidze

5. Baron Nikolaj V. Driezen

6. A. N. Benois: The act curtain at the Ancient Theatre

7. N. K. Rerix: Scenic rendering for *The Three Magi*

8. A scene from *The Three Magi*

9. A scene from *Le Miracle de Theofile*

10. V. A. Ščuko: Scenic rendering for *Present-day Brothers*

11. Costumes, props, and scenic pieces from *Le Jeu de Robin et Marion*

12. Marion (M. A. Rigler) and the Knight (P. È. Nelobin), *Le Jeu de Robin et Marion*

13. An announcement of the Ancient Theatre's first season

14. K. M. Miklaševskij as the Nephew in *An Amusing Farce about a Cuckhold's Hat*

15. N. K. Rerix: Scenic rendering for *Fuente Ovejuna*

16, 17. Two scenes from *Fuente Ovejuna*

18. I. Ja. Bilibin: Costume rendering from *Fuente Ovejuna* (The Commander)

19. A. K. Šervadšidze: Scenic rendering for *Marta la Piadosa*

20. N. K. Kalmakov: Scenic rendering for *El Gran Ducque da Moscovia*

21, 22. N. K. Kalmakov: Two costume renderings from *El Gran Ducque da Moscovia* (Tsar Ivan the Terrible and his wife)

22. N. K. Kalmakov: Costume rendering from *El Gran Ducque da Moscovia*

23. I. Ja. Bilibin: Costume rendering from *El Purgatorio de San Patricio* (An angel)

24. Z. V. Xolmskaja

25. A. R. Kugel'

26. L. A. Fenin as Strafokamil. [Inset]: The cast of
    Vampuka, African Bride

27. [(upper)] L. I. Lukin as Lodyrè; [(lower)] the emblem of the Crooked Mirror Theatre

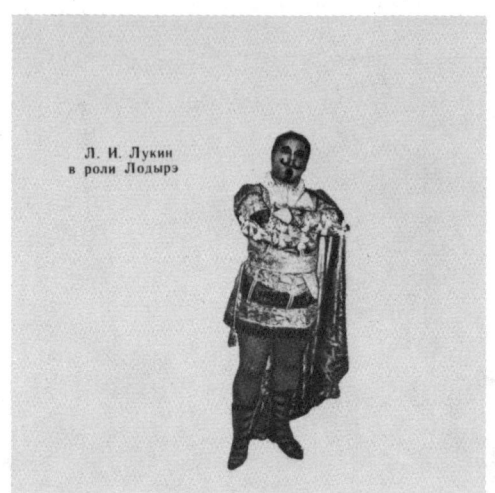

28. N. N. Evreinov (1909)

29. The White platform

30. The Red platform

31. The Red platform with connecting bridge

32. The bridge

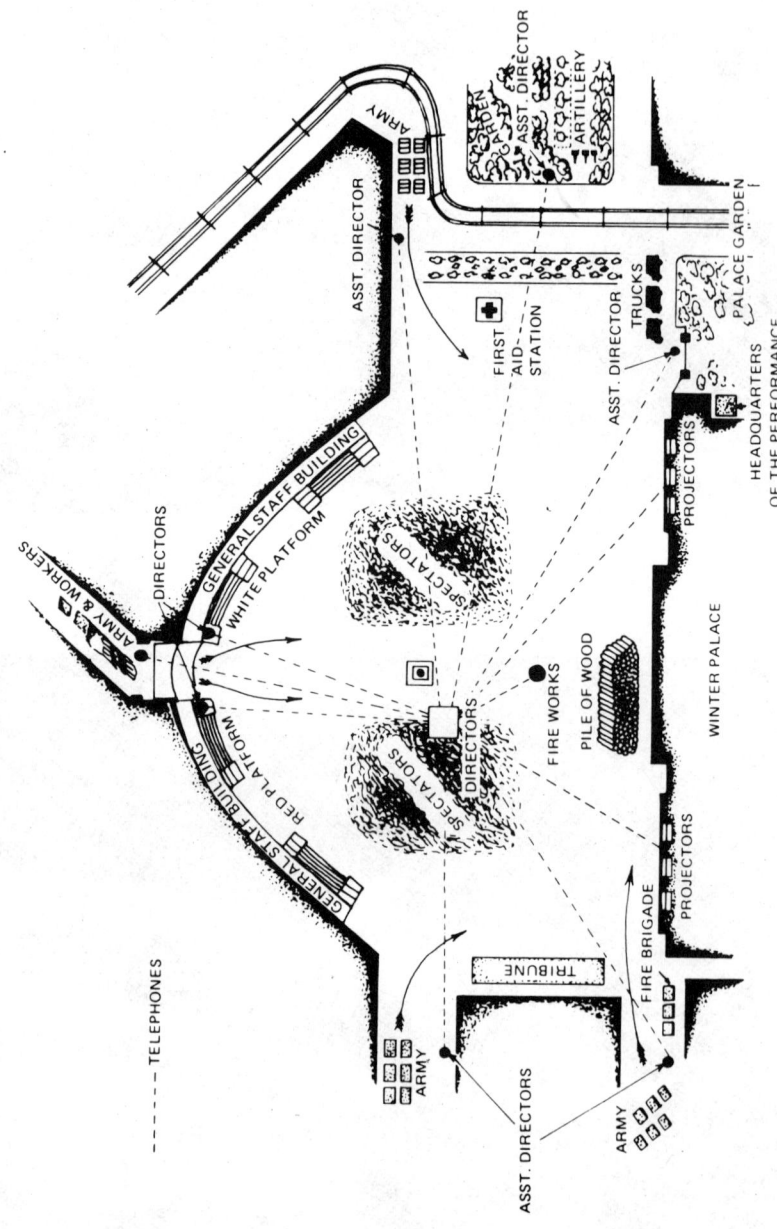

33. The general plan of *The Storming of the Winter Palace*

34. Jurij Annenkov's sketch of *The Storming of the Winter Palace*

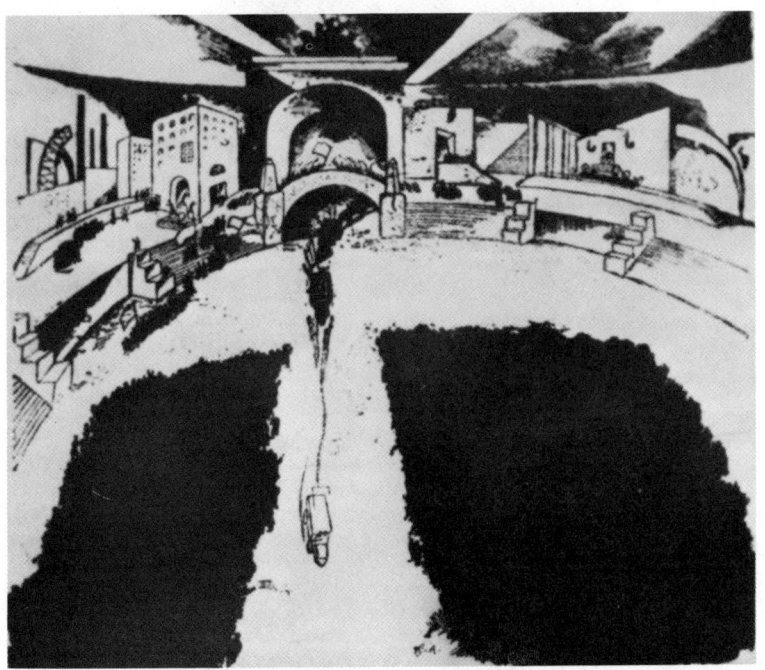

35. Portrait of Evreinov by Jurij Annenkov (1921)

5

The Ancient Theatre

No, do not summon us forward.
Backward! There life is in full swing!
There the fatal doubts that now press in upon us
Do not profane holy causes....[1]

Painters and poets turn the many-faceted mirror of world history to find in each prism a fragment of their own face.[2]

Evreinov claimed that he alone conceived the idea for the Ancient Theatre in early 1905. At that time he discussed it with a group of co-workers at the Imperial Aleksandrinskij Theatre, where his play *The Foundation of Happiness* was being performed. M. E. Darskij, S. M. Ratov, and other members of the Theatre's staff advised against such an enterprise, saying that its audience appeal would be too limited to make it commercially viable. Evreinov made no attempt to pursue his idea at this time.[3]

On 5 January 1907, Evreinov met Baron Nikolaj Vasil'evič Driezen (see fig. 5) at a banquet hosted by A. R. Kugel' commemorating the tenth anniversary of his journal *Theatre and Art*. Driezen was a director of the Imperial Theatres, a theatre censor, the editor of the *Ežegodnik Imperatorskix teatrov* — a "genuine theatre fanatic." Evreinov confided to Driezen his dream of founding an "ancient theatre" that would reconstruct the theatrical forms of the past. Driezen was intrigued by the idea and invited Evreinov to present it at a discussion circle at his apartment on Preobraženskaja Street.

A series of gatherings ensued with all manner of professors, artists, musicians, directors, theatre experts, lovers of art and especially the antique in attendance. As the meetings progressed the skeptics little by little dropped out. But Driezen supported Evreinov, and together they began to solidify plans for an Ancient Theatre in St. Petersburg.[4] Thus began a relationship that was likened by one critic to that of Mozart and Salieri. Driezen was one of several co-workers in the theatre, Kugel' being another, with whom Evreinov had a profitable but highly abrasive professional association.

The Ancient Theatre *(Starinnyj teatr)* did not represent an original idea. As we have seen there was a general impulse in the Russian arts at this time to return to the past in order to reclaim art as a vital force in the life of society. This trend was expressed in theoretical terms by the Russian symbolists, especially be Vjačeslav Ivanov whose "theatre of congregate action" was modelled on the ancient Greek theatre. The actual implementation of this impulse in the theatre was undertaken by Vsevolod Mejerxol'd in his experiments with commedia dell'arte and the theatre of the Spanish Golden Age. Others also experimented along these lines, but no one effort was as sustained, as systematic, and ultimately as influential as the Ancient Theatre of Evreinov and Baron Driezen.

Evreinov repeated throughout his life the idea that "theatre is by its very nature *uslovnyj*" and that which we call naturalness both onstage and in life is nothing but subtle theatricality. This was implicitly understood by primitive cultures as the theatres which they engendered prove. The various ancient civilizations that had strong theatrical bases—the Greek, Roman, Chinese, Hindu, Peruvian, and Mexican—all produced conventional or *uslovnye* theatres. Yet the audience believed it all and enjoyed the play because

> its theatrical instinct fills the gaps seen on the stage, co-operates with the actor, transfigures conventionality into a new reality. When the soul rebels, it does not submit to the facts imposed from without by reality; it dictates its own laws and forms to this reality. Give only a pretext, an allusion to the theatrical instinct, and it will achieve the rest: it will build magnificent palaces out of cardboard, it will transform a piece of satin into an ocean, it will make a king out of a miserable player wearing a paper crown.[5]

Evreinov now set out to prove that he was right.

The Medieval Cycle

In the 3 June 1907 issue of *Theatre and Art* there appeared a letter to the editor from Evreinov, Baron Driezen, and M. N. Burnašev (the third member of the directorate) under the heading "Prospectus for the Productions of the Ancient Theatre." It read, in part, as follows:

> Russian society's interest in the history of art embraces painting, sculpture, literature, poetry, and music. It would be a mistake to assume that it does not also include theatre. In the matter of aesthetic-historical education in the arts, we have museums, galleries, often historical concerts, special collections on the history of painting, sculpture, etc. But where is the establishment, where is the Russian book which familiarizes us with the evolution of the stage, with the evolution of the actor's art, with the artistic develop-

mental problems of the theatre of the past centuries? Our only source of information is dramatic literature. But for such an important epoch of the theatre as the Middle Ages, we have not a single play in Russian translation.

Meanwhile, theatre as a cultural force and indicator of popular tastes, morals, and world view should not occupy last place in the history of civilization.[6] Separate productions have tried with some success to fill this gap—for example, the historical production commemorating the 150th anniversary of the Imperial Theatres or the Russian historical productions organized in Moscow by N. N. Arbatov.

We have in mind a whole series of historical productions presenting in chronological order not only the history of dramatic literature but also the evolution of staging combined with the history of theatrical dance and music, costuming, makeup, etc. Archeological and historical truthfulness of staging and communication of the spirit and character of the epoch under consideration should have decided significance. Each production will transport the spectator to one or another epoch. The characteristics of the actor-audience relationship of the particular epoch will be re-created.

Those who have contributed ideas to the construction of a program for this theatre include: Assistant Professor E. V. Aničkov, Professor L. A. Saketti, directors N. N. Arbatov, Vl. Iv. Nemirovič-Dančenko, Ju. E. Ozarovskij, K. S. Stanislavskij, Ju. M. Jur'ev, N. A. Popov, writers on questions of stage art M. A. Vejkone, N. N. Dolgov, I. A. Sac, S. O. Cybul'skij, È. A. Stark and others. The programs which have been decided upon are:

1st evening—the antique theatre (Greek and Roman)

2nd evening—the Middle Ages (mysteries, miracles, street theatre, etc.)

3rd evening—the epoch of the Renaissance (pseudo-classicism, Spanish theatre, harlequinades, ballet, etc.)

4th evening—theatre of the epoch of Shakespeare (in England)

5th evening—the theatre of Molière.

The time of the theatre of Molière coincides with the appearance of theatre in Russia and so will make for a natural crossover from the Western European theatre to our own.

It goes without saying that the presentation of segments from plays would, in terms of economy of time and broadness of interests, be preferable to their presentation in toto.

As it turned out the directorate changed its mind about beginning with the cycle of plays from the Greek theatre. Professor E. V. Aničkov argued that whereas the Greek theatre was the product of a pagan civilization, the medieval theatre and the Western European thereafter reflected a Christian consciousness. Evreinov pointed out that a link existed between the Russian *skomoroxi* (clowns) and the medieval jongleurs. He found it strange that his society knew more about the Greek theatre than it did about the medieval theatre, which was closer to it in time.[7]

By the early summer of 1907 a major portion of the theatre's staff had been selected. As originally set out, Evreinov was in charge of artistic matters while Driezen handled the running of the theatre. Evreinov, who had little talent for business and less use for it, contracted a similar arrangement with A. R. Kugel' when he took over as artistic director of the Crooked Mirror Theatre. Aleksandr A. Sanin (Šenberg) was signed from the Imperial Aleksandrinskij Theatre as an additional director, primarily for his skill in staging crowd scenes. A. A. Skuratov became stage manager at the Ancient Theatre, and M. R. Bekker was also added to the production staff. The designers included I. Ja. Bilibin, M. V. Dobužinskij, E. E. Lansare, V. A. Ščuko, V. Ju. Chambers, and N. K. Rerix. A. N. Benois was commissioned to design the theatre's permanent curtain (see fig. 6).[8] V. K. Lapšin was in charge of properties.

The literary department of the theatre was under the supervision of E. V. Aničkov. The music department consisted of A. K. Glazunov (one of Evreinov's former teachers), Professor L. A. Saketti from the St. Petersburg Conservatoire, I. A. Sac, and Professor V. F. Šišmarev. M. M. Fokine was in charge of choreography.

The acting company included the following: M. I. Berseneva, N. I. Butkovskaja (Evreinov's publisher), Z. A. Dmitrenko, E. K. Dukšinskaja, E. G. Zotova, E. A. Klassovskaja, M. A. Korol'kova, M. N. Lokteva, E. A. Polocova, K. K. Potemkina, M. A. Rigler, V. A. Ščegoleva, I. M. Bereznjakov, V. O. Vreden, A. N. Grigor'ev, I. M. Il'in, F. N. Kurixin, B. X. Kastal'skij, M. N. Karakai, V. A. Karneev, Konstantin M. Miklaševskij (also a writer), N. I. Orlov, V. N. Poznjakov, and S. P. Perelygič.[9]

In the fall of 1907 *Theatre and Art* announced that the Ancient Theatre would open its season on 7 December at the New Theatre in Petersburg and would play there until 22 December. Preparations were already well underway. Rehearsals began on 1 September in a rented space in Kononovskij Hall. Ida Al'berg, a well-known performer of the day, occupied the space until midnight. The Ancient Theatre company took it over at that time and rehearsed until 8:00 A. M. rehearsals resumed at 1:00 P. M.[10]

In the meantime the directorate was engaged in gathering materials. Burnašev travelled to Paris and Cologne for materials on the history of medieval theatre. Driezen visited some Swiss monasteries and then continued on to Nuremberg and Rothenberg. Evreinov remained in Russia to work out a production style for the liturgical drama *The Three Magi (Tri volxva)* and for the street theatre of the sixteenth century.

Introductory lectures were delivered to the company to acquaint them with the period and its various art forms. Assistant Professor E. V. Aničkov spoke on the history of medieval literature, Professor L. A. Saketti on the history of music, M. V. Dobužinskij on medieval iconography, and N. N. Evreinov on the medieval actor.[11] Efforts were made to locate medieval music and wherever possible to play it on instruments of the period. Original instruments could not always be found and so were constructed. Similar care was taken with the costumes. N. K. Rerix rejected 143 costumes which had already been partially designed and started over again, working until he was satisfied with the results.

Translation likewise presented a problem. These plays had not previously been translated into Russian. To compound the problem, the extant texts were written in such dialects as Norman and Artois. They first had to be translated into literary French by Pierre Chapman, archivist-paleographer at the French Institute in Paris, and then into Russian.[12]

It was decided to divide the medieval cycle into two evenings. The plays would be chosen from the following categories: a liturgical drama from the eleventh century, a miracle play from the thirteenth century, street theatre from the fifteenth century, and farces from the sixteenth century.

In the end neither the mystery plays nor street theatre were included in the actual program. Many of the mystery plays were thought to be apocryphal and would have created difficulties with the censor and especially the Church synod. One such play, *Adamsspiel (Jeu d'Adam)* by an unknown author of the twelfth century, was disallowed by the censor on the grounds that Adam had been canonized by the Russian Orthodox Church and could not be impersonated on the stage.

Street theatre, which had originally been scheduled as the last play of the second evening, was cancelled due to an intratheatre problem. The costume designer said that the costumes would be too complicated to build in the allotted time and categorically refused to do so.[13]

Apparently the street theatre presentation, *The Fair on the Day of St. Denis, (Jarmarka na indikt sv. Denisa)* had been fully staged when the decision was made not to open it to the public. A review of the production appeared in the 11 October 1907 issue of *Theatre and Art*. The set by E. E. Lansere was judged a success. A. N. Benois designed the costumes. A. A. Sanin staged the production, and Chinizelli's acrobatic troupe performed. Evreinov, who wrote the piece with advice from Professor E. V. Aničkov and V. F. Šišmarev, painted a clear picture of life in a medieval town square. His first stage direction sets the scene:

> A town square seen in the light of evening. In the center a small fountain and round the sides multicolored little shops. In the distance is a church. In the foreground to the right is a brothel with a little light and a tempting notice. Beside the steps leading to the

entrance is a long table with benches. To the left is a small restaurant in front of which are arranged tables with barrels round them. Next to the brothel a drinking session is taking place. Some of the girls are serving, others, drunk, are sitting on the citizens' knees, while still others are embracing. To the left of the restaurant some students have also gathered on the barrels, playing dice. They too are drunk. Further back from the footlights, surrounded by a merry crowd, a puppet show owner and his assistant are giving a performance. Still further upstage, beyond the foundation, a lively round dance is taking place. Long before the curtain rises the sounds of musical instruments—gamba horns and tambourines—can be heard mingled with the stamping of feet, laughter and the confused chatter of coarse drunken conversation. Someone bangs crocks and someone else whistles. All this hubbub is dominated by the voice of the puppet show owner. As the curtain rises there is a deafening burst of laughter.[14]

As a result of the cancellation, *Le Jeu de Robin et Marion,* a pastorale from the thirteenth century, was moved from its original slot in the program of the first evening to the one that had been allocated to the street theatre presentation. Another reason offered for the change was that the directorate had second thoughts about performing a lightweight piece such as *Le Jeu de Robin et Marion* on the same evening as the liturgical drama *Le Miracle de Théofile.*

The program for the two evenings was eventually set as follows:

First Evening

1. *The Three Magi (Tri volxva).* Prologue by Evreinov. Miracle/liturgical drama, eleventh century. The prologue and mass scenes were directed by A. A. Sanin and the ritual by M. N. Burnašev. Set and costumes designed by N. K. Rerix (see fig. 7).

2. *Le Miracle de Théofile (Dejstvo o Teofile).* A miracle-trouvère, thirteenth century, by Rutebeuf (1245–1285). Translation by Aleksandr Blok. Directed by A. A. Sanin and N. V. Driezen. Set, costumes, and properties designed by I. Ja. Bilibin. Religious music from the thirteenth century arranged by Il'ja Sac.

Second Evening

1. *Present-day Brothers (Nynešnie brat'ja).* Morality, fifteenth century. Translation by Sergej Gorodeckij. Directed by N. V. Driezen and A. A. Sanin. Set and costumes by V. A. Ščuko.

2. *Le Jeu de Robin et Marion (Igra o Robine i Marion).* Pastorale, thirteenth century, by Adam de la Halle (1240-c.1290). Translation by N. M. Vencel. Directed by Evreinov. Set and costumes by M. V. Dobužinskij.

3. *Very Merry and Amusing Farces about a Tub and about a Cuckold's Hat (Očen' veselyj i smešnoj fars o čane i Očen' smešnoj i veselyj fars o šljape-rogače)*. Farces from the sixteenth century by Jean Dabondance. Translation by A. M. Trubnikov and N. N. Vrangel', respectively. Directed by M. N. Burnašev. Set and costumes by V. Ju. Chambers.[15]

The Ancient Theatre opened its first season on 8 December 1907, at 61 Mojka Canal next to the Policejskij Bridge, a space formerly occupied by L. B. Javorskaja and her acting troupe. The bill ran for one month on these premises. An additional two evenings were presented at the *Narodnyj Dom* on the *Peterburgskaja storona*. The company went on tour for four weeks in Moscow, taking up residence at the Hermitage Theatre.[16]

Anatolij Kremlev criticized the Ancient Theatre at its inception as an impractical enterprise. It lacked money, direction, and plays from the Middle Ages in Russian translation. What it had was naiveté. The directors (Kremlev was, in fact, referring to Aničkov, who was actually a lecturer-consultant) seriously believed that the barbarous Middle Ages was a "radiant" epoch, and furthermore, that they could re-create the play of medieval actors when everyone knows that re-creating the actors' play of ten to twenty years ago is impossible. Kremlev also pointed out that it is one thing to reproduce a medieval play written in the Middle Ages and quite another to stage a work written by a contemporary author that is meant to pass for a medieval play.[17]

According to Edward Stark, the ninth and tenth centuries were characterized by intense religious mysticism and fanaticism. People believed that the world would end in the year 1000. When the year 1000 came and went, the religious fanaticism remained and was carried into the eleventh century, where *The Three Magi* is set. This century had a very anxious character, which, in Stark's opinion, the production captured. As the curtain opens, there is silence onstage. It is night. The shroud of darkness covering a small, medieval town is soon to be lifted, revealing the radiant day. The thin twilight envelops a structure of gray flagstone, a cathedral at stage right at an oblique angle to the footlights with an arched doorway, a parapet, and a series of steps leading down onto the town square. To the left of the cathedral are various other stone buildings running from downstage left to upstage center and vanishing into the distance. A crowd of people are huddled together in the square and on the steps of the cathedral. These human figures—men, women, and children—seem bound together in weariness caused by travel, worries, sickness, and fear of "the eternal unknown." One old pilgrim, tormenting his body and soul in confession, has spent the entire night in prayer, on his knees, his face raised to the portal of the cathedral and his hand toward the sky.

Slowly the people rouse themselves from their deep sleep. They are awaiting the start of the liturgical drama. In this, the eleventh century, the drama is closely tied to religious ritual. They expect it to lift their souls, to work on them like a miracle, to bring them peace. Like children, their moods can change quickly.

The crowd is restless with expectation. They discuss the possibility of rain, which would cause the performance to be cancelled. Rumors of the Black Death are in the air and contribute to the general agitation. Women begin to sob and men to call out in disconnected phrases, not knowing whom to blame for this misfortune of the people. Tensions increase as a group of flagellants make their appearance. First, only the sounds of their approach are heard; then, they enter through the gate, moving through the crowd. They are half-naked, in rags, with touseled hair. Slowly they mount the steps to the parapet, whipping themselves on the back, shoulder, and sides, filling the air with their cries before disappearing behind the cathedral.

As the crowd continues to wait restlessly, preparations are begun for the presentation. An elegant carpet is brought out and placed on the steps, followed by a throne of bright copper. "It is Herod's throne! Herod's throne!," cry voices from the crowd.

Finally, the preparations are finished, and the town dignitaries make their appearance, the men moving to one side and the women to the other. The old abbot slowly appears on the parapet, and all bow down. "Silence! Silence! Praise the Lord! Silence! The presentation will begin."

The old abbot genuflects before the church doors. In the depths of the dimly lit church can be seen the crib of the Christ child. The solemn song of a choir, and the sound of an organ is heard. Monks and nuns enter. The presentation begins. The text is read and sung in Latin. Herod's appearance evokes an animated response in the crowd. The three magi enter with gifts, preceded by a child with a star on the end of a pole. They bow to Herod and proceed into the cathedral. In their place appear a bright spirit and a beautiful angel with golden hair who sings, "All that was prophesied has come to pass. Do not be informers, but return by another road."

While the angel sings, convulsive sobbing arises from the crowd. The spectators, who are already inclined toward religious harmony, are visibly moved. A messenger enters and informs Herod that he has been deceived. The magi have returned via a different road. An uneasy murmuring sweeps through the crowd. They know what Herod intends to do. They yell "Curse him!" for he is ordering the firstborn killed. The crowd rises up as one, and Herod's last words are drowned in a sea of enraged voices and the hysterical crying of women and children. The crowd is united in despair, anger, and protest, and caught up in the power of religious ecstasy; they sweep onto the parapet. All is dissolved in general disorder, the lights go out, and the performance is ended. The spell wears off, but the strength of the impression remains.[18]

Evreinov understood quite well that the medieval theatre fully engaged its audience. The medieval mystery play, for example, sometimes demanded up to five hundred participants, which meant that the director had to enlist the rabble to play roles. Evreinov referred to the naive identification medieval audiences made between actors and the characters they impersonated. Playing the role of a sinner or a martyr could be dangerous, and the audience often called for "Judas"'s death following the performance. The level of medieval acting was reflected in the simplicity of the stage directions. Medieval characters were locked into types that were consistent throughout. The medieval actor was often familiar with the crowd before which he played.

A. R. Kugel' pointed out that the body of the theatrical event at this time took place in the depths of the cathedral. He criticized Evreinov's prologue, saying that one does not know where the action of the play ends and the religious action begins. Everything here takes place on the cathedral steps and on the parapet. During the prologue the crowd continually interrupts the "actors" on the parapet with their shouts. In Kugel''s estimation this crowd was too conscious of rhythm, harmony, acting, and singing to resemble a real crowd of the Middle Ages. Kugel' conceded that this is, after all, a work of art. Still, he couldn't help wishing that from time to time the crowd would act more like a crowd.[19]

Ljubov' Gurevič drew attention in her review to the "picturesque" quality of the stage picture (see fig. 8), a quality often noted in Evreinov's productions not only at the Ancient Theatre but at other theatres as well. In this particular case Gurevič felt that this quality in the crowd scenes interfered with the performance as a whole. There was too much exaggeration. The impression conveyed was too striking in its beauty and clarity, not unlike the paintings of the European romantics in the first half of the nineteenth century. The mass scenes interfered with the play itself, which was done in soft, dull colors and restrained movements. In those moments when the crowd broke in with its passionate cries, the wholeness of the production's overall impression was fragmented.[20]

The second presentation of the evening was the thirteenth century miracle-trouvère *Le Miracle de Théofile*.[21] A fanfare announces the beginning. We are transported to the thirteenth century, when drama was no longer a part of the church service and had already lost its religious character. The drama is no longer played on the church parapet but has moved into the town square. The performers are now commoners rather than clergy. The text receives a freer treatment, with the comic element now a factor. The stage is divided into three levels: heaven, earth, and hell. The legend on which the play is based was already known in the sixth century and was reworked in the form of a poem in the tenth century by a nun.

The plot is as follows. Théofile has given up his goods to the poor and so has been deprived of his cloth by the Cardinal. He turns to the magician Saladin for advice. The latter descends into hell and sues the Devil for aid. The Devil agrees to help Théofile if he will sign a paper saying that he has forsaken God and will now serve only him. At this point, the Cardinal sends his servant Zadira after Théofile. When he finds Théofile, he returns to him his cloth. Théofile repents, and the Bright Spirit descends into hell to recover the paper from the Devil.

According to Stark, the production was absolutely charming. Bilibin designed a beautiful set in the style of a twelfth-century miniature (see fig. 9). The performances were all in the primitive style. There was a deliberate uniform tonality of speech and simplicity in the gestures. When the curtain went up, all of the characters were already seated in their places, and they remained there until the conclusion of the performance. On the upper level, representing heaven, sat the Bright Spirit with his attendants; on the middle level, representing earth, to the left was the Cardinal, right of center was Théofile, and to the far right were his friends, Pierre and Tomas. According to A. R. Kugel', these two characters "sat for the entire play without moving their lips, in the same pose, with their arms folded as in old Italian paintings." There is the flat facade of a building on either side of the stage at this level and what appears from extant photographs to be a castle stage right and a monastery stage left. A chalice rests on a stand stage center. As is the case in medieval miniatures, the human figures are large in comparison to the scenic elements. On the lower level stood Saladin. Downstage left stood the Prologue, who read the author's stage directions aloud in an impressive manner. In addition, the Prologue explained the characters inner feelings and thoughts. A reviewer writing under the pseudonym "Old Friend" *(Staryj drug)* was critical of the manner in which this convention was treated. He maintained that the Prologue, noticing that the practice of commenting aloud on the characters' thoughts and actions drew laughter from the audience, played it up. By underlining the fact that these conventions were funny, the Prologue undermined the objectivity of the production.[22]

Also on the lower level was a Hell mouth, turned up in the direction of the top of the stage. Gremlins came out of the Hell mouth. The set had the look of a flat cardboard cutout. This primitive impression was reinforced by the look of the actors, who were attired in stock character clothing (Saladin, for example, wore a floor-length robe covered with stars and a wizard's cap and carried a staff) and gestured broadly.

Stark was again enthusiastic concerning this production, but Kremlev criticized the acting—the strange, ungrammatical accents and intonations that were not quite human and the garbled running together of words in what he called "a misguided attempt to re-create medieval performance." Evreinov is incorrect in asserting that the actors of that time who played villains felt it necessary "to growl like wild animals, to bulge out their eyes, to bare their teeth and so forth. This is obviously a gross mistake."[23]

A. R. Kugel' again offered an interesting observation. He was personally in favor of the modern theatre's returning to the primitive style of performance in general. Noting that in the medieval miracle play such abstract entities as the "Bright Spirit" and "Satan" were manifested in actual form, he commented that whereas modern man lacks faith but has imagination, in medieval man the situation was just the reverse.[24]

Another reviewer pointed out this particular miracle's similarity to the Faust legend and for that reason found it to be absorbing. Ljubov' Gurevič found this to be the most significant piece of literary work of all the plays in the medieval cycle staged at the Ancient Theatre. She thought highly of Blok's translation. I. Borozdin echoed this sentiment but complained about a certain amount of unnecessary modernization of the language. Gurevič praised the set, whose primitive style she thought resembled paintings of the thirteenth and fourteenth centuries. However, she was not very impressed with the acting. The lack of technical strength in the acting company was a common enough complaint of the critics reviewing productions at the Ancient Theatre. Just as often, however, critics echoed the sentiments expressed by N. Karabanov in his 1912 review of the Spanish cycle: "What youth, vigor, boldness, and artistic beauty are projected in the productions of the Ancient Theatre."[25]

The second evening of the medieval cycle opened with the morality *Present-day Brothers (Nynešnie brat'ja)*. The curtain rises to reveal a beautiful picture in a white frame resembling a medieval miniature painting (see fig. 10). The floor is raked and covered with a pattern of small triangles. A well stands centerstage. The blue-toned walls are decorated with fleurs-de-lis, but the most original feature of the set is upstage in the rear wall. There are five curtained doors, and above each is a label—"Parents" and "Sons" to the extreme left and right respectively, and above the three others, "Conscience," "Envy," and "Brotherly Love." These labels indicate which characters will enter and exit through a given door. Below the stage is a placard indicating the subject matter of the play, and above the stage, a notice describing how the play ends.

The Prologue enters in a beautiful costume, historically accurate in its detail from the shoes to the staff he carries. He approaches the audience and invites them to give their attention to the piece about to be performed. Then, making an elegant bow, he exits, and the play begins. A small curtain draws open on the left, and the Parents enter. They begin to recite verse in a primitive tone. Then through the right door enter the three Sons. After them, through the appropriate door, follows a fine lady. So there will be no confusion in the audience's mind about who this lady is, she holds a sign aloft that bears her name, "Brotherly Love." The naiveté of the presentation produces an interesting effect as real people enter into conversation with allegorical figures.

"Envy" appears and, bending over the two Brothers who are asleep, induces them to conspire against the youngest son, their father's favorite. Before they have a chance to act, however, "Conscience" appears and dissuades them. "Envy" returns and this time succeeds in persuading the two Brothers to throw the youngest into the well. But of course this is a morality and Good must triumph. The Brothers experience pangs of conscience and, full of repentance, confess to their Father. The unhappy Father cries over the well, mourning the loss of his youngest son, whom he believes to be drowned. However, the latter's voice rises from the well. The youngest climbs out of the well in which he has spent four days and is reconciled with his family. They all agree that it is necessary to fight the temptations of "Envy" and are thankful that "Conscience" arrived in time to prevent them from going astray. The Prologue again enters and bids the audience farewell.

Stark commented on the presentation's childlike naiveté and cited that as the reason the morality had remained relevant five hundred years after it was written?[26] But not all of the critics agreed. One wrote that the fine staging by Sanin and Driezen, the effective translation by Sergej Gorodeckij, and the scenic elements and style of the play could not mitigate the sense of boredom such blatant preaching produces in a contemporary audience. Anatolij Kremlev argued that such projects as those undertaken by the Ancient Theatre were irrelevant when the contemporary theatre was so close to dying, having lost its artistic, social, and universal meaning. The energy being squandered on reviving old plays should be employed to get the contemporary public interested in their own theatre. The Ancient Theatre had to weather such attacks continually. Ljubov' Gurevič, who had been critical of the acting in the first evening's presentations, was in general pleased with the acting in the offerings of the second evening.[27]

By all accounts, the most interesting and successful of the productions in the medieval cycle was Evreinov's staging of *Le Jeu de Robin et Marion,* which was performed next. The pastorale was staged as the entertainment during a feast at a knight's castle.

The walls are hung with rich, multicolored tapestries. From left to right along either side of the hall sit gray-bearded minstrels with crowns on their heads readying their instruments. The master of ceremonies enters and invites the assembled guests to give their attention to the spectacle.

Then, before the eyes of the audience onstage and the one in the auditorium, simple preparations are made for the play. A small cardboard house representing a peasant's dwelling and some prop sheep to be tended by Robin and Marion are carried onto the stage. As in the other medieval productions these pieces have been designed less than full-scale (see fig. 11). Four servants enter with torches and stand in the corners illuminating the stage, which we imagine to be a green meadow. The master of ceremonies again enters to make sure that everything is in order, claps his hands three times, and exits. The exotic music produced by the instruments transports us to a faraway time and place.

We hear a song, and soon Marion appears, with a garland in her hair and wearing a long dress and a cloak. She is barefoot and carries a staff. The delicate, naive melody she sings is suddenly interrupted by the coarse voice of the Knight. He enters on a large wooden horse mounted on four brightly decorated wheels and covered in a white cloth spotted with fleurs-de-lis (see fig. 12). The Knight, who wears a wooden sword at his side and has a wooden falcon perched atop his arm, is immediately charmed by the shepherdess's beauty. He pays her court but in vain, since Marion is in love with Robin. The Knight exits, the horse being pulled out backwards.

Robin's voice is heard in the distance. He enters, and a pastoral idyll ensues in which the two lovers exchange tender words of love, alternately speaking and singing, and share a humble repast. They decide to arrange a celebration in the meadow, and Robin exits to enlist the aid of their friends. Marion is left alone onstage, and the Knight again appears on his horse. He is preoccupied with the loss of his falcon, which has flown away. Recognizing Marion, he again makes overtures to her. At this point, Robin returns, the falcon perched on his arm. The Knight boxes his ears and absconds with Marion as his captive.

A comic scene follows involving Robin and his two cousins, one of whom sings in a nasal voice and the other in a bass. The Knight returns. He has brought back Marion, satisfied that she will never love him. Marion calls to her lover and his cousins, who re-enter along with the peasant Guar and the shepherdess Peronella. All make merry. The play ends with a general dance under the supervision of Robin.

Stark commented upon the success of Dobužinskij's stylized set and the special contribution made to the overall atmosphere by the music composed by Il'ja Sac. The actors, trained by Evreinov, displayed admirable versatility in their mastery of singing, dancing, declamation, and mime. They also succeeded in matching the rhythm of their recited verse with the rhythm of their movements. Their naive style of play and broad characterizations corresponded with existing historical evidence on acting in the medieval theatre.[28]

Unlike the play preceding it on the bill, the significance of *Le Jeu de*

Robin et Marion as a work of dramatic literature was in general appreciated by the critics. Not only did it serve as the prototype for later pastorales and the basis for comic opera and French light comedy, but it was entertaining in and of itself. The translation was thought good, and the music and dance (staged by Fokine), sets, and costumes were considered a success. Despite what one critic called its excessive length the pastorale was not boring.[29]

Another critic noted that this presentation did not employ archeological restoration of scenic elements but instead represented "the triumph of artistic intuition and good taste." Likewise, the costumes reflected a stylized rather than an archeological approach. This same unnamed critic concluded that Adam de la Halle "was evidently quite a skeptic since his pastorale is in no way naive or sentimental."[30]

The reviewer writing under the pseudonym "Old Friend," by contrast, criticized Evreinov for exaggerating the naiveté of the play (as he said had been done in *Le Miracle de Théofile*), as if the contemporary audience needs to have things underlined in order to understand the attitude they should adopt. Indeed, each time the Knight pressed his body against the cheek of the wooden horse as an expression of fear, it got a good laugh from the audience. But the result, in the critic's opinion, was to parody the old form of the play rather than to re-create it. The impression conveyed was that of examining a miniature through a magnifying glass, and the value of the restoration was lost. The sentimental character of the pastorale was evaporated. The actors should believe more in what they are doing and be less self-conscious in their approach.[31]

If this last critic's remarks were true, they would point in the direction of Evreinov's later work at the Crooked Mirror Theatre, especially his parodies of theatrical forms which were staged there. However, the majority of the reviews give the impression that Evreinov sought to emphasize the playfulness and naiveté of the piece and not to parody these very qualities.

The last presentations in the medieval cycle, *A Very Merry and Amusing Farce about a Tub* and *A Very Merry and Amusing Farce about a Cuckold's Hat,* were not originally written, in Stark's estimation, with any literary significance or moral intent in mind. They are significant only as another form of medieval spectacle. The chief interest in the pieces springs from the role played by the two fools.

The set represents a medieval fairground booth with two boxes on either side of the stage. The fools, who are fantastically costumed and made up, sit in these boxes and deliver their humorous commentary on the action. From time to time they leap from the boxes to disrupt the action. The farces deal with the credulity of an old husband who is being deceived by his young wife. Stark noted that they are very coarse as written, and the directorate of the Ancient Theatre displayed great courage in staging them.[32] "Old Friend" wrote that the "Farce about the Tub" was funnier in retrospect than in the viewing, but not as funny as the usual contemporary play in either case. This time a different critic objected to what he called the director's "sharp and even shrill underlining which grates on the contemporary spectator."[33]

For the most part, however, the reaction of the press to the medieval cycle at the Ancient Theatre was highly favorable (see fig. 13). There was widespread praise for the great artistic taste, energy, and talent displayed by the directors of the theatre. *The Three Magi* and *Le Jeu de Robin et Marion* enjoyed the greatest success. Financially, the enterprise was less than successful, filling the house only on occasion. It attracted a devoted but limited audience of educated theatregoers. A longer period of time was necessary to educate the general public and build up a larger audience.[34]

Despite its lack of material success, A. R. Kugel' considered the course set by the Ancient Theatre important:

> It is difficult, of course, to say what will happen in the theatre in the future, whether it will return to primitives. Very probably so. I would even say that this is essential, that it is not possible to continue along the lines of factory production as the theatre is now doing.

Kugel' concluded that the Ancient Theatre is "just about the most interesting phenomenon in the life of the theatre in recent times."[35]

P. Muratov echoed these sentiments in the Moscow press. Writing in *The Russian Word (Russkoe slovo)*, he said that the Ancient Theatre was the most important event in Russian artistic life in the last two years. "It is apparent from these productions that the people involved have a deep, heartfelt understanding of art." He continued, "The Ancient Theatre quite correctly set itself the task of attaining artistic truth. Above all, it strives to convey the very spirit of the given epoch and play." Although it has carefully and scientifically assembled a wealth of material for production,

> the productions themselves are the result of free and inspired playing by the artist with the materials gathered, of that creative fantasy without which art in general is senseless. The Ancient Theatre is not afraid to introduce its own interpretation, but this [its interpretation] is the result of a long and close acquaintance with the play and the epoch.[36]

This was reflected in the design of the productions. Igor' Grabar' wrote that "what was produced was not an exact reproduction of the ancient theatre, but rather something in the nature of a fantasy on the theme of the theatre."[37]

Edward Stark stated that the aim of the Ancient Theatre was to steer clear of even the slightest trace of modernism in its work, to operate on the strictly scholarly ground of everyday historical events and archeology. It sought to cast light deep into past centuries without refracting it through the prism of the personal "I." Instead, the perspective it offered was that of the audience present at the original performance.[38] In a statement reminiscent of the chauvinism of the World of Art, which began the trend of adapting Western forms to suit Russian needs, the critic "Old Friend" argued that the real importance of the Ancient Theatre was to show the West what the Russian theatre could do in the way of restoration.[39] But the Ancient Theatre had accomplished something else a good deal more important. Stark wrote in his book on the Ancient Theatre that its work proved the thesis that is the basis of the artist's creative process: "Art creates Beauty and Beauty creates Good."[40]

The Reconstructive Method

The name given by Evreinov to the overall production approach employed at the Ancient Theatre was "artistic reconstruction" (*xudožestvennaja rekonstrukcija*). Evreinov believed that this could only be accomplished by "the reconstruction of the spectator."[41] By this he meant including an audience composed of actors in period dress onstage to watch the play. This was not to be a passive audience. It not only helped to shape the perspective of the audience in the auditorium, it played an integral part in the stage action. While the reactions of a contemporary audience could not match the emotional outpouring of the onstage (e.g., the medieval) audience to the religious and moral themes being enacted, they could be drawn further into the action. This, the innovators of the pre-Revolutionary period realized, was the most that could be expected. The twentieth-century audience lacks the sense of community, the spiritual cohesiveness of the Ancient Greek and medieval audiences.

In his book *Directorial Portraits* (*Režisserskie portrety*, 1928), G. K. Kryžickij credited Mejerxol'd with having conceived the idea of reconstructing past theatrical forms in 1906 with his reconstructive approach to the staging of *Sister Beatrice* by Maurice Maeterlinck at the Dramatic Theatre of V. F. Komissarževskaja.[42] His stage groupings resembled the bas-reliefs on the walls of medieval cathedrals. Actors spoke their lines in a rhythmic monotone, much as they had in several of Evreinov's productions.

In a 1908 article Mejerxol'd commented at length on the reconstructive approach as it was employed at the Ancient Theatre:

> The Ancient Theatre could have chosen one of two paths, either (1) having selected plays of old theatres [the Theatre] could have approached the staging via the archeologi-

cal method, that is, it could have concerned itself first and foremost with an exact scenic reconstruction or (2) having selected plays written *in the manner* of the old theatres (the old plays), it could have staged them through free composition on the theme of the primitive theatre (as, for example, the manner in which *Sister Beatrice* was staged by me at the Theatre of V. F. Komissarževskaja).

Instead, argued Mejerxol'd, the Ancient Theatre took original texts from the medieval theatre but stylized them in performance ("free composition"). Thus, says Mejerxol'd, the theatre has fallen between two stools and is neither wholly stylized nor wholly authentic. This results in acting that seems like a parody on medieval performance to a contemporary audience.[43]

Evreinov justified his use of free composition within the context of the reconstructive technique in "The Method of Artistic Reconstruction in Theatrical Stagings":

> Each director-reconstructor gives to his production his own particular touch. This is not "historio-archeological prospecting" and for that reason is not called simply "reconstruction," but "artistic reconstruction."

This concept, Evreinov claimed, opened a wide area for comparatively free creation. The director must enter into the spirit and details of the historical epoch. He should not, however, become a slave to this information. "The difference...between the simple 'reconstructive' method and the 'artistic reconstructive' method is as huge as between the methods of science and art."[44]

Mejerxol'd continued his own experiments with the reconstructive method in his 1909 production of Wagner's *Tristan und Isolde* at the Imperial Marinskij Theatre and Molière's *Don Juan,* staged at the Imperial Aleksandrinskij Theatre (1910). Mejerxol'd's extant production notes for *Don Juan* and his published second thoughts on the Ancient Theatre indicate that he and Evreinov were not very far apart in their essential outlook. Referring to his earlier review of the Ancient Theatre, Mejerxol'd wrote:

> When I spoke of the possible means of re-creating the stage conventions of the exemplary ages of drama, and of the two ways to stage plays of the theatres of the past, I omitted to mention one possible exception to the suggested rules. I said that in producing a work from a past age of the theatre it is by no means obligatory to stage it *according to the archaeological method;* in the process of reconstruction there is no need for the director to bother with the exact re-creation of the architectural character of the stage of the period in question. An authentic play at the old theatre may be staged as a *free composition* in the spirit of the theatre in which it was originally staged, but on one inflexible condition: from the old theatre one *must* select those architectural features which best convey the spirit of the work.[45]

Whatever their similarities, there were of course considerable differences between Mejerxol'd's approach to reconstruction and Evreinov's. First, Mejerxol'd emphasized with a tone of superiority that his was not intended as an "archeological reconstruction," but rather a selective one designed to convey the spirit and, one might add, the theatricality of the piece. Evreinov, on the other hand, sought to re-create the old forms in careful detail. He believed that this was essential in order to evoke both the mood and spirit of the piece. Second, although Mejerxol'd brought actors into the audience and sought other ways to involve the audience in the stage action, he did not, like Evreinov, "reconstruct the spectator." That is, he did not provide an onstage audience to serve as (1) a reflecting mirror for the contemporary audience, (2) a stimulus for the contemporary audience, or (3) a part of the action. Here again Evreinov believed that he had hit upon a necessary element in conveying the spirit of the piece in its original production. Mejerxol'd was more concerned with making his productions relevant to a contemporary audience. Evreinov preferred to give the audience the opportunity to relate to the production, to reach out for it. His approach was, in a sense, more demanding, and the limited (albeit enthusiastic) public response evoked by the productions at the Ancient Theatre was in part a result of this. Baron Driezen recognized that the highly detailed, uncompromising approach adopted by the Ancient Theatre made great demands upon the public. The nature of the productions required of them a degree of familiarity with the history of art and culture. There were, of course, other reasons for the theatre's lack of material success. The Kononovskij Hall was, according to Driezen, cold and uncomfortable. The Petersburg critics, who like that city's public were notoriously difficult to please, offered some harsh criticism, although there were many enthusiastic reviews as well. However, the Moscow tour was a great success materially as well as artistically.[46]

There was a third essential difference between the two directors' approaches. In his staging of *Don Juan,* Mejerxol'd reconstructed the production style of Molière's day, that is, the time and place in which the play was first *written and performed,* as opposed to the details of the time and place which the play *depicted.* Evreinov's approach was all of a piece. The production style sought to capture both the period in which the play was written and the period it depicted.

One final argument may be offered in response to Kryžickij's claim that credit for the reconstructive method should go to Mejerxol'd and not Evreinov. Although Mejerxol'd may have employed this method on at least one occasion prior to Evreinov's productions at the Ancient Theatre, it was Evreinov in collaboration with his codirectors who developed a unified body of stage work in illustration of this theory.[47] In the two years the

Ancient Theatre was in operation, he pursued this idea to much greater lengths than Mejerxol'd, who soon moved in the direction of stylization.

V. Vsevolodskij (Gerngross) regarded the Ancient Theatre as simply a further extension of the naturalist trend led by the Moscow Art Theatre:

> Indeed, methodologically there is no difference between the reconstruction of ordinary life in historical plays and the reconstruction of the ancient play. The experiments of the Ancient Theatre were only a facet of the naturalist school, and consequently it experienced the same failures as overtook the school as a whole.... These experiments convinced us that in the matter of reconstruction only conventional and stylized devices were applicable.[48]

Evreinov and his co-workers at the Ancient Theatre were seeking to do something quite different than were the directors of naturalistic productions. The latter strove to reproduce *life* as it is lived or was lived in times past. The essential aim of the directors at the Ancient Theatre was to recreate a *theatrical event* of the past. While the outer form created onstage was partially the same in both cases, the perspective and dynamics were not. In the Ancient Theatre the focus was on theatre and the life that surrounds its creation, for example the audience observing the performers onstage. The naturalistic theatre made an attempt to conceal the process of creating theatre and to suggest that what is happening onstage is not theatre at all, but life. For this reason the naturalistic theatre employed the concept of the fourth wall which, while giving the audience a window through which to view the performance, effectively cut off direct contact with the performers. The productions at the Ancient Theatre did away with the fourth wall and sought actively to involve the audience in the production by channelling their perceptions through those of an onstage audience who were at once observers of and participants in the process of *creating theatre*.

It might be argued that an attempt was also being made here to create an illusion, the sense that this particular act of theatre was happening for the first time for the *onstage* audience. But while the excitement of this idea did operate on the theatre audience to some extent, they were not completely taken in by it, nor were they intended to be. The onstage audience is ultimately a reminder to the spectator in the auditorium that he is in a theatre, and that he is watching an illusion in the process of being created. The particular manner in which the Ancient Theatre approached this exciting idea was unique and placed it outside the boundaries of the naturalistic tradition in theatre. Although naturalism was a means employed by the Ancient Theatre, the end it had in mind, as did all of the theatrical enterprises with which Evreinov was involved, actually ran counter to the conventions of the naturalistic theatre.

The Spanish Cycle

The Ancient Theatre ceased production for three years until in 1911 it rose again like the legendary phoenix. No reasons were given for this hiatus in any of the printed sources on the theatre's history, but some probable causes can be suggested. Evreinov spent the 1908-9 season as chief artistic director at the Dramatic Theatre of V. F. Komissarževskaja, replacing Mejerxol'd. In 1910 he became chief artistic director at the Crooked Mirror Theatre. Evreinov was without question the major creative force at the Ancient Theatre, and without his guidance it does not seem likely that it could have functioned successfully. Also, it seems reasonable to assume that the theatre's rather tenuous finances made operation on a continual basis impossible.

The original plan of the Ancient Theatre called for a Spanish cycle to follow the cycle of medieval plays. As early as 1908 Evreinov stated in an interview that he had in mind the plays of Cervantes, Lope de Vega, and Calderón de la Barca for production in the Spanish cycle, specifically *Fuente Ovejuna* by Lope de Vega and *La vida es sueña* by Calderón.[49]

In 1909 Evreinov published his article "The Spanish Actor of the XVI-XVII Centuries" *(Ispanskij akter XVI-XVII vv)*.[50] The Spanish theatre of this period embodied the principle underlying all of Evreinov's own theatrical work, theatricality, and more specifically, the theatre in life. Evreinov wrote that the Spanish theatre of this period "was not theatre, but only life striving toward theatricality, life appointed in the jingling attire of Harlequin, wanting to see under the fearful mask, the touching and devout one." He viewed the Spanish theatre as one of "tragic and merry hyperbole, enormous contrasts both heavenly and diabolic, and fairy tale motley."

The real focus of the Spanish theatre was the actor-audience relationship, which was passionate and forthright. To a great extent the actor was ruled by the crowd's demands for brightly exaggerated play. When the actor performed well, his audience responded with generous outpourings of emotion. However, if he failed to satisfy the crowd, they were likely to rush the stage and beat him.[51]

Evreinov considered the Spanish actor a genuinely great artist. This art, he suggests, has not disappeared, because the art of the actor, more than any other, continues to live in the souls of the young who witness it. "And now, when the most sensitive of us have lost our faith in the fruitfulness of the naturalistic direction and are seeking salvation for the theatre in that artistic *uslovnost'* which is still alien and incomprehensible to our public, the history of the Spanish actor acquires special interest.[52]

The Spanish theatre of the sixteenth through seventeenth centuries was also of special interest to the directorate of the Ancient Theatre, because in it they saw a direct link to the forms of the plays in the medieval cycle. But unlike the medieval cycle, which focused on primitive, poetic works for the theatre, more interesting as theatrical spectacles than as works of dramatic literature, the Spanish cycle would reflect the development of a true literature for the theatre.

When the Ancient Theatre began work on the new season in the winter of 1910-11, the directorate was without M. N. Burnašev but now included K. M. Miklaševskij, who had participated in the medieval cycle as an untrained actor (see fig. 14). N. I. Butkovskaja returned as a director and organizer along with the two cornerstones of the theatre, Baron Driezen and Evreinov.

The problem faced by the directorate was the severe lack of information about the Spanish theatre. Consequently, they again travelled abroad in search of materials. Evreinov went to Naples since this city had for many years been under Spanish domination. Driezen and Miklaševskij travelled to Spain, where they studied iconography, documents relating to the old Spanish theatre, contemporary stage productions, Spanish dances, and in general breathed the atmosphere of Spain.

Rehearsals for the second season began on 15 September 1911, in the apartment of N. I. Butkovskaja. They continued here until the *Soljanoj gorodok,* an old exhibition hall, could be readied for the company's use. The rehearsals lasted two-and-a-half months in all. In the company at this time were, among the women: Gejnc and Elena Marševa, both of whom joined Nikita Baliev's "The Bat" *(Letučaja myš')* in Moscow after the Ancient Theatre closed; Dorotea Frenc; Vera Koroleva; Ol'ga Ra, a dancer; Bella Kaza-Roza, a singer; Oksinskaja; Glinskaja; Ljudmilla Patron; Viktorija Čekan, actor-director Aleksandr A. Mgebrov's wife; and Sidorenko. Among the men were Mgebrov, whose two-volume *A Life in the Theatre* is a major source of information on the Ancient Theatre's second season; Kievskij; Sobolev; Faljutinskij, Stepnoj; Viktorov; and Gejrot. In Mgebrov's opinion the male members of the company were not as strong as the female, but all the actors brought youthful enthusiasm to their work. They all shared a "high level of culture" as well. Mgebrov and his wife, Čekan, had some previous experience with Spanish drama, both having acted in Mejerxol'd's Tower Theatre presentation of *La Devocion de la Cruz* (1910).

Mgebrov refers to the long hours spent learning gesture and movement, dance and *plastique,* in preparation for the Spanish cycle. Specialists such as Presnjakov of the Imperial Marinskij Theatre, who also staged the dances, and Andreev were brought in to train the company. The actors also took a course based upon the Dalcroze system of eurhythmics as disseminated by Prince Sergej Volkonskij.

Other specialists invited to help in the company's preparations included theatre historians P. O. Morozov and D. K. Petrov; A. K. Glazunov, S. A. Cui, and L. A. Saketti, who spoke on Spanish music; Felipe Pedrella and Fita y Colomer of the Royal Spanish Historical Society; and Don Vera, archivist of the Toledo Cathedral library. Lay and religious music was composed by Il'ja Sac and Špis Èrenberg from the materials supplied by these specialists.

Mgebrov emphasized the care and thoroughness with which Evreinov worked on tempo, rhythm, movement, and the reading of verse even in the most inconsequential of scenes. Mgebrov, who had worked under both Mejerxol'd and Evreinov, said that the latter displayed greater respect for the actor. This refutes the accusation levelled at Evreinov by a number of critics that he neither understood nor respected the actor and his craft. All of the artists and the designers at the Ancient Theatre, including Dobužinskij, Bakst, Rerix, and Bilibin, had great respect for the actor's craft and his individuality. They designed backdrops to harmonize with the actor. Mgebrov argues that the Ancient Theatre was the first proponent of the actor's revolution, placing his craft at the center of the production as the one essential element in the theatre.[53] Nevertheless, when Valerian Čudovskij reviewed the Spanish cycle at the Ancient Theatre, he said that there were no real talented actors in the company. They were amateurs and not up to the task set for them by the director. This was said in reference to Evreinov's production of *Fuente Ovejuna* but reflected a general criticism. Mgebrov's claims aside, Čudovskij called this "a director's theatre" to the highest degree.[54]

Mgebrov indicates that there was much box office activity prior to the opening of the Spanish cycle and that the company played to full houses for its entire two-month run. The first night audience included more than the usual assortment of notables. Before each performance a short introduction was delivered by D. K. Petrov on the theatre of the Spanish Golden Age, L. A. Saketti on Spanish music, and K. M. Miklaševskij on the stage techniques of the Spanish Theatre.[55]

The hall in which the productions were performed was transformed by Ščuko, Lansere, Šervadšidze, Bilibin, Rerix, and Kalmakov into a stylized representation of Spain in the sixteenth and seventeenth centuries. The walls of the foyer were hung with huge, fantastic Spanish coats of arms and bathed in a soft, even light. Everything in the auditorium was stylized, beginning with the stage and extending to the high walls and windows and the chandeliers. There was no division between the foyer and the theatre itself.[56]

The first production in the Spanish cycle, *Fuente Ovejuna (Ovečij istočnik)*, premiered on 18 November 1911.[57] It was directed by Evreinov.

The set by N. K. Rerix represented the public square of a small Spanish town of the sixteenth century where a group of travelling players has come to perform. The stage was patterned after the conventional Spanish stage of this period, made of rough-hewn wood and mounted on barrels, not very deep by modern standards but wide. There was no front curtain and no footlights. Curtains were used in the Spanish theatre only at the back of the stage like the traverses of the Elizabethan theatre to represent an interior scene. In Evreinov's production the travelling troupe brought with them a small curtain which was hung upstage. Characters entered from behind the curtain and used the closed-off space to prepare for some of the more complicated scenes. The actors changed costumes behind this curtain. Also, the curtain drew open periodically to reveal a new setting.

The travelling troupe brought no scenery with them. The Spanish considered elaborate scene changes superfluous, since neither the exactness of thought, the elegance of diction, nor the splendor of the production depended upon it. A scene change was indicated by the actors' coming through a different entrance. Lope de Vega did not divide his *comedias* into scenes, only into acts.

Upstage was a large painted backdrop depicting sullen cliffs in the distance atop which a church sat upstage right. The entire stage left side of the backdrop was filled with billowy clouds (see fig. 15).

A trumpet sounded three times, the lights went out in the hall and onstage. The director of the troupe appeared and announced the play to be performed. Evreinov altered the play somewhat, focusing on the popular uprising and eliminating all extraneous elements. The ending included a reconciliation between the people and the king that does not appear in the original text. This, suggests Christopher Moody, may have been done so the censor Baron Driezen could rest more easily.

The extant photographs of this and other productions at the Ancient Theatre depict the actors in exaggerated, melodramatic poses (see fig. 16). Although Evreinov had worked hard to capture the vocal and bodily rhythms of the Spanish actor, even Stark, who is usually highly complimentary of the Ancient Theatre's productions, admitted that not all of the performers were equally successful in capturing these qualities.

There were generally no intermissions in the Spanish theatre. Instead, between the acts were dances and intermedii, a format Evreinov retained in his production of *Fuente Ovejuna*. The dancers in Evreinov's production had been trained at the Ancient Theatre's own school of dance. According to Stark, not only did they dance in a completely natural manner, they interacted effortlessly with the audience as well. The young dancing girls peeled oranges, spitting out the pips while they bickered with the audience. They then performed a famous dance of the period called *Guardainfantes,* which had been banned by the Catholic clergy as an offense against chastity. The dancers moved about in an erotic manner and excited the imagination of the audience with their suggestive costumes, featuring flesh colored stockings that rose to a little above the knee, exposing bare thighs. K. M. Miklaševskij, in an article on the Spanish stage, wrote that the Spanish dances "seem coarse to our contemporary aesthetic consciousness" and "often conveyed an unpleasant erotic character."

In the interval between acts 2 and 3, the company performed the interlude *Los habladores (Dva boltuna)* by Cervantes. Stark wrote that in this interlude "the style of the century with its life-affirming quality, despite the oppressive political structure of the day, is reflected like a clear mirror." In it is seen the simple relationship of the people to surrounding reality and the ability of the people "to lie with childlike laughter." It was customary that the intermedii be in no way related to the main presentation. The intermedii were designed to interrupt the serious mood much in the same way that Shakespeare utilized the comic scenes in his tragedies.[58]

A. R. Kugel' called the evening a success but suggested that the boundaries of the theatre's activities needed to be solidified. Specifically, the theatre needed to define more precisely its *uslovnost'*, the limits of its *muzejnost'*, that is, its archeological reproduction, and to be more consistent in the selection of its repertoire.[59] The critic Beskin called it "a production of rare beauty which captures the mood of the period and place." He had praise for the set and costumes and for the acting—the harmonious ensemble work and Čekan specifically for her broad dramatic range and excellent *plastique*.[60]

Valerian Čudovskij felt that Evreinov had directed with great enthusiasm, a fullness of artistic conception, and consistency of general tone. The force of the original was, for the most part, successfully conveyed. He ascribed the defects of the production to its "schematic summariness," some monotony in the generally stormy tone and in the movement. The love scenes and the peacefulness of farm life were partially concealed by the general torrent of action. However, Evreinov succeeded in effectively contrasting the violence and confusion taking place in the foreground with the calmness of royal power manifesting itself in the background until the conclusion of the play, when all of the anxieties and sufferings were resolved. In Čudovskij's opinion the company was not able to meet the acting demands placed upon them.[61]

Ljubov' Gurevič used the opportunity of the opening of the Spanish cycle to offer an overall evaluation of the Ancient Theatre's activities. While Gurevič conceded the seriousness of this theatre's intentions and the conscientiousness of its quest, she said that we must still ask ourselves what the importance is of such a venture. Certainly, when archeological findings reveal to us "the timeless monuments of an ancient people," when critics in the arts call our attention to something new to us that brings us face to face with the soul of a former time, this is important. And the drama of Calderón, Lope de Vega, and Tirso de Molina does just this—it reveals to us the soul of their times. But in the theatre of former times dramaturgy was inextricably linked with the creative work of the actor. The theatre of each epoch dies together with its actors, who give it its soul and contemporaneity. You can re-create the sets, costumes, make-up, and even the style of the play of the theatre of a former epoch, but in so doing you will not re-create the soul of that theatre. The actors' style of play is tied to the particular time in which it developed and is especially characteristic of the actors who developed it, that is, their personalities and artistic traits. In staging Calderón or Shakespeare, we take from them what is eternal and universal. But we can experience the characters and situations only through the prism of the contemporary style. The productions of *Fuente Ovejuna* and *Los habladores* were extremely interesting, even enchanting from a decorative standpoint. But what was produced was a framed painting and not a living work of art (see fig. 17).

According to Gurevič, the actors did not touch the heart of the play. She repeated the frequently articulated view that the Ancient Theatre did not have strong actors, and in the production of *Fuente Ovejuna* they experienced particular difficulties. Playing to large crowds under the open sky caused the Spanish actors to employ a forced tone of delivery without any semitones. Evreinov directed his actors, playing in a small, closed hall on a small stage, to shout and stamp about. They would have done better, in Gurevič's opinion, to have captured the wild passions, the cruelty and physical torture, the real southern temperament, genuinely human pathos, and so forth. A number of critics were bothered by what they felt to be the inconsistency of this choice in the context of the overall directorial approach. Having the actors shout *as if* they were really in a town square was, in the critics' estimation, a jarring and unnecessary naturalistic touch within a stylized framework. In fairness to Evreinov, Gurevič continued, he did infect the actors with his own temperament and made the play highly theatrical. Mgebrov wrote that in *Fuente Ovejuna* "Evreinov's burning temperament had the chance to display itself in full." Unfortunately, this also caused the play to be performed at breakneck speed. In general, however, Gurevič and the spectators as a whole judged the presentation a success.[62]

Aleksandr Benois likewise took this opportunity to offer a general appraisal of the enterprise's value. There was, he said, a public for its productions, and the productions themselves were bold. The only other place to see such reconstruction was in certain operatic productions and in the work of Djagilev abroad. The directors' work showed wit and courage. But the total effect was not one of theatre but "playing at theatre." Everything was depicted not to activate the play's inner workings but rather to realize the means for their display. In this could likewise be found the reason so little attention was paid to the inner play of the actors. Although the actors were well-equipped with the external elements of performance, one did not believe what they said.

Benois insisted that he greatly respected the talents and motives of the directors and artists of this theatre, but what they were producing were illustrations of the history of literature and not dramatic action. Who is to blame? Most would say the actors, "poor school amateurs who have not mastered technique and are simply ungifted." However, Benois claimed that the real fault lay in the attitude the theatre had brought to its task. "Those concerned are too little interested in the theatrical essence, and therefore, the Ancient Theatre is not matter but only idea." Benois objected also to the name "the Ancient Theatre," arguing that "what we need is not a museum, but a temple of living art."[63]

The second evening of the Spanish cycle was presented on 28 November. The first production that evening was *Marta la Piadosa (Blagočestivaja Marta ili Vljublennaja Svjatoša)* by Tirso de Molina. This play had been staged once before in Russian during the 1898–99 season at the Imperial Mixailovskij Theatre in a translation by M. Batson. It opened the season and ran for a total of five performances. The Ancient Theatre used a new translation by T. L. Ščepkina-Kupernik. Stark, for one, believed that they would have done better to forget this play entirely in favor of Tirso de Molina's *El Burlador de Sevilla.* However, there was no translation of it in Russian. The somewhat lower attendance for the second evening's presentations indicated that this was not a particularly popular choice.

Much of the problem with the presentation stemmed from the director. Stark said that although K. M. Miklaševskij was very well-educated and highly intelligent, a man of taste and talent, he had not yet mastered the craft of directing when he undertook this assignment. He did not have control of his material, as evidenced by the fact that what should have been a merry comedy turned out to be unbearably dull.

The play was staged in a manner somewhat reminiscent of Evreinov's production of *Fuente Ovejuna.* However, in this case the performance took place in the courtyard of a public house rather than a town square, and the troupe of travelling players was somewhat poorer. The audience looked into a set that formed the two legs of a right triangle (see fig. 19). A three-story public house formed the stage right leg. A balcony at a second-story window jutted out above a stage formed by rough planks laid on top of wooden barrels. The platform was bordered on the stage left side by a high stone wall. Awnings were attached to the inn at several places. One hung down from its tile roof. Another extended down to the stage and may have been used as a rear curtain. The inn was attached to the playing platform by stone pillars that formed an arcade with one of the walls of the building. A wooden placque with the date 1607 also hung from the inn wall. Customers at the inn were seated at small tables in front of the building. Behind them were several musicians. A person selling flowers strolled by. The prompter sat in full view of the audience, notebook in hand, as was the custom of the day. A figure appeared on the balcony and threw money to the performers. Following one of the musical numbers, two of the customers, who had up until this point been peacefully drinking wine, came to blows over one of the girl dancers.

The play's three acts were presented without intermission. The intervals between acts were filled with dancing as was the custom in the Spanish theatre. All of the incidental features of the presentation, the background activity and the dancing, were effectively performed, but the play itself was not. It was too leisurely paced and displayed no temperament, the very quality for which Evreinov's *Fuente Ovejuna* had been praised. Neither the movement nor the dialogue pulsated with life. The production failed to capture the spirit of the Spanish people. Under capable direction, as in *Fuente Ovejuna,* the actors in the company had proven their ability to give good performances. However, Miklaševskij's production lacked a definite directorial style and plan.

Aside from the director's lack of experience, the production suffered from a casting problem. The actress playing Marta, Ilinskaja-Molčanova, was simply not up to it. Unfortunately, the director did not realize this until late in the rehearsal period.[64]

However, not all of the critics agreed with Stark's assessment of the production. Valerian Čudovskij wrote that Miklaševskij had directed the play "wittily, cleverly, and ingeniously with many subtle details and good general comic business." The production's defects lay in the incomplete realization of the general tone. There was too much *haute comédie* for a troupe of travelling players. There were refined love scenes instead of the simple romantic behavior characteristic of the common people. This sense of common behavior was missing from the general comportment and gesturing of the actors as well as from the costumes. The main fault of the costume design in this and the other presentations of the Spanish cycle was that they did not agree with Spanish sources. However, Čudovskij was quick to add that the dearth of Spanish sources in Petersburg made accuracy a difficult task. These complaints, he insisted, reflected only the desire of a gourmand who prefers simple, genuine peasant fare to refined culinary delights.[65]

N. Karabanov wrote that the performance was so believable, the spectator really felt as if he were in seventeenth-century Spain and wanted to call for wine and throw coins to the travelling performers.[66] However, A. Izmajlov complained that the illusion was somewhat weakened by a certain lack of refinement in the design. Specifically, he objected to what he called "the rags" hung all over the place. Izmajlov also offered a by now familiar criticism. He felt that by underlining the naive manner of play characteristic of seventeenth-century Spanish actors, the Ancient Theatre had somewhat weakened the overall impression.[67]

The second production on the bill that evening was *El Gran Ducque da Moscovia (Velikij knjaz' Moskovskij i gonimyj Imperator)* by Lope de Vega. The best single description of the play's content and staging appeared in a review for a Tiflis newspaper. The description, quoted by Stark, follows:

> The Ancient Theatre re-created perfectly the atmosphere of the original production. A small stage was placed upon a lawn and hidden behind a screen. [See fig. 20.] The screens were changed and moved—the first step towards the modern theatre with its broad range of décor. The costumes were elaborate because it was a court company. The actors portrayed court notables, their manner was aristocratic and their speeches were spoken in a high-flown tone. Their gestures were in accordance with court etiquette, and indeed in the play itself tzars and courtiers were being portrayed. The plot of the play, the murder of Tzarevich Dimitrii, was based upon Russian history, but the author had confused the chronology and the participants and so we found the Tzarevich being rescued by a German prince. On the stage the Russian Tsar was referred to as Vasilii although it was really Ivan Groznyi who was depicted. The scene of the murder of the son was represented but it was another son of the Tsar-Ivan, who was portrayed as being doltish and simple-minded. Dimitrii was saved by the German prince with the aid of the Spaniards who took him to their castle. But he was pursued by murderers sent by Boris. The prince, however, put his own son in the place of the sleeping Tzarevich Dimitrii, who was killed by Boris' soldiers in error. When they spoke one heard not Borís but Bóris, not Dimitrii, but Demetrii. Not only were the names changed, but also the costumes.
>
> The Russian Tsars and boyars were dressed in fantastic garb—short cloaks embroidered with gold. [See fig. 21.] Both the wives of the boyars and the ladies of the German princes wore the same wide crinolines. [See fig. 22.] Only the wide collars and fur hats indicated that the action was taking place in the north. But in spite of the historical travesty and the pompous monologues, the play created a powerful impression. There was a unique style, unique measured tempo and unique mode of speech. It exuded fear and gloom. The scene of the murder of the German prince, who had made friends with Dimitrii, took place behind half closed curtains, but was nevertheless frightening. Then there was the dim light of the torches which burned in the hands of the servants standing along the sides of the stage. Among the servants were Negroes, Arabs, and Turks. They stood like statues as if not noticing the action on the stage.

Upstage was the darkness of advancing night. One detail was particularly interesting: at the beginning of the play the actors advanced one after the other across the stage bowing and curtsying to the audience. Meanwhile one of the actors presented them by their real names and the names of the characters they were to portray....[68]

Stark praised the directorial work by N. I. Butkovskaja, saying that it revealed seriousness and consistency of style and approach. The gestures of the actors were carefully thought out and fully in keeping with the overall production style. Čudovskij called the production "charming" and said that it successfully captured the atmosphere at the court of Philip IV. The only failing was a certain laxity with what should have been very strict Spanish etiquette.[69]

The third and final evening of the Spanish cycle was devoted to the presentation of Calderón's *El Purgatorio de San Patricio (Xristilišča Patrikka)*.[70] This was, by Stark's account, an uninteresting choice for a reconstructive approach. Little happens in an external sense. The heart of the play is its philosophical content. The set consisted of a series of high engraved arches behind several narrow steps extending the width of the stage. A photograph of the set shows a canvas backdrop hung behind the arches with clouds from which an angel emerges. Mgebrov described one scene using this backdrop:

> The scene depicting the passing of the letter from God to St. Patrick by an angel [see fig. 23] took place in the central portal, where transparent clouds, illuminated by the sun's rays, were visible. From these clouds the angel appeared with huge wings, white like the clouds themselves. The angel appeared from behind me [Mgebrov played St. Patrick]. At that moment, I knelt upon the bottom step facing the audience, and gradually, as I conversed with the angel, ascended the steps until I reached the top as the conversation ended.

Meanwhile, a choir sang behind the scene, and Il'ja Sac improvised on the organ.[71]

Another scene contained a backdrop featuring a house and a mountainous landscape. The action took place within the arches. The painted backdrops were changed as the actors moved from one portal to another. The performance was supposed to be taking place inside the court theatre at Buen Retiro during the reign of Philip IV. The artist in residence at Buen Retiro, Cosme Loti, is said to have been the first man to use painted backdrops and such scenic effects as fire and thunder. The performing of scenes within the portals in front of painted backdrops was also a significant step in the development of the proscenium arch stage.

All of the careful historical research that went into the staging of this production could not disguise its poor performance. The manner of play, while historically accurate, was extremely uninteresting. Mgebrov was the exception, making of Patrick a striking figure. This was, in general, the company's weakest performance, perhaps owing to the psychological subtlety of the play. Naturally, this was more difficult for an acting company of limited skills to master than a highly active external manner of play.[72] Čudovskij concurred in judging this the Ancient Theatre's weakest production. There was no guiding concept, no attempt made to bring interpretative value to this highly significant religious subject (of course, the censor had to be considered). There was no awareness evident that the center of the play is the character of Ludovico and not Patrick. The latter only provides the tone of the play and colors the action. This drama, Čudovskij suggested, would have been a good deal more effective if staged as a huge auto-da-fé.[73]

The Legacy of the Past

The second cycle at the Ancient Theatre, which ran for two months, was an unqualified success with the public that attended and, in general, a critical success as well. A. R. Kugel' wrote in *Theatre and Art:*

> The Ancient Theatre is one of the most interesting theatrical undertakings of our time. One should be aware that such experiments supported by private means and undertaken on private initiative are possible only here in Russia, where the theatre has a fanatical following and where commercial interests still do not have everything in their clutches.

However, the critic "V. A.," writing in the newspaper *Speech (Reč'),* viewed Russia's relationship with the Ancient Theatre in another way:

> It was a sumptuous feast of art, a sacred act, the secret birth of forgotten beauty, the beauty of ancient times... These were unforgettable evenings, evenings of pure joy and burning delight. Some day a historian of our culture, plotting the steps in our aesthetic development, will say: "The World of Art... the Art Theatre... an historical exhibition of portraits... the Ancient Theatre." And he will reflect sadly that in Russia the means and the people were not available to make the Ancient Theatre permanent.[74]

There was always much praise for the Ancient Theatre but never much money or much of a public following.[75] The shortness of its life and the specialized nature of its offerings permitted the Ancient Theatre to become a habit only with an elite. But if the Ancient Theatre was not in operation for a long enough time to condition the public, it did strongly affect the consciousness of those who were working in the arts. A whole series of new artist-designers—among them, Rerix, Dobužinskij, Bilibin, Lansere, Ščuko and Chambers—practiced their craft at the Ancient Theatre and were thereafter introduced into the mainstream of theatrical design.[76]

The method of artistic reconstruction developed by the directors and designers at the Ancient Theatre was taken seriously and adopted by other artists in the field. It seemed logical to many to opt for a stylized rather than a strictly realistic approach to reconstruction, as had the Ancient Theatre, since the conditions that made a certain style of play the norm for the audience of a particular time cannot be fully re-created. There are two reasons for this: (1) the actor's art arises from personality and environment, and therefore cannot be transmitted, and (2) the mental set of a contemporary audience cannot be matched to that of the audience of some former time when religious and social consciousness made for a greater homogeneity of perceptions. Rather than caricaturing naturalism, the Ancient Theatre offered an "artistic idealization of true realism," which is to say that it conveyed the spirit and essence of the times being represented.[77]

In the plays it selected to produce and in its manner of staging them, the Ancient Theatre offered to its audience both the substance of history and a living commentary on it. Many of these plays and the manner in which they were performed in their day would have remained unknown had not the Ancient Theatre translated and produced them.[78] Unfortunately, the final cycle, which was to be on commedia dell'arte, had to be cancelled when the Ancient Theatre's expert on the subject, K. A. Miklaševskij, was drafted into the army. World War I changed conditions in Russia so that the Ancient Theatre would never open its doors again.

The actual demise of the Ancient Theatre has been linked to a heated dispute leading to a final rift between Evreinov and Driezen. The argument was over who should receive greater credit for the theatre's operations, the producer or director. Evreinov, to whom the issue of directors' rights was of the utmost importance—he had been writing on this theme since 1908 and would take it up again at the Crooked Mirror Theatre—was in general dissatisfied with Driezen's attitude toward him, his leadership, and his artistic intervention. Evreinov, along with Butkovskaja and Miklaševskij, refused to tour Moscow with the theatre in 1912, keeping the theatre's costumes with them in St. Petersburg. The grievances between Evreinov and Driezen were eventually brought to arbitration with each side nominating three members of the court. Evreinov nominated F. K. Sologub, K. I. Arabaznin and, surprisingly, V. È. Mejerxol'd. Driezen nominated V. N. Davydov, M. E. Darskij and A. R. Kugel', Evreinov's future employer and adversary at the Crooked Mirror Theatre. The court found Driezen "guilty" of disrespect and artistic meddling regarding Evreinov and his work. It cited Evreinov for poor judgment and disruptive behavior in the matter of the Moscow tour. The theatre never fully recovered.[79]

Mejerxol'd learned a great deal from the Ancient Theatre. He said as much in a paper delivered to a conference at the Russian Institute of Art

History on 22 June 1924, explaining that he was endeavoring to better understand the achievements of the Ancient Theatre, to study its methods in the hope of finding the means by which to alter the worthless elements in the current hackneyed "academic style" of play.[80]

As with so many developments in Russian arts of this period, it is extremely difficult to establish causal relationships between various artists and enterprises. To say, as Evreinov did, that Mejerxol'd appropriated the ideas that he realized at the Ancient Theatre is far too bold and difficult to prove. However, to say that the experiments carried out at the Ancient Theatre served as a model—both positive and negative—for the work of Mejerxol'd and others is only realistic. Artists learned a great deal from one another as they worked. Many of them were contemplating similar ideas and methods at the same time and who got there first is far less important than how a particular artist developed an idea. No one idea was completely realized in practice during the pre-Revolutionary period. This does not reflect a lack of talent on the part of the Russian innovators. On the contrary, it bespeaks the breadth and complexity of the ideas themselves.

The Ancient Theatre brought together under its banner several of the major artistic trends of the day. Perhaps the most important of these was theatricality. The Ancient Theatre depicted societies in which theatre was an integral part of life and as such transformed life. By having the contemporary audience view a play-within-a-play featuring an onstage audience, the Ancient Theatre emphasized the idea of theatre in the process of being created. Aside from erecting a stage-upon-a-stage, the Ancient Theatre abolished the footlights and broke down mental barriers between stage and audience.

For all its practical contributions to the contemporary theatre, the Ancient Theatre had an aesthete's heart that loved "beauty for beauty's sake." Stark called this theatre "a fragrant blossom of aesthetics."[81] No one label could completely capture the nature of the Ancient Theatre. It was, like its creator, paradoxical. It sought to capture the spirit of bygone days by re-creating in detail the external elements of design and actors' play. Yet even these external forms were approached with a certain poetic license and stylized. The audience was confronted with an actor who was not, like the contemporary actor, psychologically based, but was instead a master of outer form and at the same time an exaggeration of that form. He was the "condensation and generalization of life," projecting several basic character traits in a clear theatrical form.[82] The actor of ancient dramatic forms no more wanted to conceal his face behind the mask of character than his theatre wished to disguise itself as life. The fact was that theatre flowed into life and could not be separated from it as easily as it could be in contemporary society.

The Ancient Theatre was a romantic idea in the spirit of the World of Art, looking to the West for theatrical forms, then bringing Russian talents to bear so as to show the West what Russian artists could do. The tendency to look to the past, like the window on the West, predated the Ancient Theatre. However, it was the Ancient Theatre's experiments that proved to many people that such a path was possible and relevant for the contemporary theatre and the unborn theatre of the future. Some critics thought this gathering of ancient Western forms symptomatic of the cultural-historical eclecticism that infected Russian art in this period. But even these critics, when confronted with the productions staged at the Ancient Theatre, had to agree that on balance the argument for cross-cultural retrospectivism was persuasive.

The Ancient Theatre was a significant and highly characteristic stage in Nikolaj Evreinov's career. Practically speaking, his work here attracted the eye of Vera Komissarževskaja and Aleksandr Kugel', in both of whose theatres he was later to serve as chief artistic director. Evreinov's work at the Ancient Theatre also marked a significant step in the development of his major theory, the theatre in life. Evreinov used the antique theatres he studied in preparation for his productions here as examples in his theoretical treatise *The Theatre for Oneself.*

It could also be argued that his production of *The Storming of the Winter Palace* (*Vzjatie Zimnego dvorca,* 1920) owed much to his experiences at the Ancient Theatre. Like a medieval mystery play, this modern-day mass spectacle deployed its participants into groups representing the forces of Good and Evil, the revolutionaries and Kerenskij's Provisional Government, respectively. The idea was clearly underscored by setting the actions of the two camps on separate "Red" and "White" platforms, exaggerating the behavior of those on the latter to make them seem ridiculous and malevolent. There were choral elements in both the ancient and the revolutionary presentations. To the question, "Who killed the Commandant?" the Spanish townspeople answered "Fuente Ovejuna." Likewise to the question, "Who killed the Tsar?" came the response "the Russian proletariat." Naturally, there were essential differences between the productions at the Ancient Theatre and the post-Revolutionary Soviet mass spectacles. The former aimed at a more accurate, albeit not an exact, reconstruction of past forms, while the latter ventured much further into the realm of stylization. The Ancient Theatre sought to educate the public in forms that were new to them. The post-Revolutionary mass spectacle aimed at solidifying lessons the public already knew by portraying events they had helped bring about. However, both shared a certain naiveté and moral fervor. Evreinov developed the tools he would need in order to stage the mass spectacle by working first with ancient forms.

One tool Evreinov never relinquished was the reconstructive approach to the staging of old theatrical forms. He applied the lessons he learned at the Ancient Theatre to the reconstruction of Russian classics during his émigré period, 1925–53. In 1939, when Evreinov made plans to direct Denis Fonvizin's *The Minor (Nedorosl')* at the Theatre of Russian Drama in Paris, his terminology was still the same: "A theatrical work is valuable to us not only in a scenic, dramaturgical, or aesthetic sense, [not only] as *a work of art,* but equally as *a cultural indicator.*" He spoke of the necessity of capturing "the spirit of an epoch," and of conforming to the theatrical conventions of the author's day, not to those of the contemporary theatre in staging the play.[83]

Evreinov's booklet, "On the New Mask" (*O novoj maski,* 1923), combined the terminology employed at the Ancient Theatre with his monodramatic outlook in a new fashion. Evreinov here spoke of an "autobio-reconstructive mask" whereby the director is concerned with re-creating the circumstances of his own life rather than the life of some other culture. He dramatizes memories from the life of the "I" and projects them onstage for others to see. The approach is highly subjective (monodramatic) and as such runs counter to the original purpose for which the reconstructive method was developed at the Ancient Theatre. However, it reveals the rather strange path Evreinov later took in an attempt to reconcile inherently conflicting ideas coexisting in his creative consciousness.

Historian Evgenij Znosko-Borovskij wrote that the general nature and quality of Evreinov's directorial work was reflected more clearly and completely at the Ancient Theatre than at the Crooked Mirror. Although Evreinov served at the Crooked Mirror for a longer period of time, Znosko-Borovskij argues that he exercised only a single aspect of his talent and personality there—his sense of irony. This misses the point. All of Evreinov's work is ironic, although not always by design. His various projects and theories represent only different ways of seeing.

Throughout his career, Evreinov experimented with various lenses and filters through which to project his multifaceted conception of reality—its *realia* and *realiora.* Monodrama and the reconstruction of the spectator at the Ancient Theatre were Evreinov's attempts to redefine and perhaps reconstruct his own vision. In a sense, Evreinov's dual role as artist and spectator is reflected in his dramatic and theatrical devices—the onstage audience and the actor, the play and the play-within-the-play. Through these new arrangements he sought not only a new perspective but a new communion. His is a characteristically modern dilemma, the conflict between heightened perception and unintegrated consciousness. The moral absolutism and direct simplicity of faith manifested in the Middle Ages and the Spanish Golden Age represented a welcome respite for Evreinov the modern, drowning in a sea of relativism and subjectivism.

Evreinov's oft-quoted and alluded to ambivalence regarding the actor, reflected in his directorial work at the Ancient Theatre, is only in part a Craigian response conditioned by frustrated idealism and perfectionism. Evreinov's periodic casting of the actor as a foolishly and falsely naive poseur rather than as a vessel for true emotionalism and inner belief can be read as a veiled attempt to suppress a disturbing reflection of his own extreme subjectivism and apparent egoism. Evreinov's own practical naiveté, which many of his critics perceived correctly as a pose, was an ill-fitting mantle to conceal what he feared to be sterile intellectualism and an inability to feel or achieve anything real through art.

History, that most talented of ironists, gave even the most profoundly distressed of artist-intellectuals—the visionary seekers after life philosophies and alternative faiths—a chance for redemption. They were free to embrace the simple faith of the Revolution. However, as Evreinov realized early on and Mejerxol'd discovered too late, the extreme individualism that forms a vital part of the artist-seer's condition prevents him in advance from entering into the paradise of the true, unconflicted believer.

Evreinov tried to affect a spiritual communion with the people at large and through them with himself via his own informal channels, his theories and experiments relating to theatre as event and theatre in life. By erasing the borders separating stage from audience and the actor's realm of imagining from the spectator's via monodrama and artistic reconstruction, Evreinov sought a kind of blessing.

In this regard, the Ancient Theatre's official emblem seems almost prophetic (see fig. 13). It features an antique actor's mask beneath which one can see a goat's head wearing a darkly shaded domino. Below this is a black mask behind which no face of any sort appears. One sees here a sampling of the many masks created and worn by Nikolaj Evreinov, classicist and modern—preoccupied with origins and essences, antique forms and conventions, theatre's archetypal patterns and roles and their implications—and the actor-creator's function in all of this. The masks diminish in size from top to bottom and the face, any face, disappears, but where to? Into art? Into life? Into nothingness?

One senses in Evreinov as in other artists the strong need not only to validate himself through his audience but also through this same connection to save himself. Critics responded with confusion to Evreinov's theory of monodrama, which seemed to be even more highly manipulative than traditional approaches to the theatre, even as it espoused total integration of stage and audience. What monodrama is, in fact, is a way for the artist to use the audience so that he can commune with himself. He does this in order to be eventually able to transcend the self and achieve salvation. It offers only *one* ticket to heaven.

This process is not fully conscious and is not unmitigated by guilt, anxiety and confusion. Evreinov truly seems to believe that he *wants* to share, to achieve communion with his audience. However, he cannot resist "playing the audience," because he cannot silence his own need, nor can he accept his awesome responsibility as scapegoat-priest. His work at the Ancient Theatre, like his explorations into ritual and popular theatre, are restatements of this same problem. It is impossible for him and perhaps for anyone to achieve an honest, unmanipulative theatrical vision. His work is punctuated by frank admissions of this fact. He exposes his own theories as performances in print, playful egoism masquerading as serious scholarship. Neither Harlequin in *A Merry Death* nor Paraclete in *The Chief Thing,* both of whom rail against the living death of stultifying convention, can truly save anyone. In each case, they undermine their own pretentions to sainthood by quick-change artistry and frank admissions of theatrical deceit. The artist's chosen persona, the Harlequin-Christ, represents an uneasy union between belief and disbelief, truth and illusion.

Evreinov's theatre, like Artaud's and Pirandello's, is born of strongly personalized historical conflict. Behind the cross stands the Devil. The first actor was the serpent in the Garden of Eden. Read in this light, Evreinov's ironic detachment becomes something much more than the aesthete's jaded world-weariness or even the romantic's sense of having been born out of time as has been previously suggested. The latter was in part Evreinov's romantic fantasy of himself as "beautiful despot," a "retrospective dreamer" at war with the present, the preservation of beauty being his call to arms. His work, which seems on the surface to represent a sustained and focused attempt to dramatize a self into being, might just as easily be the opposite. Evreinov's transformation of strongly imagined landscapes of the past into romantic dreamscapes, his escape into alter egos, into a kind of continuous, present-tense narrative is a not-always-calculated attempt to be absorbed back into life by making himself as large as life. He aspires to become selfless, and since he has equated the theatre with his self, the two reach the vanishing point simultaneously.

Ironically, it was Evreinov's nemesis-to-be at the Crooked Mirror Theatre, Aleksandr Kugel', who put his finger on the problem. Modern man, he had said in response to the medieval cycle of plays at the Ancient Theatre, is long on imagination but short on faith. The periods and cultures that Evreinov sought to render as art were just the opposite. He sought to reconcile what were for him two opposing tendencies—to imagine romantically and to believe naively (remember that he was an atheist)—by such notions as pre-aestheticism, a pre-conscious realm in which the two could be integrated. However, his infernal modern consciousness would not have it so. Evreinov brought the problems of the modern condition to premodern man. The strange result was that Evreinov seemed to be parodying the faithful believer when what he really wanted, and needed, was to share in his belief.

6

The Crooked Mirror Theatre

> *Least of all would I like to be
> considered a serious man.*
> —Evreinov[1]

The Theatre of Small Forms

As a man of wit, Evreinov had reason to view the age in which he lived with chagrin. Following the abortive revolution of 1905 the Russian people were sorely in need of humor, but satire was a risky business. Nikolaj II had disbanded the Second Duma on 3 June 1907, a period of reaction had set in, and the censor had his eye out for satirical literature of a progressive nature.

All the satirical journals of the period immediately following the 1905 revolution employed a system of allegories and symbols through which they criticized the tsarist regime. From such conditions was born a unique brand of humor in Russian literature—"laughter from adversity" (*smex sredi ruin*). Such satirical journals of the period as *Satyricon* (*Satyrikon*), *The Spectator* (*Zritel'*), *The Hammer* (*Molot*), *The Machine Gun* (*Pulemet*), *The Signal* (*Signal*), *Arrows* (*Strely*), *The Bugbear* (*Župel*), *The Alarm Clock* (*Budil'nik*), *The Fool* (*Šut*) and *Splinters* (*Oskolki*), were, while they lasted, the only weapons at the disposal of a generally passive intelligentsia.[2]

The year 1908 saw an analogous line of development in the theatre. There sprang up almost simultaneously in Moscow and St. Petersburg cabaret theatres of "small forms," most of which had a strongly satirical bent. These represented a continuation of the general trend to quest and question so prevalent at this time, as well as an attempt to save the self-appointed saviors of society and the arts in particular from their own pretense.

Perhaps the most famous of the enterprises was "The Bat" (*Letučaja myš'*) founded by Nikita Baliev. It opened on 29 February 1908 (and closed in 1922) as an after-hours haunt for the personnel of the Moscow Art Theatre. Here they could partake of light entertainment similar to the "cabbage parties" (*kapustniki*) which took place periodically in the theatre proper.³

In the years prior to Russia's entry into World War I, the theatre of small forms spread as far as Odessa.⁴ Petersburg alone had more than ten theatres of this type, including the "Assembly" (*Assambleja*), the "Palace-Miniature" (*Palass-miniatjur*), the "Renaissance" (*Renissans*), the "Theatre Valentin Lin" (*Teatr Valentin Lin*), the "Vaudeville" (*Vodevil'*), the "New Theatre" (*Novyj teatr*), the "Theatre Pavilion de Paris" (*Teatr Pavil'on de Pari* — now the movie theatre *Molodežnyj*), and the "Troickij Theatre of Small Forms" (*Troickij teatr miniatjur*) where now stands the Malyj Dramatic Theatre (18 Ulica Rubinščtina). These featured poetry readings, "eccentric" acts, parodies, impressionists, dramatic skits and gypsy romances.

To play in the theatre of small forms was not easy. The actor did not develop a characterization gradually but rather revealed his character to the audience all at once (*vo ves' rost*), at the moment of his first appearance onstage. Therefore the miniature demanded from the actor distinct delineation and clarity of execution. He needed a broad range and good technique since he was often called upon to play dramatic as well as comic roles in the same night (generally, two shows per night). Among the performers who met such requirements were Nererova, Lenar, Peregonetz, Kurixin, Nevolin, Vol'skij, Ermlov, Mirovič, E. A. Mosolova, and O. M. Antonova. These last two artists performed at the Litejnyj Theatre and at the Intimnyj Theatre respectively, which were considered to be the strongest among the Petersburg theatres of small forms.⁵

The Russian theatre of small forms was modelled after the many cabarets that had sprung up across Western Europe at this time, the most influential of which were the German cabarets such as Ernst von Wolzogen's *Überbrettel*, founded in Berlin in 1901. Although there was nothing of real literary value in the repertoire of these cabarets, there was the hint of a newly developing theatrical form which the Germans named *Kleinkunst*.⁶

A. R. Kugel' theorized that in the very principle of breaking down the complex organism of the contemporary theatre into component elements, there was something of value, even of historical necessity. Very often the process of evolution demands a disintegration in order to yield the possibility of further development. The complicated mechanization and growth of the theatre had increased to such a degree that theatrical art had become routinized. It was necessary to discover a new form, to break the theatre into its primary elements, to compress and concentrate it.

Both Malyj Theatre actress Zinajda V. Xolmskaja (Timofeeva) (see fig. 24) and director Vsevolod Mejerxol'd recognized the importance of the theatre of small forms and dreamed of opening one of their own. By chance they decided to open their respective theatres at approximately the same time, and a decision had to be made to whom to grant a license for operations. Kugel' (see fig. 25), who helped his wife Xolmskaja to found her theatre, claimed that Mejerxol'd was given first priority because he had the ability to promote himself and his projects. He was at this time already a very modish director and produced an "extraordinary noise." Although it was decided to open the two theatres simultaneously, the "real" theatre was to be Mejerxol'd's, and its productions would go on at the usual time. After its show was over, Xolmskaja's cabaret would be given the stage.[7]

What Xolmskaja had in mind, however was not cabaret in its present form. She and Kugel' had travelled to Berlin, Vienna, and Paris to examine various cabarets. While she liked the lightness and spontaneity of execution, the intimacy, simplicity, and perceptiveness of the forms she found there, she did not much care for the structure of the programs. They revolved around a master of ceremonies who served as host, amusing his guests with jokes, puns, and foolishness. The individual numbers making up the program served only as the garnish for the main course served up by the emcee.

Xolmskaja decided to found a merry, original theatre of grotesque and artistic parody, without a master of ceremonies. It would feature a company of performers playing together in a more integrated manner. Even her husband Kugel' doubted the feasibility of such a project and considered it a feminine whim.

Many dramatists and feuilletonists were immediately attracted to Xolmskaja's proposed theatre without really understanding what she had in mind. They contributed old forms such as vaudevilles, farces, and reviews. But Xolmskaja wanted a new form of comedy, thoughtful and cultured. She took her idea to the Theatrical Club of Prince Jusupov on Litejnyj Prospekt, site of the former Jusupov Palace, where she discussed it with Kugel', the dramatist V. A. Tixonov, and I. N. Potapenko, a writer and dramatist whose satire *The Unfortunate* (*Mnogostradal'naja*) later enjoyed great success at the proposed theatre. It was supposedly here that a name for the new theatre was offered to Xolmskaja by A. A. Izmajlov, a theatre critic and author of a collection of literary parodies on Bal'mont, Gippius, Vjačeslav Ivanov, Blok, Kuzmin and others, entitled *The Crooked Mirror* (*Krivoe zerkalo*).[8]

The name struck a chord in Kugel', who recalled Gogol''s epigraph for *The Inspector General:* "Don't blame the mirror if your mug is crooked." Xolmskaja was reminded of Hans Christian Andersen's fairy tale *The*

Snow Queen in which a magic mirror reflected distorted images of people and things.[9]

Both theatres had their premieres on Saturday, 6 December 1908, at the Theatrical Club on Litejnyj Prospekt. Mejerxol'd's theatre was called The Strand (*Lukomor'e*), a reference to the opening line of Puškin's fairy tale verse epic, *Ruslan and Ljudmilla*. For his theatre's debut, Mejerxol'd enlisted the aid of well-known professionals, the designers Bilibin and Dobužinskij and the famous actress Varlamova and her troupe. They offered a program consisting of a piece entitled *Prologue (Prolog)* by Arkadij Averčenko; *Petruška* by Potemkin (set and costumes by Dobužinskij); a one-act tragedy adapted from Edgar Allan Poe's "The Fall of the House of Usher" entitled *The Last of Usher* (*Poslednij iz Usherov*), designed by Dobužinskij and Chambers, with music by Karatygin; concert numbers; and a one-act play entitled *Honor and Revenge* (*Cest' i mest'*) by Count Vladimir Sollogub, designed by Bilibin. The program ran from 8:00 to 11:00 P.M. and drew a lukewarm response. Most of the audience was bored. Although the external trappings of the program were beautiful, it was all form and no content.

The curtain went up again at midnight on the rather inelegantly named Crooked Mirror Theatre. Actually, the late starting time proved advantageous to Xolmskaja. It allowed her to enlist the services of the best actors and actresses in Petersburg, who by that time had completed their performances in other theatres. The Crooked Mirror program ran until 2:00 A.M. and included dances, songs, imitations, a play by Vladimir A. Azov, a parody by Kugel' (written under a pseudonym) on Leonid Andreev's play *Days of Our Lives* (*Dni našej žizni*) directed by Lev Geben, a parody of contemporary choreography entitled *Salome's Funeral (Poxorony Salome)*, and Nadežda A. Teffi's *Love Through the Centuries*, which satirized the current concern with sexual problems, depicting the evolution of love from the time of the apes to the twenty-first century.[10]

The Crooked Mirror's rather primitive, stylized sets were poor and comical next to those of Mejerxol'd's Strand, but the texts it employed were light and the company played in high spirits. It was a welcome relief to an audience that had been lulled by the aestheticism and self-important air of Mejerxol'd's program. The Crooked Mirror's fare was more appropriate for late-night entertainment. The Strand closed after one night, a victim of its own pretentiousness and preoccupation with external beauty. The Crooked Mirror, which aimed at economy of form, lightness in play, and *uslovnost'* in design with its presentation of parody and grotesque, began a career that would continue with one interruption (1918–22), until 1931.

The Crooked Mirror billed itself as "a theatre of literary artistic parody." It depended on literature, theatrical routine, and dramaturgy for sustenance. But its subjects were drawn from daily life, current forms and trends in addition to the conventions that rigidify life and art. Only rarely were its presentations political. Although parodies of theatrical forms constituted only about one quarter of the total repertory at the Crooked Mirror in the pre-Revolutionary years, they were the theatre's strong suit.[11]

Actors were drawn from different theatre companies and had various specialties. For example, the artist Nikolaj Fedorovič Barabanov was originally invited to the Crooked Mirror to perform his parody of Isadora Duncan and stayed on as a member of the company. He worked during the day as a clerk at one of the ministries and danced nights at the Crooked Mirror under the stage name "Ikar," nearly always in female dress. Other members of the company who were not employed elsewhere during the day as performers likewise held nontheatrical jobs to supplement the five rubles per evening paid them by the Crooked Mirror. Members of the acting company in the early days included V. V. Aleksandrinskij, a famous provincial actor who worked at the Dramatic Theatre of V. F. Komissarževskaja as a comic before joining the original company of the Crooked Mirror Theatre; S. I. Antimonov, who became one of the leading actors at the Crooked Mirror, creating a series of vivid grotesque and parody roles (after the demise of the Crooked Mirror, he joined Tairov's Kamernyj Theatre); Kurixin, a brilliant comedian and one of the best actors at the Crooked Mirror in its first year; A. P. Los', "the fat comic," who acted at Suvorin's theatre (later merged with the Crooked Mirror), and remained with the company until his death in 1914; L. I. Lukin, one of the leading actors at the Crooked Mirror, who worked there throughout its duration, creating leading roles in *Vampuka* and *Ryčalov's Tour* (*Gastrol' Ryčalova*), two of the theatre's earliest and most durable successes; E. A. Nelidova, who played coquettes and young heroines; A. E. Saxonov, who created another leading role in *Vampuka*. Rounding out the company were Z. Xolmskaja (the Theatre's founder), M. Jarockaja, A. S. Abramjan (the original Vampuka), Svetlova, L. Lukin, L. Fenin, A. Xovanskij, S. Vexov, A. Lebedinskij, Gibsman, Egorov, Donskoj, Salkovskij, Granovskij, Volnovskij, Mal'šet, and others. They were a highly intelligent and cultured group.[12]

Especially notable among this original group was Nikolaj Nikolaevič Urvancov, formerly an actor at the Dramatic Theatre of V. F. Komissarževskaja, where he specialized in character roles. As a writer-director at the Crooked Mirror from its first season to its last, he had several successes and apparently a certain degree of influence. His first success, *Jacques Nuar or Henri Zaverni,* was a parody of melodrama featuring a deft performance by Antimonov as the villain. Urvancov contributed several more parodies, including an operetta entitled *Love's Delights* (*Vostorgi ljubvi*). Kugel' referred to Urvancov, along with Evreinov, as "my two-miracle-working Nikolajs."

Specialists were brought in according to the needs of a particular production. When it staged dance parodies, for example, the Crooked Mirror had no trouble enlisting professionally-trained dancers and directors such as Nikolaj Mixajlovič Foregger, whose specialty was ballet.[13]

Xolmskaja tells how various actors, writers, artists, and composers gravitated to the Crooked Mirror Theatre. N. N. Ventcel' (*Benedikt*), the famous feuilletonist and poet, who had never written anything for the stage, contributed a satire to the second program at the Crooked Mirror entitled *A Play About Mr. Ivanov* (*Licedejstvo o gospodine Ivanove*). Subtitled *A Twentieth-Century Moralité*, the play satirized modernist poetry and the pornographic trend in contemporary Russian literature.

The theatre appreciated youth with its fresh amateur quality, and even accepted scripts from unknown students. There was a genuine communal spirit among the workers at the Crooked Mirror, a sense of vitality and the appearance of youthful naiveté that concealed a deep sense of irony. Evreinov wrote: "Under the Crooked Mirror scalpel were revealed many organic deficiencies and inner ills being harbored in such apparently healthy and attractive forms as contemporary 'Comedy,' 'Drama,' 'Opera,' 'Ballet,' and so forth."

Ballet was a deserving target at this time. Evreinov points out in his memoirs that it is difficult for people whose only contact with ballet came after the reforms of Mixail Fokine to realize just how ridiculous the Russian ballet once was. The dance critic V. A. Nelidov wrote that ballet was ruled by dogma:

> In Ballet you danced and nothing more. Inspiration was not discussed. Neither the heartfelt experiencing of emotion nor even talented mimicry and play were demanded. No one thought it incongruous for the hero or heroine on the verge of death to dance some light-spirited waltz. To talk of ensemble was even more ridiculous in ballet than in opera at this time. Stereotypes and routine ruled like a despot. For example, a poet always appeared in a frock with a head of long blond hair, blond mustaches, and a small beard. An Englishman was portrayed in a checked costume with binoculars in a safari hat, even if the action was taking place at the North Pole. He always wore red side whiskers. The villain customarily rolled his eyes, the lover sighed deeply, and so on.
>
> The balletic language of gestures was extraordinarily primitive and banal. "She is beautiful" was expressed by opening the hand so that four fingers were on one side of the face and the thumb on the other. "She is my bride" was expressed first by pointing to the girl then with the index finger of the right hand pointing to the ring finger of her left hand. "Love" was indicated by a hand to heart gesture, "courage" by taking two steps forward, and "fear" by taking two steps back.

The scenic elements were likewise simplistic. Sets were often lifted directly from operas. For costumes, the prima ballerina was given a tutu with gold braid, the second lead something paler, and the corps de ballet something in light blue, pink, or green.

As bad as the external trappings of the ballet were, the internal considerations were even worse. People burst out laughing if you argued that music is an organic part of ballet and that there ought to be a synthesis of the music with the content of the ballet. The only concern was whether or not the music was easy to dance to.

The Crooked Mirror began its satirical barrage against ballet with Lev Geben's *The Enchanted and Disenchanted Forest* (*Očarovannyj i razočarovannyj les*) and followed with parodies of *Giselle, Swan Lake,* and *Esmeralda*, which had audiences laughing until they cried. The first appearance of Isadora Duncan in Petersburg in 1908 caused the Crooked Mirror to turn its attention from classical ballet to modern dance. The theatre's resident "prima ballerina," Z. F. Ikar, appeared in parodies of dancers, singers and actresses that included *Duncan, Prima Ballerina, Chanteuse, Maud Allan* and *Sarah Bernhardt*.[14] However, The Crooked Mirror scalpel was wielded with real authority for the first time over the decaying organism that was contemporary opera.

The inspiration was provided by one of the theatre's founding members, Vladimir G. Èrenberg, virtually an unknown quantity when he came to the Crooked Mirror. Although a serious composer with a predilection for sad, lyrical melodies, all the music he wrote for the Crooked Mirror came out light and merry. Kugel' said that the Crooked Mirror Theatre came into the world not quite formed. Its early traits and tendencies first coalesced to form a recognizable artistic identity with Èrenberg's first major work at the theatre, a parody of windy Italian opera à la Verdi (specifically *Aida*), entitled *Vampuka, African Bride* (*Vampuka, nevesta afrikanskaja*; see figs. 26-27). Prince M. N. Volkonskij provided the libretto. The famous satirist N. Šekiev wrote that *Vampuka* illustrated "how one must not compose an opera, must not stage an opera and must not sing an opera." In 1927 it celebrated its one-thousandth performance.

Reports on the exact derivation of the title *Vampuka* vary slightly. The most commonly accepted, as reported by P. P. Gnedič, concerns the occasion of Prince Ol'denburgskij's visit to the Smol'nyj Institute at which time he was handed a bouquet of flowers. The students making the offering quoted a famous line from Giacomo Meyerbeer's (Jakob Liebmann Meyer Beer, 1791-1864) opera *Robert le diable* (*Robert the Devil*, 1981). The line reads: "Vam puk, vam puk, vam puk cvetov podnosim" ("for you a bunch, for you a bunch, for you a bunch of flowers we are bringing").

On hearing of this and of the related question posed by a relative of Gnedič's wife—"Can there really be such a name as Vampuk?"—Volkonskij exclaimed, "Eureka! A name for my heroine has been found! It shall be *Vampuka.*"

The *Robert le diable* story is especially appropriate since *Vampuka* took much of its story from Meyerbeer's *L'Africaine* (*The African*), and among the many musical works it quoted were several others by the same author. Meyerbeer's blend of medieval romance and supernatural goings-on was for a time quite popular and became the model for French grand opera. Among those he influenced were Verdi and Puccini. *Vampuka* was then as much a parody of Meyerbeer as it was of Verdi and Verdism.[15]

Act 1 of *Vampuka, African Bride* is set in an African desert with a luxuriously upholstered red divan center stage and two or three painted palm trees in the background. The wicked king Strafokamil IV (Greek for Ostrich, played by L. A. Fenin and A. Šaxalov) has imprisoned the beautiful Vampuka (A. S. Abramjan and de Gorn) and is planning to force her to marry him. We are told of this in a song by a chorus of four typically dull extras who are indifferent to everything. Dressed in red tights and standing behind huge fig leaves they sing:

> My v pu—, my v pu—, v pustyne my živëm,
> i kak—, i kak—, i kaktusy žuem!
> (We in the des—, we in the des—, in the desert we live,
> and cac—, and cac—, and cacti we chew!)

Vampuka's father has been killed in battle by Strafokamil, but the fight is carried on by a sensitive Hispano-Italian warrior named Merinos. He tells Vampuka that her father's ashes are buried in the desert, which causes her to faint. There follows Merinos's famous aria, which he sings with all manner of vocal embellishment: "Gde najti—dostat', dostat'—najti stakan vody?" ("Where to find—to get, to get—to find a glass of water?"). After a big finish in which he raises his hands to the heavens and hits a high note, having circled the entire stage, Merinos triumphantly exits singing: "Tuda, tuda-a-a-, gde est' voda!" ("There, the-e-e-re, there is water!")

Lodyrè, the hero (played by L. I. Lukin), enters, sits beside Vampuka, and they sing the following duet: "Èto ty, Lodyrè? —Èto ja, Lodyrè! Èto ty zdes', Lodyrè? —Èto ja, zdes', Lodyrè! Èto ty? —Èto ja! Èto ty? —Èto ja." ("Is it you, Lodyrè? —It is I, Lodyrè! Is it you here, Lodyrè? —It is I, here, Lodyrè! Is it you? —It is I! Is it you? —It is I.") Having established that Lodyrè is indeed there, they both sing: "Èto my!" ("It is we!"). Lukin, in the worst tradition of the egocentric Italian tenor, rushes to the footlights each time he is to deliver a high note, then remembering Vampuka, runs back to her. Having heard the voices of their enemies singing in the wings, the lovers, who are ensconced on the sofa, begin another duet: "Za nami pogonja, bežim–spešim!" ("They are pursuing us, let us run—let us hurry!").... They then exit slowly, flashing a charming smile at the audience and waving goodbye with their fingers.

The second act is again set in the desert, but in place of the divan there are two thrones and an executioner's block. A procession of soldiers, played by the same four extras who formed the chorus in the first act, march one behind the other in the upstage area, then dart into the wings on one side of the stage only to jump out of the wings on the opposite side a moment later.

In the meantime Vampuka and Strafokamil have sat down on the thrones and are being entertained by a classical ballet in which Ikar (N. Barabanov) parodies the gestures and movements of a prima ballerina. Lodyrè enters carrying a lyre. The King recognizes him and challenges him to a duel. With that, Merinos charges onto the stage and says that he will fight the King. Merinos emerges victorious and orders the execution of Strafokamil. Placing his head on the executioner's block, the King begins an endless aria in imitation of Boris Godunov consisting of two phrases: "Lišajuc' sil, lišajuc' sil, sejčas umret Strafokamil." ("I am losing strength, I am losing strength, now dies Strafokamil.") Losing his patience, the executioner (A. P. Los') raises his prop sword several times over the head of his victim, but each time the King stays his arm so that he may finish singing the phrase.

The opera ends with the ensemble parodying the inane finales of Italian operas, absurdly mouthing the libretto. Everyone sings: "Slavim geroja, pav na koleni, —pav na geroja, slavim koleni." ("All hail the hero, fall on your knees, —fall on the hero, all hail your knees.")[16]

This production was, by Xolmskaja's account, a truly collaborative effort on the part of cast. At one point in the action, L. A. Fenin as Strafokamil leaned against the backdrop representing the sky and wiped his nose with a handkerchief which he took from his nearly naked body. Fenin himself suggested this bit of business in imitation of the great Russian opera star Fedor Šaljapin. The entire production was characterized by a sort of exuberant lunacy. Kryžickij claims Èrenberg was so worried about what the audience's response to his mock opera might be that he conducted the orchestra in a wig and false beard. Kugel', who rarely acted, played the role of the priest at the premiere in a red beard but without make-up. Reportedly Èrenberg laughed so hard at this that he could barely hold on to his baton.[17]

Vampuka was a great success and added some new words to the Russian lexicon, among them the title itself and such derivatives as *Vampučit'* and *Vampuknost'*. More importantly, it helped to awaken the consciousness of a segment of the Russian public and especially of the artistic community to the stultifying and ridiculous conventions that had infested the staging of Italian opera in Russia. Another term, *krivozerkal'nost'*, also worked its way into the Russian language, signifying a creative work of satirical content, form, and style of performance.[18]

Despite the favorable reception of *Vampuka*, some critics voiced reservations about the future of the Crooked Mirror Theatre. V. V. Vorovskij warned of two dangers ahead. On the one hand, an exclusive circle such as the Crooked Mirror could never become a really significant artistic force. However, on the other, should the theatre seek to reach a wider public, it would no doubt compromise the taste and quality of its work.[19]

Apparently Kugel' and Xolmskaja themselves sensed that their theatre had reached a crossroads in its development. *Vampuka* had established the Crooked Mirror as a talented theatre of parody, but even in this genre its experiments had so far been limited. The directorate looked for the means whereby their theatre could expand its scope. For this they needed a new building to house a larger theatre and a new director who could bring to this theatre a clear artistic vision.[20]

The Reformed Crooked Mirror

One summer morning in 1910, Nikolaj Evreinov (see fig. 28) received a short note from A. R. Kugel' which read as follows: "If it would not be too much of an inconvenience, could you please drop by the editorial offices of *Theatre and Art* on a matter of some urgency and importance." Evreinov suspected even before meeting with Kugel' that the latter intended to offer him the position of chief artistic director of the Crooked Mirror Theatre.

Evreinov credits his work at the Ancient Theatre for his selection by Kugel' for this new post. It had, after all, given him a certain degree of celebrity in artistic circles. Still, Kugel' might not have felt that he was the right man to determine the future course of the Crooked Mirror Theatre had he not witnessed Evreinov's work at the Merry Theatre for Grown-up Children (*Veselyj teatr dlja požilyx detej*). This short-lived venture (what David Zolotnickij calls a "theatre-butterfly"), begotten primarily to produce Evreinov's *A Merry Death,* was somewhat similar in spirit and purpose to the Crooked Mirror Theatre.

The idea for the Merry Theatre came to Evreinov and Fedor F. Komissarževskij, at the close of the 1908–9 season at the Dramatic Theatre of V. F. Komissarževskaja, where they were both working as directors. Vera Fedorovna and the rest of the company had left on a long tour of the provinces, and the two directors decided to make the most of the free time and space to stage a series of productions: *Čereposlov* by Koz'ma Prutkov, one of Evreinov's favorite authors whose work and spirit would figure prominently in the Crooked Mirror's repertory[21]; *Beautiful Galatea (Prekrasnaja Galatea)*, a 44-year-old opera by Franz Zuppe; an opera parody by Il'ja Sac entitled *The Ring of Guadelupe* or *Love's Revenge (Kol'co Guadelupe ili mest' ljubvi)*; Bernard Shaw's *Caesar and Cleopatra*; *The Diabolical Masquerade (D'jabol'skij maskarad)* by Count Aleksej Tolstoj; *Divertissement*, a series of parody-grotesques; and Evreinov's harlequinade, *A Merry Death*. Although Evreinov's work at the Merry Theatre was short-lived, it helped to focus his craft as a parodist, which would stand him in good stead at the Crooked Mirror.

Evreinov and Kugel' met at the offices of *Theatre and Art* at 14 Voznesenskij Prospekt, thereby initiating a new stage in the development of the Crooked Mirror Theatre and in Evreinov's artistic career. Kugel' remembered well Evreinov's theory of monodrama, having attended his lecture at the Theatrical Club, and asked him at their meeting where he intended to stage plays of this genre. By Evreinov's account, Kugel', who had still not directly offered him the post of artistic director, answered his own question by saying that there was no place but the Crooked Mirror Theatre suitable to Evreinov's peculiar, multifaceted talent. Kugel' and Evreinov succeeded in charming one another at this meeting. But their first flush of mutual admiration did not last for long.[22]

From the outset Evreinov placed certain conditions upon his acceptance of the job. He wanted a staff that would include another high-quality director from the theatrical avant garde, and a designer of the "new school." He chose Mixail Nikolaevič Jakovlev to head the design department at the Crooked Mirror and Il'ja Sac to head the music department. Evreinov also wanted a guarantee that he would be able to devote himself to organizing and staging the programs without having to be bothered with the daily business of running the theatre. There was a certain amount of squabbling over salary arrangements which became a permanent feature of the Evreinov-Kugel' relationship. Evreinov insisted that Kugel' was notoriously closed fisted in money matters.

The major condition upon which Evreinov accepted the position was that the Crooked Mirror change its status from a late-night cabaret (which despite its founders' intentions, it still was) to a full-fledged theatre of parody and satire performing at regular hours (8:30 P.M. was the starting time on which they eventually agreed) in more substantial premises. Kugel' was quick to agree to this condition since he himself desired such a change.[23] It is conceivable that the Crooked Mirror might never have taken this major step and once having taken it would not have sustained this new direction without Evreinov's influence. Kugel' and Evreinov set out to find new lodgings for the Crooked Mirror Theatre. They were greatly impressed by the Ekaterininskij Theatre at 60 Ekaterininskij (now Griboedov) Canal. The theatre, located above a club, held from 650 to 800 (accounts vary). The seats were upholstered in sky-blue velvet. There was a large, deep stage with fly apparatus and ample storage space. The Crooked Mirror company moved in and stayed.[24]

During his tenure as artistic director of the Crooked Mirror, Evreinov, "the prophet of eccentrism," was to experiment with a number of forms and genres. He served as artistic director for six seasons, although he was formally affiliated with the theatre for seven, from 1910 to 1917.[25] During the 1915–16 season, Evreinov worked on his three-volume theoretical work, *The Theatre for Oneself*, at his dacha in Finland, while his plays continued to be performed at the Crooked Mirror.[26] Evreinov estimates that he was involved as director, author, translator, or in some advisory capacity in about one hundred plays produced at this theatre, although he remembers only fifty by name. He directed about eighty productions, a figure he derives from the fact that each season at the Crooked Mirror saw three to four premieres, each premiere consisting of three to four plays. During his six years in residence at the Crooked Mirror, he directed the majority of the productions in the repertory, including about fourteen successful productions of his own plays, some of which were original works, some adaptations, and some collaborations.[27]

The Crooked Mirror Theatre opened its first season under Evreinov's directorship at the Ekaterininskij Theatre on 1 October 1910, with the following company: Abramjan, Batorskaja, Wagner, Lukina, Naumovskaja, Nelidova, Svetlova, Xolmskaja, Jarockaja, Antimonov, Volnovskij, Granovskij, Donskoj, Egorov, Ikar, Los', Lukin, Kirsanov, Kiselev, Mal'šet, Osvecimskij, Podgornyj, Fenin and Šestakovskij.[28]

Viewing the programs of the 1910-11 season, the critics concurred that the Crooked Mirror Theatre had undergone a significant transformation. M. Vejkone wrote in the October 1910 issue of the newspaper *Speech* (*Reč'*):

> The directors of the theatre have made an attempt to widen the boundaries of its former platforms and to deepen its content. The first steps in this direction are of significant interest. There is the sense of a firm directorial hand at work. The staging, sets, costumes, and make-up are superb. The public desiring to find in the Crooked Mirror a "cabaret" will be disappointed, but people seeking to find even in trifles a reflection of true art with its indispensable element of talent undoubtedly discerned in the first appearance of the reformed Crooked Mirror the precursor of a new, original phenomenon in the realm of stage art.[29]

Critics commented that "the troupe of the theatre has been welded into an ensemble of rare, impeccable harmony." Perhaps best of all, they said, even a frequent visitor to the Crooked Mirror would be continually surprised by some new, unexplored theatrical thought or scenic approach.

Evreinov conceived of the Crooked Mirror as Aristophanic in spirit, dedicated to creating a positive work of art out of a subject's negative qualities. Kugel' described the Crooked Mirror as a "theatre of skepticism and negation."[30]

The theatre was not afraid to tackle serious contemporary themes, some of which had philosophical overtones, in addition to dramatic pieces. There were also burlesques, caricatures, grotesques and satirical monodramas. This last category, which enabled the author to express veiled criticism from behind a satirical mask and so confound the government censor, included Boris Fedorovič Gejer's *Reminiscences* (*Vospominanija*, 1911), *Aqua Vitae* (*Voda žizni*, 1911) and *Dream* (*Son*, 1912); Evreinov's *The Presentation of Love* and *In the Stage-Wings of the Soul,* and *Aeolian Harps* (*Èolovye arfy,* 1915), co-authored by Gejer and Evreinov[31] The authorship of *Aeolian Harps* was originally credited to Gejer alone. However, Evreinov protested to the directorate of the Crooked Mirror Theatre that Gejer had not only appropriated the form devised by Evreinov—monodrama—but the subject as well. It seems that Evreinov had earlier proposed a parody of theatre critics. Eventually, the dispute was resolved and Gejer and Evreinov were listed as co-authors of the play.

Aeolian Harps, as well as Gejer's solo work in the same vein, was less monodrama in the narrow sense and more "polydrama." This type of play offers not one but several protagonists whose highly individual and subjective perspectives transform the reality we see being dramatized.[32] Although not as intellectually ambitious as Evreinov's earlier monodramas, these variants were written in the spirit of playful parody that characterized most of the work at the Crooked Mirror and so are of interest.

Aeolian Harps demonstrated the highly subjective reactions of different theatre critics to the same production (monodrama is impossible without a single person or thing to precipitate conflicting perceptions). The title *Aeolian Harps* (the play the reviewers were watching) is a humorous allusion to a popular play of the time by I. Surčučev entitled *Autumn Violins* (*Osennie skripky*). The play begins with a scene from this syrupy play as it would be perceived "objectively." Next, we see the same scene through the eyes of three different critics: the first benevolent, the second malevolent, the third drunk. The benevolent critic regards the play as a splendid symphony and is especially glad when the actress with whom he is in love comes onstage to deliver her one line, "Dinner is served." Since the enamored critic has eyes only for her, the rest of the stage is plunged into darkness at this point. The critic who wishes the play ill envisions the leading actor losing his dentures. A knock at the door causes the door to fall off its hinges, and the prompter drowns out the actors with his shouting, not unlike the *Quo Vadis?* rehearsal scene in Evreinov's *The Chief Thing.* For the drunk critic the whole stage is covered in white muslin to indicate his deadened senses. A scene recalling a good time spent in some restaurant is inserted into the production. The actors speak nonsense while behind the scenes champagne corks pop and a drunken voice calls out: "Sir, the bill!"

Gejer's own *Reminiscences*, which Evreinov dubbed his masterpiece, re-creates a typical bourgeois wedding as it is remembered by five of its participants—bride and groom; two wedding guests, one somber and one merry (i.e., drunk); and the bride's mother.

Gejer's *Aqua Vitae*, which Evreinov directed, depicts the manner in which a barroom scene changes as a man drinks progressively more beer. Kugel' credited this production with conveying the idea of monodrama "from the world of cloudy abstractions into the realm of clarity and persuasiveness."[33]

Also of note in another vein was Gejer's *The Evolution of Theatre (Evoljucija teatra*, 1910), a parodistic treatment of the crisis in the theatre and a direct response to S. Rafalovič's article of the same name in the anthology *Theatre: A Book on the New Theatre* (1908). Gejer's play consists of four sections parodying four different authors: Gogol' (his play *Marriage*), Ostrovskij (*The Storm, The Forest*, etc.), Čexov (*Ivanov*) and Leonid Andreev (*Anathema, The Life of Man, The Black Masks* and *He Who Gets Slapped*). The vignettes are introduced by a lecturer who, much to our relief, offers them in place of a series of more formal addresses on the subject, "The Evolution of Theatre."[34]

The Crooked Mirror can also be credited with the creation of a new genre, the "ceremonial conference" (*toržestvennoe zasedanie*). This was an evening of speeches and performances of a particular author's work, such as the one which Evreinov staged (14 January 1913) in honor of his favorite nineteenth-century comic writer and satirist, Koz'ma Prutkov.

Koz'ma Prutkov was the creation of Aleksej Tolstoj and the Žemčužnikov brothers—Aleksej M., Vladimir M. and Aleksandr M. The real authors, by inventing this fictitious author, for whom they created an elaborate biography, were able to criticize certain aspects of Russian society in the latter part of the nineteenth century. Prutkov wrote vaudevilles, dramatic proverbs and social and romantic drama of a pretentious sort. As a youth Evreinov shared his father's enthusiasm for Prutkov's works, reading and enacting them at home. This interest was reinforced by Evreinov's discovery while at the Imperial School of Jurisprudence that one of the Žemčužnikov brothers had been a student there. Evreinov became a Prutkov cultist at the school and acted the role of Nina Xristianovna in a production of *Čereposlov* at which Aleksej M. Žemčužnikov and philosopher Vladimir Solov'ev were in attendance.

The Prutkov evening was esentially a polydrama in two parts. The "scholarly" half of the program consisted of a lecture entitled "Prutkov and the Antichrist," spoofing such mystics as Merežkovskij, Gippius, and Filosofov, and an old general's reminiscences about Koz'ma Prutkov, whom he erroneously referred to as Kirill Prytkov. The "artistic" half of the program consisted of a performance of odes in honor of Prutkov, romances composed to his words, a duet entitled "At the Seashore" ("The market-gardener stands sullenly picking his nose with his finger."), a quartet offering their parody of Prutkov's famous words, "Do you love cheese, they once asked the canting hypocrite", and finally Koz'ma Prutkov "himself" reading the prologue to his comedy *The Hasty Turk* (*Oprometčivyj turk*).[35]

The "conference" format was utilized by other authors to develop a particular theme rather than to interpret the work of a specific person. Leonid Andreev, who contributed several works to the repertory of the Crooked Mirror Theatre, made use of the format in *Monument*, which satirized the stupid and cowardly behavior of local officials preparing to erect a monument to Puškin. Andreev, even after he himself was parodied in Gejer's *The Evolution of the Theatre*, continued to contribute work to the Crooked Mirror. One of his works, *The Sabine Women* (*Prekrasnye sabinjanki*), was a political satire in which Andreev "pilloried the *Kadets* as the feckless Sabines who were prepared only to employ ineffective legal means to retrieve their wives (freedom) from the Romans (the Government) who had abducted them." Somehow the play managed to pass the scrutiny of the censor.[36]

Falling somewhere between the polydrama, ceremonial conference and theatrical parody genres at the Crooked Mirror were two of Evreinov's more amusing plays. The second and critically less successful of the two was *A Feast of Laughter* (*Kuxnja smexa*, 1913), subtitled *The World Contest of Wit* (*Mirovoj konkurs ostroumija*), which concerns an event allegedly organized by an unnamed theatre in order to fill the gaps in its repertory with a good, representative collection of contemporary comedies in translation. A selection panel has been named to judge the entries according to how well they have captured their national brands of humor.

The story premise the various entrants have been assigned to write about is appropriately trivial and redolent of Gogolian humor. Many of Gogol''s tales show us how, as Donald Fanger explains, "an innocent blowhard is discomfited in the interests not of poetic justice but of simple exhibition."[37] It seems that among the bored cavaliers at the festive ball there was a merry fellow who loved to amuse himself at the expense of others. He went into the smoking room and began to brag about his manual dexterity, claiming that he could tear the buttons off a coat and sew them back on in exactly two minutes. Everyone said that this was impossible, and so he offered to bet 100 rubles that he could do as he claimed. A count, who was noted for his miserliness, took the bet but lowered it to 50 kopecks. The fellow then proceeded to rip all of the buttons off the count's waistcoat but could not sew them back on in two minutes. "What? You have lost?" said the count. "Unfortunately," answered the merry fellow, handing him the 50 kopeck piece amid the loud laughter of those watching. Everyone hurried off to their ladies, except the count, whose waistcoat was in terrible disarray.

The chairman of the selection panel offers a series of prologues to the performance of the winning plays in which he explains more specifically how and why each play won. The German entry, *Die Bienenliebe,* or *Was soll es bedeuten,* by Georg Meyer, is, as the chairman tells us, characteristic of its nation's humor in its moral intent, its militant tone, its sensitivity to nature and its use of such familiar comic types as the stutterer, the very tall man and the very short man.

The French entry, *Les Boutons d'amour,* or *Oh-la-la* or *A Quarter of an Hour with Georgette,* by Julia Korbot, we are told carries an untranslatable play on words in its title, which the chairman then translates as both "The Bride of Love" and "The Buttons of Love." The author of this play included such typical French devices as puns, risqué double entendres, well-aimed bon mots and piquant quid pro quo, an appropriate lightness and gracefullness of tone, and the obligatory references to French cooking being done always in a suet. One panel member nonetheless voted instead for *Mimi Forgot Her Pantaloons.*

The American selection, *The Betting of Two Red Devils,* or *Time is Money,* by William Medge, is an appropriately "hyperbolic grotesque, neoplacard, trans-comedy, super-caricature" or more precisely, an "eccentro-caricature." The play contains such "characteristically Anglo-Saxon traits" as the ideal of sportsmanship, a witty exchange of slaps in the face, a subtle satirical moment which takes place on a toilet, a checked handkerchief in which a huge red nose is blown, an ironic manner of play and the capitalist spirit of utilitarianism.

The Russian entry, *Sčast'e Trogloditova* (*Trogloditov's Luck*), by the humorist Osip Arkadčenko, features such unfortunate Russian social types as the drunk, the mother-in-law, the suburban husband, the sorrowful figure of the office clerk, and the Jew speaking in his "typical" Odessa dialect, created by Russian humorists from elements of Jewish jargon, the Russian language and their own fantasies. This play, which is "not without political overtones," followed the usual long and winding course before finally reaching the stage. It was first published as separate stories in the satirical journal *Satyricon,* which were reprinted in one of the organs of the provincial press, then in the almanacs of another satirical journal, in a volume of the author's complete works, in a cheap library edition and only then adapted for the stage. By then the work which was once fresh and new had gone stale.

The second Russian entry, *Gorderdergor,* or *Ugucusmex,* by a Soviet collective, foreshadows the post-1917 mass spectacles in which Evreinov figured prominently. The play, we are told, is designed to be played under the open sky with the participation of infantry, cavalry, artillery, air force, military elephants and artists from theatre, opera, ballet and circus under the control of a staff of directors who communicate with each other via telegraph, light projections and flags.

The title *Gorderdergor* is an acronym created from the first letters of the Russian words for city (*gorod*) and village or country (*derevnja*). Soviet theatre historian David Zolotnickij sees Evreinov's purpose in this section of the play as twofold: to spoof the grandiose Soviet mass spectacles staged under the open sky with their elaborate quasi-military command posts and complicated communication systems and to ridicule the epoch's impoverished way of life (*byt*). Evreinov credited V. A. Azov with co-authoring this section. Azov and S. I. Antimonov were featured performers in *A Feast of Laughter*. Although Evreinov invented such authors' names as Georg Meyer and Julia Korbot, the name Osip Arkadčenko, author of *Trogloditov's Luck*, is an amalgam of two then well-known authors' names — Osip Dymov and Arkadij Averčenko. These two writers were a part of the abundant parodistic one-act play and dramatic joke (*p'esy-šutki*) trend in the period 1900–10.[38]

A Feast of Laughter received mixed notices, but as Evreinov acknowledged, he was more interested here in experimenting with form than with content. Of course, this is not entirely true. This humorous compendium brings together several of Evreinov's favorite themes: (1) relativism versus the absolutism brought about by unimaginative, literal-minded thinking which manifests itself in clichéd character types and dramatic forms; (2) the distinction between comedy and true wit or thoughtful laughter; (3) the tiredness of the contemporary theatre; (4) his own excessiveness in hyperbolic mode of expression (no less than "The *World* Contest of Wit"), one-upmanship, and the effort to get to the bottom of such insoluble ideas as what makes one thing funny and another not; (5) his effort to get original readings from established ideas and forms; (6) artistic chauvinism and isolationism; and (7), as always, his own pretense in systematizing art and building grandiose edifices on the slightest of premises.[39]

As to the form to which Evreinov alluded, he had already been far more successful with his highly original adaptation of Gogol''s *The Inspector General* (Evreinov's *Revizor*, 1912) which became his most popular work as a dramatist at the Crooked Mirror. Kugel' credited Xolmskaja with the original idea for the production and himself with having written the prologue; he considered the play as a whole a collaborative effort. Evreinov acknowledged Kugel''s contributions to the editing of the script and his help in creating the character of the "Clerk (Narrator) from the Special Commission Delegated by the Directorate of the Crooked Mirror Theatre," who appears in the introduction to each segment, but that is all the credit he begrudged his adversary-employer.[40]

These conflicting claims notwithstanding, the play is unmistakably Evreinov's in the same way that Gogol' borrowed Puškin's original idea as a premise for his *The Inspector General* and fashioned a wholly original play. Gogol''s memorable protagonist Xlestakov never appears in Evreinov's version. In a sense Evreinov has appropriated the Xlestakov role, fulfilling the latter's dream to write a comedy on his strange experiences in Gogol''s provincial town. Xlestakov-Harlequin is a role with which Evreinov was by now comfortable and familiar.[41]

Evreinov's serious purpose in writing this parody was to prove the director's right to be named author of the stage production, a cause to which he had long dedicated himself. In 1909 he responded to an article in Kugel''s director-baiting journal *Theatre and Art* which had called petty and destructive those contemporary directors who were preoccupied with their creative rights.

Evreinov was sensitive to the issue of directors' stealing ideas and production concepts from their colleagues, having been victimized by this himself on at least one occasion.[42] Kugel''s journal argued that you cannot steal a director's creativity if he is secure in it; you can only borrow at most the outer form it takes. Evreinov claimed that the director has the right to be co-author of the stage directions, which the journal saw as a direct infringement upon the author's rights. Evreinov distinguished between the writer as author of the literary, dramatic work and the director as author of the theatrical work.

Evreinov later outlined what he felt constituted the director's functions:

1. Above all, the detailed *interpreter* of the author's work
2. *Translator* of the written text into the living language of gesture and mimicry
3. *Artist/designer* who sketches the original scene design (as Evreinov had done with *Stage-Wings*)
4. *Composer* of the melody of stage speech, its common music, tempo, nuances, pauses and instrumentation
5. *Sculptor* of live material, creating independent value in the area of plastic art
6. *Actor-teacher,* himself playing all the roles through the souls of his actors.

Evreinov believed that the director must possess the power to put "invisible blinders on the eyes of the audience," an image that is consistent with his conception of art as a form of hypnosis. In order to accomplish this, says Evreinov, a true director should possess almost universal knowledge, especially in the areas of art, philosophy and cultural history. He must be the fulcrum upon which is balanced the often antithetical views of the producers and the actors.[43] His hand should be subtle but his vision pervasive. He must be able to make the complicated seem simple to the spectator, a requirement which Evreinov's spiritually naive productions satisfy whereas those of the directors under attack in *The Inspector General*, in his opinion, do not.

Evreinov's "directorial buffonade" offers interpretations of Gogol''s text by disciples of Stanislavskij, Gordon Craig, Max Reinhardt and the silent film. Typically, Evreinov is here spoofing close to home, much as Xlestakov risks unmasking by composing an incriminating letter to a friend in which he satirizes the townspeople he has duped. But then, as Jan Kott reminds us, "this little copying clerk had a writer's soul." He himself tells us, "I, I must admit, live by literature." Evreinov too thinks it worth the risk in order to teach by what he perceives as negative examples.

Of his contemporaries, the major Russian director-innovators, Evreinov respected Stanislavskij and thought him one of a kind, although he refuted his artistic path. He disliked Mejerxol'd, of course, whom he thought very talented but unoriginal, stealing each new phase of his work from someone else. Evreinov liked Tairov, whom he considered less talented than Mejerxol'd but more honest, pursuing his own path effectively. Evreinov admired and respected Vaxtangov, whom he considered his pupil. Specifically, Evreinov felt that Vaxtangov's production of *Princess Turandot* (1922) owed much to his use of commedia in *The Chief Thing* (1921). One assumes that Evreinov's decision not to parody Mejerxol'd in *The Inspector General* (whose Germanness he parodies elsewhere) was intended as a slight or, Evreinov would say, a judgment on Mejerxol'd's relative lack of importance among these other innovators. Following the premiere of Mejerxol'd's production of Gogol''s *Inspector General* (1926), however, Kugel' took it upon himself to add a section parodying Mejerxol'd to Evreinov's play.

One might consider the Gordon Craig parody in part as Evreinov's response to the Craig-Stanislavskij alliance that resulted in a monodramatic *Hamlet*. Evreinov could claim credit for influencing Craig in his approach (although he had no real proof for this), but he must have felt somewhat encroached upon nonetheless. The theme of Craig's production— which logged 142 rehearsals but only 47 performances between 23 December 1911 and 26 February 1914, with Vasilij I. Kačalov in the title role— was said to be the victory of the spiritual over the material. According to

Russian historian Evgenij Znosko-Borovskij, Evreinov never staged the last two sections of *The Inspector General* at the Crooked Mirror Theatre.[44]

Each segment of Evreinov's play begins with the appearance before the curtain of a narrator, dressed as one of Gogol''s clerks, who offers an introduction to what we are about to see so as "to facilitate the audience's perception of the stage event."[45] This device was frequently and self-consciously employed by Evreinov to clue in the reader/spectator on how the ensuing play should be perceived. It is a useful instrument for parody, setting up some pseudoscholar or specialist as a straw man to whom we can feel superior. The device draws attention to the author by underlining the theatricality and artificiality of the event about to take place. The stage curtain should be the dividing line between reality and illusion, but it is not because the speaker, who is himself a *fictitious* character, appears in front of it. Ringing down the curtain on the play is made *a part of the action* rather than its conclusion. Pirandello made use of the same technique.

In response to those critics who have recommended a return to the classics as a solution to the current crisis in theatre, the narrator tells us, the Crooked Mirror has embarked upon an experiment to multiply the number of classic plays. It will offer five widely variant directorial interpretations of each classic, united by the directors' common goal of making the author's original work unrecognizable.

As soon becomes apparent, the various interpretative renderings of the play serve as mere pretexts for the narrator's lengthy explications of the directors' backgrounds and production concepts. Evreinov, as has often been his custom, is here utilizing a first person voice directed squarely at the audience to settle accounts, denigrating current artistic tendencies which he opposes, offering his own solutions and in general holding forth wittily in a self-conscious evocation of the long-winded doctor from Bologna. Evreinov was never one to spare himself ridicule; he asked only to be spared the ridicule of others. The so-called narcissist Evreinov at times approaches self-effacement by the very manner in which he draws attention to himself as a negative comic example of the pedant who goes on too heatedly for too long. So too, by continually drawing the audience's attention away from the play, which is, after all, "the [chief] thing," Evreinov calls into question the notion of there being a chief thing at all, and if there is, what it might be. Evreinov's use of the interrupted dramatic narrative is distinctly modern. It is the ironist's way of representing the incomplete stories of unfinished men, the torturous reasonings and conversational fetishes of men who are unable to act upon or prove anything. Yet, Evreinov's single-minded promulgation of his theatre-in-life philosophy as mankind's salvation suggests that the ironist and the visionary reformer were locked into a relationship of necessity.

The purpose of the traditional nineteenth-century staging that begins the proceedings is, the narrator tells us, to reacquaint the audience with the scene under consideration (the play's opening scene announcing the imminent arrival of the Inspector General) and to give us an "objective" standard against which to measure all experiments. All of the characters sit in chairs near the footlights with the mayor in the middle. They are in somewhat fancy dress with poorly done wigs. Their performances are "presentational" in the nineteenth-century sense of the term, words and gestures projected toward the audience without the "pause for mood" and other such modernist devices. In other words, this is the type of staging that Stanislavskijan realism was meant to replace.[46]

The Stanislavskijan rendering is staged by a director who originally graduated from the agricultural school in Yaroslaval province, where he studied tree planting and the cultivation of rare strains of apples. "But once while sitting on the banks of the Volga he heard the miraculous song of a nightingale." It was as if something had awakened in him, and from that point on he lost all peace of mind.[47] He threw aside all of his agricultural work and travelled to Moscow to become a pupil of the great master. There he studied mood for a month and a half and theatre as life (not to be confused with Evreinov's own theories) for two years. At night he worked on pauses. His dissertation, dedicated to Stanislavskij, was entitled "The Semipause and Pause for Mood." Its thesis was that the "square" of mood is inversely proportional to the distance of the theatre from life.

In a direct jibe at what he felt to be the hypocrisy of Stanislavskij's basic approach to theatre, Evreinov had the narrator add: "As is well-known, the highly artistic productions at MXAT are distinguished in the first place by the fact that everything onstage happens as in life and in the second, that everything does not happen as in life but as in 'mood.'" In other words, what results is not a sharp reproduction of life as it really is but a hazy, emotional, artistic rendering.

From a brief reference by the Mayor to the location and appearance of the town, the director has gone to great and absurd lengths to reconstruct it in detail. By consulting Gogol''s correspondence he found that the action originated in the city of Mirgorod, which at present has ten thousand inhabitants, two tallow-melting factories, and one leather-dressing plant. Having himself visited this city and studied its history through its architecture, the director has precisely reconstructed the house where the mayor lived at the time in which the action of the play is set.[48] A similar attempt has been made to capture the character of local Russian speech at this time. For this reason the Mayor speaks with a Ukrainian accent, "not loud and not soft, but just as in life."

In terms of "mood," "the action presents the lighthearted life of the city, quiet and almost devoid of industry. But gradually there develops a 'mood' of dispiritedness in expectation of the arrival of the Inspector General."

The director has rendered all of Gogol''s imagery in literal fashion. Thus Zemljanika, who is described by the author as "a veritable swine in a skull-cap," actually wears a skull-cap. Like his teacher, the director values his interpretative detail work more than the play itself.

Although, says the narrator, it is impossible to ascertain precisely the kind of weather the town had on the day of Xlestakov's arrival, the director has made an educated guess. He based his assumption on the line from the play which reads, "the garrison marched down the street in full-dress uniforms" and "they wore nothing under their uniforms." Thus, the narrator speaking for the director tells us, "we may assume that it was a warm, cloudless day. In the end a light rain falls as a last artistic touch for the creation of an inconsolably sad mood."[49]

As the curtain rises, it is almost completely dark. A sofa is turned with its back to the audience, a visual reference to Stanislavskij's concept of "the fourth wall." We are immediately struck by a barrage of auditory and visual effects in the best — or worst — MXAT tradition. At the dramatic moment in which the Mayor reads the letter announcing the arrival of the Inspector General, his words are drowned out by the tolling of church bells. The text of the play is unaltered, and it is played in a realistic manner. However, what is most interesting to the reader is the fact that the stage directions which have been inserted by the director are lengthier and more elaborate than the play itself.

The second staging, "in the spirit of Max Reinhardt," is, the narrator tells us, by a director raised in poverty on a meager diet of potatoes which led to the development of rickets. Yet in spite of this and even though he had one leg shorter than the other, he successfully studied rhythmic gymnastics in school according to the system of Dalcroze. He approached *The Inspector General* with "typically German seriousness." Gogol''s text was reworked along the lines of the literature of Hugo von Hofmannsthal as interpreted by Reinhardt. The incidental music, in the style of Engelbert Humperdinck, was based on a letter written by Belinskij which began with the words: "Music, music, to hell with you!"

The staging contains a number of Reinhardt's familiar devices, crammed together into a small time frame as were Stanislavskij's in the first segment: the circus arena calculated to seat five thousand under the open sky, character entrances through the audience, and a cerebral production concept based upon Gogol''s statement that the one honest face that watched over his play was the face of laughter. In order "to placate the ghost of the great writer," the director decided to present the character "Laughter" onstage in the person of a charming girl, accompanied by her customary companions, "Satire" and "Humor."

The scene depicts the facade of a house built "in the new Russian style as understood by the Munich Secession."[50] The orchestra plays an especially written overture on a Russian theme. As the curtain rises, "Laughter," "Satire," and "Humor" are performing a symbolic dance "in the Russian spirit as understood by Humperdinck." When the Mayor enters, the three spirits sit at his feet.

The dialogue is written in rhymed verse which Evreinov credited to the actor S. I. Antimonov. Following the Mayor's first speech, a bravura march is heard. The office clerks march in step through the audience, in full regimental attire. The Mayor's wife and daughter are dressed in operatic fashion on a Ukrainian theme. At the conclusion of the scene, "Laughter," "Satire," and "Humor" dance around the confused Mayor.

The pupil of Gordon Craig, "well-known to us for his mystical, cubistic production of *Hamlet*," has, like the preceding directors, based his interpretation upon the author's own words. Gogol' said that the town of Mirgorod (which means literally "World City") is a spiritual place found in all of us. Likewise, the Inspector General represents our sleeping conscience. Thus, the action, as envisioned by this director, takes place "at some point in interplanetary space."

The "infinite space" represented onstage is bordered by "blacks." Upstage there are poles and pipes flooded with "a deathly light." Downstage, angels blow trumpets at the audience, behind them, then into the wings, and finally at each other. Doleful organ music plays as the Mayor enters, followed by the other characters in the scene, some in masks, others completely wrapped in black cloaks.

The Mayor reads his speech "mystically" and "melodiously" from a long scroll. A bell rings between his lines, and at one point he is interrupted by a powerful choir backstage singing a part of the "Requiem." A scene between the Mayor's wife and daughter, which has been included in each version, is cut very short. They enter in white confessional dresses, crying in despair. Realizing that they have been abandoned by the Mayor, they freeze in "a pose of inconsolable grief." We hear the tender sounds of violins, drowned out by the trumpeting of the angels. The scene ends with the measured tolling of the bell and the solemn sounds of the organ under which is heard the penitential choir.

The final scene, created for the cinema "in the spirit of the famous company Pathé" is subtitled, "A Foolish Fellow in the Role of Mayor." The director is one of the ablest pupils of the famous Max Linder, and has applied cinematic technique to all of the tricks suggested by Gogol''s text.

The characters sit huddled around the Mayor, who takes the letter from his pocket and waves it in the air. Everyone acts startled, stands up, sits down, changes places, and heatedly gesticulates. When the Mayor reads the letter, it fills the screen. All say goodbye to the Mayor, who puts the case to his hat on his head, his left glove on his right hand, and vice versa. He falls to his knees, quickly prays, and starts to run out left, when from the right in comic dishabille appear his wife, daughter, and the coquettish maid. The wife grabs her husband by his coattails, which tear, and a chase ensues. The characters run across the stage, one character stumbling and each falling on the other in turn.[51]

The curious history of Xlestakov and company repeated itself most auspiciously for the Crooked Mirror Theatre. The fame of Evreinov's production of *The Inspector General* became so widespread that Tsar Nikolaj II expressed a desire to see it just as his forbear Nikolaj I came to the premiere of Gogol''s original at Petersburg's Aleksandrinskij Theatre (19 April 1836). Tsar Nikolaj II greatly loved Gogol' and was said to have known this particular play almost by heart. He could not come to the Ekaterininskij Theatre to see the production because the theatre lacked a royal box. Instead he extended an invitation to the entire company to perform *The Inspector General* at the Kitajskij theatre at Tsarskoe selo. Only Kugel', whose writings had displeased the Tsar, was excluded. The Crooked Mirror company accepted the invitation and performed both *The Inspector General* and *Ryčalov's Tour* at Tsarkoe Selo early in 1913. Evreinov, Èrenberg, and the administrator, E. A. Markov, each received a gold watch from the Tsar. Kugel' remembered this bitterly along with the fact that the oldest worker, a confirmed *Menševik*, received a silver watch. All of the actors in major roles were rewarded with gifts as well.[52]

Kugel' was not the only person to be put out by this production. Evreinov's cordial relationship with Stanislavskij ended as well. Evreinov claimed that Stanislavskij felt compelled to re-stage *The Inspector General* at MXAT as a result of this parody treatment of his original staging. He also credited his concept of theatricality set forth in *The Theatre as Such* with influencing Stanislavskij to redo his production. Evreinov later qualified this, saying that it was Evgenij Vaxtangov's productions of *Princess Turandot* and *Erik XIV* that so influenced Stanislavskij. Of course, said Evreinov, it was *he* who had influenced Vaxtangov.

Of the many parodies on theatrical forms written for and staged at the Crooked Mirror, several were directed at Stanislavskij and Mejerxol'd. Kugel' claimed that these productions were extensions of the views he expressed in his articles in *Theatre and Art*, particularly regarding the smothering of the actor by the modern director-tyrants. However, Evreinov's artistic and personal biases were most clearly at work here.

Evreinov's *The School of the Stars* (*Škola ètualej*, premiere 11 November 1911), which concerns a school for *chansonettes*, features a Stanislavskijan director lecturing his students to the effect that the theatre is a school and a temple and as such demands of them ever more psychological realism. "It," he says, "is the main [chief] thing. And then rhythm. Rhythm, rhythm rhythm."[53] A would-be dancer in the Duncan mode is told that the most important aspect of this technique is to take off her shoes. However, when her shoes come off it is revealed that she has corns. The teacher instructs the Duncanist in the following manner:

> First pose: "Striving toward the ideal...." Stick out the elbows. More delicately, of course. Like so. Second: "I cannot accept this sacrifice." Stick out the behind. You have got some fat there. You need a massage. Absolutely. Third pose: "I worship you my beloved." More expression. [You must] Personify beauty. Lower your heel. God, what a callus! Do not forget: 24 Marat Street [the address of the school's chiropodist]. At once! "Striving toward the ideal." Just so. "I cannot accept this sacrifice." "I worship you my beloved."[54]

Evreinov greatly loved and admired Duncan but was less enamored of the imitative schools that sprang up in her wake. The poses here described sound as hollow as those of the Russian classical ballet that were parodied in other Crooked Mirror productions.

Evreinov returned again and again to what he considered the ludicrous excesses of Stanislavskij's school of psychological realism. He was apparently quite familiar with the sort of techniques that were employed at MXAT, as he indicated to Anaïs Nin in bemused fashion when they met in Paris in the 1930s. Pointing to his toes and leaning over, Evreinov explained, "In the Moscow Art Theatre one was taught to conceal the outward marks of timidity. For example, a singer, instead of twisting her hand was taught to twist her toe."[55] In Evreinov's play *The Theatre of Eternal War* (*Teatr večnoj vojny*, 1928), a teacher of dramatic arts at a theatrical institute corrects a student:

> Why are you wringing your hands? Have you forgotten how to conceal nervousness? How many times have we told you: curl your toes, press down on your big toe! No one will see inside your shoe, and the relief you get from tension is the same as you get from wringing your hands.

Evreinov, the excessive personality, was critical of excess wherever else he found it. In his memoirs he quotes at length from *The Technique of Perfecting the Stage Production* (*Texnika obrabotki sceničeskogo zrelišča*, 1922), in which actor-director Valentin Smyšljaev discusses the process whereby an actor of the Stanislavskijan school would prepare to play the role of Faust.

Stanislavskij instructs the actor that this can be done in stages. He must first converse with the doorman whom he meets on his way into the theatre, a man who has no awareness of the elusive laws of the cosmos which so torment and tear at the heart of Faust. Entering into his dressing room, the actor should seat himself before a mirror. By concentrating on the tiny wrinkles in his face he may turn them into the deep-set furrows characteristic of old age and thus begin to see the signs of approaching death. Once the actor feels that he is in the proper state of mind, he can leave his dressing room for the stage, where he will converse with the stagehands. But he does so not as he would in everyday life, but as would the character of Faust, who he is in the process of becoming.

At this point the stage should be completely set and emptied of people who do not belong there. The actor playing Faust feels a special closeness to the furnishings in his (Faust's) study. Sitting in his armchair as the curtain goes up for the first scene, the actor *is* Faust. Evreinov says of this approach: "From this example, which serves as a powerful magnifying glass for the pretentiousness of the Stanislavskij-worshippers, it is but a short step to parody in a formal sense."[57]

As impatient as he was with his fellow theatrical innovators, Evreinov had absolutely no use for their disciples, imitators and adaptors, a fact amply illustrated by the fact that his *Inspector General* parodies only the *students* of great men. In this vein, one of Evreinov's most popular plays for the Crooked Mirror Theatre, *The Fourth Wall* (*Četvërtaja stena*, 1915), parodied in knowing detail the misapplication of Stanislavskij's naturalistic acting and staging techniques by untalented imitators to the wholly imcompatible form of opera. Such an approach was actually being applied in Evreinov's day by the Theatre of Musical Drama in St. Petersburg. Evreinov's fictional theatre company, in the process of staging Gounod's opera *Faust*, gradually strips it of all theatrical and specifically operatic elements. The opera is first transformed into a "musical drama," then into a drama with music and finally into a realistic drama without any music at all.[58]

Every effort is made to make Faust a real person. To this end poetic language is replaced with prose, and Faust does not sing. The actor playing the role of Faust is told that he was cast on the basis of his age rather than his voice. The Director exults that even the actor's voice is hoarse and cracked as befits a man of Faust's age. He encourages the actor, who has a cold, to give him "more wheezing, hoarseness, choking, coughing and nose-blowing. In other words, reveal Faust's old age to us a bit more naturally." The Producer supports these instructions with the following argument: "Indeed, if an old man on the stage is not an old man with all of the infirmities characteristic of old men in general, then what, I ask you is realism in acting!"[59] The actions of real people dictate the lives of characters who are, after all, fictitious creations.[60] Of course, it is ludicrous that directors who are so preoccupied with naturalism should have chosen to stage an opera, with all its highly artificial conventions, in the first place.

Like many of Evreinov's plays, this one shows us theatre in the making. The din made by a crowd of people in motion is suggested by hitting the lowest notes on an organ. A prompter's box like the one at the Moscow Art Theatre rises downstage center, strangely juxtaposed with carefully reconstructed specimens of sixteenth-century German architecture upstage. Daylight is produced with the aid of a projector beaming rays through a window of the damp, rat-infested study, where the actor playing Faust is being forced to sleep. There the poor man sits in a medieval bathrobe (but wearing a false beard) eating his breakfast and reading a Petrograd newspaper. The Director angrily confiscates the newspaper, instructing the actor instead to study the ancient manuscript, an alchemical treatise on homunculi, which has been given to him so that he may better assimilate his role. The actor objects, stating that he entered into the acting profession because as a schoolboy he could not master chemistry, let alone alchemy. He is even more ruffled when the property man brings on a chalice filled with real poison which Faust is to drink in the course of the play. "Is this real poison?" asks the actor, trembling. "We do not engage in falsifications," the director proudly responds. Of course, the fact that it is real poison will force the actor to only pretend that he is drinking. In seeking to avoid falsification of material elements, the Producer and Director are forcing a falsification of the dramatic action. Despite the attempts that have been made to create a realistic atmosphere for the actor to soak up, Faust continues to play in a high tragic manner. "Sing with your back! Your back!" they instruct him. "Forget about the audience!"

Mephistopheles appears out of the hatch dressed according to the findings of the latest archeological research. No sooner does he appear than the actor playing Mephistopheles is relieved of the role. The Producer explains that a recent reading of Eckermann has convinced him that Mephistopheles is actually Faust's negative alter ego as in the relationship between the Devil and Ivan Karamazov.[61] Therefore, the Producer concludes, the actor playing Faust must also play Mephistopheles. The actor must sing both the tenor role of Faust and the basso role of Mephistopheles, struggling to imagine that the latter is his internal voice, "a voice from the other side." The Producer sees this as a real triumph:

> Henceforth, the problem of presenting Mephistopheles on the stage should be considered solved...without any of those antirealistic appearances from under the stage floor, fiery lighting effects and other such foolishness, unworthy of a serious theatre which adheres to the slogan, "everything as in life."

Evreinov is here aiming at two specific targets. In his article on *Faust* in the book *Conversations with Goethe* (*Razgovory s Goethe*) Fedor Komissarževskij wrote: "Mephistopheles in Goethe's tragedy *Faust* is for me the second 'I' of Faust. He is the devil, but a special devil, namely a Faustian devil.... I would even like it if the face and figure of Mephistopheles depicted onstage reminded me of Faust." Vasilij I. Kačalov, portraying Ivan Karamazov in Stanislavskij's 1910 production of *The Brothers Karamazov* at MXAT, converted Ivan's dialogue with the devil into a monologue. The critic Nikolaj E. Èfros, writing in his book *The Moscow Art Theatre 1898–1923* (Moskva-Petrograd, 1924) recalls: "Ivan spoke his own words and then those which in the novel are ascribed to the devil. This was a colossally difficult technical feat."[62] Evreinov had, of course, already offered a different and to his mind better solution. In monodrama, separate actors play the various characters but with make-up, costuming, *plastique*, deployment, vocal inflections, and scenic treatment making it clear that they are being presented as aspects of the protagonist or his perceptions of the world around him.

As the Producer and the Director continually exhort the actor playing Faust to forget about the audience, it becomes clear that the illusion of reality they seek to create is designed solely for the actor's benefit. The very notion of play and performance is distasteful to them. All of their directions are designed to wall up the presentation on the stage side of the footlights, to make the actor experience the role without conveying anything to the audience paying to see him perform it. The Director proposes in the interests of realism to permeate the theatre with "some kind of mixture which will transmit the smell of decrepitude, snuff, mothballs and some other things." This is to be done in an effort to bring the audience closer to Faust since the Director reasons, "old men always smell a little." (And so do old convention-bound theatres, Evreinov would suggest.)

The logical conclusion to this illogical process is to build a real wall along the curtain line. The audience will view all of the action of the play, which by this time amounts to very little, through a window in the wall. The Producer hails this as a brilliant idea, "the dawn of a new theatre!", a theatre freed from lies and compromises.

Unbeknown to the Producer and the Director, the Assistant Director, whose suggestion it was to build the fourth wall, was being facetious. In confessing the ruse to the Prompter and the Propman, the Assistant Director acknowledges that creating real art where fantasy and beauty reign is one thing, "but to render everything as in life is fraudulent imitation.... Any fool could do that!... What kind of art is that!" But what if it is an historical theme? asks the Prompter. The Assistant Director answers: "And what then are picture books for?... Now with every worthless archeological discovery they snap photographs and even print them in books!... That's not enough. You must know your basics."[63]

Thus, Evreinov characteristically returns to defend one of his basic positions, artistic reconstruction. There were those who tried to make his experiments at the Ancient Theatre look like exercises in archeological research and to tie his work to the MXAT school of stage naturalism. To those who misunderstood him and who persisted in interpreting his work in light of standard approaches to theatre, Evreinov offered a reminder that there were essential differences.

The second part of the play depicts the fruits of the production staff's labors over *Faust*. It is also a fairly typical example of Evreinov's writing for the theatre. His regular use of the play-within-a-play device is illustrated as the musicians enter in tuxedos and take their places in the orchestra pit of the actual theatre where *The Fourth Wall* is being performed. The Director appears a moment later in tuxedo and white gloves to announce to the audience that what they are about to see represents "the most glorious event in the universal history of dramatic art." He instructs the audience to "regard it with the kind of feeling which it justly deserves." Whatever the judgement, the Director expresses his satisfaction that they have fulfilled an important obligation: "an obligation not to prefer, in the end, the charms of theatrical deception over the truth of sober reality." Characteristically, Evreinov here hits two widely separate targets with a single shot, Stanislavskij's theatrical reverence and his own grandiloquent and even messianic proclamations concerning the theatre.

The Director exits, and the orchestra strikes up the overture to *Faust*, during which the curtain opens to reveal a second curtain. Here is depicted the image of Truth as a plain, pallid old woman, throwing off a wig before a mirror and stamping on a pile of masks with her feet. Shields are at both her sides, and there are laurels which bear the legends *Amicus Cato, sed magis amica Veritas* and "Eat Bread and Salt, and Speak the Truth." The overture ends, the conductor departs, and the second curtain rises.[64]

There on the stage stands the notorious fourth wall, built according to the latest archeological findings on sixteenth-century German architecture. The audience catches a glimpse of Faust through a window where light flickers from an oil lamp. A band of drunken artisans staggers by singing in ancient German. Faust sticks his head out the window, nods in the direction of the departed young people and, having become tearful at the soul-filling thoughts of youth, blows his nose loudly. Faust again disappears, and we are treated to a scene from daily life involving a street sweeper, a boy-ragamuffin intent on relieving himself on the wall of Faust's abode, and a homely woman who pours a bucket of slops, intended for the boy, from a second floor window on the unsuspecting sweeper. Some typical German burgher women appear with groceries, and the auditorium is filled with the smell of smoked fish, onions, and pork. Backstage the choir of drunks sings in German to the tune, "The flowers allure me with their beauty."

Margarita and Marta appear from stage right. They have been stripped of their customary operatic costumes and dressed in rags. Margarita is barefoot and carries a spinning wheel in her arms. Stopping beneath Faust's window, the two women converse in German. Faust, who has been drawn to his window by the sound of Margarita's sensual, coarse laughter, is holding the chalice of poison. Abruptly turning to the audience, he shouts, "I can't go on like this any longer!... Ladies and gentlemen, you are my witnesses!" He downs the chalice of poison and staggers back down into his study apparently to die.

Confusion breaks out onstage, and someone is heard to call for a doctor. The curtain quickly falls, and the Assistant Director, who has from the outset provided the only voice of reason, appears slightly inebriated. Standing before the curtain, he bows to the audience and clears his throat:

> And so, ladies and gentlemen, owing to the acute lunacy of the actor playing Faust, we are unable to continue with the opera...(He looks at the crib sheet in his hand.)...a fact which I hereby bring to the attention of our highly respected audience. (He bows and exits.)[65]

Evreinov on Wit and Humor

Evreinov considered himself a student of comedy, and his own theories greatly influenced the work done at the Crooked Mirror, which he called his "school of wit and laughter." Evreinov prided himself on the fact that his work as a director and dramatist embodied wit rather than purely comic values. The child laughs at something comic (in the sense of funny) for its own sake. Wit, however, is a more thoughtful sort of humor. It is the product of a refined, subtle, imaginative, and resourceful mind. Evreinov associates it with such qualities as style, taste, and originality, the qualities that distinguish the true artist, for example, himself, from the imitators, the dilettantes, and the workmanlike minds, such as Kugel', Driezen, and all too many others. Whereas wit depends on the element of surprise, mere amazement is sufficient in order for something to be funny. To be amazed or dumbfounded is a momentary and often automatic reaction, whereas the element of surprise entails reflection. He offers an etymological argument to further his point. The word for something funny or ridiculous in Russian is *smešnoj*. Evreinov suggests that this derives from the word for confusion, *smešenie*. Thus, he argues, the logic of wit is the logic of the sensible (thought), while the logic of the comic is the logic of the absurd, (confusion, amazement).[66]

Amazement is, according to Evreinov, the critical moment in our psyche that leads either to an ominous premonition of some unexpected unpleasantness and produces in us *anxiety* or to a realization that no threat or danger exists, which produces in us *joy*. The tension accompanying amazement will translate in the first instance into a shout or hysterics and in the second into laughter or even hysterical laughter. "Surprise," said Aleksandr Belenson (quoted by Evreinov), "is an insufficient reason for laughter! Amazement is another matter. When surprised we do not fall into a *state of confusion*. However, amazement always brings *confusion*."

In developing his theory of wit versus the comic, Evreinov drew heavily on the teachings of Sigmund Freud and especially Henri Bergson. Freud's discussion of art and humor as they relate to the subconscious struck a chord in Evreinov, whose theories of monodrama and the theatre for oneself covered similar ground. Freud had written (in *Jokes and Their Relationship to the Unconscious,* 1905) that thought covers itself with wit in order to attract our attention and so as to be able to convey to us with a minimum of stress something of value and significance. Wit must be regarded as a powerful factor, capable of tilting the scale in our unconscious from one side to another.

Evreinov stated, "there is no deadlier weapon than laughter," an insight that allied him with the philosophical position of Henri Bergson.[67] Bergson had called laughter a corrective, a remedy for vanity. But the real connection between Evreinov and Bergson lay in their perception of theatre as it relates to life. Bergson wrote that comedy "lies midway between art and life" and oscillates between the two. It is not disinterested because it "cannot by its very nature exist outside the pale of what is strictly human." He continued:

> A landscape may be beautiful, charming, and sublime, or insignificant and ugly; it will never be laughable. You may laugh at an animal, but only because you have detected in it some human attitude or expression. You may laugh at a hat, but what you are making fun of, in this case, is not the piece of felt or straw, but the shape that men have given it—the human caprice whose mould it has assumed.

To be comic one must sense a human presence, but to laugh at this presence one must be indifferent to it, and suspend one's emotion. Laughter's appeal is to the *intelligence* and is evoked, according to Bergson, by "the momentary transformation of a person into a thing." This process extends not only to some outside target of the humorist but back to the humorist himself. "When the humorist laughs at himself, he is really acting a double part; the self who laughs is indeed conscious, but not the self who is laughed at." Like Freud, Bergson suggested the inner reaches of comedy whereby the consciousness of the artist (in this case, the humorist) becomes fragmented in its relationship to reality, and emotion ebbs and flows according to the ratio of the comic to the serious. Evreinov found in both Bergson and Freud an understanding of the comic as a serious matter, the result of a systematic, psychological process. Individual statements by Bergson in his famous essay "Laughter" (1900), evoke the spirit and, in some cases, the letter of Evreinov's own theatrical positions. Bergson writes:

> There is something aesthetic about it [the comic], because it comes into being just when society and the individual, freed from worry of self-preservation, begin to regard themselves as *works of art* [my emphasis].
>
> . . . .
>
> It is only in its lower aspects, in light comedy and farce that comedy is in striking contrast to reality: the higher it rises the more it approximates life...the elements of comic character on the stage and in actual life will be the same.

Bergson's discussion of wit sealed the union between Evreinov's mode of thinking and his own.

> In the broader meaning of the word, it would seem that what is called wit is a certain *dramatic* way of thinking. Instead of treating his ideas as mere symbols, the wit sees them, he hears them, and above all, makes them converse with one another like persons. He puts them on the stage, and himself to some extent, into the bargain.

Bergson concluded that the poet can turn into a wit by simply resolving to be no longer a poet in feeling, but only in intelligence. Thus, Bergson not only ties wit to thought but to "a certain dramatic way of thinking," of seeing things *sub specie theatri*.

Bergson offered an explanation of the creative process that speaks directly to the monodrama of Nikolaj Evreinov:

> If the characters created by a poet give us the impression of life, it is only because they are the poet himself — a multiplication or division of the poet, the poet plumbing the depths of his own nature in so powerful an effort of inner observation that he lays hold of the potential in the real and takes up what nature has left as a mere outline or sketch in his soul in order to make it a finished work of art.[68]

Evreinov divided wit into *parody, satire, political caricature, living caricature (živaja karikatura)*, *burlesque*, and *grotesque*. He likewise catalogued the lower forms of comedy, such as *farce* (based as much on the vulgarly comic as on the vulgarly erotic), *vaudeville, musical comedy* and *operetta, circus clowning, music hall revues*, and *cabaret sketches*. Always playing the serious historical scholar, Evreinov listed the theatres he believed to have glorified the cult of wit:

1. The Theatre of Aristophanes
2. The Theatre of Atellan Farce
3. The Theatre of Adam de la Halle (thirteenth century, whose pastorale *Le Jeu de Robin et Marion* Evreinov produced at the Ancient Theatre)
4. The Theatre of Hans Sachs (sixteenth century)
5. The Theatre of French Farce (which developed in the eleventh and twelfth centuries from parodies on church liturgy and blossomed into a full-bodied genre in the sixteenth and seventeenth centuries with the appearance of some five thousand farces)
6. The Theatre of Italian Comedy (the *commedia dell'arte* of the sixteenth and seventeenth centuries, which heavily influenced Molière)
7. Puppet and marionette theatre (growing out of the ancient theatre and receiving its concrete form in the commedia dell'arte. Evreinov made special note of Punchinello in Italy, Punch in England, Hanswurst in Germany, Karagez in the Near East, and Russia's own Petruška. He wrote a play entitled *Karagez*, which he directed at the Crooked Mirror Theatre during the 1915-16 season.)
8. The Theatre of Jacques Offenbach (sixteenth century) (Kugel' compared the fate of the Crooked Mirror Theatre to that of the operetta of Offenbach. In its theatrical parodies, the Crooked Mirror laughed at the feelings, ideals, and virtues that inspired the old theatre. Then, as happened with Offenbach, the idea was vulgarized by imitators.)
9. And naturally, the Crooked Mirror Theatre itself, which in Evreinov's opinion developed new forms of satirical art and offered subtle craftsmanship.[69]

The Crooked Mirror made its greatest contribution in the realm of parody. More specifically, the Crooked Mirror excelled in the creation of synthetic parody by which Evreinov meant satirizing the play not just as written but as it was usually performed. He offered the following list of parodied forms that were favored at the Crooked Mirror:

1. melodrama — *Jaques Nuar* by N. N. Urvancev; *The Handkerchief of the Baroness* (*Nosovoj platok baronessy*) by B. F. Gejer
2. operetta — *Love's Delights* (*Vostorgi ljubvi*) by V. G. Èrenberg
3. ballet — *The Enchanted and Disenchanted Forest* by Lev Geben; *La Dame aux camélias* by Alexandre Dumas *fils* Music by Giuseppe Verdi. Dances by Ikar

4. vaudeville—*Vasil' Vasil'ič Reconciled* (*Vasil' Vasil'ič pomirilsja*) by Lev Urvancev
5. Ibsen's dramaturgy—*The Veterinarian (Veterinarnyj vrač)* by Lev Urvancev[70]
6. Cinematic drama—*A Victim of Love's Passion* (*Žertva ljubovnoj strasti*) or *The Adventures of an Unhappy Worker (Priključenija nesčastnoj rabotnicy)* by B. F. Gejer
7. Plays from the Repertory of the Community Center Temperance Society—*The Moral Bases of Man* (*Nravstvennye osnovy čeloveka*)by N. Smirnov and S. S. Ščerbakov
8. "Potboilers" (*Xalturnye spektakli*)—*The Riddle and the Solution* (*Zagadka i razgadka*) by Traxtenberg; *A Wonderful Presentation* (*Zamečatel'noe predstavlenie*) by Mancenilov; *Ryčalov's Tour* by Mancenilov (M. N. Volkonskij)
9. Russian opera—*Don't Shoot Your Mouth off Before Going into Battle* (*Ne xvalis iduci na rat'*) by Il'ja Sac
10. "Realistic" opera—*The Action Surrounding a Disputed Promissory Note and the Court Order Concerning It* (*Dejstvo o protestovannom veksele i ispolnitel'nomu po onomu liste*) by Vladimir Azov; *A Sweet Pastry* (*Sladkij pirog*) by Lev Urvancov and N. N. Evreinov; *The Fourth Wall* by N. N. Evreinov
11. Farce—*To the Accompaniment of a Trombone* (*Pod zvuki trombona*) by K. N. Saxarov
12. Futurist dramaturgy—*Sausage from Butterflies* (*Kolbasa iz baboček*) by N. G. Smirnov and S. S. Ščerbakov.
13. Leading figures in Russian dramaturgy—*The Evolution of the Theatre* by B. F. Gejer
14. Leading directors—*The Inspector General* by N. N. Evreinov
15. The comedic conventions of different peoples—*A Feast of Laughter* or *The World Contest of Wit* by N. N. Evreinov
16. Pulp literature (*Lubočnye proizvdenija*)—*Eastern Delights* (*Vostočnye sladosti*), an opera caricature (*opera-šarž*)by Il'ja Sac[71]

Evreinov sought to clarify the concept of the grotesque, which he felt had been clouded by the vague definitions of others. He likened the grotesque to "gallows humor" or "black comedy," of which there were examples in the repertory of the Crooked Mirror Theatre. He cited his own play, *The Foundation of Happiness,* as representative of this genre.

A major problem in defining the grotesque is that it does not seem to have any reference points outside of its own highly original idiosyncratic realm. It does not conform to any laws. Evreinov believed that the grotesque should carry within itself a comic effect. Our understanding of the grotesque has been confused by such Russian "originals" (Evreinov's word) as Mejerxol'd, who viewed it as not only comic in its effect, but tragic as well. The works of artists such as Goya and Poe, which have been referred to as "tragic grotesques" are, according to Evreinov, nothing more than nightmarish fantasies. Fantastic terror is not embodied in the grotesque. The grotesque is always aimed at eliciting laughter, which is dependent upon the element of amazement. Amazement results when the listener or spectator is prepared for a serious or even tragic ending but encounters a comic one instead. A contrast in form and content will result in a comic effect, and so it too is essential to the grotesque. It is not surprising that Evreinov viewed paradox as an essential element of the grotesque. Another element basic to the grotesque as well as to caricature and parody is that of taboo. Evreinov claimed that his production of Oscar Wilde's *Salomé* at the Dramatic Theatre of V. F. Komissarževskaja (1908) was the first example in Russia of an approach he called "the grotesque as such" (*grotesk, kak takovoj*). As with "the theatre as such," this concept implies exploring the very essence of the grotesque for its own sake rather than for any value it might possess as an element in various art forms.

In exploring the realm of the grotesque, how far can public mockery, ridicule, and offense be taken? Where must the line be drawn beyond which laughter cannot pass? Evreinov responded that there are no such borders in the realm of the grotesque so long as the mode of presentation remains *uslovnyj*. *Uslovnost'* frees the grotesque from taboo.[72] In the end Evreinov succeeded only in giving an impression of what he meant by the grotesque without ever really defining it.

Evreinov also examined the meaning of "parody," again drawing heavily on Freud and Bergson. He argued that imitation of a model is nearly always comic, especially when the imitator pretends to some authority. "The occasion of the ludicrous is the *degradation* of some person or interest possessing dignity." Evreinov invoked Freud and Alexander Bain (*Emotions and the Will*, 1859) to support his case. He might also have looked to Bergson who wrote: "To imitate anyone is to bring out the element of automatism he has allowed to creep into his person. And as this is the very essence of the ludicrous, it is no wonder that imitation gives rise to laughter."

Bergson based his theory of laughter and the comic on the idea of automatism and its characteristic devices of repetition, inversion, and the reciprocal interference of series. Imitation, stasis, petrification, and the like contribute to the production of automatism. Thus, one begins with Pascal's maxim: "Two faces that are alike, although neither of them excites laughter by itself, make us laugh when together, on account of their likeness." Repetition makes us laugh, and one form of repetition is disguise, in which man attempts to become unlike himself and like someone else. Society at large may engage in disguise, in which case this social masquerade will be laughable and a fit target for parody. Any ceremony or convention becomes comic when we focus our attention solely on the ceremonial element within it, that is, its form, and forget about its content. In so doing, we forget the serious object of the ceremony or occasion and begin to view those who are taking part in it as puppets or automatons. In short, "something mechanical encrusted upon the living," will always be laughable and comic. Since parody, according to Bergson, is nearly always comic, it grows up in the same fertile soil of the automatistic, the pretentious, and the conventional.[73]

Evreinov did not, however, agree with Bergson on all points. In fact he questioned Bergson's definition of comedy in terms of automatism, borrowing his argument from the critic Vladimir M. Vol'kenstein. Bergson had said that one way in which automatism results in comedy is when people relate to others as if they were marionettes. Vol'kenstein argued that while this may be true in vaudeville, it is not the case in *Othello*, where Iago cruelly manipulates the hero in just such a way. The result here is horrific rather than comic.

There is a similar weakness in Bergson's argument concerning repetition as a comic element. While it is true that the repetition of the same scene with groups of different characters is comical in Molière's *George Dandin,* it is not at all so when Macbeth repeats the same action, murdering Duncan, then Banquo, and finally attempts but fails to murder Macduff. Again the effect is horrific.

Bergson asserts that the automatism of a character blindly pursuing his ideals is comical, giving Don Quixote as an example. True, says Vol'kenstein, but one could cite Calderón's constant prince, whose blind pursuit of his ideal results in tragedy. Thus, Vol'kenstein concludes, the idea of automatism is not comic in and of itself.[74]

Evreinov conceded that Vol'kenstein was persuasive when he criticized Bergson. However, Evreinov was concerned with getting to the root of the concepts with which he worked in the process of transforming theories of art into works of art. His dissatisfaction with Bergson as well as with Vol'kenstein stemmed from the fact that, in the final analysis, neither could clearly explain to him the essence of the comic, what specifically causes it, what must be there in order for it to develop. His entire philosophy of the theatre derived from this same search for the essence of the art, its source and its character.

The soul of parody is irony, and this, more than anything else, was the flame in which the Crooked Mirror scalpel was tempered. The object of parody, argued Evreinov, citing formalist critic and historian Jurij Tynjanov for support, is to penetrate to the "second plane" of a form or work of art (as for example, those listed by Evreinov) and to illuminate it using irony as a tool.[75] This concept of the "second plane" is reminiscent of Bergson's statement:

> Art has no other object than to brush aside the utilitarian symbols, the conventional and socially accepted generalities, in short, everything that veils reality from us, in order to bring us face to face with reality itself.... Art is only a more direct vision of reality.[76]

The symbolists were at this time engaged in a somber, poetic search for *realiora*, the inner, transcendent reality. Evreinov alternated between two moods, the comic and the serious, in his own search for ultimate reality.

Evreinov's references to Jurij N. Tynjanov (1894–1943) tells us something significant about his level of scholarly ambition if not expertise and his ability to recognize ideas from other disciplines close enough to his in spirit to be fit into his grand design for theatre. Tynjanov's sense of a literary work was as a "dynamic integration" rather than "a close symmetrical whole." Instead of being fixed in a form, he theorized, literature mutates periodically, making the boundary between itself and life fluid. "Literature never mirrors life," Tynjanov states in his highly influential *Archaists and Innovators* (*Arxaisty i novatory*, Leningrad, 1928), "but it often overlaps with it." He speaks in terms that at times strike quite close to Evreinov's theory of theatre in life. Thus in his *Problem of Verse Language* (*Problema stixotvornogo jazyka*, 1923), Tynjanov writes:

> I do not deny the existence of the links between literature and life. I merely doubt whether the problem is posed correctly. Can we talk about "life vs. art," when art too, is life? Do we need to prove the social usefulness of art, if we do not bother to demonstrate the usefulness of life?

In his *Gogol' and Dostoevskij. Toward a Theory of Parody* (*Gogol' i Dostoevskij. K teorii parodii*, Petrograd, 1921), the work to which Evreinov is referring in his argument, Tynjanov discusses the role of parody and stylization in bringing about literary change. Victor Erlich, in explaining Tynjanov's view of parody, makes him sound, unintentionally of course, very much like a *krivozerkalec* and as a defender of the Evreinov modus operandi. He writes: "By poking fun at a specific set of conventions which tend to degenerate into stale clichés the artist paves the way for a new, more "perceptible" set of conventions—a new style." Parody was to Tynjanov, in Erlich's terms, "a sign of emancipation, indeed an act of literary warfare."[77]

Evreinov differed with Jurij Tynjanov on two key points concerning the nature of parody. Tynjanov said that from stylization to parody is but one small step, that stylization when justified or underlined in a comic manner becomes parody. Evreinov argued that stylization is in fact, the opposite of parody.[78] He subscribed to Mejerxol'd's definition of stylization. Mejerxol'd worte in *On Theatre (O teatre,* 1913): "To 'stylize' a given period or phenomenon means to employ every possible means of expression in order to reveal the inner synthesis of that period or phenomenon, to bring out those hidden features which are to be found deeply embedded in the style of any work of art."[79] Evreinov maintained that to make this definition complete one need only add reference to the artist's subjective understanding of these "hidden features" in the work being stylized.

The distance between parody and stylization, argued Evreinov, is a good deal greater than that between stylization and the grotesque, which have caricature in common. Evreinov countered critics who claimed that parody could be noncomic or even tragic in content and effect. The comic and the tragic, he said, spring from different sources. They embody contradictory architectonics, and under no conditions can their goals and the manner in which they are realized onstage be confused.[80]

In distinguishing between parody on the one hand and stylization, caricature, and the grotesque, on the other, as well as in seeking to purge the concept of parody of impure and inaccurate claims, Evreinov had a definite purpose in mind. His idea was to make a case for parody as the highest form of wit, thus ennobling the efforts of the Crooked Mirror Theatre, and specifically his own at this theatre, which were given over almost exclusively to work in this particular genre. Parody is after all the most self-conscious of literary modes, merging, as Robert Alter reminds us, creation with critique. This is the particular knife point upon which Evreinov perenially liked to balance, appealing as it did to his desire for distorted scale, elevation, and heightened danger.[81]

Evreinov's efforts to devise a theory which would define the phenomena of wit and humor only serve to dramatize once again his shortcomings as a theatre philosopher in the narrow sense. He balances the theories of various psychologists and philosophers, addressing himself to aspects of these theories which he likes or does not like. But this eclecticism does not constitute a philosophical position in itself as Evreinov would have us believe. His "show me" attitude vis-à-vis the attempts by other theorists to define the nature of the comic moves him no closer to finding a definition of his own.

The Waning Years

The Crooked Mirror suspended operations in 1918 because of the civil war then raging in Russia. The theatre was hit hard by the mobilization, losing many of its actors to the army. It did not reopen its doors until 1922.

David Zolotnickij credits the Moscow theatre of small forms, the Crooked Jimmy (*Krivoj Džimmi*, 1921-24, located in the former premises of the Bat) with persuading Kugel' and Xolmskaja to reopen their theatre. On 27 September 1922, the Crooked Jimmy announced that Evreinov would serve as its chief director, an arrangement that lasted no more than three months. Several of Evreinov's plays were mounted here, including *In the Stage-Wings of the Soul* with Crooked Mirror actor S. I. Antimonov in the role of the professor (a number of Crooked Mirror actors were employed in this theatre), *Such a Woman*, with M. N. Morskaja and A. P. Čaadaevaja in major roles, and *A Columbine of Today*, directed by M. G. Dyskovskij, with E. D. Lenskaja as Columbine and D. L. Kara-Dmitriev as Pierrot. In addition, the Crooked Jimmy began staging old Crooked Mirror hits such as *Vampuka* and N. N. Urvancov's *Jacques Nuar and Henri Zaverni*. As a result, the Crooked Mirror reopened on 30 December 1922, in the uncomfortable former Pavlova Hall at Troickaja, 13, Petrograd (the Ekaterininskij Theatre was no longer available).[82] In the 1923-24 season the theatre was in residence at the *Slavjanskij Bazaar* in Moscow. Kryžickij wrote that the company played the old repertoire but in a new tone which was not at first successful. (He did not elaborate on the nature of this "new tone.") However, the theatre as always met with success on its tours of the Russian provinces, which it now resumed.

In 1924 Kugel' invited Evreinov, who had left the Crooked Mirror following the 1916-17 season, to rejoin the theatre for a tour of Warsaw and, if successful, other European capitals. The tour was a disaster. Some members of the Russian émigré press in Poland viewed the tour as a Soviet propaganda ploy, while others sought to persuade the company to defect. Relations between Kugel' and Evreinov were strained. The "orthodox" Crooked Mirror program, consisting of *Vampuka, Ryčalov's Tour, The Evolution of the Theatre,* and the like, was largely boycotted by the public, which had been biased against the theatre by the press.

Kugel' waged a personal campaign to villify Evreinov in the Soviet press. He claimed that upon the arrival of the theatre in Poland, Evreinov announced that he did not intend to return to Russia and abandoned the troupe without any means of support. This, said Kugel', incited the Russian émigrés and the anti-Soviet press all the more to urge the company to defect en masse. Kugel' reported that he and the collective refused and that he arranged with the Soviet government for the company's return to Leningrad. And so, concluded Kugel', to the derisive cries of the counterrevolutionaries and the white émigré collective, the Crooked Mirror returned home. Kugel''s defense of his own actions and the accusations which he levelled at Evreinov must be considered suspect. The political climate of the day apparently did contribute to the failure of the tour, but so too did the depreciated quality of the Crooked Mirror's work.

Fall 1925 found the Crooked Mirror in residence in the basement of the former Palace Theatre in Leningrad, where it remained for six years. Many of the theatre's older members felt a strong attachment to Moscow and so had quit and were replaced by Leningrad youths. Fenin, Jarockaja, and Antimonov were among those of the old cadre who elected to stay in Moscow. The company at this time included V. Lepko, F. Polvjanov, A. Vetvenickaja, S. Raxmanova, L. Kop'ev, A. Šubin, A. Avvakumov, P. Strigušenko, Maria Ponna, and Aleksandr Kaverzin. Kugel' and Xolmskaja were still at the helm, but Evreinov had stayed abroad. The directors then on staff were N. N. Urvancov, N. M. Forreger, A. V. Šubin, and G. K. Kryžickij. Rounding out the staff, Nestor Surin replaced Jurij Annenkov, who had emigrated in 1924, as the theatre's designer, and D. Astradancev took over the musical direction from Gejer and Èrenberg, who had died. Two of the theatre's older authors, N. G. Smirnov and S. S. Ščerbakov, stayed on, working together with young Soviet writers.

The remainder of the theatre's career was rather lackluster when compared with its former successes. Some of the latter were again pressed into duty—*Vampuka, Ryčalov's Tour, The Fate of a Man, In the Stage-Wings of the Soul, The School of the Stars* among them. Evreinov's parody version of *The Inspector General* was revised to include more topical targets for parody.

The theatre produced a series of failures until several satires on Soviet life and rule brought it a measure of success. *A Decree on the Abolition of Love* (*Dekret ob otmene ljubvi*) by N. G. Smirnov, directed by G. K. Kryžickij, was a burlesque set in the twenty-first century, which confronted the question of how and where human feelings fit into the new Soviet order. *The Legalization of Daily Life* (*Oformlenie byta*) by K. Mazovskij, directed by N. N. Urvancov, satirized old church rituals.

Theatrical parody remained the favorite genre at the Crooked Mirror. The mid-1920s witnessed the widespread reworking of librettos from old operas. This tendency was parodied in the Crooked Mirror's production of *Arzanaja's Love* (*Ljubov' Arzanaja*) with music by A. Curmilen. Other theatrical parodies then in the repertory were *Woe from Wit*, written in the then modish "criminal jargon." and *Among the Red Muscovities* (*U krasnyx moskovitov*), which illustrated how Soviet life is depicted in French theatre. Kryžickij adapted a Japanese work into a two-act tragicomedy entitled *Apple Blossom (Cvet jablonnyj)*, which utilized such devices of the oriental theatre as the "unseen" prop and costume-changers. Rounding out the repertory were the pantomime *The Monastic Gardener,* based upon Boccaccio's *Decameron,* for which Kugel' wrote the libretto; two successful vaudevilles, *The Quick-Witted Stockingmakers* (*Soobrazitel'nye čuločnicy*) and *The Renounced Fiancés (Zarečatannye* ženixi), both on contemporary themes; a witty comedy of student life, *Love with a Bird Cherry* (*Ljubov' s čeremuxoj*) by N. G. Smirnov and S. S. Ščerbakov; another in the continuing tradition of conferences (*zasedanija*), this one entitled *A Solemn Conference on the Question of Economic Policies* (*Toržestvennoe zasedanie po voprosu o režime èkonomii*).[82]

A. R. Kugel' died in 1928 and so, for all intents and purposes, did the Crooked Mirror Theatre. Its doors remained open until 1931, but it lacked inspiration and effective leadership. According to A. G. Avvakumov, an actor in the company at this time, the government did not close the Crooked Mirror; it closed itself. The directors of the theatre decided that it was no longer necessary. What was necessary was "Soviet satire." Without consulting the company as a whole, the directors selected those actors they wanted for the future theatre of satire. O. N. Malozemova, an actress who specialized in balletic presentations at the Crooked Mirror, stated that the theatre of small forms did not die out, but rather evolved into the Soviet political theatre of small forms. But this was another era with different goals and sensibilities.[83]

The Crooked Mirror had served its times well. It provided thoughtful laughter for the frustrated Russian intelligentsia in the years of reaction, employing irony to point out the grotesqueries and trivialities of social life. The actor N. N. Xodotov wrote: "In the years of reaction [the Crooked Mirror] made us feel the absurdity of our everyday life. It lashed out at dullness, conceit, and complacency. It mocked...the hypocrisy of the bureaucratic system of ranks and always pushed and summoned us forward."

The major artistic importance of the crooked Mirror Theatre lay in its development of the parody genre. Work was, of course, being done in this area in France, Germany, Italy, and elsewhere prior to the Crooked Mirror. But whereas many of these theatres parodied individual works, the Crooked Mirror pursued a particular direction in art. Experimentation in subject matter and written forms proceeded alongside the development of new scenic forms. As Kugel' stated, the Crooked Mirror may not have invented a new psychological law for humor, but it did conceive new and interesting means for presenting humor on the stage.

The Crooked Mirror taught lessons regarding the relativity of human perception, an idea close to Evreinov's heart. G. K. Kryžickij credited the Crooked Mirror with "battling philistinism in life, routine and tastelessness in art, [and] standing up for realism in the tough skirmishes with the pseudo-innovators, decadents, naturalists, and futurists." The Crooked Mirror cultivated a new genre of comic literature built on bold grotesque and caricature that took the comic to the limit. Evreinov compared it to the miniature engraving, which in the smallest possible space makes things stand out in bold relief.[84]

Mozart and Salieri, Again

There are a number of indicators which could be cited to reflect the influence of Evreinov's leadership on the development of the Crooked Mirror Theatre as a producing body. Evreinov's carefully thought-out theoretical positions helped to create a unified, consistent framework within which productions could be conceived. His skills as a director, dramatist, and composer helped to shape the theatre's repertory to a great extent. Certainly one indication of the theatre's growth under Evreinov's guidance is the fact that the vast majority of its most successful productions were staged during his tenure. A list of these productions with the lengths of their runs, according to Evreinov's recollection, follows:

Vampuka   1909-17
Ryčalov's Tour   1911-17
The Four Corpses of Fiametta   1911-16
The Inspector General (Evreinov's version)   1912-17
In the Stage-Wings of the Soul   1912-17
The Cinematograph   1911-15
A Solemn Public Conference in Memory of Koz'ma Prutkov   1913-17
The Riddle and the Solution   1909-12
Jacques Nuar   1909-12
The Enchanted and Disenchanted Forest   1909-12
Reminiscences   1909-12
Love's Delights   1909-11
Don't Shoot Your Mouth off Before Going into Battle   1910-12
About Ballet in Ancient Times   1910-12
Model Spouses   1915-17
The Fate of a Man   1915-17
Grae-grae-voropae   1910-11
A Wonderful Presentation   1910-11
Eastern Delights   1911-12
The Moral Bases of Man   1911-12
The School of the Stars   1911-12
A Columbine of Today   1915-16[85]

Of the plays listed above, Evreinov directed fourteen, wrote six, and composed the music for one. All but seven of the productions listed premiered during his tenure as artistic director of the theatre. Under Evreinov's leadership the Crooked Mirror greatly expanded its repertoire and assembled its own stable of writers, many of whom were also actors, who created original, contemporary works.[86]

The Crooked Mirror's popularity, like that of the Ancient Theatre, was limited to certain circles. Many observers, including Evreinov, made reference to the aloofness of Petersburg audiences. Petersburg residents prided themselves on their refined taste and high level of culture. Evreinov's arguments regarding the subtlety of parody as a genre notwithstanding, the Crooked Mirror's brand of humor did not suit everyone. Aleksandr Dejč (whose adaptation of Gogol''s short story, "The Nose," premiered at the Crooked Mirror in October 1915) wrote that while each success brought new luster to the Crooked Mirror, the amount of actual attention it drew decreased. The small auditorium on the Ekaterininskij canal was not always filled.[87]

The tours the Crooked Mirror made of the provinces were continually successful. However, the Crooked Mirror was entirely unique and at times somewhat confusing to the populace of the towns it toured. Many small-town audiences were not aware that this was a theatre of satire. As a result, one schoolteacher wrote a letter to the newspapers in which he complained that in the Crooked Mirror production he saw the actors mixed up the text, lost their wigs onstage, struck absurd poses, and in some moments seemed to fall asleep. This, he complained, was not what he expected from a realistic production.[88]

It seems paradoxical that the more cultured Petersburg audiences would not find the parodies at the Crooked Mirror more congenial than the less knowing provincial audiences did, although the theatre certainly had supporters among the critics and intelligentsia in Petersburg as well as detractors in the provinces. But the Crooked Mirror was a strange hybrid, blending high purpose and subtle humor with often primitive production values and broad performance. Then too the satirist is often least loved by those most likely to understand him.

Evreinov maintained throughout that Kugel' envied him, his talents and his successes at the Crooked Mirror Theatre. Kugel' was, said Evreinov, a failed dramatist, and a dilettante as a director and philosopher of the theatre. Evreinov pointed out that Kugel' did not conceive of one original theory, whereas he (Evreinov) was responsible for several, including monodrama, theatricality, and reconstructivism. Kugel' did not understand the director's work and the idea that style dictates the logic of the production. His orientation to the stage was completely theoretical. Xolmskaja, on the other hand, did understand, having been for many years a talented actress and a woman of taste. Kugel', according to Evreinov, never realized that directing involves special mastery, the ability to carefully create and plan a mise-en-scène prior to the start of the rehearsal process. When he directed, Kugel' was all too willing to listen to and to accept the suggestions and improvisations of actors in rehearsal. The director's word, according to Evreinov, must be law.[89] This image of Kugel' as the actor's fool is disputed by L. S. Ljubaševskij. He describes Kugel' as having been a menacing presence in rehearsals with his Assyro-Babylonian head of hair and beard and ever-present walking stick. Kugel' was, he maintains, respected by the actors, of whom he demanded the utmost and who gave it to him rather than risk being made the targets for his fearsome temper. However, Ljubaševskij was with the company and observed Kugel' only during the 1922–23 season, some five years after Evreinov's departure.[90] Kryžickij, who also worked with Kugel' during this period, said of him, "Himself a director-hater, he became a director-despot."

Kryžickij refutes the claim that Evreinov was the moving force at the Crooked Mirror Theatre, asserting that the reins of power lay in Kugel''s hands. Kryžickij admits that "without a doubt he [Evreinov] brought quite a bit to the work of the theatre." He calls Evreinov a cultured man of solid erudition, although his theoretical positions were based on erroneous concepts. Nevertheless, he had excellent taste, inventiveness, imagination, a keen wit, and refined sense of humor. Kryžickij also credits Evreinov with having had a greater capacity to "fall in love" with the actor during the work process than Mejerxol'd. However, his ability to fall in love with the actor did not mean that Evreinov could work with him. He was able to conceive an interesting production concept with which to captivate the actors, but never having been an actor himself (actually he had been one for a short time), he could not show the actor what he wanted. Kryžickij quotes Kugel' to the effect that Evreinov was particularly good at imparting a witty form to the thoughts of another.

Despite the imperfect reliability of these reports, one nevertheless senses the possibility that Kugel' and Evreinov ultimately differed less from one another than either would have wished to believe.

Evreinov claimed that Kugel' resisted his efforts to hire for the Crooked Mirror Theatre the new wave of scene designers whose work he (Evreinov) had introduced at the Ancient Theatre. Kugel', who Evreinov considered had no understanding of scenic elements, distrusted them explaining that they hindered the play of the actors.

Kugel' resented Evreinov's claim that he was responsible for making the Crooked Mirror Theatre into a self-sustaining enterprise, arguing that the theatre had already become one prior to Evreinov's entrance on the scene.[91] Evreinov and Kugel' were each demanding and difficult personalities with a history of conflict. Only one man was a more frequent target for Kugel''s criticism than Evreinov and that was Evreinov's nemesis, Mejerxol'd. Nevertheless, Kugel' admitted to having a weak spot for Evreinov. He was, after all, a charming man, but Kugel' felt that he indulged him too much. This mistake, he said, allowed Evreinov to become vain and light-minded. Kugel' never denied that Evreinov was exceptionally gifted, but he thought Evreinov could never understand that the art of the theatre is only successful when individual wills are kept in check and coordinated for the good of the collective. Kugel' stated that in his last attempts to work with Evreinov, the latter was too engaged in erecting an altar to himself to be able to collaborate.

Kugel' asserts that Evreinov never understood why his tenure as artistic director of the Crooked Mirror Theatre was the most creative period of his life and why he could not duplicate this success in other theatres. It was, said Kugel', the intellectually stable environment at the Crooked Mirror Theatre that made Evreinov's best work possible. Evreinov admitted to having spent the best years of his creative life at the Crooked Mirror Theatre (1910–17) but said that he did so in spite of Kugel's presence and not because of it.[92]

The accounts offered by both men are suspect and certainly exaggerated. It should be remembered that Evreinov offered the same complaint—the exploitation and misunderstanding of the creative artist by the boorish organizer—in his conflict with Baron Driezen at the Ancient Theatre.

Evreinov's stint as artistic director of the Crooked Mirror Theatre proved beneficial to both the artist and the enterprise. Beyond his practical work in various capacities, he set a course for the theatre that embodied high artistic ideals. In return, Evreinov was given a forum in which to express his ideas and a laboratory in which to turn these ideas into theatrical realities. In a letter to the Chekhov Publishing House in New York dated 25 March 1953, Evreinov discussed his memoirs, *In the School of Wit (V škole ostroumija)* which he was still completing. Evreinov said of the Crooked Mirror:

> During my seven years' work in the theatre, I developed not only my art as a writer and director of satire but a full understanding of those theoretical bases on which should rest the teaching of "comical" phenomena—an understanding which drew me nearer to the secret of wherein lies the essence of wit.[93]

Again we return to Evreinov's preoccupation with essence. In seeking to find the essence of laughter, the comic, and the theatre, Evreinov hoped to uncover nothing less than "the secret of true happiness on earth." In order to be really happy, man must be able to define accurately life's priorities, to separate essences from extraneous elements. It is a theme to which Evreinov returned in nearly all of his plays (most notably, in *The Chief Thing*) and which underlay his theoretical, historical, and quasi-philosophical works. But while his practical work in the theatre helped him to sense where these essences lay, it seems that Evreinov never succeeded in defining them.

Aside from its importance in the overall scheme of his directorial work, the Crooked Mirror gave Evreinov the opportunity to express a vital part of his artistic personality. If anything saved Evreinov from being dragged down by his own pretense, it was his highly ironic sense of humor. It is no accident that Evreinov spoke of both humor and theatricality as seasonings. Each whets our appetite for life and in this sense is vital to the health and fulfillment of man. Perhaps even more than this, however, Evreinov's whetting of our appetite is a tease predicated on the belief that theatre and life both habitually send us away from the table less than satiated. The Crooked Mirror Theatre was itself a kind of refined, delightful tease perpetrated by some skilled and intelligent artists engaged in serious play. The Crooked Mirror parodies were in a sense calculated sorties into the theatre of truth and commitment. The purpose of the Crooked Mirror's work was to expose pretense, outmoded conventions, antitheatrical abstractions and to experiment with alternatives. However, there was never any real program for reform of the theatre or society at large.

The Crooked Mirror Theatre was a good place for Evreinov-Xlestakov, that infernal "incognito," to exercise his ways and means. Travelling in a realm of sanctioned transformation and paradox, of quick-change artistry, he could blend his concerns for a time with an organization that at least seemed to be moving in the same direction as he. In fact, Evreinov used this opportunity to experiment with his beloved essences in his very own laboratory of wit and humor, even as the rest of the theatre's staff played with forms and themes. Here, Evreinov, like the satyr holding the mirror up to his face in the Crooked Mirror logo (see fig. 27), could continue to offer his audience a series of masks in lieu of a true self. In this he succeeded only too well.

7

The Storming of the Winter Palace and After

At first glance, *The Storming of the Winter Palace* seems something of an anomaly in the pattern of Evreinov's theory and practice. Evreinov's work glorified individuality, and he espoused no cause more fervently than himself. Evreinov could no more subscribe to a political faith than he could a formal religious one. Such a commitment would mean submerging his own identity in the collective and more than this, abnegating his own self-appointed mission.

Why then did Evreinov become involved with so blatantly political an enterprise and so alien a form as the Soviet mass spectacle? The image of Evreinov directing a paean to the proletariat, to industrialization and political revolution is confusing only if one assumes that his perception of the spectacle's function coincided with that of the Soviet government. Needless to say, it did not. The nature of the Soviet mass spectacle was such that it brought together parties with antithetical points of view in a marriage of convenience. But for Evreinov there was no compromise.

Two centuries after the changes wrought by Tsar Petr I, whom Evreinov had named "the Great Transformer," there came the greatest transformation in Russian history, — the Revolution of 1917. This transformation also had a hero, Vladimir Il'ič Lenin, but unlike Petr, he had a large cast of supporting players. The proclaimed goal of the Revolution was the exaltation of the masses instead of the individual, the so-called dictatorship of the proletariat. The Revolution illustrated what Evreinov had long argued, that human life is in itself dramatic and that the boundary between the theatre and life is insubstantial.

The first years following the Revolution saw a number of efforts to theatricalize the life of the masses and to portray a new mass hero who would lead Russia into a new era of prosperity in a classless society. Huntly Carter, an English drama critic who visited Russia during this period, romantically and somewhat ingenuously saw the new theatre in the process of developing as a

> positivist church in which the people as a whole undergo conversion to a positivist faith as enunciated by the bolshevist leaders. The stage is an altar on which is sacrificed the old social evil in order to purge the community of unrighteousness that they may enter upon a new epoch animated by the new spirit.

The Bolševiks realized that the theatre was a powerful means of influencing the masses, and, so the masses were encouraged by their leaders to think in theatrical terms. But it was clear that the theatre of the pre-Revolutionary years would no longer do. As early as 1908, Anatolij Lunačarskij, who in the Soviet period became the first People's Commissar of Enlightenment, called for

> a theatre of rapid action, major passions, rare contrasts, whole characters, powerful sufferings, and lofty ecstasy. Yes, it will be a theatre of ideas. [This ideal] new theatre will get rid of nuances, details, and all the flavors needed by the refined and hysterical palates of our "cultured" public. It will thunder, glitter, be noisy, rapid-flying, and crude both for the nervous young ladies and the soured "cream" of society. Its satire will strike one's cheeks loudly: its woe will make one sob. Its joy will make one forget himself and dance; its villainy will be terrifying.

Lunačarskij believed that the theatre of the future would be a barbarian theatre, for "the salvation of civilization is in its barbarians. They are the bearers of real culture; they discover the light, long paths, while the so-called rotten society withers away."[1] The time for that real culture had now come.

The masses, for their part, had adopted the theatre as a means of escaping the hardships and uncertainties of life. But it was no longer enough for the people to sit passively and watch a theatrical performance. After all, they had been responsible for the creation of the major theatrical event in Russian history. They wanted to argue and to shout at the performers and, even more, to be performers themselves.

The people and their leaders both desired a life-centered theatre, the people in the interests of greater liberation and the leaders in the interests of greater control. The Bolševik leaders conceived of the new mass theatre not as pageantry in the Western European sense (although such pageants were studied) but as a means of encouraging the people to fight the battles of the Revolution over again. In the process of theatricalizing their own lives, the masses were also keeping the spirit of the Revolution alive and reabsorbing its lessons.

The earliest mass spectacles theatricalized revolutions, historical and contemporary. While the Bolševik leaders challenged the past, they still looked to it to provide romantic revolutionary heroes such as the seventeenth- and eighteenth-century peasant rebellion leaders Stepan Razin and Emeljan Pugačev. The largest of the mass sepctacles involved imitations of actual victorious battles. They were held in the open air with simple scenarios and a certain amount of improvised action. Professionals from the theatre and opera were joined by soldiers, government representatives, workers, and peasants who performed against the backdrop of a large public building such as the Winter Palace or the Stock Exchange. Scenery was usually primitive in style. Vehicles were stopped and used as platforms by agitators, workers, students, and revolutionary poets in order to get the masses involved in the spirit of the presentation.

An important source of information and suggestions for the new popular theatre was Romain Rolland's study of mass spectacles, *The People's Theatre*, which had been translated into Russian in 1916. Rolland offered the following useful advice:

1. The poet should select historical subjects that are already well-known so that exposition can be condensed.
2. Everything must be done on a large scale—vast, festively arranged pictures, marches, sacrifices, battles, dances, pantomimes. All of these scenes and occurrences should flow quickly if in terms of the sense of the presentation they are only of secondary importance.
3. All poetic parts of the presentations and those involving song should be simple, imbued with a single feeling. Otherwise, it will sap too much precious energy from these highly demanding presentations. The musician should therefore limit himself exclusively to expressing the poet's thought in long notes. He should employ broad harmony and melody. His orchestration should be kept free from subtle details since the spectator will be listening to the music from afar.
4. The actor should stand at the edge of the stage and pronounce each word distinctly.
5. In this type of theatre it is necessary to simplify the action, to broaden the dialogue, using fewer words, fewer gestures but greater expressiveness.
6. In general there must be a concentration of feeling, action, and style.
7. Music is very useful but only as background.
8. Theatre of this type requires powerful effects in the genre of fresco.
9. The crowds will be employed as an individual as in the ancient theatre.
10. Dialogue will be arranged between two or three choral groups.
11. The place of individual intrigues will little by little be usurped by mass conflicts in which only general characteristics will be represented.

12. Strong dramatic contrasts will be exploited.
13. Heavy use will be made of light and shadow to produce strong effects.
14. The vast size of these theatres will permit separate episodes to be presented simultaneously.[2]

The most influential native theorist in the Russian people's theatre movement was Platon Keržencev (Platon Mixajlovič Lebedev, 1881-1940), "cultural worker and diplomat," whose book, *Creative Theatre. The Paths of the Socialist Theatre (Tvorčeskij teatr. Puti socialističeskogo teatra*, 1919), went through five printings and was "the catechism of the proletcult stage." The proletcult theatre was an extension of the proletcult organization, founded in 1906 for the purpose of disseminating proletarian culture. Proletcult theatre was, said Keržencev, never intended to masquerade as a genuine art form. It was more concerned with expressing the new psychology and theatrical instinct of the working class so as to make theatre more democratic. To this end, the prolecult theatre was staffed with lay people rather than theatre professionals. Performances were aimed at a proletarian audience rather than at an educated, cultural elite of the sort that dominated the pre-Revolutionary Russian theatre and was still an insidious presence. Keržencev fondly recalled Evreinov, who he said "with great wit shows how strong the theatrical instinct is in man."

Besides discussing and disputing Rolland's guidelines and Keržencev's proletarian theory, the would-be creators of a Russian popular theatre asked what was to be the role of the actor, dramatist and director in the creation of the mass spectacle. Sergej Radlov, who codirected one such mass spectacle, *In Favor of a World Commune* (*K mirovoj kommune*, July 1920), along with Nikolaj Petrov, Vladimir Solov'ev and Adrian Piotrovskij, posed the question: Does the mass spectacle aim at destroying the theatre of the single actor, the platform on which is presented the physical freedom and the spiritual beauty of man? No, he answered, socialism does not want to kill our admiration for the fine proportions of man, the rhythm of his movement, the softness of his voice. Of course, practically speaking, this is exactly what did happen. The new heroic Soviet man represented in post-Revolutionary arts was a perfect specimen of anonymity. It is interesting to compare the pre-Revolutionary preoccupation with commedia wherein man is made to seem Fate's pawn with post-Revolutionary dogmatic art in which he appears as History's maker but is in fact its messenger at best.

Radlov rejected the idea that a spectacle given for the masses must of necessity be massive in scale. Demanding that a historical event created by a large number of people be re-enacted in theatrical form by a similar multitude, was, according to Radlov, a mistake of "naive realism." It is akin to

Čexov, who in his attempt to depict the melancholy and boredom oppressing his heroes, plunged the spectators into boredom. A single actor can hold sway over a crowd, be it tragedy or comedy. Radlov cited as examples the circus clown and the Greek actor, who played to a public of from twenty to thirty thousand spectators.

Radlov asserted that several weeks to a month are necessary in order to coordinate the movement of the crowds in the mass spectacle. The use of professional actors compounds the director's problems since each wants to play an individual role. This interferes with the overall movement patterns. There is, he pointed out, an important psychological difference between theatricalized parade in which sailors play sailors and theatrical transformation in which sailors play kings or policemen in the tsar's service. The first type of presentation appeals to anyone who takes pride in belonging to the military, to a particular professional organization, and so on. The second appeals only to people who have a taste for acting.[3]

Theatre scholar Konstantin N. Deržavin suggested that the cognitive meaning of words in a mass spectacle amounts to zero. The mass spectacle is instead built on acoustic effects. He cited the failure of Reinhardt to achieve a desired effect in his 1910 Berlin production of *Oedipus Rex*. He instructed five hundred people to shout the word "plague" at one point, with each person trying to articulate it. He would have done better, Deržavin suggests, to have employed sounds rather than actual words. Regarding the proper design for the mass spectacle, Deržavin favored simple painted backgrounds with different broken geometrical lines to highlight the contours of the actor's body. Although there were a wide variety of practical suggestions offered from various quarters, nearly all agreed that an entirely new aesthetic must be applied to this type of theatre.[4]

The 30–31 October edition of the newspaper *The Life of Art (Žizn' iskusstva)* carried a background article by Nikolaj Evreinov on the mass spectacle *The Storming of the Winter Palace (Vzjatie Zimnego Dvorca)* which was scheduled to take place on 7 November 1920, on Urickij Square in Petrograd to commemorate the third anniversary of the October Revolution. At least nine mass spectacles had already been staged in Petrograd with *The Storming* serving in some people's minds as the final part of a trilogy that began with *The Mystery of Freed Labor* (*Misterija ili Gimn osvoboždenogo truda*, 1 May 1920) and the aforementioned *In Favor of a World Commune*. Although Evreinov was listed as chief author and director of the spectacle, he spoke of the collective authorship of ten people working together in harmony on this exercise of "unprecedented complexity."

The article said that the action would take place on three stages simultaneously—two "*uslovnye* theatrical" and one authentically historical. On the White platform (to the right as one looked out from the Winter Palace; see fig. 29) the action would be staged in a comic style, on the Red platform (to the left; see figs. 30–31) in the tone of a heroic drama, and on the third stage, Urickij Square itself, in the tone of a battle display. The production approach would be one of artistic simplification. The audience's attention would be directed from one stage to another by means of lighting. One searchlight was to be attached to the top of the Aleksandrinskaja column in the middle of the square. The action would transpire also on a bridge connecting the two constructed platforms as well as in the sky overhead (see fig. 32).

Some ten thousand performers were scheduled to take part in the presentation, including groups of professional actors, dancers, and circus performers, drama students, members of the proletcult clubs and theatre societies, whole sectors of the Red Army and the Baltic Fleet, as well as groups of workers and all manner of machinery and transports.

The Winter Palace would itself serve as a giant actor, expressing its inner life. "The director," said Evreinov, "must arrange it so the stones themselves seem to talk," so that the spectator feels what is transpiring behind these cold Red walls. This would be accomplished, according to Evreinov, by adopting a technique common to cinematography. The spectator would see some moments in the internal life of the Winter Palace through each of the building's fifty windows, where figures will appear in action for an instant. Silhouetted groups would be revealed in a flash and as quickly disappear into the darkness on the square just prior to the finale, which would feature gunshots, whistles, sirens, flags, and fireworks. The banquet to follow the spectacle would feature a speech by K. I. Čukovskij expressing the idea that the Revolution provided Russia with a scale of unprecedented size and boldness by which to measure the magnitude of events. Evreinov likewise viewed this production as employing a scale unprecedented in theatrical history.[5]

The handbill-libretto for the presentation provides several important bits of information. The directors state that their intention is not *exactly* to re-create the events that constitute their subject, since it is "uncharacteristic" of the theatre to offer such exact reproduction. Here Evreinov's voice can be clearly heard. He developed his concept of "artistic reconstruction" at the Ancient Theatre "to avoid the temptation of creating museum replicas and to give the theatre its due in dealing with past forms and events." Evreinov's emphasis here on the theatricality of the piece rather than simply extolling its authenticity gives a clue to his intentions in undertaking this project. He pointed out that this presentation is significant not only as a recording of a historical event but as a step in the development of the mass spectacle as a theatrical event. Finally, the directors ask the

The Storming of the Winter Palace *and After* 197

spectators to note that the great masses of people used in the crowd scenes are not merely a body of trained actors but represent a single collective actor, much as Evreinov's work on such Ancient Theatre pieces as *Fuente Ovejuna* featured a mass protagonist. Far from having abandoned his earlier ideas, Evreinov was getting ready to create a monodramatic theatre-in-life spectacle on a grand scale.

It was Evreinov who first conceived the idea for *The Storming* and who remained the moving force throughout the preparations. The idea was further developed by A. R. Kugel' (it is unclear why these two decided to work together on another project) who passed it on to Nikolaj V. Petrov, Jurij P. Annenkov, Hugo Varlix and Dimitrij I. Temkin (the noted émigré composer).[6]

As the spectacle's general director, Evreinov was responsible for coordinating the efforts of the directorate with the various other sectors devoted to the writing of the scenario, the mobilization, transportation, feeding, and equipping of the participants, the construction of the set, and so forth. Rehearsals ran for three weeks at night in the Gervovyj Hall of the Winter Palace.[7] Nikolaj Gorčakov described the organization of such spectacles:

> Every thousand participants was divided into units of ten, and each unit had its own "foreman." The rehearsals took place, for the most part, with only the directors and "foremen" present. The latter would then train their groups and take charge of them for the show. Furthermore, there were leaders for every group of characters, for every episode in the action, and for every part of the square during the show. The "mass performance" was divided into short, effective bits, such as entrances, turns, and individual gestures. There were 170 such "measures" used to stage *In Favor of a World Commune*. They were all included in the "score" of the mass action that the director's staff used to indicate the development of the plot and the movements of groups and characters. The staff took their places on the captain's bridge and were connected with all the platforms of action through a system of signal lights and field telephones. The guides would receive the signal from the captain's bridge and would pass it along to their "foremen," who in turn would pass it along to their own subordinates. The director was on the podium, and he controlled tempos, rhythms, pauses, retards, and accelerations.[8]

That information regarding signal relays, the breakdown of the presentation into episodes under the supervision of group leaders, the division of directorial responsibilities, and so forth involved in the preparations for *The Storming* has been well documented. What is uncertain is the exact nature of the rehearsal arrangements, how many of the performers actually took part in the rehearsals, and how they were run.

It rained through the night and into the morning of 7 November. There was frost and apparently even some snow, because by the time the presentation was ready to begin at 10:30 P.M. the square was covered with slush. The atmosphere created by the weather reminded one observer of Gogol''s short story *Nevskij Prospekt*.

By the time the signal came from the director's command bridge (a raised platform in the middle of the square) for the production to begin, the square had become inundated with some one hundred thousand people. Sectors were roped off on either side of the Aleksandrinskaja column for the spectators (they stood with their backs to the Winter Palace) so that they would not interfere with the action (see figs. 33–34). This did not prevent them from giving their rapt attention to the performance and offering their vocal support whenever the moment seemed to demand it. Groups of peasants had flocked to the spectacle from the villages. They huddled close together behind the ropes, afraid of getting lost in the crowd and frightened by the noise and the projectors, which shot beams of light across the cloudy sky.[9]

Evreinov had assigned several directors to each of the two major platforms. In charge of the Red were Leonid S. Viv'en, Nikolaj V. Petrov and N. I. Miševev. Directing the action on the White were Aleksandr R. Kugel', Konstantin N. Deržavin and Aleksandr G. Movšenson. Hugo Varlix conducted the five-hundred-member orchestra whose music accompanied the action. The set was designed by Jurij Annenkov, the lighting effects by Professor Majzel'.

Visually, the spectacle resembled a medieval mystery translated into twentieth-century expressionist art. The flats which backed the Red and the White platforms were slanted at sharp irregular angles. Those on the White platform were off-white, pink, and light brown in color. Those on the Red platform were all brick red, representing factory works. Smokestacks popped up amidst the factory walls, which were dotted with rows of windows containing a painted yellow light. Long runs of broad steps led up to both the Red and the White platforms, producing heroic and ludicrous impressions respectively. The Winter Palace itself was kept free of constructed pieces.

The critic V. G. Samojlov had questioned Annenkov's use of flats and platforms in juxtaposition to the existing architecture on the square. The critic had argued that any constructed scenery should harmonize with the existing architecture without being swallowed up by it. Although Annenkov's design was perfectly consistent with his own highly geometric style, it clashed noticeably with the real surroundings, offering a strange, fantastic perspective on historical events.[10] This, of course, also reflected the methods of Evreinov, the spectacle's chief director, whose earlier work had been said to have mixed tragedy and farce like wine with poison.

This scenic tension was extended into the area of costuming. Romain Rolland had instructed the builders of the popular theatre to present the

The Storming of the Winter Palace *and After* 199

proletariat in an uncaricatured, optimistic manner, but this did not rule out ridiculing the bourgeoisie. Evreinov, Annenkov, and company dressed the bourgeoisie in elegant but exaggerated and frivolous costumes suggestive of a masquerade ball, a kind of capitalist commedia dell'arte. Bankers in gold and silver top hats wearing gigantic carnations on the lapels of their evening attire straddled huge money bags labelled with the equally huge sums they supposedly contained. Their wives wore long dresses and stylish bonnets and carried large fur muffs in which to warm their white hands. They were joined by military officers in dress uniforms, cocked hats, white sashes, monacles, and medals. All of this contrasted sharply with the honest proletarian dress and drab uniforms of the real aristocrats on the Red platform and in the jeeps and trucks that came racing through the arch of the General Staff Headquarters onto the square. The dignified comportment of the bourgeoisie, now so ludicrously irrelevant, likewise contrasted dramatically with the scenes of workers, including women, children, and cripples, trudging up flights of stairs, bent over from the weight of tools on their backs.

Among both the Red and the White contingents there was great uniformity in movement and gesture, and repetition was used to great effect. This device was effectively employed in presenting the two major figures in the production, Kerenskij and Lenin. Twenty-five Kerenskijs, played by ballet dancers, read a speech three times in succession. The generals and dignitaries on the White platform approved each sentence by slowly and rhythmically tapping hammers. They also shouted their hurrahs, handkerchiefs and cocked hats held aloft to punctuate each cheer. This episode was heightened further by the playing of three selections from the *Marseillaise*. The Kerenskijs sat at a table covered with a pale pink cloth as 100 dignitaries, played by circus artistes, passed in review. This was followed by a parade of cadets and generals (200 theatrical extras and 50 government employees respectively). The next wave to sweep in was composed of bankers and merchants (245 theatrical extras and 100 government employees respectively with 5 professional actors of supporting roles scattered among them) bearing aloft a banner that read "Seize Freedom" and dragging sacks of gold. Amidst general exultation on the White platform the Kerenskijs struck a heroic pose, and the bankers and merchants sat down at the table in unison.

As the name of Lenin was murmured ever more urgently and distinctly from the still unilluminated Red platform, those on the White stage became more visibly restless, uneasy, and indecisive. The ministers, who were all clad in gray, rocked in unison on their bench, first to the right and then with a sudden jerk to the left. This action was repeated several times, each time more violently, as the Red forces' singing of the *Internationale* was heard coming closer and closer. The women's battalions shouted *Moriturae te salutant* to Kerenskij as they moved in a grotesquely stylized manner up the stairs to the stage.

As the lights on the White platform were cut off, those on the Red platform were brought up to reveal 200 workers entering from the flatly painted factories, hammers in hand, shouting as if to greet the Red dawn. Half of the workers proceeded to simulate work while the other half stood in bas-relief. The sound of hammers striking anvils provided the musical accompaniment for the scenes on this platform. Workers and soldiers, women and children, crowded around a gigantic red flag. Several moments later, the masses advanced to the edge of the Red platform as if listening for something. Suddenly cries rang out from the square, at first 10, then 50, 140, and finally 200—"Lenin!" Thirty "Lenins" entered the Red platform to the strains of martial music. The Lenins, like the Kerenskijs, delivered a speech. It elicited a great vocal response and led into yet another of the frequent repetitions of the *Internationale*.

The searchlight next illuminated the White platform, where the ministerial bench could be seen rocking back and forth and finally crashing to the ground. Two cars sped in from a side street, their horns blaring, and pulled up alongside the White stage. The desperate Kerenskij and his ministers rushed down the steps and jumped into the vehicles. They sped through the gates of the Winter Palace which had opened quickly to admit them and then closed as quickly behind them.

As the battle raged on between Red and White soldiers on the bridge and machine gun fire filled the air, the lights inside the Winter Palace flashed on and off intermittently, illuminating various scenes as Evreinov had foretold. The White soldiers on the outside having been defeated, the Red army, fed by additional forces entering by the side streets, now marched on the Winter Palace singing the *Internationale*. The guns of the battleship Aurora, anchored as it had been during the actual historical event, bombarded the Winter Palace and kept bombarding it even after the call to halt due to a signal mix-up. Kerenskij, disguised as a woman, escaped the Winter Palace, with his ministers in tow, by car.

By 12:00 P.M. the Winter Palace had been taken and the rain which had marked the day prior to the performance was replaced by the traditional rain of red stars, golden rain, and silver fires that poured down on the crowd in a moment as light as day, a new day.[11]

The question of why Evreinov agreed to direct a Soviet mass spectacle is not as puzzling as it initially seems. It is highly plausible, as Tamara Baikova Poggi suggests, that Evreinov was invited to direct a mass spectacle on the strength of his work at the Ancient Theatre, despite the fact that the crowd scenes she cites as having especially qualified him in Soviet eyes were from the Ancient Theatre's production of *Three Magi* and directed by A. A. Sanin, who was brought in specifically to perform this task.

Less palatable is Poggi's contention that Evreinov staged the mass spectacle to dramatize his rejection of "the aristocrat of the theatre" concept set forth in his *Theatre for Oneself.*[12] After all, according to Evreinov's definition, one can still be an "aristocrat" in a crowd. Nor did Evreinov's staging of the mass spectacle mean that he had embraced socialism. In fact, three of the major creative forces involved in *The Storming*—Evreinov, Annenkov and Temkin—later emigrated from Soviet Russia. Their purpose in staging the mass spectacle was clearly not political. It is more reasonable to assume that they worked on the spectacle in spite of its political message.[13]

One must then look elsewhere for an explanation, to the nature of Evreinov's art and the stages in its development. Although somewhat more stylized than Evreinov's productions at the Ancient Theatre, the mass spectacle nevertheless embodied a similar scenic as well as spiritual and ideological naiveté. *The Storming of the Winter Palace* depicted the struggle between Good (the Reds) and Evil (the Whites), "the expulsion of the Satanic host under the banner of capitalism from the world which the Bolsheviks were working to transform into a proletarian paradise."[14]

Both the medieval productions and the mass spectacles were events designed to reaffirm the beliefs of the already converted. Although the medieval presentations drew upon liturgical drama while Soviet agitprop was secular and even antireligious, each offered in Evreinov's mind theatre in life as consolatory faith to a modern-day audience, a return to shared mystery and communion. The inclusion of actual participants from the storming of the Winter Palace in Evreinov's commemorative spectacle made his concept of theatre in life even more palpable. Finally Evreinov had found a life-size canvas he could paint, possessed of a spirituality and cosmic scope borrowed from the Ancient Theatre. And through the use of a mass protagonist, a device he had earlier employed in staging Spanish and medieval drama, Evreinov at least partially realized the principle of monodrama, that is, totally involving the audience in the various manifestations of a single "character's" psyche. At the same time, with the mass spectacle Evreinov moved further than ever toward transcending the concept of "character" altogether, substituting agents as he had done earlier in his monodrama, *In the Stage-Wings of the Soul*. Moreover, Evreinov had always been interested in the grotesque. It became a sort of nexus for his sense of humor, his examination of primitive forms, his highly subjective outlook on art and life, and above all, his sense of theatricality. The mass spectacle provided an opportunity for the creation of *Übergrotesks* which could be made to walk in the footsteps of history.

The mass spectacle was the most dramatic move in a direction that had long been surveyed by Evreinov, the extension of the theatre into life, the emancipation of theatre from convention to serve a higher purpose. Theatre is not *an* art, it is *the* art, as big as life and capable of transforming it. In light of this the question becomes not how Evreinov could have agreed to stage a mass spectacle but rather, how he could have resisted. It was his last bold theatrical effort prior to his emigration in 1925 and the one for which he is best remembered in the Soviet Union and around the world. Although the project was, in fact, consistent with Evreinov's inner beliefs, the apparent paradox it suggests to most observers of Evreinov's life and work is a fitting last testament to a man whose career was motivated by the spirit of contradiction.

The period between 1920 and 1925 was relatively unimportant as a new stage in Evreinov's creative development. Instead Evreinov used these years following his staging of *The Storming of the Winter Palace* and prior to his emigration to consolidate his major theoretical ideas and to do further research before publishing them in book-length works. Evreinov did a large amount of historical research during this period, which is evident in his completed books. In such works as *The Origin of Drama* (*Proisxoždenie dramy*, 1921), *The Primordial Drama of the Germanic Peoples* (*Pervobytnaja drama germancev*, 1922), *Azazel and Dionysos* (*Azazel i Dionis*, 1924), *Serf Actors* (*Krepostnye aktery*, 1925), and others, Evreinov applied his theoretical ideas to history. By so doing he both justified these ideas and discovered for them new implications. This was a further step in what was for Evreinov a lifelong effort to place the theatre in the broadest and most significant context — life.

On 22 July 1921, Evreinov married Anna Aleksandrovna Kašina, a divorcée twenty years his junior. They were of widely disparate temperaments. Anna Kašina had a more stable and practical nature, owing in some part to her merchant origins. She devoted herself to keeping her more volatile, unpredictable, and basically unhappy husband in check both financially and emotionally.[15]

Since he was devoted to more scholarly work during this period, Evreinov carefully selected from the various directorial offers that came to him. He was interested in staging operas and did so during his last five years in Russia and, following his emigration, in Western Europe. He accepted an offer to stage Wagner's opera *Der Ring* and Offenbach's *La Belle Élène* in the reconstructive style of the Ancient Theatre in 1920. In

1922 he directed *Manon* by Massanet and Mozart's *Die Entführung aus dem Serail* at the Mixailovskij Theatre. He worked on the Mozart piece for two years, but it was performed only after his emigration.

In 1922 Evreinov recieved passports for himself and his wife to travel abroad as part of an agreement with Mixail Razumnij, to direct a program of Crooked Mirror plays at the Moscow theatre "Crooked Jimmy." Razumnij, a former actor at the Crooked Mirror and now director of several Moscow theatres, was able to secure the passports because he was rumored to be the lover of Olga Kameneva, wife of Lev Borisovič Kamenev (a powerful political figure) and Lev Trockij's sister. Evreinov and his wife toured Berlin and Paris for three months and then returned to the Soviet Union. Evreinov had no intention of staying abroad at this time; his mother was ill and he did not wish to leave her.[16] It was only during his own frequent illnesses, when he felt depressed, unappreciated, and poorly provided for by the Soviet government that Evreinov discussed in personal correspondence the possibility of permanent emigration. In 1921 Evreinov wrote a letter to, of all people, Mejerxol'd, in which he said: "If the U.S.S.R. cannot feed me sufficiently to maintain my works, my health, I will be compelled to make plans to go abroad, something which I do not want to do now, despite the fact that my plays are being produced there and my books being translated."[17] This letter and others of this period written by Evreinov to Mejerxol'd convey a feeling of desperation. It seems strange that Evreinov would turn to his lifelong rival at this late date. But Mejerxol'd was, after all, a fellow artist who happened to occupy a position of some influence in the Soviet regime, while Evreinov, a nonpolitical artist, was kept at arm's length by the ruling powers of the new society. In a characteristically paradoxical action, Evreinov had already rejected Mejerxol'd's aid on an earlier occasion. In autumn of 1921 Mejerxol'd had sent Evreinov a telegram asking him to assume control of a new theatre, RSFSR 2. Mejerxol'd himself planned to undertake the direction of RSFSR 1. Along with the position, Evreinov was offered travel expenses for himself and his library. Evreinov's rejection of the offer no doubt sprang in part from his ambiguous relationship with Mejerxol'd.

Evreinov was dismayed by Soviet theatre and felt out of place in post-Revolutionary society. With the exception of his work on *The Storming of the Winter Palace,* Evreinov avoided associating himself with the Soviet regime. He rejected Lunačarskij's offer (April 1921) to stage the First of May spectacle in Moscow.[18] In general Evreinov kept what was for him a low profile. However, he did head a committee for the reorganization of the academic theatres at the invitation of Lunačarskij in 1921. He was, in general, on good personal terms with Lunačarskij (whose brother he knew in his civil service days) but was unwilling to solidify their relationship, as Mejerxol'd had, by devoting his art to propagandizing for social and political causes.

While in Moscow in 1923, Evreinov met a Pole who informed him that his plays were doing well in Warsaw, and considerable royalties awaited him. He contracted with the Pole to supervise the handling of his royalties and when he learned in 1924 that A. R. Kugel' was proposing to take the Crooked Mirror to Warsaw and perhaps to other cities as well, he signed on as director of a program of his own devising.

The Evreinovs boarded a train for Warsaw on 30 January 1925, with the intention of remaining abroad for sometime. Evreinov's mother had died, which made this decision possible. However, the Evreinovs still did not intend their stay abroad to be permanent, as evidenced by the fact that they took with them only as much as they could carry, including as many books as possible. Many of Evreinov's books and personal manuscripts were left behind in Russia. Some were collected by the government and housed in the central archives, but many were lost.

Following the disastrous Crooked Mirror tour of Warsaw, during which Evreinov and Kugel' made a final break, the Evreinovs travelled to Paris via Prague. They reached Paris in May 1925, eventually setting up quarters at 7 rue Boileau, where Evreinov lived until his death in 1953.[19]

Evreinov's émigré career is well documented in the newspapers of the day as well as in his study of the Russian émigré theatre in Paris, *A Memorial to the Transient* (*Pamjatnik mimoletnomu*) from *The History of the Émigré Theatre in Paris* (1953), and in his memoirs *In the School of Wit* (*V škole ostroumija*). In the latter Evreinov listed the following as the major productions he directed during this period:

The Fairy Tale about Tsar Saltan (*Skazka o tsare Saltane*), an opera by N. A. Rimskij-Korsakov from Puškin with the Russian opera company at the Theatre of the Elysian Fields in Paris (1925)

Les amours de Jean-Pierre, Le joyeux van der Polaff, Tin'ol, Marionettes (Marionetki), The Robber and the Rose (*Razboinik i roza*), *Demylera's Daughter* (*Doč' Demylera*), *Toys* (*Igruški*), *The Stairway of Life* (*Lestnica žizni*), and *La revolte de Gai-Rou* at the Bat (*Letučaja myš'*) Theatre in Paris (1928)

The Snowmaiden (*Sneguročka*), an opera by N. A. Rimskij-Korsakov from Ostrovskij, with the Russian Opera Company at the Theatre of the Elysian Fields in Paris (1929)

Ruslan and Ljudmilla (Ruslan i Ljudmilla) by M. M. Glinka from Puškin with the Russian Opera Company at the Theatre of the Elysian Fields in Paris (1930)

Woe from Wit (Gore ot uma) by A. S. Griboedov at the National Theatre in Prague (1935)

The Minor (*Nedorosl'*) by D. I. Fonvizin at the Russian Theatre in Paris (1938–39)

Belučina's Marriage (*Ženit'ba Belučina*) by A. N. Ostrovskij and N. Ja. Solov'ev at the Theatre of Russian Drama in Paris (1943–44)

The Living Corpse (*Živoj trup*) by L. N. Tolstoj at the Theatre of Russian Drama in Paris (1944) (Evreinov made plans to direct this, but it is uncertain whether he actually did stage it.)

Eugene Onegin (*Evgenij Onegin*) by P. I. Čaikovskij from Puškin, *Orphée* by C. W. Gluck and *La Bohème* by Puccini with the opera class at the Paris Conservatoire (1952).[20]

In 1934 Evreinov was involved in an enterprise called *The Wandering Comedians (Brodjačie komedianty)* as artistic director. V. A. Kostrova was the theatre's producer. M. A. Razumnij, the one-time influential friend (Trockij was no longer in favor) who had helped Evreinov to secure his passport to go abroad in 1922 was also involved. The enterprise was designed along the lines of the Crooked Mirror Theatre. Evreinov said: "Our problem is to relieve émigré boredom.... Our productions are designed for a select audience, for an elite, for critics, for snobbish scoffers...and simply for merry fellows and wits of all types...the program is designed to take into account the indifference of the jaded public toward the old values of the theatre, etc." This enterprise was short-lived, presenting only two series of productions.

Beginning in 1935 Evreinov was affiliated with the Society of Russian Artists (*Obščestvo russkix artistov*). Following two months of rehearsal the Society staged Evreinov's *The Chief Thing,* his one great world-wide dramaturgical success. The play was a great success as performed by the Society.

In 1943 Evreinov was invited by Sergej Lifar' to become the chief artistic director of the Theatre of Russian Drama in Paris. At this theatre, in addition to the plays already cited, Evreinov directed *Tsar Pëtr and*

Prince Aleksej (*Car Pëtr i Carevič Aleksej*) by D. S. Merežkovskij, *My Family* (*Svoja sem'ja*) by Griboedov, and the nineteenth-century farce *The Queen's Furnished Rooms* (*Meblirovannye komnaty koroleva*) by S. Uraiskij. The Germans heavily censored these plays. Performances could not end later than 11:00 P.M. Jews were not allowed to perform. The great actress E. O. Skokan was almost banned from playing a role in *The Chief Thing*, when it was erroneously suggested that she had Jewish blood. Evreinov was also watched closely by the Germans on account of his affiliation with Freemasonry.[21]

During his emigration Evreinov wrote the following new plays: *Love under the Microscope (Ljubov' pod mikroskopom,* 1931), a play performed in Poland and Yugoslavia

The Theatre of Eternal War (1928), the third part of Evreinov's dramaturgical theatre-in-life trilogy, which also includes *The Chief Thing* and *The Ship of the Righteous*

Le Triangle Immortal (date unknown)

Truer than the Truth (date unknown)

The Steps of Nemesis (*Šagi nemezidy*) or *I Do Not Know Another Country Like This One,* a full-length play concerning life in the Soviet Union (1936–38), published in 1956)

The Nameless (*Čemu net imeni*), a full-length play (1965).

Evreinov wrote and staged three ballets:

Les Bronzes, with music by Nicolas Stein, presented in Paris in 1937

In Bessarabia, with music by Illjašenko, first presented at the Theatre de la Monnaie in Brussels in 1938

Chota Roustaveli, "epopée chorégraphique," with music by Honegger, A. Čerepnin, and Harsanyl (1946).[22]

In the spring of 1945 Evreinov delivered a series of nine lectures on Parisian radio under the collective title *Les grandes figures artistiques de la Russie Contemporaine,* personal memories of Stanislavskij, Rimskij-Korsakov, Aleksej Tolstoj, Mixail Zoščenko, Mixail Fokine, Majakovskij, Gorkij, Tairov, and (Evreinov) himself. Also in 1945 Evreinov began writing *Histoire du Théâtre Russe,* which was published in 1947. This account of the Russian theatre from its folk and ritual origins to the pre-Revolutionary period reflected as always Evreinov's major concerns and biases. He drew heavily from his previous works on the origins of drama both in Russia and abroad and on the Russian serf actor. His account of Russian theatre in the pre-Revolutionary period is more personal memoir than historical record. Predictably, he extolls his own contributions to the Russian theatre while depreciating Stanislavskij's and villifying Mejerxol'd as a German alien and political opportunist. The *Histoire* originally ended with a fifty-page survey of the Soviet theatre in the first years of the new regime, but this was cut from the Russian edition published in the United States (1955).[23]

Evreinov began writing his last major theoretical work, *The Revelation of Art (Otkrovenie iskusstva),* in 1934. Its aim was to fathom the essence of the process of artistic creation. This final attempt to discover the philosopher's stone was unfinished at the time of his death in 1953.

Despite the apparent breadth of his activities during his years as an émigré, life must have been extremely frustrating for Evreinov. Plagued by ill health and subjected to the privations of life in occupied Paris, Evreinov could never return to St. Petersburg, the stage on which he had performed his paradoxical harlequinade. The magic of Petersburg was lost forever even for those who remained in Russia.

Evreinov's directorial work during this period consisted for the most part of isolated projects involving classics in drama and ballet. He also advised on productions of his plays throughout the West. There was no theatre akin to his spirit that could serve as laboratory and forum for his ideas as the Ancient Theatre and the Crooked Mirror had. He developed no new ideas as a director or a writer and did not modify to any significant extent his already existing ones. He continued to propagandize for the theories and directorial approaches he had devised in Russia. But Evreinov's voice no longer seemed as significant as it had in pre-Revolutionary Russia when great plans were being made for the theatre of the future. His new plays dealt with familiar Evreinovian themes but neither so strikingly as *In the Stage-Wings of the Soul* nor so completely as *The Chief Thing*. The whimsical and ironic elements that gave his earlier dramatic works their unique quality were replaced by an earnestness and social dogmatism that reflected his concern with the fate of the country he had left.

Although Evreinov's earlier plays were widely produced abroad, Western critics did not really understand this strangely paradoxical figure. They could measure his achievements only within the context of Western artists, and his work was considered by most Western critics to be derivative. They attributed his personality and his writings for the theatre to his "Russianness," a term they never concretely defined. Russian and Soviet artists were alien beings to the West, and to make matters worse, Evreinov's consciousness was formed in a time and place that had already passed into history.

8

Conclusion: Evreinov at the Vanishing Point

Harlequin always serves two masters, the second of which is human nature.
— Jan Kott[1]

Having already explored the negative capabilities of the Evreinov persona, I wish here to offer another equally valid and coexistent reading of his work and its implications. There is no one right answer to Evreinov nor to any man, and one is well-advised in the particular case of so self-conscious a creator to follow his lead. By evolving a position from multiple angles of perception, one creates a fittingly relative profile of the artist as self-creator and self-observer. It remains then to see how the artist's malady and even that part of his nature which was less than idealistic may have been subverted by art, transformed by its mysterious power into something good, useful and honorable. This is both a necessary feature of the specifically Evreinovian paradox and, in general, restitution made to the visionary artist by life and art.

Evreinov wrote of a conversation he had in Paris with his friend I. S. Traxterev, President of the Union of Russian Lawyers, who had often subsidized artistic enterprises in Paris. Traxterev asked Evreinov why his play *The Chief Thing* played over two hundred times in the avant-garde theatres of Paris but not once in Russian. Traxterev wondered, "Why do you think that our countrymen [i.e., the Russian émigrés] perform all of the favorite plays here except yours?" Evreinov replied, half-joking and half-serious, "No man is a prophet in his own country."[2]

Throughout his life, Evreinov sought to play the prophet through his chosen persona, the Harlequin-Christ. His sense of displacement in the twentieth century made him seek out a romantically imagined past even as he considered himself to be ahead of his time. The "retrospective dreamer" fantasized about a past that never was. The Middle Ages had its pestilence and illiteracy, the Spanish Golden Age its religious and intellectual intolerance. These ages, for all their theatricality, were less life-affirming than they were, by necessity, preoccupied with mortality. Had he chosen to recognize it, this could have proved a disastrous contradiction even for a man who thrived on paradoxes, because throughout his life Evreinov had equated theatricality with life and happiness.

Evreinov then took refuge from the ravages of historical time in his created persona and the stage time which it inhabited. He perceived his personal identity crisis and that of the theatre as one and the same. He viewed theatre as an expression of the "I." Returning to its origins was equivalent to exploring the mysteries and secrets of childhood. From this subconscious realm, man brings back the essence of theatre and human life—play, the ability to transform.

Given his need to solidify and assert his identity through a theatrical vision, his antipathy toward Mejerxol'd, the great theatrical figure of his day, brilliant and ubiquitous, seems only natural. Sadly yet appropriately, the two met for the last time not in Russia, where they could never comfortably coexist, but in Paris, where Evreinov had established his new domicile and sought his own uncontested sphere of influence. Evreinov and his wife were sitting at a café window by a cinema which they planned soon to attend when Anna Aleksandrovna thought that she recognized the familiar faces of Mejerxol'd and his wife, actress Zinajda Rajx. While waiting in the ticket line going into the theatre, Anna Evreinova again sighted Mejerxol'd and Rajx and excitedly whispered this to her husband. Coincidentally, Evreinov and Mejerxol'd turned in each other's direction at the same instant, and their eyes met. Each made a movement in the other's direction as if to exchange salutations, but in the next moment, stopped short, turned back to their respective lines and passed into the theatre without saying a word to one another. They avoided each other on the way out as well.[3] It was their last chance for reconciliation. Evreinov never returned to Russia. Mejerxol'd remained in his homeland where he continued for a time to believe in the Revolution's promise to create the theatre of the future. But like Evreinov, Mejerxol'd too finally proved not to be the prophet his times required. He was arrested on 20 June 1939, and is believed to have died in prison in 1940 of still undisclosed causes.

Throughout his theatrical career, Evreinov remained a primitive in style and spirit, and, one could say, as a matter of principle. He was a rare combination of artist and scholar, able craftsman and charismatic, improvisatory performer who, by his grand passion, his talent for storytelling, his vividly sympathetic imaginings, his grace and wit, transformed history into a first-person narrative and the world into his audience. Evreinov, who always came to play rehearsals brightly waistcoated and with a flower in his lapel, was a seductive presence.[4] More than a stage director, Evreinov was a director-personality. Like the hypnotic charlatan Rasputin, the man who played God, Evreinov could both anger and enthrall with his rare power to persuade and manipulate. As a result, his career seems to the observer to balance precariously between art and artifice, magic and sham.

All of Evreinov's varied theatrical efforts were, to some extent, compromised by his didacticism, even while they were ennobled by the obsessive passion that informed his constant preaching. Evreinov, like others before him and since, was caught between the abstract realm of the philosopher and the concrete realm of the theatre professional. He borrowed from history, science, and philosophy the necessary scholarly apparel in which to dress his beloved theatre, only to proclaim that theatre is beautiful (and necessary) as is and does not need the hand-me-down clothing of other disciplines.

Evreinov's learned and often mock-serious treatises, lectures and disputes, his stage productions and personal performances, paid allegiance to two masters, often simultaneously: a deeply committed theatrical vision and an equal and (at least to all appearances) opposite sense of bemused and devious play. The two poles were actually closer together than the public guessed. Evreinov was, after all, the most knowingly sophisticated of theatrical primitives, whose naiveté was in the service of his refined skills at bending all wills to his own. He transformed his peculiar talents and predispositions into the theories of monodrama, the theatre for oneself and the theatre in life, and thus legitimized them.

Anna Evreinov maintains that her husband did not care much for actors, because, he believed, they are not *intelligent* creators.[5] And yet Evreinov and the actor (as several of his actors have attested) could as easily be said to have loved each other or at least to have been in love with the performer-image they had of one another. However, even as he spoke of returning the theatre to the actor's dominion, Evreinov was busily inventing devices that would make the actor curiously irrelevant. His body of dramatic theory is not so much actor-affirming as actor-proof, whether by conscious design or unconscious disposition.

Evreinov's complex, ambivalent attitude toward actors, other directors and theorists, women (whom he would woo but not marry; idolize and blaspheme), God, and ultimately himself, reflects an instinctive feeling for the paradox of mankind, living between reason and faith, self-possession and self-denial. The eternal conflict between man's desire to realize his own will and the will of a higher power or being to control him links Evreinov's concerns to the theatre of ancient Greece and the theatre of the absurd, to retrospectivism and modernism. His art and life embody the tragicomic push-pull of the harlequinade, an improvisation on the themes of art and life, transience, and seduction and the many configurations they may assume.

Obsessed with beginnings, Evreinov was suspicious and positively fearful of ends. As a result, his work is long on premises but short on proofs. It seeks to fully inhabit and even define a moment but quickly attenuates when moments are strung together sequentially. The density his images and arguments suggest seems to evaporate on exposure to careful analysis.

We are charmed by Evreinov but unsure that we are convinced. We cannot finally ascertain whether his originality is a pose or whether his seemingly eclectic Harlequin's motley of other people's ideas constitutes something truly original. He infects us with his ambivalence so that we have difficulty gauging the proper response to his curiously unfinished performance. However, if we deny Evreinov a place in his own "commission of experts," we risk being redundant, since self-mockery was inherent in its creation.

Evreinov's mask, like its commedia models, may ultimately reveal more than it conceals if we have the patience and perhaps the imagination necessary to play his game. In the end, he may have told us less than he knew, but if he teaches us how to become more aware of what we already know and need to know, then he deserves consideration alongside the visionary artists who have fared better than he in this century with fewer real accomplishments to their credit.

In a very real sense, Evreinov is our contemporary, and contrary to expectation, not merely in terms of spirit or tonality, with irony the dominant chord. The theatre of personality that ran like a film loop through both his actual professional work and the professional career he made of his life is distinctly modern. This act of what the Soviets call "anarchic personality" was ultimately less a decadent pose or a dilettante's game than a statement of alienation from a culture changing too quickly to allow for considered adaptation.[6] At times subliminally and often openly, Evreinov confronted life itself, which always moves too quickly and unexpectedly for man to fathom or properly inhabit. Evreinov actively sought a way for man to become absorbed back into life. Evreinov's life and work embody the investigative and transformative approaches to theatre characteristic of this century. In Evreinov we see the process whereby man reinvents himself through theatre and theatre reinvents itself through the basic masks, rituals, and archetypes that engendered it, whether classical Greek or Italian commedia dell'arte. Evreinov was one of the first and most insistent modern exponents of the will to play as an instinct basic to mankind, and therefore the theatre as not a pastime but a necessity.

Evreinov offers us a philosophy of the theatre, legitimizing theatre as a subject for serious scholarly investigation, an example followed by artist-scholars of succeeding generations. He explored not only the functions of theatre as had been the rule in dramatic criticism for centuries, but the idea of theatre. He relocated the basis of theatre in its theatricality which he helped to reclaim for modern times. The notion of theatricality as opposed to stylization or the external theatricalization of theatre through devices (which he also helped pioneer) became perhaps the dominant force in twentieth-century theatrical theory and practice.

Evreinov made theatrical performance the subject of his drama and writings about the drama. His tragi-farces, in drawing attention to form, dramatized the death of outmoded social and artistic forms. Similarly, his intensification of the self was aimed at setting free the soul from the confines of the ego. He bridged the gap between existence and essence, the respective domains of realism and symbolism. He likewise fused the search for individuation with the search for oneness, perhaps the two main impulses to art. His highly sensory theatre explored and attacked the boundaries of perception.

Evreinov also involved himself actively with gaining an understanding of wit and humor, a line of investigation sometimes bypassed by all but the most serious artist-scholars. In fact the parodistic nature of Evreinov's own artistic stance is largely responsible for his relative disregard and partial misinterpretation. Either he is not taken seriously enough or he is taken too seriously, that is, literally at his word even when he is being purposely coy or hyperbolic.

Evreinov's satirizing of the other leading innovators of his day—Stanislavskij, Mejerxol'd, Reinhardt, Craig, Sologub, Andreev, the symbolists, and others—represents another important aspect of his legacy to modern theatre: as a historical and cultural indicator. Although Evreinov often exemplified more than he accomplished, perhaps no other single figure embodied so completely the cultural currents of Russian theatre's "golden age": retrospectivism and artistic reconstruction (the Ancient Theatre); cabaret and theatre of small forms (The Crooked Mirror Theatre); mass spectacle (*The Storming of the Winter Palace*); extreme subjectivism (monodrama); extreme aestheticism (theatre for oneself); theatre of ritual and folk theatre (*The Theatre and the Scaffold* and his many published theoretical-historical works); *commedia dell'arte* and tragi-farce (his many plays); the cult of the body and of silence (his pantomimes); theatre as play (the Merry Theatre for Grown-up Children); and threads of many then-current aesthetic-poetic movements and tendencies, from symbolist myth-creation and congregate action to sociological, psychological and anthropological investigations into the nature of art to give it legitimate foundations in scientific methodology. Evreinov demysticized the symbolist jargon of Sologub, Andreev and others while injecting a quasi-scientific language of his own. Evreinov had a knack for taking tendencies and turning them into forms (e.g., monodrama, theatre for oneself). His multifaceted theatre of paradox and transformation was characteristic of the healthy debate and cross-fertilization within and among disciplines that made the culture of his day so extraordinary. He was a much-quoted and respected figure whose secondary position in the artistic hierarchy of his generation is more a judgment of subsequent history than of his own time.

The anarchic personality regards everything he touches and which touches him as part of his art, because he is not only an artist but the very stuff of art. The nexus of monodrama, theatre for oneself and the theatre in life is manifested by the happenings, performance art, and celebrity-as-art tendencies that have been in vogue with some intensity for the past twenty years but actually date from considerably earlier. Evreinov's *The Storming of the Winter Palace* is certainly a happening of gigantic proportions, utilizing the most evocative of found spaces and thousands of lay people as amateur performance artists, reinventing life as art.

The self-conscious image-making, contrapuntal tempo-rhythm and subjective camera perspective of contemporary life was anticipated by Evreinov in dramatic theory, theatrical practice, and personal example. Evreinov's investigations into antiquity were really modernist experiments in the creation of the most immediate form of *uslovnyj* theatre. Here, the purposeful tension created between antique and modern perspectives is meant neither to alienate the viewer à la Brecht nor to purge him by paroxysm à la Artaud, but rather to confront him with the quandary of the mind-body, mind-spirit dichotomies that plague mankind, as each new epoch confronts the problem of its modernity.

The theory of the theatre in life suggests that man's natural state is involvement rather than alienation and that true purgation is a false promise. Awareness brings neither freedom nor salvation but some measure of release from the Scylla and Charybdis of life as impenetrable mystery and uninhabitable vacuum.

Without accepting his premises or their possible implications, Evreinov's successors in the Soviet theatre have made use of his devices. Many Soviet productions, especially at Moscow's innovative Taganka theatre—whose director Jurij Ljubimov names Stanislavskij, Mejerxol'd, Vaxtangov and Brecht as his artistic godfathers—shape productions from the art-life concordance of actual historical protagonists such as Puškin, Gogol', Lermontov, Majakovskij and Bulgakov. As many as a half-dozen actors may impersonate the protagonist, offering a multiplicity of perspectives on the subject and demonstrating the various roles he played in his life. Even Lenin has come in for such treatment in contemporary Soviet drama, although this has not met with official acceptance.

This play of perspectives, the simultaneous experiencing of contradiction and paradox in the fullness of the moment, risks confusion and worse.

Evreinov was sympathetic to those who, like himself, engaged the insoluble dilemma of life with a measure of irrational optimism, what some mistook for light-mindedness.

Ultimately how aware was Evreinov? It *seems* at times too much and at times too little, and never exactly enough. Although he was insistent, he did not probe insistently, preoccupied as he was with his own performance. Like the media personality, the modern Narcissus who becomes enamored of his public image to the detriment of his art, Evreinov became his own occupation and preoccupation, and in the end, he may have lost track of himself. More and more he ceased to be Nikolaj Evreinov, a maker of works that were hybrids of fact and fiction and became instead "Nikolaj Evreinov," a tyrannical persona constituted through his writings and his own life's drama. How was he to control this unruly "Evreinov," this bender of wills, when his own was among the wills being bent? It seemed that Evreinov successfully harnessed Art's hypnotic power to create a perfectly realized monodrama of self-hypnosis in which the artist as creator-performer entrances the artist as perceiver. The paradox of Evreinov's transformational theories and his monodrama is that, at least in the present moment, they limit more than they set free. No one seems to suffer greater constraints than the artist himself, unless it is we who are kept from giving the artist outright the approbation he seems to demand (and we in general want to give) by his tireless efforts to tie our sympathies and understanding into knots.

Evreinov was saved repeatedly from himself by the sound of his own laughter, just as Gogol'-Xlestakov was saved from the Devil by his comic muse, the one true hero of his art. But whose laughter is it that we hear at the colloquium that concludes *The Original on the Portraitists* and runs like an undercurrent through "In the Commission of Experts" and his various Harlequin-based works? Is it Evreinov's own or rather that of the other "Evreinov," and at whose expense is "he" laughing?

Evreinov was compromised in the view of his critics by the freedom he allowed himself and mankind to reason at will in all directions. He would appear to have seduced himself, martyred himself in fact, to his own cause in a manner which even he could not have anticipated. However, we must never underestimate the cunning and foresight of the supremely self-conscious, visionary artist. As has been previously suggested, Evreinov's ultimate goal was for the self to vanish, to give way to the soul, to essence. Seen in this light, the public spectacle of Evreinov's artistic suicide (his theatre on the scaffold) is nothing more than a faked death. He kills only the other "Evreinov," while the artist himself, his essence in tow, changes here for "Newville" and life eternal.

That Evreinov and Gogol' should eventually cross paths and specifically at a point defined by *The Inspector General*, suggests, as does so much in Evreinov's career, a kind of programmed inevitability. In his excellent study of Gogol''s *oeuvre* as a sustained and gradual act of self-creation, Donald Fanger employs a structuring principle and system of terminology that could double as a profile of Evreinov.

It would of course be ingenuous to draw anything like an equation between Gogol' and Evreinov. In the first place, as the French critic Melchior de Vogüé suggested over a century ago (in a statement most often credited to Dostoevskij), Gogol''s overcoat is commodious enough to accommodate all manner of Russian artists who came after and absorbed his influence. In the second place, to put it bluntly, Evreinov is in no sense Gogol''s equal, although his facility with the language of the theatre is nevertheless something Gogol' might well have admired. However, proceeding with these reservations, a comparison of the two artists has much to recommend it, since they suffered from a somewhat similar condition and were given to seeking remedies in artistic devices. Gogol' too had reason to say "The prophet is without honor is his homeland."

Both Gogol' and Evreinov seem to make up themselves and their art, the story of the self and of the self recast as Other, as they go along. They make frequent use of framing devices and the improvisation or "Xlestakovization" of play structure (characters watching characters, scenes watching scenes). They make time and space wear a purposely artificial grimace. Character is abstracted to the level of mask and motivation reduced to the level of puppet show. Then having called the entire matter of fixed identity and inviolable structure into question in life and art respectively, they seem almost to surprise themselves in mid-device by focusing a cold spotlight upon their own artifice. There it stands frozen and objectified like the con artist's victim who, having been robbed of his possessions, is then stripped of his remaining dignity and illusions when the obviousness of the ruse perpetrated upon him is exposed. (See the conclusions to *The Inspector General* and *A Merry Death*). In effect, it is we the audience who have been conned, trapped in the author's net along with his convention-bound characters.

In both Gogol' and Evreinov we see the artist's personal identity crisis being wrestled into a richly imagined, self-contained world of art—Gogol''s *Mirgorod* and its environs and Evreinov's commedia puppet-stage (*balagančik*). The soul of each world is the vitality of humanness and the fix that humanity is in with respect to reality. The authors' respective characters, functioning as agents, escape into a dream world ruled by the demands placed upon it by wish-fulfillment—the dream of potency. Gogol''s problem with the nineteenth century, which he described as an age of "coldly dreadful egoism" and "mercantile souls," is mirrored in Evreinov's similar assessment of the twentieth century in which these tendencies became intensified.⁷ History for these two artists was the stuff of myth, not fact, a beautiful but falsely remembered dream of harmony that made both Gogol' and Evreinov inspired dreamers but marginal historians.

The revenge of the imaginative artist against the confinement of historical fact is hyperbole, which was raised to an art in Gogol' and mirrored in appropriately crooked fashion in Evreinov. As parodists and social satirists, they took their revenge further, employing the Old Comedy of Aristophanes as a model. Each imagined himself in the select company of geniuses, a dream fulfilled by Evreinov in his audacious "In the Commission of Experts."⁸ "A happy dream," writes Evreinov at the beginning of this exercise in philosophical monodrama, "is the gift, perhaps the only gift, with which Fate rewards honest seekers of truth, fearless divers for spiritual pearls, and perspiring brick layers of philosophy for their heroic sufferings and sacrifices."

One hears the echo in this voice of other voices — Gogol''s and that of E. T. A. Hoffmann who inspired them both (he sits on Evreinov's "Commission of Experts"). The narrator in Hoffmann's "Ritter Gluck" speaks of the joy of "abandoning myself to playful reveries in which sympathetic figures appear with whom I chat about learning, art, everything that is supposedly dearest to man" and, one might add, to the dreamer.⁹

The structuring principle of the dream has been well documented in Gogol''s work but not in Evreinov's. In Evreinov's *The Theatre as Such* the dream is portrayed as the stage on which the soul creates a magical life, representative of wish-fulfillment. It was the dream that first suggested to primitive man the existence of the soul and the possibility of theatricalizing life. Monodrama represents a wish-fulfilling dream in the sense that the world sees things through the eyes of the individual, who becomes the author-director-hero of the theatre which is life.

The freedom of the dreamer is, however, only an illusion, for just as the characters in Evreinov's and Gogol''s works are little more than puppets whose strings are manipulated by their creators' hands, so are the authors themselves in the employ of some other master. For both artists this "master" is approximately defined as their own intense agitation over God and the Devil who are locked in an eternal struggle for supremacy on earth and in the soul of man, a struggle whose outcome remains in doubt. Seated both at Gogol''s table and on Evreinov's "Commission" is Ludwig Tieck, musing on marionetteness. The tension between the illusory freedom of wish-fulfillment and the self-restraints that bind as tightly as some external fate makes Evreinov and his protagonists into a company of Hamlet-Pierrots seeking the transforming power of Promethean Harlequins.

We sense in both Gogol' and Evreinov a profound sense of existential peril—a fear for their souls and their selfhood (made explicit in Evreinov's *Stage-Wings*). Both go to great, even extreme lengths to affirm their Russianness, which together with their self-advertisement and what Fanger, referring to Gogol', calls "eminence by association," constitutes an effort to capture a self or more properly, at least in Evreinov's case, the Self or essence. The preponderance of shadows and doubleness in their work in terms of character, perspective, language and conventions commenting upon themselves (irony) illustrates how easily the self can be lost.[10] This accounts in part for the artists' "prescriptive tendencies." Their dogmatic teaching and retreat into quasi-religious stances represent attempted stop-gap measures in a game in which the stakes are high and the outcome irreversible.

Along with retreat there is active and aggressive invention and mystification on the artists' part, transformation and paradox. Gogol', the "literary magpie" and "double ventriloquist"—inventing "a hypothetical reader" who is then "filtered through the voice of a fictive narrator"—is again mirrored in Evreinov the self-proclaimed original, weighed down with other people's belongings, and Evreinov the self-styled Harlequin with the great talent and overriding need to play the audience (Gogol''s "baring the device").[11]

The story of the self obscured by sly but necessary play and by the author's close to fetishistic infatuation with his own narrative voice, remains, in the case of both authors, unfinished, with some essential part unrevealed.[12] This may help to account in part for the sense of incompleteness one experiences (at times quite maddeningly) in Evreinov's work. Even Evreinov's most ardent supporter, his wife, admitted that although her husband believed theatre could and should console humanity with its balm-giving illusionism, he was uncertain exactly how and to what extent this beneficial effect could be achieved. There is perhaps to be read into this admission a partial explanation of Evreinov's vague and unresolved "program" for salvation. The emotional Self preaches what the rational Self knows to be little more than a wish-fulfilling dream. The rational Self adopts irony as both a weapon and a protective shield but in the end cannot kill the faith of the emotional Self. Paradoxically, the atheist is saved by his faith and a message if not a methodology may be conveyed to mankind; life becomes an exemplary monodrama, a commedia of the soul.

Paraclete, Evreinov's obvious alterego in *The Chief Thing,* plays the role of consoler with some measure of success, although ultimately the action of the play breaks down into commedia dell'arte and Paraclete's role in it into that of the lithe and limber trickster Harlequin.[13] Is Paraclete and his creator Evreinov then a Christlike savior having the power to transform or a Harlequin whose transformation is nothing more than a theatrical effect, an illusion?

Ultimately, judging Evreinov's fakery, his Xlestakovism, is not really the issue. Certainly his career contains enough real accomplishments and suggestive insights for the modern theatre to acknowledge his importance. The question is more one of motive, namely, why did Evreinov seem to confirm his critics in their attacks upon his artistic integrity by his contrariness, magnification of self and blatant insincerity? To answer this, we must again venture into informed speculation.

Evreinov's intention seemed to have been to broaden our area of doubt so as to deepen our awareness of and active engagement in possibilities. He purposely spoke in quotation marks, pretending to be a plain dealer while transparently functioning as a double dealer. Via this process, the audience, in a sense, becomes an actor just as the artist becomes in effect an audience for his own performance. Each becomes a mirror image of the other.

Evreinov's life and work were finally most concerned with the idea of borders—crossing, illuminating, and skirting suggestively along the edges of them. He often drew attention to borders by his process of purposeful obfuscation and his avowed goal of final annihilation of all such barriers. Interestingly, two sources of inspiration for Evreinov, medieval art and the retrospective artists of the World of Art group, while sharing his preoccupation with borders, differed markedly in their goal, which was clarity, the strict delineation of boundaries, contours and outlines. There was within Evreinov that invisible but profoundly experienced border common to some degree to all thinking artists. It is the line of demarcation in the artist's ambigious perception of art as guilty pleasure and saving grace, the artist as confesser (false teacher-prophet) and confessor (scapegoat-priest). This dichotomy is a constant which grows apace with the sensitive man's perpetual self-consciousness and self-analysis of the design and efficacy of his motives. Evreinov projected himself into this dual role, characterizing the artistic seer as Christ and the hypnotist-charlatan as Harlequin. It was his insatiable hunger for Truth in an absolute sense which made Evreinov willing to deal in apparent falsehoods.

The preponderance of hyphenates employed in this study—Evreinov-Harlequin, Harlequin-Christ, Evreinov-Paraclete, Evreinov-Xlestakov—like the number of eminent associations employed by friend and foe alike to characterize the elusive artist—Evreinov-Wilde, Evreinov-Pirandello, Evreinov-Craig, Evreinov-Artaud, Evreinov-Gogol'—and even like the professional functions which Evreinov assayed—Evreinov-director, Evreinov-dramatist, Evreinov-theorist, Evreinov-composer, Evreinov-historian—suggests the extent of the Evreinovian conundrum. Two questions suggest themselves as the markers within whose boundaries lies the chief thing: "How many masks are there?" and "Which is the *real* mask?" To discover the answer to one or both of these questions would be akin to the mathematician suddenly unravelling several of the long-standing riddles on his short list of unsolved problems. The question is identity and the answer, which seems always to be just around the corner, remains, as always, safely out of reach.

The record shows that Evreinov neither sought an easy path through life nor believed that one existed. His conception of life as a theatre of eternal war, engendered in him, no doubt, by childhood experience, caused him to foster discord so as to feel himself in the thick of life's natural condition, to experience it to full effect in all its immediacy.

Evreinov the egoist and mesmerizer saw (or fancied) himself a weak man unable to control the "evil force" within him which led him to extremes of indulgence and denial.[14] His Harlequin mask was superimposed upon the face of what its creator thought or feared to be a true Pierrot. One suspects that Evreinov was not as generously forgiving of himself as his egocentric posturing leads us to believe. Instead this egocentricity was itself the modern masquerade of the *Untermensch* adorned in the classical trappings of mask, chiton and cothurni so as to resemble the *Übermensch*.

It remains for us to be as generously forgiving of Evreinov as he was of mankind in his vision of a theatre that is at once aristocratic and egalitarian, professional and amateur, communal and private, transformative and curative.

Theatre was shamanistic for Evreinov, the means by which man might discover his own godhead. The seeming aestheticism and elitism of his theatre actually was meant to distinguish and engage a deeply felt humanism. Evreinov's notion of a benign theatrical deity to dispel the chaos of modern times with white magic seems too romantic and idealistic for a world that has known the terrors of the Holocaust and the threat of nuclear destruction. The vision of Artaud and the absurdists that presumed a god who was either indifferent or else cruel and savage seems better suited to us than Evreinov's vision of hope and succor. However, so long as man will contemplate the focusing power of art not merely to reflect life but somehow to change it, Evreinov's name will be mentioned. Today we invoke Stanislavskij as the father of modern psychological realism in acting and Mejerxol'd as the leading practitioner of stylization and theatrical grotesque in directing. Evreinov should be cited as both a great synthesizer of these and other modern artistic tendencies and as our spiritual and ideological forbear in the idealistic theatre of sources and possibilities, which describes as well the borders of our lives.

Appendix A

Theatres of Pre-Revolutionary St. Petersburg

The following theatres ran advertisements in the theatrical journals during the years 1905–1909:[1]

1. The Imperial Theatres: the Mariinskij, the Aleksandrinskij, and the Mixailovskij.
2. The Theatre "Passage" (*Teatr "Passaž"*). Located at 19 Ital'janskaja Street; later the "Passage" Farce of S. F. Saburov *("Passaž" fars S. F. Saburova)*.
3. The Theatre of the Literary-Artistic Society (*Teatr literaturno-xudožestvennogo obščestva*) at 65 Fontanka Canal.
4. The Nevskij Farce (*Nevskij fars*). Later called the Contemporary Theatre (*Sovremennyj teatr*). 56 Nevskij Prospekt.
5. The Winter Bouffe *(Zimnij buff)*.
6. The Ekaterininskij Theatre of N. G. Severskij *(Ekaterininskij teatr N. G. Severskogo)*. 90 Ekaterininskij Canal.
7. The New Theatre of Nekrasova-Kolginskaja *(Novyj teatr Nekrasovoj-Kolginskoj)*. 61 Mojka Canal.
8. The Free Theatre *(Vol'nyj teatr)*. Moxovaja Canal.
9. The Theatre Founded by L. E. Sadovnikov-Rostovskij *(Teatr učreždennyj L. E. Sadovnikovym-Rostovskim)*. Vasil'evskij Island.
10. The New Vasil'evskij Theatre *(Novyj Vasileostrovskij teatr)* under the direction of N. A. Popov. Vasil'evskij Island, Srednij Prospekt.
11. The Theatre of Nemetti *(Teatr Nemetti)*. On the *Peterburgskaja* (now *Petrogradskaja*) side of the city.
12. The Theatre Bouffe *(Teatr "Buffe")* on the Admiralty Embankment.
13. The Dramatic Theatre of V. F. Komissarževskaja *(Dramatičeskij teatr V. F. Komissarževskoj)*. 39 Oficerskaja Street.
14. The Mester Theatre *(Mester-teatr)*.
15. The People's House of Emperor Nikolaj II *(Narodnyj dom imperatora Nikolaja II-go)*. Performances of Russian opera and drama.
16. The Theatre Moderne of V. Kazanskij *(Teatr modern V. Kazanskogo)*. 78 Nevskij Prospekt at Litejnyj Street (now Litejnyj Prospekt).
17. The Summer Bouffe *(Letnij buff)*. 114 Fontanka Canal.
18. The Tavričevskij Gardens *(Tavričevskij sad)*. Contained a theatre.
19. The Express Theatre *(Èkspress teatr)*. 48 Nevskij Prospekt in the Passage *(Passaž)* building.
20. The Theatre and Aquarium Gardens *(Teatr i sad Akvarium)*. Often presenting French performers and forms of entertainment.

21. The Zoological Gardens *(Zoologičeskij sad)*. Contained a theatre.
22. The Popular Theatre—The People's House of Countess E. V. Panina *(Obščedostupnyj teatr—Narodnyj dom graf. E. V. Paninoj)*. Priluskskaja Street at 10-61 Tambovskaja Street.
23. The New Hall of the Theatrical Club *(Novyj zal teatral'nogo kluba)*. 42 Litejnyj Prospekt.
24. The Merry Theatre for Grown-up Children *(Veselyj teatr požilyx detej)*. Under the direction of N. N. Evreinov and F. F. Komissarževskij. On the premises of the Dramatic Theatre of V. F. Komissarževskaja, 39 Oficerskaja Street.
25. The Moulin Rouge *(Mulen-Ruž)*. 51 Nevskij Prospekt.
26. The Krestovskij Gardens *(Krestovskij sad)*. Contained a theatre.
27. The Summer Farce *(Letnij fars)*. 39 Oficerskaja Street.
28. The New Summer Theatre *(Novyj letnij teatr)*.
29. The Theatre "Hermitage" *(Teatr "Èrmitaž")*.
30. The Litejnyj Theatre *(Litejny teatr)*.
31. The Music Conservatoire *(Konservatorija)*.

The following eight theatres that were previously unlisted during the period 1905-1909 ran advertisements for the 1915-1917 seasons:

1. The Suvorinskij *(Malyj)* Theatre.
2. The Theatre of Musical Drama *(Teatr musykal'noj dramy)*.
3. The Theatre of Smoljakov *(Teatr Smoljakova)*.
4. The Theatre of L. B. Javorskaja (The Winter Moon Park). Teatr L. B. Javorskoj *(Zimnij Luna-Park)*. 39 Oficerskaja Street.
5. The "Trocadero" *(Trokadero)*. The *Petrogradskaja* side of the city. 42 Bolšoj Prospekt. Presenting "operetta, farce, comedy, divertissement, and the latest newsreels."
6. The Troickij Theatre *(Troickij teatr)*. 18 Troickaja Street.
7. The Intimate Theatre *(Intimnyj teatr)*.
8. The Crooked Mirror Theatre of Z. V. Xolmskaja *(Teatr "Krivoe zerkalo" Z. V. Xolmskoj)*. Performing on the premises of the Ekaterininskij Theatre. 90 Ekaterininskij Canal.

Not all of these theatres offered strictly dramatic fare. Some presented opera, ballet, and various forms of light entertainment—operetta, variety shows, and the like. Some were seasonal, operating only during the winter or summer months. On the other hand, this number includes only those theatres that welcomed a paying public and advertised to secure their business. Not included are the various dramatic circles that were closed to all but the artistic elite. Such groups would swell the list of theatres appreciably if included. Other theatres appeared and disappeared during this period. Some changed names and locations. The stages of theatrical Petersburg were many and bustling with activity.

Appendix B

Cast Lists of Productions at the Ancient Theatre

The Medieval Cycle (1907–8)

First Evening (7 December 1907)
1. *The Three Magi (Tri volxva),* prologue by Evreinov.[1]
2. *Le Miracle de Théofile (Dejstvo o Teofile)* by Rutebeuf
    Théofile   Nelobin
    The Cardinal   Kaslal'skij
    Zadira, his servant   Orlov
    The Bright Spirit   Vreden
    Saladin, a magician   Sazonov
    The Devil   Perelygin
    Pierre } friends of Théofile   Mišlevskij
    Tomas   Al'minskij
    Prologue   Kvjatkovskij[2]

Second Evening
1. *Present-day Brothers (Nynešnye brat'ja)*
    Prologue   Al'minskij
    The Father   Perelygin
    The Mother   Lorox
    First Son   Sazonov
    Second Son   Dal'nev
    Third Son   Vreden
    Brotherly Love   Rigler
    Envy   Loxteva
    The Pangs of Conscience   Dmitrenko[3]
2. *Le Jeu de Robin et Marion (Igra o Robine i Marion)* by Adam de la Halle
    Marion, a young shepherdess, sweetheart of Robin   Rigler
    Robin, a young shepherd, sweetheart of Marion   Al'minskij
    The Knight   Nelobin
        [In the 23 March 1908 edition of the journal *Theatre* (Teatr), Nelobin was listed as playing Robin's cousin Bodin. However, production photographs show him in the role of the Knight.]
    Bodin, a young peasant, Robin's cousin
    Peronella, a young shepherdess, Marion's girlfriend   Butkovskaja

224   Cast Lists of Productions at the Ancient Theatre

    Guar, a young peasant, Robin's friend   Orlov
    Two musicians
    The Master of Ceremonies   Perelygin[4]

3. *A Very Merry and Amusing Farce about a Tub (Očen' veselyj i smešnoj fars o čane)* by Jean Dabondance

    The Husband   Nelobin
    His Wife   Dmitrenko
    His Mother-in-Law   Kvjatkovskij

    A Very Merry and Amusing Farce about a Cuckold's Hat (Očen' smešnoj i veselyj fars o šljape-rogače) by Jean Dabondance

    The Husband   Kastal'skij
    His Wife   Lokteva
    First Nephew   Kvjatkovskij
    Second Nephew   Miševskij
    Servant   Vreden
    First Fool   Orlov
    Second Fool   Dal'nev[5]

The Spanish Cycle (1911-12)

First Evening (18 November 1911)

1. *Fuente Ovejuna (Ovečij istočnik)* by Lope de Vega

    King Ferdinand of Aragon   Razumovskij
    Queen Isabella of Castille   Jasnovskaja
    Don Roderigo Téllez Girón   Smirnova
    Don Roderigo Manrike de Lara   Verescagin
    Don Fernando Gómez de Guzmán   Murav'ev
    Flores } servants to the commander   Faljutinskij
    Ortuno }   Orlov
    Cimbranos, a soldier   Ardašev
    Esteban, alcalde of Fuente Ovejuna   Galinskij[6]
    Rekhidor   Gol'denberg
    Mengo   Stepnoj
    Barrildo } peasant ploughmen   Nazarov
    Juan Ryžij }   Volynskij
    Frondo   Gejrot
    Judge   Korolev
    Laurencia, daughter of Esteban   Gercfel'd[7]
    Pascuala   Sidorenko[8]

The remainder of the company participated in the crowd scenes and in the dances during the intervals. The production was directed by Evreinov, the set designed by N. K. Rerix, and the costumes by I. Ja. Bilibin. The music was composed by Il'ja Sac. The translation was by Sergej Jur'ev.

2. *Los habladores* (Interlude) *(Dva boltuna)* by Cervantes

    Doña Beatrice   Jasnovskaja
    Sarmiento   Faljutinskij
    Roldan   Orlov
    Alyvazil   Volynskij
    Inez   Nazimova

Second Evening (28 November 1911)
1. Marta la Piadosa *(Blagočestivaja Marta ili Vljublennaja Svjatoša)* by Tirso de Molina

Don Gomez	Razumovskij
Doña Marta	Gercfel'd
Doña Lucia	Smirneva
Doña Inez	Nazimova
Captain Urbina	Volynskij
Alferec	Orlov
Don Felippe de Aiala	Gejrot
Pastrana	Stepnoj
Director of the troupe	Volynskij
Prompter	Korolev
First dancer	Gejnc
Second dancer	Marševa
Xitana	Čekan
Tavern keeper	Kasjutinskij
First guest	Adašev
Second guest	Kal'kovskij
Third guest	Gippel'son

Translation by T. L. Ščepkina-Kupernik. Directed by K. M. Miklaševskij. Set design by Prince A. K. Servadšidze. Old Spanish music arranged by Il'ja Sac.

2. El Gran Ducque da Moscovia *(Velikij knjaz' Moskovskij i gonimyj Imperator)* by Lope de Vega

Vasilij Velikij knjaz' Moskovskij	Razumovskij
Theodore } His sons	Gejrot
Juan }	Stepnoj
Dimitri	Smirnova
Christina, Theodore's wife	
Boris, her brother	Korolev
Isabella, Juan's wife	Sidorenko
Lambert, a German knight	Galinskij
Tibalda, his wife	Jasnovskaja
Cesar, their son	Gejnc
Conrad } knights	Volynskij
Rudolf }	Kievskij
Rufino, a Spaniard	Vereščagin

Translation by P. O. Marozov. Directed by N. I. Butkovskaja. Set and Costumes designed by N. K. Kalmakov. Music by Il'ja Sac.

Third Evening (6 December 1911)
1. El Purgatorio de San Patricio *(Čistilišče Patrikka)* by Calderón de la Barca

Elerio, King of Ireland	Vereščagin
Patrick	Mgebrov
Ludovico Enio	Galinskij
Pauline, a peasant	Volynskij
Lepario	Nazarov
Filippo	Gejrot
Captain	Razumovskij
An unnamed person	Gol'denberg
First monk	Faljutinskij
Second monk	Nikolaev

Old peasant	Orlov
A kind genius	Nazimov
An evil genius	Faljutinskij
Polonea	Simonova
Lecebea	Gercfel'd
Lucia	Sidorenko

Translation by K. D. Bal'mont. Directed by N. V. Driezen. Set designed by V. A. Ščuko and E. E. Lansere. Costumes designed by I. Ja. Bilibin. Music by I. A. Sac.[9]

Appendix C

Premieres at the Crooked Mirror Theatre During Evreinov's Tenure as Artistic Director, 1910-1917[1]

Third Season, 1910-1911

First Program: 1 October 1910
1. *Someone Else's Wife and Husband under the Bed (Čužaja žena i muž pod krovat'ju)* by F. M. Dostoevskij. Dramatization by S. I. Antimonov in two scenes. Designer M. N. Jakovlev.
2. *A Little Bit of Music (Nemnožko muzyki),* a grotesque in one act.
3. *About Six Beautiful Women who Don't Resemble One Another (O šesti krasavicax ne poxožix drug na druga).* A fairy tale by Mohammed El-Bassri. Dramatization and music by N. N. Evreinov. Scene and costume design by M. N. Jakovlev. Featured a narrator reading the stage directions à la Sologub's suggestion in "The Theatre of One Will."
4. *A Small Misunderstanding (Malen'koe nedorazumenie).* A short scene in verse presented as silhouettes projected upon a white screen. Translation by Vojnov.
5. *Imitations of Music-Hall Singers of Different Nationalities (Imitacija šansonetnyx pevic raznyx nacional'nostej).* Performed by Z. F. Ikar (N. F. Barabanov).
6. *Don't Shoot Your Mouth off Before Going into Battle (Ne xvalis' iduči na rat').* An opera-vaudeville in one act spoofing the naturalistic trend in Russian drama. Music and libretto by Il'ja Sac. Directed by N. N. Evreinov.

Second Program: 18 October 1910
1. *A Wooden Tragicomedy (Derevjannaja tragikomedija).* A one-act parody in verse by Benedikt, spoofing old theatrical conventions and character types. The set was designed to resemble a puppet stage with the actors moving like marionettes.
2. *Songs of Bilitis (Pesni Bilitis).* A story by Pierre Louÿs, concerning a follower of Sappho. Translated by Kondrat'ev. Music by N. N. Evreinov. Designed by M. N. Jakovlev. Silhouettes of feminine figures on a white background suggested antique terra cotta vases.
3. *A Page from a Novel (Stranička romana).* A farce *(balagan)* by Èsterejx, translated by E. Mattern.
4. *Wise Čaruatta (Mudryj Čaruatta).* A musical tragicomedy in three acts. Music by V. G. Èrenberg.
5. *A Wonderful Presentation (Zamečatel'noe predstavlenie).* A travelling circus in one act.

Third Program: *"The Gentle Sex,"* 2 November 1910
1. *The Gentle Sex (Slabyj pol)* by Gustav Vid. Dramatization by Z. V. Xolmskaja. *Mademoiselle Matilda (M-l' Matilda).* A satire in one act; same as above.
2. *A Mute Wife (Nemaja žena).* A comedy by Anatole France. A free translation by A. Kosortov. Directed by N. N. Evreinov in "Molièresque tones," using a stylized setting.
3. *Woman and Death (Ženščina i smert').* A slander in one act by S. I. Antimonov (an actor in the company). Sets and costumes by M. N. Jakovlev in the style of Beardsley. An experiment in the schematization of Strindberg's misogyny.
4. *Silhouettes of Dances (Siluèty tancev).* Another of the experiments with black on white projections.
5. *Don Limonado de Gazec.* A comic opera in two scenes, based on Mejerxol'd's 1910 production of *Don Juan.* Music by Lev Geben, libretto by V. P. Burenin. Design by M. N. Jakovlev. Directed by N. N. Evreinov.

Fourth Program: *"Merry Dramas,"* 10 December 1910

1. *The Elements of Life (Elementy žizni).* Short scenes in one act with an introduction and a conclusion by B. F. Gejer. A morality play depicting the transformation of an idealistic youth as he confronts the world's harsh realities.
2. *An Ideal Tenant (Ideal'nyj kvartirant).* A merry anecdote.
3. *The Four* (Četvero). Dramatization of a story by Arkadij Averčenko.
4. *A Night in a Harem (Noč' v gareme).* A grotesque by Vep. Music by L. Geben.
5. *About Ballet in Ancient Times (Okolo baleta v starinu)* by Z. Boner. Music by Godar. Another silhouette presentation, set in the epoch of Louis XIV.
6. *Grae-grae voropae.* A revival.

Fifth Program: 21 December 1910; an extraordinary presentation commemorating the third anniversary of the Crooked Mirror Theatre.
1. *The History of the "Crooked Mirror" (Istorija "Krivogo zerkala").* A sketch by Sčepkina-Kupernik based on Hans Christian Andersen's fairy tale *The Snow Queen.*
2. *The Many-headed Monster (Čudišče mnogogolovoe).* A fantasy in one act by Benedikt.
3. *A Solemn Act Commemorating the Second Anniversary of the "Crooked Mirror" (Toržestvennyj akt po slučaju dvuxletnogo jubileja "Krivogo zerkala")* by N. N. Evreinov.
4. *The Three lovers of the Queen or The Page's Revenge (Troe vljublennyx v korolevu ili mest' paža).* A mime melo-tragidrama in one scene. Text by B. F. Gejer. Music by V. G. Èrenberg.
5. *A Corner of the Parterre (Ugolok partera).* A caricature in one act by "Black Cat" *(Černyj kot).*
6. *Fata Morgana.* An anniversary medley almost without action.

Sixth Program: 7 January 1911. "The Strong Sex"—Negatives in Four Scenes *(Sil'nyj pol—komedijnye negativy v četyrex kartinax)* by N. Krašeninnkov.
1. *Porfirij Nikitič* (No author listed).
2. *Dirty Work (Černyj trud)* based on a short story by Guy de Maupassant.
3. *In a Study (V kabinete).* Same as above.
4. *Xlykin*—based on a story by Čexov. "The Last of the Female Mohicans" *(Poslednjaja mogikanša).*

Seventh Program: 24 January 1911
1. *The Decameron Hour (Dekamarona čas).* An étude in one act by Boccaccio. Dramatization by S. Ljubošic-Ljubovnaja. A tragicomedy.

2. *The Moral Bases of Man (Nravstvennye osnovy čeloveka).* A parody of the syrupy, wretchedly banal plays of the popular theatre, in one act with an introduction, an apotheosis, songs and music. Text by "Valentina Moreau" (N. G. Smirnov and S. S. Ščerbakov).
3. *Hamlet and Little George (Gamlet i Žoržik)* by Vladimir Traxtenberg. Hamlet as seen through the eyes of a child.
4. *Statues Coming to Life (Oživajuščie statui)* by N. N. Evreinov. Designed by M. N. Jakovlev.
5. *Beautiful Galatea (Prekrasnaja Galateja).* A comic opera by Franz Zuppe, earlier staged by Evreinov and F. F. Komissarževskij at the Merry Theatre for Grown-up Children.

Eighth Program (No date given)

1. *How They Write (Kak oni pišut).* A parody on yellow journalism in America by S. S. Timofeev, based upon a story by Mark Twain.
2. *The 1002d Night (1002-aja noc').* An Arabian fairy tale in one act by Mjurgit.
3. "The Cinematograph or The Innocent Victim of Senseless Passion and Bloody Love of an Old Man," a powerfully dramatic drama, approximately 11764 meters long in colorful colors with nature captured [photographed] in conversation by B. F. Gejer ("Kinematograf ili nevinnaja žertva bezumnoj strasti i krovavaja ljubov' starika," sil'no dramatičeskaja drama dlinoju v 11764 metra v cvetnyx kraskax s natural'noj prirody s razgovorom snimal B. F. Gejer). This play ran through 1915. Directed by N. N. Evreinov. Designed by M. N. Jakovlev.

Fourth Season, 1911–1912

First Program: 18 September 1911
1. *Vasil' Vasilič Reconciled (Vasil' Vasilič pomirilsja).* A restored vaudeville by Lev Urvancev.
2. *Aqua Vitae (Voda žizni).* A play in four decanters by B. F. Gejer. A monodrama (polydrama) staged by N. N. Evreinov.
3. *The Four Corpses of Fiametta (Četyre mertveca Fiametty).* A pantomime to music by V. A. Vigdaj, based on a story by Milo. A parody on a libretto with pantomime with all of the usual romantic excesses.
4. *A Grandmother's Fairy Tale (Babuškina skazka).* A black-on-white silhouette.
5. *Ryčalov's Tour (Gastrol' Ryčalova).* A play in two acts. Text by Ančar Mancenilov (M. N. Volkonskij). Music by V. G. Èrenberg. The first act takes place in the wings of the theatre. The second act is a play-within-a-play. Directed by N. N. Evreinov. Designed by M. N. Jakovlev. The play remained in the repertoire through 1917.

Second Program: 20 October 1911
1. *Posthumous Letters (Posmertnye pis'ma).* A caricature *(šarž)* by Ne-Gorev, B. K.
2. *Shouldn't we lower the curtain? (A ne opustit' li nam zanavesku?).* A scene in one window *(scena v odnom okne)* by P. P. Potemkin. This play was performed over 100 times. *Solo Numbers (Sol'nye No. No.).* Romances by Abramjan and imitations by Ikar of a bawd, a marchioness, and a music-hall singer.
3. *Such is Woman (Takova ženščina).* A musical satire. Text by Vl. Podgornyj. Music by V. G. Èrenberg.
4. *The Handkerchief of the Baroness (Nosovoj platok baronessy).* A clichéd drama from high society life for provincial benefit performances of both sexes by B. F. Gejer. Directed by N. N. Evreinov. Designed by M. N. Jakovlev.

Third Program: 13 November 1911
1. *Love for One's Neighbour (Ljubov' k bližnemu)*. A satirical miniature by L. N. Andreev.
2. *Twenty-two Misfortunes (22 nesčastija)*. An Egyptian subject in verse (a borrowed subject) by A. A. Izmajlov.
3. *Reminiscences (Vospominanija)*. An illustrative tale. A monodrama by B. F. Gejer, consisting of (1) Reality, (2) Reminiscences of the bridegroom, (3) Reminiscences of the bride, (4) Reminiscences of a merry wedding guest, (5) Reminiscences of a somber wedding guest, (6) Reminiscences of the mother, and (7) Epilogue. This play ran through 1914.
4. *The Barometer of Coppelius (Barometr Koppeliusa)*. A short musical scene by P. Potemkin. Designed by M. N. Jakovlev. Music by V. G. Èrenberg.
5. *The School of the Stars (Škola ètualej)*. A parody-grotesque in one act. An episode from the life of Annuška the maid. Written by N. N. Evreinov. This play ran for two seasons.

Fourth Program: 12 December 1911
1. *The Sabine Women (Prekrasnye sabinjanki)*. A political satire and historical presentation in two acts and three scenes by L. N. Andreev. Music by V. G. Èrenberg. Directed by N. N. Evreinov. Designed by M. N. Jakovlev.
2. *Anja and Vanja (Anja i Vanja)*. A parody on children's plays by N. G. Smirnov and S. S. Ščerbakov. Music by V. Èrenberg. Directed by N. N. Evreinov.
3. *Eastern Delights (Vostočnye sladosti)* or *The Russian's Battle with the Kabardinians (Bitva russkix s kabardincami)*. An opera-farce in two acts. Music by Il'ja Sac. Libretto by V. Podgornyj and I. Sac. Directed by N. N. Evreinov. Designed by M. N. Jakovlev. Dances by E. A. Xovanskaja.
This program included romances by A. S. Abramjan and imitations by Ikar.

Fifth Program: 23 January 1912
1. *Vanka's Literature (Van'kina literatura)*. A creative process in one act by B. F. Gejer.
2. *The 86th of Martober (Martobrja 86 dnja)*. A play by V. A. Vyškov.
3. *Sumurun*. A pantomime from the fairy tales of Scheherazade (also in the repertoire of Max Reinhardt's theatre) in five scenes. Music by V. G. Èrenberg. Designed by M. N. Jakovlev. Ballet master — Presnjakov. Directed by N. N. Evreinov.
[The Crooked Mirror was on tour for the second half of this season.]

Fifth Season, 1912–1913

First Program: 18 September 1912. General title: "Napoleon at the Crooked Mirror" *(Napoleon v Krivom zerkale)*
1. *Napoleon and Love (Napoleon i ljubov')* by B. F. Gejer.
2. *Contemporaries (Sovremenniki)* by P. P. Potemkin.
3. *A Family of Muscovites (Sem'ja moskovitov)* by M. Dezož'e. Translated by M. M. Potapenko. A restorative staging of a play by Dezož'e. Music by Gretri, Bual'd'e, Snontin. Directed by N. N. Evreinov.
Apotheosis (Apofeoz): A story about a goat, given as a gift to a French-Russian family, reared as a child whose mother's milk went sour from fear. Presented in pseudoclassical style. Designed by M. N. Jakovlev. Directed by N. N. Evreinov.
4. *Napoleon*. A symphonic poem in five parts. A parody by V. G. Èrenberg.
5. *A Biography of Napoleon Bonaparte (Žizneopisanie Napoleona Buonaparta)*. An historical play in four scenes by Banquo's Ghost *(Dux-Banko)* (D. Glikman). Music by V. G. Èrenberg. Designed by Miss.

Premieres at the Crooked Mirror Theatre 1910–1917   *231*

Second Program: 21 October 1912. General title: "Tragi-farces"
1. *The Life of a Cultured Man (Žizn' kul'turnogo čeloveka)* or *Philistine Dramas (Meščanskie dramy)*. Five pieces from the sewing machine of N. N. Krašennikov.
2. *Dream (Son)*. A realistic phantasmagoria by B. F. Gejer.
3. *In the Stage-Wings of the Soul (V kulisax duši)*. A monodrama in one act by N. N. Evreinov with a prologue. Designed by M. P. Bobyšov. The total time of the action is one-half minute.
4. *A Sweet Pastry (Sladkij pirog)*. A lyrical naturalistic opera in one act. Libretto by Lev Urvancev. Music by N. N. Evreinov.

Third Program: 15 November 1912
1. *An Intermission is Announced (Ob'javljaetsja pereryv)*. A humoresque by Jonson. Directed by N. N. Evreinov.
2. *The Legend of the Holy Black Swan (Legenda o svjaščennom černom lebede)*. A satire in two acts by B. F. Gejer. Music by V. G. Èrenberg. Ballet master: Leont'ev.
3. *Everyday Affairs (Vsegdašny šašni)*. A popular song *(pesennyj ljubok)*, a dramatic fairy tale in twenty-four scenes by F. K. Sologub. Designed by M. P. Bobyšov. Directed by N. N. Evreinov.

Fourth Program: 2 December 1912
1. *White Tea (Belyj čaj)* by Banquo's ghost *(Dux-Banko)* (D. Glikman). A sketch from student life of the nineties in one act.
2. *Lulu's Happiness (Sčast'e Lulu)*. From the life of a doll. Written by R. A. Ungern.
3. *The Inspector General (Revizor)*. A directorial buffonade in five constructions *(postroenijax)* on one cutting. Written and directed by N. N. Evreinov. Designed by M. P. Bobyšov.
4. *A Ballet Reborn (Vozroždennyj balet)* or *La Dame aux camélias (Dama c kamelijami)* by Alexandre Dumas *fils*. Music by Guiseppe Verdi. The dances are performed by Z. F. Ikar.

Fifth Program: 14 January 1913
1. *A Solemn Public Conference Commemorating Koz'ma Prutkov on the Fifth Anniversary of His Death (Toržestvennoe publičnoe zasedanie pamjati Koz'my Prutkova po slučaju pjatiletija ego končiny)*. Written by N. G. Smirnov and S. S. Ščerbakov.
2. *The Hasty Turk (Oprometčivyj turk)* or *Is it Pleasant to be a Grandson? (Prijatno li byt' vnukom?)*. A naturally conversational presentation by Koz'ma Prutkov. Directed by N. N. Evreinov.

10 February 1913: A Special presentation for Tsar Nikolaj II at the Chinese Theatre, Tsarskoe Selo.
1. *A Solemn Public Conference Commemorating Koz'ma Prutkov on the Fifth Anniversary of His Death*.
2. *Individual Concert Numbers*.
3. *The Inspector General* by N. N. Evreinov.
4. *Ryčalov's Tour*.

Sixth Season, 1913–1914

First Program: 23 September 1913
1. *Preferaneov and Son (Preferaneov i syn)*. A scene from the daily life of undertakers and sewage-disposal men by N. G. Smirnov and S. S. Ščerbakov.

2. *A Lecture on Alcoholism (Lekcija ob alkogolizme)*. Accompanied by magic lantern slides.
3. *Yellow Jacket (Želtaja kofta)*. A Chinese play reworked for the London stage.
4. *The Wedding (Svad'ba)*. A musical illustration of *The Wedding* by Čexov. A one-act opera by V. G. Èrenberg.

Second Program: 23 October 1913
1. *The Golden Mean (Zolotaja seredina)*. A play in one act and two scenes by M. A. Ljubimov. The title refers to a newspaper; the cast includes a female dancer, an actor, a modernist poet, and a professor.
2. *When Knights Were Brave (Kogda rycari byli otvažny)*, a pantomime by B. F. Gejer. Music by V. G. Èrenberg. A mime melo-tragidrama in one scene.
3. *A Feast of Laughter. The World Contest of Wit (Kuxnja smexa. Mirovoj konkurs ostroumija)*. A parody in four jokes *(šaržy)* by N. N. Evreinov. Directed by N. N. Evreinov.

Third Program: 14 December 1913
1. *The Gold Mine (Zolotoe dno)*. A satire, translated from the French.
2. *Under the Power of Pan (Pod vlast'ju Pana)*. An English comedy, translated by Z. Vengerova. Dramatization by N. N. Evreinov.
3. *Homo sapiens*. A play be Benedikt (N. Vencel'). A parody on mystical symbolism in the style of Hofmannsthal.
4. *Tat'jana Larina*. A cinematic treatment of *Eugene Onegin* by the firm "Crocodile" in one act. Written by B. F. Gejer.

Fourth Program: 29 January 1914
1. *The Stylized Branch of the Department of Expectations (Stilizovannoe otdelenie departamenta ožidani)*. A satire.
2. *The Son of Two Mothers (Syn dvux materej)*. The real, original Russian operetta. Libretto by K. N. Saxarov. Music by V. G. Èrenberg.
3. *Utopia (Utopija)*. A play by Banquo's Ghost (D. Glikman). Set and costume designs by N. N. Evreinov.
4. *Sausage from Butterflies (Kolbasa iz baboček)*. A parody of futurist art by N. G. Smirnov and S. S. Ščerbakov.
The Symphony of Digestion (Simfonija piščevarenija) by V. G. Èrenberg.
[War with Germany. Members of the Crooked Mirror are abroad; Evreinov in Egypt.]

Seventh Season, 1914–1915

First Program: 1 October 1914
1. *A German Idyll (Nemeckaja idillija)*. A satire in one act by B. F. Gejer.
2. *1914–1814*. A dramatic ètude by Banquo's Ghost (D. Glikman) with a prologue and epilogue.
3. *Mal'brug is Ready for the Campaign (Mal'brug v poxod sobralsja)*. A grotesque buffonade by A. K.
4. *The Circle of Life of One Conqueror (Krug žizni odnogo zavoevatelja)*. A pantomime-caricature in three scenes. Text by A. B. Music by V. G. Èrenberg.

Second Program: 3 November 1914
1. *Idols of the Sacred Mountain (Idoly svjaščennoj gory)*. A satire in three scenes by Lord Dunsany. Translated from the English by M. A. Potapenko.

2. *The Action Surrounding a Disputed Promissory Note and the Court Order Concerning It (Dejstvo o protestovannom veksele i ispolnitel'nom po onomu liste).* A mystery. Libretto by Vladimirov. Music by V. G. Èrenberg.
3. *Max and Morris (Maks i Moric).* A little fairy tale on contemporary events à la S. Timofeev.
4. *The Pearl of Madrid (Žemčužina Madrita).* A behind the scenes story in one act and two scenes by Džen. Translated by A. K.

Third Program: 16 December 1914
1. *What They Say, What They Think (Čto govorjat, čto dumajut).* A psychological experiment in one act by B. F. Gejer.
2. *The Lost Silk Hat (Zabytyj cilindr).* A sketch by Lord Dunsany. Translated from the English by M. Potapenko.
3. *A Presentation about Tsar Vasil'jan,* "How He Planned to Subdue the Entire World and Convert It to His Own Religion" (*Predstavlenie o care Vasil'jane, o tom, kak on zadumal ves' svet pokorit' i v svoju veru obratit'*). A patriotic presentation (an imitation of *Emperor Maximillian*) by N. G. Smirnov.

Fourth Program: 19 January 1915
1. *A Hyperborean Drink (Giperborejskij napitok).* (Based on a story by Jack London.) A play in one act and three scenes by S. S. Timofeev.
2. *Bird's Milk (Ptič'e moloko).* A symbolic presentation, a miniature in three parts (one act) by Vladimir Azov.
3. *Moral Upbringing (Nravstvennoe vospitanie).* A scene from a child's life in one act. A tragicomedy by Banquo's Ghost (D. Glikman).
4. *Dramatizations of Romances (Inscenirovki romansov).*

Eighth Season, 1915–1916

First Program: 4 October 1915
1. *Model Spouses (Primernye suprugi).* A farce in one act and two scenes. A borrowed subject. Translated by Z. Vengerova. Directed by N. N. Evreinov. Designed by Ju. P. Annenkov. This play remained in the repertoire through 1917.
2. *The Nose (Nos).* Based on Gogol''s short story. Dramatization by A. I. Dejč. A grotesque in five transformations with an epilogue. An unusual event. Directed by N. N. Urvancov.
3. *The Fate of A Man (Sud'ba muzčiny).* A psychological drama of the future. A farce by N. N. Urvancov.
4. *Romances by A. S. Abramjan (Romansy A. S. Abramjan).*

Second Program: 16 November 1915
1. *In a Neutral Little Restaurant (V nejtral'nom kabačke)* by V. Ja. Ireckij (Glikman). With songs and dances.
2. *Šura the Sufferer or Yankel the Musician. (Stradalica Šura ili Jankel'—muzykant).* A parody on Yiddish plays by N. N. Urvancov.
3. *A Columbine of Today (Kolumbina segodnja).* A pantomime by N. N. Evreinov and Miss. Music by N. N. Evreinov. Set and costume designs by Miss. Directed by N. N. Evreinov and A. A. Naulov. Dances staged by ballet-master Presnjakov.
4. *Aeolian Harps (Èolovy arfy).* A play in three reviews with an introduction and a conclusion. Written by B. F. Gejer and N. N. Evreinov. Directed by N. N. Evreinov.

234 Premieres at the Crooked Mirror Theatre 1910–1917

Third Program: 21 December 1915
1. *Darkness (T'ma)*. An opera-pantomime by V. G. Èrenberg. *Pastorale (Pastoral')* by Abramjan Černenko.
2. *The Paths of Good and Evil (Puti dobra i zla)*. A didactic play in one act by N. G. Smirnov, satirizing Lev Tolstoj's idea of non-resistance to evil.
3. *The Fourth Wall (Četvërtaja stena)*. A buffonade in two parts by N. N. Evreinov.

Ninth Season, 1916–1917

First Program: 30 September 1916
1. *Karagez*. A presentation of the Turkish Petruška in two scenes. Dramatization by N. N. Evreinov. Set and costumes designed by Ju. P. Annenkov. Dances staged by B. G. Romanov.
2. *To the Accompaniment of a Trombone (Pod zvuki trombona)*. A parody on a farce by K. Saxarov.

Second Program: 4 November 1916
1. *The Glory of Consul Duilija (Slava koncula Duilija)*. An ancient Roman story. A satirical grotesque by N. N. Urvancov.
2. *Vel'zar, the King of Vizija (Vel'zar, korol' Vizii)*. A tragedy in five acts and six scenes by William Shakespeare. Translated by Antip Snegov.
3. *The Figure and the Voice (Stan i golos)*. A fable by Koz'ma Prutkov. Dramatization and music by V. G. Èrenberg.
4. *The Four Corpses of Fiametta (Četyre mertveca Fiametty)*. A pantomime with music by V. A. Vigdaj. (A repeat performance).

Third Program: 19 December 1916
1. *The Doctor's Dilemma*. A tragedy in four acts by Bernard Shaw. Translated from the English and reworked by N. N. Evreinov. Directed by N. N. Evreinov. Designed by Ju. P. Annenkov.
2. *The Eternal Dancer (Večnaja tancovščica)*. A choreographic mystery in seven scenes by N. N. Evreinov and Miss. Music by N. N. Evreinov. Dances staged by ballet master Presnjakov.

Fourth Program: 4 February 1917
1. *The Evolution of the Devil (Èvoljucija d'javola)*. Six scenes in verse by N. A. Teffi. Directed by N. N. Evreinov. Music by N. N. Evreinov. Designed by Grandi.
2. *Under the Mask (Pod maskoj)* by Eric.
3. *Tiger Skin (Tigrovaja škura)*. A parody by N. G. Smirnov.
4. *A Contemporary Symphony (Sovremennaja simfonija)* by V. G. Èrenberg.

Fifth Program: 19 March 1917
1. *Prince Lutonja (Princ Lutonja)*. A satire-fairy tale by V. S. Kuročkin; written in 1872 but unpublished in the author's lifetime.
2. *An Uncensored Play: Egyptian Punishment (Necenzurnaja p'esa: kazn' Egipetskaja)* by N. N. Urvancov.

Sixth Program: 30 September 1917
Long Live Justice! (Da zdravstvuet pravosudie!) A satire in three acts.

Seventh Program: 12 November 1917
La Ronde (Xorovod). A novella in ten dialogues by Arthur Schnitzler. Directed by S. N. Nadeždin.

Eighth Program: 28 December 1917
A Journey around Equality (Putešestvie vokrug ravenstva), in four acts.

Appendix D

Productions Staged by N. N. Evreinov at the Crooked Mirror Theatre

Dramatic and Musical Compositions by N. N. Evreinov

1. *In the Stage-Wings of the Soul (V kulisax duši)*. A monodrama in one act.
2. *The Inspector General (Revizor)*. A directorial buffonade in five constructions on one cutting.
3. *The School of the Stars (Škola ètualej)*. A parody-grotesque in one act.
4. *A Feast of Laughter. The World Contest of Wit (Kuxnja smexa. Mirovoj konkurs ostroumija)*. A parody in four jests *(šaržy)*.
5. *A Columbine of Today (Kolombina segodnja)*. A pantomime in one act (music by N. N. Evreinov).
6. *The Eternal Dancer (Večnaja tancovščica)*. A choreographic mystery in seven scenes.
7. *The Fourth wall (Četvërtaja stena)*. A buffonade in two scenes.

Dramatizations by N. N. Evreinov

8. *About Six Beautiful Women who Don't Resemble One Another (O šesti krasavicax ne poxožix drug na druga)*. A fairy tale by Mohammed El-Bassri (in one act).
9. *Under the Power of Pan (Pod vlast'ju Pana)*. Translated from the English by Zinaida Vengerova (in one act).
10. *Songs of Bilitis (Pesni Bilitis)*. A silhouette in one scene.
11. *The Fan (Veer)*. A silhouette in one scene.
12. *Karagez*. A Turkish presentation of Petruška in two scenes.
13. *The Doctor's Dilemma*. A tragedy in four acts by Bernard Shaw.

Plays Written by N. N. Evreinov in Collaboration with Another Author

14. a) *Aeolian Harps (Èolovye arfy)*. A monodrama in four acts (with B. F. Gejer).
    b) *A Colombine of Today* and *The Eternal Dancer*. Both co-authored with Miss. Music for both by N. N. Evreinov.
15. *A Sweet Pastry (Sladkij pirog)*. A naturalistic opera in one act. Libretto by Lev Urvancev. Music by N. N. Evreinov.

Plays by Other Authors

By Leonid Andreev:

16. *Love for One's Neighbour (Ljubov' k bližnemu).* In one act.
17. *The Sabine Women (Prekrasnye sabinjanki).* In three acts.
18. *Monument.* In one act.

By B. F. Gejer:

19. *Aqua Vitae (Voda žizni).* In four decanters.
20. *Dream (Son).* In one act.
21. *Reminiscences (Vospominanija).* In five scenes.
22. *The Legend of the Holy Black Swan (Legenda o svj'aščennom černom lebede).* In two acts. Music by V. G. Èrenberg.
23. *Reflections of Sunrays (Solnečnye zajčiki).* In one act (rehearsed but not performed owing to the uninterrupted success of Evreinov's *The Inspector General).*
24. *The Handerchief of the Baroness (Nosovoj platok baronessy).* A boulevard play in ten scenes.

By Koz'ma Prutkov (and plays dedicated to him):

25. *The Hasty Turk (Oprometčivyj turk)* or *Is it Pleasant to be a Grandson? (Prijatno li byt' vnukom?).* A naturally conversational presentation.
26. *A Solemn Public Conference Commemorating Koz'ma Prutkov on the Fifth Anniversary of His Death (Toržestvennoe publičnoe zasedanie pamjati Koz'my Prutkova po slučaju pjatiletija ego končiny).* Written by N. G. Smirnov and S. Ščerbakov.

By Viktor Vyškov:

27. *The 29th of Martober.* In one act. Listed elsewhere by Evreinov as *The 86th of Martober* (See Appendix A, First Program, 23 January 1912).

By Fedor Sologub:

28. *Everyday Affairs (Vsegdašnie šašni).* In four scenes. Music by Senilov.

By N. A. Teffi:

29. *The Evolution of the Devil (Èvoljucija d'javola).* In six scenes. Music by N. N. Evreinov.

By Arkadij Averčenko:

30. *The Four (Četvero).* In one act.
31. *A Wonderful Presentation (Zamečatel'noe predstavlenie).* A parody of a circus performance in the provinces. In one act.
32. *Ryčalov's Tour (Gastrol' Ryčalova).* In two acts. Music by V. G. Èrenberg.

By N. G. Smirnov and S. S. Ščerbakov:

33. *The Moral Bases of Man (Nravstvennye osnovy čeloveka)*. A parody on the repertoire of the Community Centers.
34. *Sausage from Butterflies (Kolbasa iz baboček)*. A futurist play in one act.
35. *The Bureau of Funeral Services (Bjuro poxoronnyx processij)*. In one act.

By Lev Urvancev:

36. a) *Vasil' Vasilič Reconciled (Vasil' Vasilič pomirilsja)*. A parody on vaudeville in one act.
    b) *A Sweet Pastry*. Libretto. (Music by N. N. Evreinov).

By Il'ja Sac (operas):

37. *Don't Shoot Your Mouth off Before Going into Battle (Ne xvalis' iduči na rat')*.
38. *Eastern Delights (Vostočnye sladosti)* or *The Russians' Battle with the Kabardinians (Bitva russkix s kabardincami)*. In two acts (text by V. A. Podgornyj).

By Vl. G. Èrenberg (musical works):

39. *A Chivalrous Ballad (Rycarskaja ballada)*. A pantomime in one act.
40. *In Versailles (V Versale)* (Text by Lev Nikulin). In one act.
41. *Sumurun* (a musical accompaniment). In ten scenes. (From the repertoire of the Deutsches Theatre of Max Reinhardt).
42. *A Festive Cantata (Toržestvennaja kantata)*. In one act.
43. *Yellow Jacket (Želtaja kofta)*. (A musical accompaniment). A multi-act Chinese play.
44. *Love's Delights (Vostorgi ljubvi)*. An operetta in one act. A parody.
45. *The Sage of Čatamutra (Mudrec Čatamutra)*. In two acts. (Text by V. A. Podgornyj).

By Sergej Iv. Antimonov:

46. *Woman and Death (Ženščina i smert')*. A symbolic play in one act.
47. *Someone Else's Wife and Husband under the Bed (Čužaja žena i muž pod krovat'ju)* by F. M. Dostoevskij. In two acts.
48. *Husbands and Wives (Muž'ja i ženy)*. In one act.

By Pëtr P. Potemkin

49. *Shouldn't We Lower the Curtain? (A ne opustit' li nam zanavesku?)*. A sketch in one act.
50. *Barometer (Barometr)*. A miniature in one act.
51. *Old-Timers 1812-1912 (Starožily 1812-1912gg)*. A farce in one act.

By K. N. Saxarov:

52. *To the Accompaniment of a Trombone (Pod zvuki trombona)*. A farce in one act.

By Anatole France:

53. *A Mute Wife (Nemaja žena)*. In two acts.

By Ben Jonson:

54. *An Intermission is Announced (Ob'javljaetsja pereryv)*. In one act.

By Other Foreign Authors:

55. *Model Spouses (Primernye suprugi)*. In two scenes.
56. *A Page from a Novel (Stranička romana)*. From the German by Èsterejx.
57. *Vaudeville of 1812 (Vodevil' 1812 goda)*. In one act.
58. *La Ronde (Xorovod)* by Arthur Schnitzler.
59. *Decameron Hour (Dekamerona čas)*. Dramatization by S. Ljubošic-Ljubovnaja.

Notes

Note for Epigraph

1. Nikolai Gogol, *The Inspector General,* in *The Collected Tales and Plays of Nikolai Gogol,* edited and translated by Leonard J. Kent and translated by Constance Garnett (New York: Farrar, Straus and Giroux/Octagon Books, 1978), 633.

Notes for Chapter 1

1. Anna Axmatova, "Cabaret Artistique," in *Modern Russian Poetry,* edited and translated by Vladimir Markov and Merrill Sparks (New York: The Bobbs-Merrill Company, 1966), 263. Axmatova's poem was originally published in *Apollon* 3 (1913): 31-39. Denis Mickiewicz, "*Apollo* and Modernist Poetics," in *The Silver Age of Russian Culture: An Anthology,* ed. Carl and Ellendea Proffer (Ann Arbor: Ardis, 1971), 395 n.59.

2. Oscar Wilde persuaded his friends to wear a green carnation to the premiere of his play, *Lady Windemere's Fan* (1892). When his friends asked why they should do this, Wilde replied, to annoy the public. George Woodcock, *The Paradox of Oscar Wilde* (New York: The Macmillan Company, 1950), 207, 221; Vladimir Markov, *Russian Futurism: A History* (London: MacGibbon and Kee, 1968), 138.

3. A. A. Mgebrov, *Žizn' v teatre* (Moskva-Leningrad: Academia, 1932), 2:176-77; V. P. Verigina, *Vospominanija* (Leningrad: Iskusstvo, 1974), 98. "The Serapions" included the following writers, a number of whom would later enjoy substantial individual success: Veniamin Kaverin, Lev Lunts, Viktor Šklovskij, Nikolaj Nikitin, Vsevolod Ivanov, Konstantin Fedin, Mixail Zoščenko, Mixail Slonimskij, and Il'ja Gruzdev. Gary Kern and Christopher Collins, eds., *The Serapion Brothers: A Critical Anthology of Stories* (Ann Arbor: Ardis, 1975), ix-xxxviii; Victor Erlich, *Russian Formalism: History-Doctrine* (New Haven: Yale University Press, 1981), 113, 150-53.

4. Mejerxol'd staged *The Fairground Booth* on three separate occasions, in 1906, 1908 and 1913. The last two stagings were part of his "unofficial" directorial work during his tenure as artistic director of the Imperial Theatres of opera and drama in St. Petersburg (1908-1918). It was for this work that he adopted the name "Doctor Dapertutto" (at Mixail Kuzmin's suggestion) from Hoffmann's "Adventures of New Year's Eve" as an alias. The two Pierrot portraits were painted by Aleksandr Golovin (1917) and Nikolaj Ul'janov (1908), the latter commemorating Mejerxol'd's performance as Pierrot in Blok's play (1906). Marjorie L. Hoover, *Meyerhold: The Art of Conscious Theatre*

(Amherst: University of Massachusetts Press, 1974), 10; Michael Green, "Mikhail Kuzmin and the Theatre," *Russian Literature Triquarterly* 7 (Fall 1973): 259; Verigina, *Vospominanija*, 98, 107, 142 and 235. Valentina Petrovna Verigina was an actress in Mejerxol'd's company during his brief tenure as artistic director of the Dramatic Theatre of V. F. Komissarževskaja in St. Petersburg (1906). Mejerxol'd once told Verigina, "I always wear a mask."

5. V. Vsevolodskij (Gerngross), *Istorija russkogo teatra*, (Leningrad-Moskva, 1929), 2:217.

6. Quoted in Edward Braun, trans. and ed., *Meyerhold on Theatre* (New York: Hill and Wang, 1969), 137. Mejerxol'd's completed essay, "The Fairground Booth" *(Balagančik)*, appeared in his collection *O teatre* (1913).

7. Aleksandr Rafailovič Kugel' (1864-1928) was the editor and critic of the influential journal *Theatre and Art (Teatr i iskusstvo)* and co-founder-producer with his wife Zinajda Vasil'evna (Timofeeva) Xolmskaja (1892-1966) of St. Petersburg's Crooked Mirror Theatre *(Teatr "Krivoe zerkalo,"* 1908-1931). He also authored several books of memoirs and theatre criticism. Painter Leon Bakst put the blame for the trend toward individualism and egoism not on the dissolution of society and its institutions in general but rather squarely on the shoulders of the artists. Their isolation from one another and from their past, he said, led to the dissipation of their common heritage and with it to an unhealthy degree of self-involvement. A. R. Kugel' (*Homo Novus*), *List'ja s dereva. Vospominanija* (Leningrad: Vremja, 1926), 152, Mickiewicz, "*Apollo* and Modernist Poetics," 378.

8. B. V. Kazanskij, *Metod teatra (Analiz sistemy N. N. Evreinova)* (Leningrad: Academia, 1925), 27-28.

9. This original group was joined by Z. N. Gippius (pseudonym Anton Krainy), D. S. Merežkovskij, N. M. Minskij (pseudonym Vilen Kin), V. V. Rozanov, Andrej Belyj and Valerij Brjusov (in 1902), I. Ja. Bilibin, M. V. Dobužinskij and V. A. Serov, A. Ja. Golovin and others. Although the World of Art was an elite group, its net was flung fairly wide among the Petersburg artistic intelligentsia, taking in many more "peripheral" members. This is accounted for in part by the fact that there was no formal membership in the World of Art in that it was not a society in a legal sense. Operating in a spirit of enlightened dilettantism, the World of Art group prided itself on embracing seemingly contradictory interests and orientations to art. It demanded only that art not become mired in the reproduction of daily reality. Its paradoxical nature caused Zinaida Gippius to proclaim that the World of Art "could have been born only in St. Petersburg." John E. Bowlt, "The World of Art," in *The Silver Age of Russian Culture: An Anthology*, ed. Carl and Ellendea Proffer (Ann Arbor, 1971), 398, 400-01; Z. Gippius, "Poliksena Solov'eva." *Vozroždenie* 89 (1959): 118-24, quoted in T. Pachmuss, *Zinaida Gippius* (Carbondale, 1971), 8 and Bowlt, "The World of Art," 398. Aleksandr Benois, *Vozniknovenie "Mira iskusstva"* (Leningrad, 1928), 8-9.

10. As John E. Bowlt points out, the journal *The World of Art,* although an artistic success, never attracted a wide audience, its subscribers rarely numbering more than one thousand. As a result of this and failed sponsorship, it was in constant financial peril. Djagilev was the journal's general editor, Benois its art director and Filosofov a "literary factotum." Bowlt, "The World of Art," 403.

11. Djagilev discontinued the World of Art exhibitions of work from abroad following a final exhibition held on 13 February 1903 at 11 Fontanka Canal. Believing that the

energies which he had reawakened at home could now sustain themselves, he turned to exhibiting Russian art abroad, beginning in 1906. Benois, *Vozniknovenie "Mira iskusstva,"* 53; Natalija Sokolova, *Mir iskusstva* (Leningrad-Moskva, 1934), 188.

12. Benois, *Vozniknovenie "Mira iskusstva,"* 8-9, 11-12, 19, 29-30, 38, 40, 49-53, 55, 68; Sokolova, *Mir iskusstva,* 13, 18, 62, 188.

13. Martin P. Rice, *Valery Briusov and the Rise of Russian Symbolism* (Ann Arbor: Ardis, 1975), 39, 68-69, 73-74, 79, 87, 136.

14. Sokolova, *Mir iskusstva,* 77, 94, 97-98; Constantin de Grunwald, *Peter the Great* (New York: The Macmillan Company, 1956), 154.

15. Sokolova, *Mir iskusstva,* 158 and 184.

16. One of Mejerxol'd's major attempts at reconstructivism was his production of *La devocion de la cruz* by Calderón de la Barca at the Tower Theatre on 19 April 1910. The Tower Theatre was a dramatic circle organized during the 1905-6 season by Vjačeslav Ivanov. Here, as the philosopher N. A. Berdjaev recorded, the leading lights of Petersburg's cultural life—"mystical anarchists and Russian Orthodox believers, neo-Christians and Social Democrats, artists and thinkers, actors and social workers..."—gathered every Wednesday to discuss "literary, artistic, philosophical, religious and occult themes, the latest literary news and the cosmic problems of existence." Andrej Belyj and the future People's Commissar of Enlightenment, Anatolij Lunačarskij, were among those who attended, the latter on a periodic basis. The theatre was located in the apartment of Ivanov and his wife, the poetess, Lydija D. Zinov'evaja-Anibal on the corner of Tavričeskaja Street. The Tower Theatre acquired its name from the shape of the building in which its top floor headquarters was located. Nikolaj Volkov, *Mejerxol'd,* vol. 2, *1908-1917* (Moskva-Leningrad: Academia, 1929), 94, 217-18.

17. While experimenting with commedia forms and techniques, Mejerxol'd was also documenting and analyzing the history and literature of the Italian comedy of masks in his journal *Love for Three Oranges. The Journal of Doctor Dapertutto (Ljubov' k trem apel'sinam. Žurnal Doktora Dapertutto,)* beginning in January 1914. The journal's title suggests its twin sources of inspiration—Carlo Gozzi and E. T. A. Hoffmann. Contributors to the journal included: A. Axmatova, A. Blok, Ju. Vexovskij, V. Pjast, Z. Gippius, F. Sologub, Vl. Knjažnin, V. Parnok, S. Radlov and K. Èrberg among the poets. Blok edited this section. In addition to poetry, there were short articles, bibliographical notes, news items (especially relating to the studios being run by the journal's contributors), and the texts of plays. Solov'ev's work on commedia was first published here. Vsevolod Mejerxol'd, ed., *Ljubov' k trem apel'sinam. Žurnal Doktora Dapertutto* 4-5 (1914): 109; Vsevolodskij (Gerngross), *Istorija russkogo teatra,* 2:253; Laurence Senelick, trans. and ed., *Russian Dramatic Theory from Pushkin to the Symbolists: An Anthology* (Austin: University of Texas Press, 1981), 296 n.19.

18. "Prospero," "Temy dnja (O režissere N. N. Evreinov)," *Teatr* 1477 (March 23, 1914): 9.

19. See Appendix A for a representative listing.

20. Vsevolodskij (Gerngross), *Istorija russkogo teatra,* 184.

21. A. O. Boguslavskij, V. A. Diev, *Russkaja sovetskaja dramaturgija. Osnovnye problemy razvitija, 1917-1935* (Moskva, 1963), 10; Oscar G. Brockett and Robert R. Findlay, *Century of Innovation: A History of European and American Theatre and Drama Since 1870* (Englewood Cliffs: Prentice-Hall, 1973), 211.

22. The best Russian language source on *Apollo* is the memoirs of its founder and editor, Sergej K. Makovskij. *Apollo* was an elegantly appointed, modernist journal which studiously avoided allying itself with any specific artistic movement or political cause. The publishing house *Scorpion* attracted many of the first-generation symbolists, the so-called aestheticists. *Musaget,* founded in 1910, was especially interested in modernist philosophy and ideology as they related to the discovery of the primary truths of mankind. S. K. Makovskij, *Na parnase serebrianogo veka* (Munich, 1961); Mickiewicz, "*Apollo* and Modernist Poetics," 360, 363, 372-3, 392 n.9; Volkov, *Mejerxol'd,* 2:60-61; *Zolotoe runo* (Moskva, for the year 1907).

23. Nikolaj Volkov, *Mejerxol'd,* vol. 1, *1874-1898* (Moskva-Leningrad: Academia, 1929), 258-59.

24. One of modernism's forebears and unallied "elder statesmen," poet-critic Innokentij F. Annenskij (1856-1909), accused Vjačeslav Ivanov of having reached a stage of such complexity with his mythological theorizing that these myths were no longer universal. Innokentij Annenskij, "O sovremennom lirizme," *(Oni),* 16-17; Mickiewicz, "*Apollo* and Modernist Poetics," 362; D. S. Mirsky, *A History of Russian Literature,* ed. Francis J. Whitefield (New York: Alfred A. Knopf, 1949), 446-48.

25. Volkov, *Mejerxol'd,* 1:281-83; Boguslavskij, Diev, *Russkaja sovetskaja dramaturgija...*, 9.

26. Vsevolod Mejerxol'd, "Teatr (K istorii i texnike)," in *Teatr: kniga o novom teatre* (St. Petersburg: Šipovnik, 1908), 174-75.

27. Fedor Sologub, "Teatr odnoj voli," in *Teatr: kniga o novom teatre,* 179-98.

28. *Mir iskusstva* (1902), cited in Vsevolodskij (Gerngross), *Istorija russkogo teatra,* 258.

29. Anatolij Nelidov, "Uslovnost' v teatre," *Teatr* 1350 (28 September 1913): 6.

30. B. Alpers, *Teatr social'noj maski* (Moskva-Leningrad, 1931), 16-17.

31. The figure of Mixail Alekseevič Kuzmin (1875-1936), aside from being highly representative of fin de siècle Russia and St. Petersburg cultural life in particular, seems especially relevant to the study of Nikolaj Evreinov. Like Evreinov, Kuzmin was a Renaissance man of his age, originally trained in musical composition by Rimskij-Korsakov (like Evreinov) whose lessons he later applied to drama and music for the theatre (like Evreinov) and, of course, to poetry as well. Each was infected by Petersburg aestheticism and aristocratism, the legacy of the World of Art. Their aesthetics each had a symbolist-decadent slant, tending toward the sacred and transcendental on one side and the sensual and profane on the other. Both were fascinated by the sexually taboo (Kuzmin was homosexual), the hermaphroditic and the paradoxical, especially by the decadent theme of the "harlot-saint"—Woman as demon temptress and Woman as Pre-Raphaelite virgin-child. They were each similarly divided internally between ironist and romanticist; between the belief that beauty is truth in itself and that art must seek to transform life; between masquerade and a kind of veiled god-seeking, reflected in their work in cabaret, harlequinade and theatre of small forms on the one hand and their investigation into historical, mystical and quasi-religious themes on the other. Each revealed a fascination for childhood fantasy as theme and metaphor, reflected in their work as writers of pantomimes, children's plays and theatrical parodies. Both conceived of life as a theatrical spectacle, a tragic *balagan* and their own lives as self-created works of theatricalist art. Mejerxol'd credited Kuzmin with writing "plays in the spirit of medieval drama" as well as "reconstructing the French comic theatre," recalling Evrei-

nov's own experiments at the Ancient Theatre. They differed in that Kuzmin viewed Mejerxol'd (for whom he composed the piano score for Blok's *The Fairground Booth*) as a theatrical savior whereas Evreinov considered him a talented but unoriginal rival and a pretender to theatrical divinity. Kuzmin seems to have been better in forming artistic alliances than Evreinov, who was something of a nonjoiner by nature. Kuzmin was more directly involved in symbolist activities, attending Vjačeslav Ivanov's "Wednesdays." He also wrote a regular column for the journal *Apollon* entitled "Notes on Russian Belles-lettres" and belonged to the journal's adjunct Society of Adepts of the Artistic Word. The many similarities which these two highly individual artists shared were less coincidences than characteristics of a relatively circumscribed cultural elite and the interests and concerns which became inbred within it. Green, "Mikhail Kuzmin and the Theatre," 243-66; Mickiewicz, *"Apollo* and Modernist Poetics," 366 and 392 n.13. M. Kuzmin, *Uslovnost'. Stat'i ob iskusstve* (Petrograd, 1923). 31.

32. Volkov, *Mejerxol'd,* 1:385-86; N. V-ij, "Naturalizm ili simvolizm," *Rampa* 4 (1909): 49.

33. Julij Ajxenval'd, "Otricanie teatra" (Publičnaja lekcija, pročitannaja pod zaglaviem "Literatura i teatra," v Moskve 16 marta 1913 g.), in *V sporax o teatre* (Moskva, 1914), 12-14, 27.

34. Volkov, *Mejerxol'd,* 2:85, 276-77.

35. Volkov, *Mejerxol'd,* 1:191.

36. N. N. Evreinov, *V škole ostroumija. O teatre "Krivoe zerkalo."* Archival materials from Central'nyj gosudarstvennyj arxiv literatury i iskusstva SSSR (CGALI SSSR), 61-62.

37. There was, at this time in Russia, a relationship between the "cult of the body" and the "cult of silence." Pantomime became an important art form in itself as well as playing an integral part in theatrical productions. The first important event in the area of theatrical pantomime was Mejerxol'd's production of *Columbine's Scarf (Šarf kolombiny),* based on a story by Arthur Schnitzler, with music by Donani and performed at the Petersburg House of Interludes (*Dom intermedii*) in 1910. The production incorporated elements of the grotesque, buffonade and tragic *balagan.* The "cult of silence" found its clearest expression in the work of the symbolist dramatists who subscribed to the nineteenth-century poet Fedor Tjutčev's dictum that "a thought once uttered is a lie." These two cults together constituted a response to the physical inarticulateness and intellectual blind alleys encountered in the naturalistic theatre and formed a part of the movement to imitate antique models. Mgebrov, *Žizn v teatre,* 2:60-61; Vsevolodskij (Gerngross), *Istorija russkogo teatra,* 256; Kn. Sergej Volkonskij, *Čelovek na scene* (St. Petersburg: Apollon, 1912), 159-60; A. Rumnev, *O pantomime, teatre, kino* (Moskva: Iskusstvo, 1964), 133-34, 137-38; James West, *Russian Symbolism: A Study of Vyacheslav Ivanov and the Russian Symbolist Aesthetic* (London: Methuen and Co., 1970), 118.

38. Volkov, *Mejerxol'd* 2:63.

39. Craig defined acting as a "series of accidental confessions." Edward Gordon Craig, *On the Art of the Theatre* (London: William Heinemann, 1912), 11-13, 35, 58, 80-85, 287; Constantin Stanislavski, *My Life in Art,* trans. J. J. Robbins (New York: Theatre Arts Books, 1952), 509-10.

40. Mejerxol'd, like so many other innovative Russian artists of his time, was greatly influenced by the Belgian symbolist writer Maurice Maeterlinck, who stated in *Menus propos, Le Theatre* (1890) that "every masterpiece is a symbol, and a symbol cannot

bear the active presence of man," and who employed the masked drama of the ancient Greeks as a model. In the matter of rhythm, among Mejerxol'd's major influences were the Oriental theatre and the works of Georg Fuchs, artistic director of the Munich Artists Theatre. In his *Theatre of the Future* (1904) and *Revolution in the Theatre* (1909), Fuchs said that the aim of the stage production is catharsis and that the path to this catharsis is rhythm embodied by the actor who had his origins in dance. E. T. Kirby, "Abstract Man: The Essence of Total Theatre," in *Total Theatre* (New York: E. P. Dutton and Co., 1969), 30-31; Braun, trans. and ed., *Meyerhold on Theatre,* 19-20, 183, 199-201; Volkov, *Mejerxol'd,* 1:240-44; V. È. Mejerxol'd, "Balagan (1912g.)," in *Stat'i, pis'ma, reči, besedy, čast' pervaja 1891-1917,* ed. B. I. Rostockij (Moskva: Iskusstvo, 1968), 212; James M. Symons, *Meyerhold's Theatre of the Grotesque* (Coral Gables: University of Miami Press, 1971), 34, 73, 83.

41. Kugel' opposed the "anarchic individualism" of the author which, he insisted, transformed the actor into a mere mouthpiece, resulting in lifeless theatre. A. Kugel', *Teatral'nye portrety,* ed. M. O. Jankovskij (Leningrad: Iskusstvo, 1967), 33-34; Volkonskij, *Čelovek na scene,* 16, 66, 72, 120.

42. Kugel', *List'ja s dereva,* 7-8.

43. Nikolai Gogol, *The Inspector General,* in *Nineteenth-Century Russian Plays,* ed. and trans. by Franklin D. Reeve (New York: W. W. Norton & Co., 1961), 273.

44. N. N. Evreinov, *Teatr kak takovoj* (St. Petersburg: Sovremennoe iskusstvo, 1912), 109-10.

Notes for Chapter 2

1. Allardyce Nicoll, *The World of Harlequin: A Critical Study of the Commedia dell'Arte* (London: Cambridge University Press, 1963), 70.

2. Mgebrov, *Žizn' v teatre,* 2:315-16, quoted in (and translated by) Christopher Moody, "Nikolai Nikolaevich Evreinov 1879-1953," *Russian Literature Triquarterly* 13 (Fall 1975): 673.

3. N. Evreinov, "Demon teatral'nosti. Leonid Andreev i problema teatral'nosti v žizni," *Žizn' iskusstva* 7 (February 14, 1922): 2; Vl. Prokof'ev, "Nužno li realizm dopolnjat' teatral'nost'ju?," *V sporax o Stanislavskom* (Moskva: Iskusstvo, 1962), 173; A. E. Red'ko, "Otkrovenija o žizni i teatre," *Russkie zapiski* 3 (March, 1916): 294; Andrej Levinson, "Recenzija: Teatr dlja sebja. *Čast' pervaja,*" *Severnye zapiski* 3 (March, 1916): 220.

4. Evg. Bezpjatov, "Novye knigi o teatre," *Teatr i iskustvo* 8 (February 24, 1913): 183. See chapter 8 for a discussion of Evreinov-Xlestakov.

5. G. K. Kryžickij, *Režisserskie portrety* (Moskva-Leningrad: Teakinopečat', 1928), 38.

6. Mgebrov, *Žizn' v teatre,* 2:312.

7. Much of the information in this chapter concerning Evreinov's biography comes from two sources: Vasilij Kamenskij, *Kniga o Evreinove* (Petrograd: Sovremennoe iskusstvo, 1917) and Moody, "Nikolai Nikolaevich Evreinov 1879-1953," *Russian Literature Triquarterly,* 659-95.

8. Another fascinating detail of Evreinov's extremely active and colorful childhood was his participation in a children's volunteer fire-fighting unit. Of his many childhood activi-

ties, however, Evreinov most liked making paper flowers. Kamenskij, *Kniga o Evreinove,* 16.

9. N. N. Evreinov, "Dan' marionetkam (Avtobiografičeskaja)," in *Teatral'nye novacii* (Petrograd: Tret'ja straža, 1922), 99.

10. Evreinov's "career" as a professional actor was the least developed of his various artistic pursuits, owing to what he perceivd as his personal limitations—a hoarse vocal quality and short stature, placing him at a disadvantage vis-à-vis his leading ladies. Having made these realizations in 1903, while under contract to L. B. Yavorskaja, he quit the acting profession and dedicated himself instead to making his life into a performance. Moody, "Nikolai Nikolaevich Evreinov 1879-1953," 663.

11. N. N. Evreinov, "Čem ja objazan Sobinovu," in *Leonid Vitalievič Sobinov 1893-1923,* ed. Vl. I. Nemirovič-Dančenko (Moskva, 1923), 61-62.

12. N. N. Evreinov, *Bolvany, kumirskie bogi,* in *Dramatičeskie sočinenija,* vol. 1, ed. Evreinov (St. Petersburg, 1908).

13. Evreinov would say later in life that he worshipped the theatrical god, "Theatrarch," "the Great Director of the Theatre of Life." We are, Evreinov said, all actors in His monodrama, carved from His image and vision of life. Evreinov's great fascination with the concept of the mask springs in part from this. As originally conceived in ancient rituals, for example, the ceremony of Dionysos, the mask or persona represented a likeness of the Deity.

14. Interview with A. A. Kašina-Evreinova, Leningrad, U.S.S.R., August 1975.

15. Ibid.

16. Ju. Beljaev, "Teatr i muzyka," *Novoe vremja* 10696 (24 December 1905): 5; "Teatr i muzyka," *Novoe vremja* 10373 (21 January 1905): 5; Ju. Beljaev, "Teatr i muzyka: 'Krasivyj despot,' " *Novoe vremja* 11064 (21 December 1906): 5; N. N. Evreinov, "Predislovie," *dramatičeskie sočinenija,* vol. 2 (St. Petersburg: Sovremennoe iskusstvo, 1914); G. K. Kryžickij, *Strel'skaja* (Leningrad, 1920), 127.

17. Christopher Collins, "Nikolai Evreinov as a Playwright," in *Life as Theater: Five Modern Plays by Nikolai Evreinov,* trans. and ed. Christopher Collins (Ann Arbor: Ardis Publishers, 1973), xx.

18. Friedrich Nietzsche, "The Birth of Tragedy," in *The Birth of Tragedy and The Genealogy of Morals,* trans. Francis Golffing (Garden City, N.Y.: Doubleday and Co., 1956), 24.

19. In an article on the composer Il'ja Sac, Evreinov asserts that *all* art can be understood as theatrical. In painting, the artist creates a place of action and characters "with whom the viewer communes in a pantomime." A literary work is a "play" being performed on the printed page. That Evreinov considered writing to be a theatrical form of self-expression is particularly apparent in his major theoretical works in which he makes widespread use of theatrical terminology and motifs. Each chapter is for him a scene. Opening the book corresponds to raising the curtain, closing the book to lowering it. N. N. Evreinov, "Satiričeskaja dominanta v tvorčestve Il'i Saca," in *Il'ja Saca* (Moskva-Leningrad, 1923), 27-29.

20. Evreinov's monograph *Beardsley. A Critical Sketch (Berdslej. Kritičeskij očerk)* was published in St. Petersburg (1912).

21. A. P. Zonov in Mgebrov, *Žizn v teatre,* vol. 2, quoted in Moody, "Nikolai Nikolaevich Evreinov 1879-1953, 669. Moody treats this incident in some detail.
22. Evreinov, *Beardsley,* 1-5, 8-9, 21-22.
23. Ibid., 11-12, 15, 31.
24. *Rops. A Critical Sketch (Rops. Kritičeskij očerk)* was published in St. Petersburg (1910).
25. Evreinov, *Rops,* 8-10; A. A. Kašina-Evreinova, cited in Christopher Moody, "Nikolai Nikolaevich Evreinov 1879-1953," 659.
26. Evreinov, *Rops,* 10, 14, 29.
27. This article was later included in the anthology, *Nudity on the Stage (Nagota na scene)* (St. Petersburg: Novoe vremja, 1911). Evreinov's stand on nudity gained him for a time the notoriety that he continually sought. A lively exchange on the subject was featured in the press, and in 1909 *Theatre and Art* carried a portrait of Evreinov by M. P. Bobyšov (who would later design *In the Stage-Wings of the Soul* at the Crooked Mirror Theatre) stripped to the waist and holding a flower. *Teatr i iskusstvo* 50 (1909): 1028, mentioned in Moody, "Nikolai Nikolaevich Evreinov 1879-1953," 672.
28. Evreinov, *Nagota na scene,* 42-44. At the Dramatic Studio of M. A. Rigler-Voronkova at No. 5 Soldackij Pereulok in St. Petersburg, where he taught from 1908 to spring, 1911, Evreinov conducted experiments with the naked body for which he was treated with derision in the press. This was part of a curriculum designed to train the body and the voice as instruments via choreography, musical theory, and gymnastic games. Intelligence, technique, taste, musicality, and *plastique* were the qualities which Evreinov hoped to develop here in the artists of the Theatre of the Future. Evreinov and Rigler-Voronkova, a former actress at the Ancient Theatre, were romantically involved between 1910 and 1913. She wanted to marry him, but that desire was not mutual. Kamenskij, *Kniga o Evreinove,* 24-25; Moody, "Nikolai Nikolaevich Evreinov 1879-1953," 675.
29. N. N. Evreinov, "O nagote" (Lekcija, 1929), CGALI SSSR, fond no. 982, ed. xr. no. 48, opis' no. 1, p. 21.
30. Evreinov, *Rops,* 41-42, 46-47.
31. N. N. Evreinov, "Pervye šagi," *V škole ostroumija,* fond no. 982, ed. xr. no. 5, opis' no. 1, pp. 61-63.
32. Evreinov, *Rops,* 57.
33. N. N. Evreinov, "Ja o sebe" (Avtobiografija), pis'mo Evreinova, Nikolaja Nikolaeviča k G. V. Švarcu, Rukopisnyj otdel—Gosudarstvennyj central'nyj teatral'nyj muzej im. A. A. Baxrušina, fond no. 96, no. postuplenija 192. 153, p. 2; Interview with A. A. Kašina-Evreinova, Leningrad, August 1975.
34. Evreinov, *Rops,* 7, 13, 15.
35. *Nesterov. A Sketch (Nesterov. Očerk)* was published in Petrograd in 1922.
36. Ibid., 6.
37. Ibid., 32, 55, 73-74; Pis'mo Evreinova, Nikolaja Nikolaeviča k Boris Nikolaeviču Rubinštein, CGALI SSSR, fond no. 982, ed. xr. no. 131, opis' no. 1.

38. Interview with A. A. Kašina-Evreinova, Leningrad, U.S.S.R., August 1975.
39. Despite the great influence Western European thought had on his artistic consciousness, Evreinov was very proud of and closely attuned to his Russianness. This was evident in his painstaking efforts to document Russian folk customs, rituals, and ceremonies through tireless reading, travel and observation. All previous attempts to return the theatre to its origins, Evreinov argued, drew upon the theatrical legacy of Western Europe and the Mediterranean countries, that is, Greece and Italy. Evreinov was among the few artists interested in preserving and revitalizing those artistic forms that were uniquely Russian, specifically under the heading of Russian popular theatre.
40. Evreinov, *Nesterov,* 30, 41, 56, 77, 79.
41. Kazanskij, *Metod teatra (Analiz sistemy N. N. Evreinova)* 30 and 80.
42. Nicolas Evreinoff (Nikolaj Evreinov), *The Theatre in Life,* ed. and trans. Alexander I. Nazaroff (London: George Harrap and Co., 1927), 123.
43. Quoted in Woodcock, *The Paradox of Oscar Wilde,* 116–17.
44. Evreinov, *Nesterov,* 52.
45. Kazanskij, *Metod teatra,* 9 and 11.
46. N. N. Evreinov, *Teatralizacija žizni (Poét, teatraliziruŝči žizn')* (Moskva: Vremja, 1922). Evreinov's admiring work on Kamenskij was in part repayment for Kamenskij's laudatory *Kniga o Evreinove* (1917).
47. N. N. Evreinov, *Original o portretistax (K probleme subbektivizma v iskusstve)* (Moskva, 1922), 11–13, 15–17.
48. Ibid., 44, 49, 54.
49. Ibid., 67–71. *Kul'bin* was published in 1912 by the Society of Intimate Theatre.
50. Included in this discussion among the portraitists are the the following: M. Dobužinskij, M. Verbova, V. Majakovskij, Miss, O. Dymov, E. Bizjukinoj, I. Grandi, N. Kalmakov, Denisov, Ljubimov, V. Kamenskij, M. Bobyšov, I. Krasovskij, A. Ermakova, Ju. Annenkov, I. Repin, V. Xlebnikov, Re-mi, S. Sorin, D. Burljuk. Evreinov had already employed a similar conceit in his colloquium of famous artists and philosphers, "In the Commission of Experts" (in *The Theatre for Oneself, Part 3,* 1917), which is convened by him to discuss his theory of the theatre in life, to settle accounts with enemies (e.g., Mejerxol'd disguised as the German Nietzsche) and to write himself into history while he was still alive so as to enjoy society's approbation. However, Evreinov at least has the good grace to deprecate the proceedings (which amount to a kind of philosophical monodrama) by banalizing them, allowing great men to engage in petty bickering in a dream vision imagined while Evreinov sits imperially in his living room.
51. Robert Alter, *Partial Magic. The Novel as a Self-Conscious Genre* (Berkeley: University of California Press, 1975), 8.
52. Quoted in Robert Brustein, "Luigi Pirandello," *The Theatre of Revolt* (Boston: Little, Brown and Company, 1964), 290.
53. See Donald Fanger's use of the Russian phrase *ne to* (in Russian "not that" or "wrong") to signify the sense of absence in Gogol''s work. He defines *ne to* as a "constant denial of what appears in the represented reality and in the representation itself." More

directly, it is "the suggestion that a thing is not what it seems to be, not what it should be, not what you expect." Fanger labels hyperbole "a variety of *ne to,* most obviously when the expression evokes the inexpressible." This principle may relate to a personality as much as to a work of art. Donald Fanger, *The Creation of Nikolai Gogol* (Cambridge: The Belknap Press of Harvard University Press, 1979), 209, 212, 214, 233, 257-59; Jan Kott, "The Eating of 'The Government Inspector,' " *Theatre Quarterly* 17 (March-May 1975): 23, 25.

Notes for Chapter 3

1. Evreinov, *Teatr kak takovoj,* 119.
2. Evreinov suggested that monodrama originated with the Greeks. Other critics and theorists make no mention of it prior to the eighteenth century when, as Evreinov maintains, the form was "crystallized." However, the *Bol'šaja sovetskaja ènciklopedija* corroborates Evreinov's opinion, dating the advent of monodrama from the pre-Aeschylean tragedy of Thespis in which one actor played several characters by changing costumes and masks. The Soviet encyclopedia, in discussing the twentieth-century concept of monodrama, makes no mention of Evreinov, however, referring only to unnamed symbolist and expressionist dramatists who made use of this device. Perhaps the most important corroboration of Evreinov's position is provided by Friedrich Nietzsche in "The Birth of Tragedy" (1871). As a matter of fact, his description of Greek monodrama is much closer in spirit to Evreinov's theory than the eighteenth-century concept. Nietzsche wrote:

   > It is an unimpeachable tradition that in its earliest form Greek tragedy records only the sufferings of Dionysos, and that he was the only actor. But it may be claimed with equal justice that, up to Euripides, Dionysos *remains* the sole dramatic protagonist, and all the famous characters of the Greek stage, Prometheus, Oedipus, etc. are only masks of the original hero.

   Bol'šaja sovetskaja ènciklopedija, 1954 edition, 28:236; Nietzsche, "The Birth of Tragedy," 65-66.
3. Kazanskij, *Metod teatra,* 130.
4. He repeated the lecture on 21 February 1909, at the Theatrical Club and 4 March 1909, at the Dramatic Theatre of V. F. Komissarževskaja, both in St. Petersburg. The paper was next printed in condensed form in the journal *Theatre and Art* (March-April 1909). It was published in its entirety as *Introduction to Monodrama (Vvedenie v monodramu)* (St. Petersburg: Sovremennoe iskusstvo, 1909), edited by N. I. Butkovskaja.
5. Kazanskij, *Metod teatra (Analiz sistemy N. N. Evreinova),* 26, 52; N. N. Evreinov, "O nekotoryx xodjačix terminax (k pereizdaniju Teatra kak takavogo)," *Žizn' iskusstva* 44 (5 November 1922): 6; A. R. Kugel', "Teatral'nye zametki," *Teatr i iskusstvo* 39 (25 September 1911): 726-28; Evg. Bezpjatov, *Ežegodnik Imperatorskix teatrov* (March, 1909): 75-81; D. Filosov, "Teatr i muzyka," *Naša gazeta,* 6; B. Glagolin, "Russkij argonavt," *Žurnal teatra Literaturno-xudožestvennogo obščestva* 1 (1909-10): 19-20; Evg. Znosko-Borovskij, *Russkij teatr načala XX veka* (Prague: Plamja, 1925), 320.
6. N. N. Evreinov, "O satiričeskoj monodrame i ispol'zovanii ee na scene 'Krivogo zerkala,' " *V škole ostroumija,* 6-7, 13-14; N. N. Evreinov, "K postanovke *Gore ot uma* A. S. Griboedova (1935)," CGALI SSSR, fond no. 982, ed. xr. no. 38, opis' no. 1, pp. 9-12.

7. František Deák aptly compares this use of light and shadow to Evreinov's treatment of the Red (Bolševik) and White (Provisional Government) platforms, respectively, in his 1920 mass spectacle, *The Storming of the Winter Palace*. František Deák, "Russian Mass Spectacles," *The Drama Review* 19 (June 1975): 20.

8. Edward Stark, "Recenzija *Francesca da Rimini*," *Teatr i iskusstvo* 17 (28 April 1913): 376-77; Kn. Sergej Volkonskij, *Otkliki teatra* (Petrograd, 1914), 20-22; A. R. Kugel', "Recenzija: *Francesca da Rimini*," *Novaja Rus'* 52 (6 October 1908): 3-4; Smolenskij, "Okolo rampy: Teatr g-ži Komissarževskoj — *Francesca da Rimini* G. D'Annunzio," *Birževye vedomosti* 10743 (6 October 1908): 4; B. T. "*Francesca da Rimini* na scene teatra Komissarževskoj (Beseda s N. N. Evreinovym)," *Rannee utro* 236 (30 August 1908): 4; "Staryj drug," "Vtoraja *Francesca*," *Teatr* 259 (6 September 1908): 3-7.

9. N. N. Evreinov, "O smexe s prepjatstvijami. K poznaniju groteska i jumora visel'nikov," *V škole ostroumija*. CGALI SSSR, fond no. 982, ed. xr. no. 12, opis' no. 1, p. 6.

10. N. N. Evreinov, *Fundament sčast'ja, Dramatičeskieسočinenija*, (St. Petersburg, 1908), 1:273, 281-82.

11. Vsevolod Mejerxol'd stated that having set forth the theory of monodrama, Evreinov should not himself have written any if he did not have the power to create exceptional images. Mejerxol'd claimed that Evreinov's *The Presentation of Love* carried within it all of the elements of Leonid Andreev's earlier play, *The Life of Man (Žizn' čeloveka)*, which he (Mejerxol'd) directed in Komissarževskaja's theatre in 1907. V. È. Mejerxol'd, "Recenzija," *Birževye vedomosti* (10 February 1917).

12. Evreinov, "Predislovie k *Predstavlenie ljubvi*," *Predstavlenie ljubvi*, 51, 57.

13. Evreinov, "O satiričeskoj monodrame i ispol'zovanii ee na scene 'Krivogo zerkala,' " 10.

14. Evreinov, *Predstavlenie ljubvi*, 75-78, 82.

15. Ibid., 103, 105-7.

16. See Appendix C for a complete listing of premieres at the Crooked Mirror Theatre during Evreinov's tenure as artistic director.

17. N. N. Evreinov, "O satiričeskoj monodrame i ispol'zovanii ee na scene 'Krivogo zerkala,' " 23. Despite the apparent awkwardness of the various scenic elements, eyewitnesses (A. G. Avvakumov and S. A. Raxmanova, members of the Crooked Mirror Company) attest to the production's success. Interview with A. G. Avvakumov and S. A. Raxmanova, Leningrad, U.S.S.R., winter, 1976. A different approach was taken to the staging in a New York production of the play (under the title *The Theatre of the Soul*, 1926). M. Yushkievitch wrote:

> There were three characters, but little was seen of them beyond their faces appearing at different levels out of intense darkness. A pulsating red light represented the heart, and the various concepts of the actors were seen in the foreground, brilliantly lighted. The play created something of a sensation.

From all indications the Crooked Mirror production left the actors playing the Selves, like the internal organs, fully exposed to the audience's view at all times. M. Yuskievitch, *New York Evening Post*, 27 March 1926.

18. Petr Ju, "Krivoe zerkalo," *Teatr i iskusstvo* 43 (21 October 1912): 817.

19. N. N. Evreinov, *The Theater of the Soul*, in *Life as Theater: Five Modern Plays*, trans. and ed. Christopher Collins (Ann Arbor: Ardis, 1973), 29.

20. Ibid., 29-30.

21. Interview with A. A. Kašina-Evreinova, Paris, France, June 1976.

22. When he became aware that his wife was being unfaithful to him, Evreinov cautioned her, "I am not a Pierrot." The Evreinovs' own "love comedy" was apparently played out with a high degree of theatrical variety, the wife costuming herself at her husband's request as a succession of girls from different countries for their romantic encounters. Interview with A. A. Kašina-Evreinova; Leningrad, U.S.S.R.; August 1975; Interview with A. A. Kašina-Evreinova; Paris, France; June 1976.

23. Interview with A. A. Kašina-Evreinova; Paris, France; June 1976.

24. In the advertisements for the Berlin production (27 April 1929), *Stage-Wings* was actually referred to as having been a precursor of expressionism. Evreinov, "O satiričeskoj monodrame i ispol'zovanii ee na scene 'Krivogo zerkala,' " 24. Soviet film director Sergej Eisenstein, who was conversant with Evreinov's cinematic experiments in monodrama and later the mass spectacle, sought his advice prior to beginning production on Jack London's *Mexicans*. Sergei M. Eisenstein, *Immoral Memories: An Autobiography,* trans. Herbert Marshall (Boston: Houghton Mifflin Company, 1983), 76-77; Moody, "Nikolai Nikolaevich Evreinov 1879-1953," 687.

25. Ibid., 7; Kazanskij, *Metod teatra,* 131.

26. Bakshy, *The Path of the Russian Stage,* 81-82.

27. Evreinov is not himself immune to such criticism. *See* chapter 8 for a dicussion of Evreinov's use of the dream and wish-fulfillment which, although not strictly Freudian, deals with some of Freud's concerns.

28. Evreinov's harlequinade, *A Merry Death,* has likewise been designated as an example of early theatre of the absurd. Martin Esslin, *The Theatre of the Absurd* (Garden City, NY: Doubleday and Co., 1969), 43-44; Albert Camus, *Le Myth de Sisyphe* (Paris: Gallimard, 1942), 18, quoted in Esslin, *The Theatre of the Absurd,* 5; D. Zolotnickij, *Zori teatral'nogo oktjabrja* (Leningrad: Iskusstvo, 1976), 158.

29. Evreinoff (Evreinov), "Trying on Deaths," in *The Theatre in Life,* 283.

30. Nikolai Evreinov, *A Merry Death,* in *Life as Theater: Five Modern Plays,* trans. and ed. Christopher Collins (Ann Arbor: Ardis, 1973), 5. All textual references are from this source.

31. Ibid., 6.

32. Will Durant, "Henri Bergson," in *The Story of Philosophy* (New York: Simon and Schuster, 1926), 341-3.

33. Evreinov, *A Merry Death,* 9, 10.

34. Ibid., 17, 18.

35. Ibid., 5, 18, 19.

Notes for Chapter 4

1. N. N. Evreinov, quoted in Kazanskij, *Metod teatra (Analiz sistemy N. N. Evreinova),* 16, 20-24, 26-27, 31; S. Makovskij, "Retrospektivnye mečtateli," *Stranicy*

Notes for Chapter 4   253

xudožestvennoj kritiki (St. Petersburg, 1909), Book 2, 114-41; Bowlt, "The World of Art," 401, 431 n.9.

2. Evreinov, *Teatr kak takovoj,* 7-8, 77.

3. N. N. Evreinov, *Teatr dlja sebja. Čast' pervaja* (Petrograd: Sovremennoe iskusstvo, 1915), 77.

4. Evreinoff, *The Theatre in Life,* 23-28; Evreinov, *Teatr kak takovoj,* 34-35.

5. Kazanskij, *Metod teatra,* 36-38.

6. Evreinov, *Pro Scena Sua* (Petrograd: Prometej, 1914), 25-26.

7. Evreinov, *Teatr dlja sebja. Čast' pervaja,* 114-15. In *The Interpretation of Dreams* (1900), Sigmund Freud studied the manner in which we transform reality in our dreams, suppressing our desires and embodying them in forms not immediately recognizable to the superego. Evreinov's prologue to *In the Stage-Wings of the Soul* contains a direct reference to Freud, so it is evident that he was familiar with the famous psychologist's theory of the divided consciousness. Evreinov discussed the attractiveness of nightmarish visions in sleep in *Pro Scena Sua* (1914). See chapter 8.

8. Evreinov, *The Theatre in Life,* 31.

9. Ajxenval'd, "Otricanie teatra," 32-34, 37-38.

10. Evreinov, *Pro Scena Sua,* 36-37.

11. Kazanskij, *Metod teatra,* 36-38.

12. Evreinov, *Pro Scena Sua,* 18.

13. Evreinov took great satisfaction in what he considered to be a victory over his critics on the tenth anniversary of the book's publication. What seemed ten years ago to be incredible—his doctrine of theatricality—was now widely accepted. Evreinov claimed that his book significantly influenced other prominent theatrical innovators, among them Mejerxol'd and Tairov. Prior to the appearance of the *Apology for Theatricality,* Mejerxol'd had written that: "The new theatre will grow out of literature." Following its publication, Mejerxol'd wrote: "In order to *save* Russian theatre from its tendency of becoming the slave of literature, it is necessary to return the cult of the *Kabotinaž* (i.e., the circus performer) to the stage." Evreinov called Tairov a "talented imitator," who in propagandizing for "the theatricalization of the theatre" was repeating in his own words the essence of *The Theatre as Such.* N. N. Evreinov, "O nekotoryx xodjačix terminax (k pereizdaniju *Teatra kak takovogo*)," *Žizn' iskusstva* 44 (5 November 1922): 6.

14. L. Antimonov, "*Teatr dlja sebja* (o knige N. N. Evreinova)," *Teatr i iskusstvo* 47 (November 22, 1915): 884.

15. Ju. Ajxenval'd, "Novye knigi: *Teatr dlja sebja (Čast' pervaja),*" *Utro* 334 (5 December 1915): 5.

16. Ajxenval'd, "Novye knigi: *Teatr dlja sebja (Čast' pervaja),*" 5; Petr Pil'skij, "Kritičeskie stroki," *Solnce Rossii* 17 (April 1916): 9; A. Benois, "Xudožestvennye pis'ma: Reč' Arlekina," *Reč'* 45 (15 February 1913): 2; A. E. Red'ko, *Literaturno-xudožestvennye iskanija v konce XIX-načale XX vv.* (Leningrad: Sejatel', 1924), 158-59.

17. Evreinov, *Teatr dlja sebja. Čast' pervaja,* 6.

18. Evreinov recalled a time when Stanislavskij said that the day theatricality installed itself at MXAT he would leave the theatre. One year later (1911), Knut Hamsun's *In Life's*

Clutches (U žizni v lapax) opened at MXAT. This play, according to Evreinov, propagandized for his idea of theatricality. Evreinov claimed that Stanislavskij later admitted to him his terrible mistake in condemning theatricality. N. N. Evreinov, *Teatr dlja sebja. Čast' vtoraja,* (Petrograd: Sovremennoe iskusstvo, 1916), 7, 10-11, 17-18, 23, 31, 33-36, 41, 47, 65-67.

19. Evreinov, *Teatr dlja sebja. Čast' pervaja,* 40-42; Evreinov, *The Theatre in Life,* 35-37, 42.

20. N. N. Evreinov, *Teatr dlja sebja. Čast' tret'ja* (Petrograd: Sovremennoe iskusstvo, 1917), 16-17.

21. Kazanskij, *Metod teatra,* 38, 58.

22. Evreinov, *Teatr dlja sebja. Čast' pervaja,* 46, 86-88, 90-91.

23. N. N. Evreinov, *Tajna Rasputina. O mifologičeskoj maske* (Petrograd: Byloe, 1924), 49, 58-60, 75; Evreinov, *Teatr dlja sebja. Čast' pervaja,* 68, 109, 148, 159, 174.

24. Fyodor Dostoyevsky, *Notes From Underground,* trans. Andrew R. MacAndrew (New York: New American Library, 1961), 105-10, 118.

25. Evreinov, *Teatr dlja sebja. Čast' pervaja,* 58-59.

26. All information relating to *The Theatre and the Scaffold (Teatr i èšafot)* comes from the A. A. Baxrušin State Central Theatrical Museum (Gosudarstvennyj central'nyj teatral'nyj muzej imeni A. A. Baxrušina), fond no. 96 (Evreinov, N. N.), no. postuplenija 192. 161-192. 162, *Teatr i èšafot* (materialy, zametki, vyrezki). Among his notes for *The Theatre and the Scaffold,* Evreinov has written in, "Monodrama—co-experiencing with the sacrifice."

27. Evreinov, says his wife, considered himself an Aristotelian. Aristotle's theory of catharsis was at the root of Evreinov's founding of the Ancient Theatre which was to have begun with a cycle of Greek drama. Interview with A. A. Kašina-Evreinova; Paris, France; June 1976.

28. N. N. Evreinov, "K poznaniju teatral'noj parodii," *V škole ostroumija,* O teatre 'Krivoe zerkalo,' " CGALI SSSR, fond no. 982, opis' no. 1, ed. xr. no. 9, p. 53.

29. Evreinov wrote that the person chosen for sacrifice upon the scaffold should be interesting. The murder of a king or a tsar is generally more interesting than the murder of a common man.

30. In developing his theory of the scapegoat as the link between Semitic culture and Greek tragedy, Evreinov went so far as to study the ancestry of the various breeds of goat. This research also served as preparation for the book he planned to write on the Russian popular theatre, for which he travelled across the country compiling information (*See* chapter 2, note 38). An extant outline for the book and a bibliography of some one hundred published sources attests to the seriousness of Evreinov's intent and the thoroughness of his preparation for this project. Although there is no evidence that the work was ever actually written, some of the data Evreinov unearthed found its way into the early sections of his *Histoire du Théâtre Russe* (1947). Materials from the Manuscript Division (Rukopisnyj otdel) of the Leningrad State Theatrical Museum (Leningradskij gosudarstvennyj teatral'nyj muzej); N. N. Evreinov, *Azazel i Dionis. O proisxoždenii sceny v svjazi s začatkami dramy u semitov* (Leningrad: Academia, 1924), 13, 46, 65, 67, 92-97, 105-6, 156; N. N. Evreinov, *Pervobytnaja drama germancev (Iz*

pra-istorii teatra germano-skandinavskix narodov) (Petrograd: Poljarnaja zvezda, 1922), 5-8.

31. Zolotnickij, *Zori teatral'nogo oktjabrja,* 272; N. N. Evreinov, *Samoe glavnoe* (Petrograd: Gosudarstvennoe izdatel'stvo, 1921); Evreinov, "Demon teatral'nosti. Leonid Andreev i problema teatral'nosti v žizni," 2; G. K. Kryžickij, *Xristos ili Arlekin?* (Leningrad, 1924), 1, 39-41, 49, 58-60, 63; Interview with Jurij Konstantinovič Gerasimov (LGITMiK; Leningrad, U.S.S.R.; winter, 1975); Roger Shattuck, Introduction to *Selected Works of Alfred Jarry,* ed. Roger Shattuck and Simon Watson Taylor (New York: Grove Press, 1965), 11, 13-14, 17-19.

32. Zolotnickij, *Zori teatral'nogo oktjabrja,* 272; E. W. Osborn, "Theatres," *New York City Evening World,* 27 March 1926; Metcalfe, "A Bit of Russian," *The Wall Street Journal* (New York), 27 March 1926.

33. Nikolai Evreinov, *The Main Thing,* in *Life as Theater: Five Modern Plays by Nikolai Evreinov,* trans. and ed. Christopher Collins (Ann Arbor: Ardis Publishers, 1973), 39. All references to *The Chief Thing* are from this source.

34. Interview with A. A. Kašina-Evreinova; Paris, France; June 1976. In fact the original title of the play when staged in France was *La comedie du bonheur (The Comedy of Happiness).* The film version, made in Italy in 1939, was similarly titled.

35. Evreinov, *The Main Thing,* 46-48.

36. Leopold Fregoli (1867-1936), whom Evreinov mentions in his *Introduction to Monodrama,* was an Italian quick-change artist who toured European music halls in sketches requiring him to play a number of different characters by means of split-second transformations. Evreinov's character is thus aptly and ironically named, given his higher purpose as described in the play. The appellation "Doctor" suggests several contrasting possibilities: learned professor, windy professor ("Il Dottore" from *commedia*), charlatan in a cheap vaudeville, Mejerxol'd's alias, "Doctor Dapertutto," and E. T. A. Hoffmann who was the source for Mejerxol'd's pseudonym. Senelick, trans. and ed., *Russian Dramatic Theory from Pushkin to the Symbolists,* 292 n.4.

37. Henryk Sinkiewicz's novel, published in 1896, was a runaway best-seller in what was to become Evreinov's adopted homeland, France, and won its author the Nobel Prize. The novel contrasts Nero's decadent pagan empire with a less scintillating but more moral, naive (i.e., primitive) Christianity. The novel's theme and its career make it an appropriate object for Evreinovian parody. Christopher Moody suggests that Evreinov got the idea to write *The Chief Thing* after staging the opera *Quo Vadis?* in 1912. Evreinov is clearly spoofing theatrical *pošlost'* in the *Quo Vadis?* scene much as he is attacking *pošlost'* in life in *The Chief Thing* as a whole. *Pošlost',* a term most often associated with Gogol', refers to the gaudily coarse, tasteless, vulgar, and banal. Evreinov no doubt also had in mind the long-running Crooked Mirror hit, *Ryčalov's Tour (Gastrol' Ryčalova,* 1911) by M. N. Volkonskij (Evreinov directed it), which spoofs provincial theatres, when he penned his *Quo Vadis?* scene. Czesław Miłosz, *The History of Polish Literature* (London: The Macmillan Company, 1969), 313; Moody, "Nikolai Nikolaevich Evreinov 1879-1953," 39; Zolotnickij, *Zori teatral'nogo oktjabrja,* 271, 273; Senelick, *Russian Dramatic Theory...,* 63.

38. In a wonderfully appropriate example of life imitating theatre, the roles of Nero and the Prompter in the 1926 Theatre Guild production of *The Chief Thing* were played by Harold Clurman and Lee Strasberg, respectively. These two American disciples of Stan-

islavskij were joined by one of America's best realistic film actors, Edward G. Robinson, in the role of the Regisseur. McKay Morris played Paraclete. The production was directed by Philip Moeller "with the cooperation of the author" who was in America for the rehearsals.

39. Evreinov, *The Main Thing*, 66.
40. Ibid., 67-68.
41. Ibid., 98.
42. Ibid., 113-15.
43. Various alternative endings were acted out at Evreinov's suggestion in the Theatre Guild production.
44. Adrian Piotrovskij, "Teatry kotoryx uže net...Listki vospominanji," *Rabočij i teatr* 29-30 (November, 1932): 6-7, quoted in Zolotniickij, *Zori teatral'nogo oktjabrja*, 273; *N. Evreinoff et son rôle dans le Théâtre du XXe Siecle* (commemorative pamphlet).
45. M. F. Andreeva was also Maxim Gorkij's wife and the founder of the Theatre of Free Comedy, "with the support of the Political Administration of the Baltic Fleet." The Theatre of Free Comedy specialized in producing contemporary plays, especially political satire. Andreeva opposed doing *The Chief Thing*, but Nikolaj Petrov argued ardently and successfully in its favor. Although Petrov later recanted and tried to minimize the significance of *The Chief Thing* to his theatre (agreeing with the official view of it as an apolitical satire inconsistent with his theatre's aim), Evreinov and the Theatre of Free Comedy shared a special relationship. Both before and after Petrov's production of *The Chief Thing*, for which Evreinov served as the advisor, Evreinov and his fellow *krivozerkalec*, designer Jurij Annenkov, exercised their finely honed parodistic techniques at the Theatre of Free Comedy. In fact, Evreinov was at one time considered to be that theatre's number one dramatist. Aside from *The Chief Thing*, which played one hundred times and was the backbone of the repertory, the theatre performed Evreinov's *In the Stage-Wings of the Soul* (1920), *A Feast of Laughter* (fall, 1921) and *The School of the Stars* (July 1922), this last as part of an Evreinov week in which the author directed his own plays, sang his own songs and performed his own music. On 10 January 1922, the theatre commemorated Evreinov's fifteen-year career as a dramatist with a jubilee celebration consisting of three of his plays: *Such a Woman* (with N. S. Raševskaja in the title role), *A Merry Death* (with Petrov playing Harlequin and Timošenko as Pierrot), and the pantomime *A Columbine of Today*. The event, which also included the usual "parade" of salutations, addresses, reading of letters and speeches, handshakes, hugs and kisses, was said to have unintentionally resembled Evreinov's production of the Crooked Mirror parody of provincial *pošlost'*, *Ryčalov's Tour*, which likewise takes place in a theatre. Zolotnickij, *Zori teatral'nogo oktjabrja*, 208, 273, 277 and 281; Nikolaj Petrov, *50 i 500* (Moskva: Vserossijskoe Teatral'noe Obščestvo, 1960), 209; Collins, "Nikolai Evreinov as a Playwright," in *Life as Theater...*, xviii.
46. Julia Ivanovna was actually Evreinov's former maid and his ward. She was said to have been in love with him, but he regarded himself solely as her guardian. He seemed also to consider his young charge to be *his* teacher. Moody, "Nikolai Nikolaevich Evreinov 1879-1953," 684; Evreinov, *The Main Thing*, in *Life as Theater...*, 35, and 67; Ellendea Proffer, ed., *Evreinov: A Pictorial Biography* (Ann Arbor: Ardis, 1981), 66.

47. N. Nilli, "O teatre buduščego (Mysli o teatre buduščego)," *Zapiski peredvižnego teatra* 20 (1919): 5-8; Evreinov, *The Main Thing,* 67.

48. L. Arns, "N. N. Evreinov (k 15-tiletiju ego literaturnoj i sceničeskoj dejatel'nosti)," *Žizn' iskusstva* 5 (17 January 1922): 2; Abram Èfros, "Otraženiju: N. Evreinov," *Teatral'noe obozrenie* 2 (1921): 5; Aleksandr Belenson, "Samoe glavnoe o *Samom glavnom,*" *Žizn' iskusstva* 682-84 (2-4 March 1921): 1.

49. A. A. Kašina-Evreinova, "Predislovie," in N. N. Evreinov, *V škole ostroumija,* CGALI SSSR, fond no. 982, ed. xr. no. 4, opis' no. 1, p. 1; Interview with A. A. Kašina-Evreinova; Paris, France; June 1976; interview with Jurij Gerasimov; Leningrad, U.S.S.R.; winter, 1975.

50. Stephen L. Baehr, "The Masonic Component in Eighteenth-Century Russian Literature," in *Russian Literature in the Age of Catherine the Great,* ed. A. G. Cross (Oxford: Meeuws, 1976), 121-23; interview with A. A. Kašina-Evreinova; Leningrad, U.S.S.R.: August 1975.

51. Baehr, "The Masonic Component in Eighteenth-Century Russian Literature," 123-4; Evreinov, *The Theatre in Life,* 285, 291-92.

52. Baehr, "The Masonic component...," 125-7; interview with A. A. Kašina-Evreinova; Paris, France; June 1976.

Notes for Chapter 5

1. "Staryj drug," "U kolybeli teatra," *Teatr* 213 (25 March 1908): 15.

2. M. A. Vološin, "Arxaizm v russkoj živopisi," *Apollon* 1 (1909): 43. Vološin's quote is from an article dealing with the trend of historical retrospectivism, specifically as it relates to the use of symbols in the work of three World of Art painters—L. S. Bakst (1866-1924), K. F. Bogaevskij (1872-1943) and N. K. Rerix (1874-1948). Maximilian A. Vološin (1877-1932) was himself an artist, art critic, poet, and amateur archeologist. He belonged to the World of Art group. Mickiewicz, "*Apollo* and Modernist Poetics," 366, 377-78, 392 n.13; Bowlt, "The World of Art," 415.

3. *Teatr* (23 March 1903): 6; Edward Stark, *Starinnyj teatr* (Petrograd: Tret'ja straža, 1922), 7. This is the major source of information on the Ancient Theatre.

4. Stark, *Starinnyj teatr,* 5-9; Viktorija Čekan, "Starinnyj teatr: Ispansikj cikl, Evreinov-Driezen," *Žizn' iskusstva* 21 (29 May 1922): 4.

5. Evreinov, *Teatr kak takovoj,* 18-19, 32-33.

6. Evreinov repeated these sentiments on several occasions, most notably in *Theatrical Innovations* (*Teatral'nye novacii,* Petrograd, 1922), a collection of journal and newspaper articles which he had written. In the section entitled "The Method of Creative Reconstruction for Theatrical Stagings" (p. 79), Evreinov wrote:

> A theatrical work is valuable to us not only in a scenic, dramaturgical, or aesthetic sense, i.e., not only as a definite object of art, but equally as a cultural indicator—spiritual and material in equal degree—of the culture of that epoch which with a natural inevitability—or more precisely, with historical necessity—any theatrical work reflects.

7. Stark, *Starinnyj teatr,* 9.

Notes for Chapter 5

8. The permanent curtain designed for the Ancient Theatre by Benois represented a tapestry from the thirteenth century, inscribed with favorite medieval motifs. A knight stood on the stage left side of the curtain. Stage right was a maiden gently petting a unicorn. This tapestry was parted in three places: stage right by an angel, stage left by a demon, and stage center by Adam and Eve. Stark, *Starinnyj teatr,* 15. (*See* fig. 6).

9. Evreinov was romantically involved with N. I. Butkovskaja from 1907 to 1911. Butkovskaja, the daughter of a wealthy Polish Jewish family, wanted to marry Evreinov, but the desire was not mutual. She gave up acting and eventually married the painter Servadsidze but remained on friendly terms with Evreinov. She published several of his books, commissioned his monographs on Rops and Beardsley and translated *Salomé* for Evreinov's production at Komissarževskaja's theatre. Moody, "Nikolai Nikolaevich Evreinov 1879-1953," 674; Stark, *Starinnyj teatr,* 12-14; "Xronika," *Teatr i iskusstvo* 45 (11 November 1907): 732.

10. Baron N. V. Driezen, "Starinnyj teatr (Vospominanija)," *Stolica i usad'ba* 71 (1 December 1917): 11. No reason has been given for the company's enduring such an unusually rigorous schedule just to have access to this particular space.

11. Evreinov read this lecture again at the Literary Artistic Circle of Y. P. Polonskaja on 30 November at an evening devoted to the Ancient Theatre. It was later published in the journal *Theatre and Art* and in Evreinov's collection of articles *Pro Scena Sua* (1914).

12. Stark, *Starinnyj teatr,* 11-12, 14.

13. Anatolij Kremlev, "Popytka restavracii srednevekovogo teatra," *Teatr i iskusstvo* 7 (17 February 1908): 134.

14. N. N. Evreinov, *Jarmarka na indikt sv. Denisa* in *Dramatičeskie sočinenija,* vol. 2 (St. Petersburg: Sovremennoe iskusstvo, 1914), translated by and quoted in Christopher Moody, "The Ancient Theatre in St. Petersburg 1907-8 and 1911-12," 23. Moody's article was published in *New Zealand Slavonic Journal* 2:33-54. My pagination refers to a xerox of the original typed copy of the article which the author graciously made available to me.

15. Moody, "The Ancient Theatre," 14-17; *Teatr* 212 (23 March 1908): 12-13.

16. Stark, *Starinnyj teatr,* 15, 29, 32.

17. Anatolij Kremlev, "Popytka restavracii srednevekovogo teatra," *Teatr i iskusstvo* 7 (17 February 1908): 135-37; Anatolij Kremlev, "Popytka restavracii srednevekogo teatra (conclusion)," *Teatr i iskusstvo* 8 (24 February 1908): 151-53.

18. Stark, *Starinnyj teatr,* 15-18.

19. A. R. Kugel', "Teatral'nye zametki," *Teatr i iskusstvo* 50 (16 December 1907): 845-47; Evreinov, *Pro Scena Sua,* 70-72, 74-75.

20. Ljubov' Gurevič, "Starinnyj teatr v. S.-Peterburge," *Russkie vedomosti* 293 (22 December 1907): 5. The cast of *The Three Magi* numbered 120 and so the play could not be taken on to Moscow with the rest of the repertory in March 1908. Stark, *Starinnyj teatr,* 32.

21. The cast lists for the various productions in the medieval and Spanish cycles at the Ancient Theatre appear in Appendix B.

22. "Staryj drug," "U kolybeli teatra," *Teatr* 213 (25 March 1908): 15-18.

23. Kremlev, "Popytka restavracii srednevekogo teatra (conclusion)," 151-53.

24. Kugel', "Teatral'nye zametki," 846.

25. Ju. Veselovskij, "Otkrytie spektaklej 'Starinnogo teatra,'" *Russkie vedomesti* 71 (25 March 1908); Gurevič, "Starinnyj teatr v. S.-Peterburge," 5; Valerian Čudovskij, "O Starinnom teatre," *Russakaja xudožestvennaja letopis'* 4 (February 1912): 62; N. Karabanov, "Starinnyj teatr," *Teatr* 1025 (22 February 1912); I. Borozdin, "Srednevekovyj teatr. Po povodu moskovskix gastrolej S.-Peterburgskogo Starinnogo teatra," *Vesy* 4 (1908): 96-98.

26. Stark, *Starinnyj teatr,* 22-24.

27. Kremlev, "Popytka restavracii srednevekovogo teatra," 134; Gurevič, "Starinnyj teatr v. S.-Peterburge," 5; L. Vas-ij, "Teatr i muzyka: Starinnyj teatr," *Reč'* 298 (18 December 1907): 5.

28. Stark, *Starinnyj teatr,* 24-27.

29. L. Vas-ij, "Teatr i muzyka: Starinnyj teatr," 5.

30. "Starinnyj teatr," *Teatr* 139 (22 December 1907): 13-19.

31. "Staryj drug," "U kolybeli teatra," 17-18.

32. Stark, *Starinnyj teatr,* 27-28.

33. "Staryj drug," "U kolybeli teatra," 17.

34. Stark, *Starinnyj teatr,* 29-32.

35. Quoted in Stark, *Starinnyj teatr,* 31.

36. P. Muratov, *Russkoe slovo* (27 March 1908): 5.

37. Igor' Grabar', "Teatr i xudožniki," *Vesy* 4 (1908): 95.

38. Edward Stark, "Otkrytie 'Starinnogo teatra,'" *Obozrenie teatrov* 274 (9 December 1907): 14.

39. "Staryj drug," "U kolybeli teatra," 18.

40. Stark, *Starinnyj teatr,* 35.

41. Kazanskij, *Metod teatra,* 103.

42. Kryžickij is not the most objective source for information on Evreinov. There was no love lost between these two men, and they were constantly sniping at each other in print. Kryžickij worked for a time at the Crooked Mirror Theatre following Evreinov's departure, and his divorce from Evreinov's sister-in-law produced hard feelings. Interview with A. A. Kašina-Evreinova; Leningrad, U.S.S.R.; August 1975.

43. Vsevelod Mejerxol'd, "Starinnyj teatr v S.-Peterburge," *O teatre* (St. Petersburg, 1913), 117-20.

44. Evreinov, *Teatral'nye novacii,* 81.

45. Mejerxol'd, "Starinnyj teatr v S.-Peterburge," *O teatre,* 117-20; *Meyerhold on Theatre,* 101-2.

46. Stark, *Starinnyj teatr,* 64; Baron N. V. Driezen, "Starinnyj teatr (Vospominanija)," 12.

47. Mejerxol'd and his supporters argued that his production of Calderón's *La Devocion de la Cruz* (1910) at Vjačeslav Ivanov's private Tower Theatre predated Evreinov's work with the reconstructive method in the Spanish cycle at the Ancient Theatre. Discrepancies in the exact dates of the performances in question make this dispute difficult to resolve. In any case Mejerxol'd's production was done with limited means and did not, from all evidence, aim at archeological reconstruction, or what he called a "lifeless copy of the past." *Apollon* 8 (1910): 35; *Apollon* 7 (1912): 32; Mejerxol'd, *O teatre*, 255.

48. V. Vsevolodskij (Gerngross), *Istorija russkogo teatra*, 2:243-44, quoted in and translated by Moody, "The Ancient Theatre....," 45-46.

49. *Teatr* 257 (1908): 6; *Obozrenie teatrov* 411 (1908): 7.

50. Christopher Moody writes:

> "There is no evidence to suggest that Evreinov was familiar with the work of the American hispanist Hugo Rennert in 1909, the year in which the latter published his *The Spanish Theatre in the Time of Lope de Vega* [Hugo Albert Rennert. *The Spanish Stage in the Time of Lope de Vega with an Alphabetical List of Spanish Actors and Actresses, 1560-1680*. New York: The Hispanic Society of America, 1909]. By the time he came to put on Spanish plays, however, he almost certainly was."

Moody, "The Ancient Theatre," 28. Evreinov's article was later reproduced in the book *The Spanish Theatre (Ispanskij teatr). Articles by Baron N. V. Driezen, K. Miklaševskij, and N. Evreinov*, St. Petersburg, 1912. The article reappeared in Evreinov's *Pro Scena Sua* (1914).

51. Evreinov, "Ispanskij akter XVI-XVII vv.," *Pro Scena Sua*, 80-81, 92-95, 98. Evreinov credited Spain's location in Southern Europe with instilling in the Spanish character the qualities of imagination, creativity, and erotic languor.

52. N. N. Evreinov, "Ispanskij akter XVI-XVII vv." (Novaja redakcija stat'i promeščennoj), *Ežegodnik Imperatorskix teatrov*, vypusk 617 (1909): 20-21, 39.

53. A. A. Mgebrov, *Žizn' v teatre*, 2:35-44, 47, 60, 64-65, 67-78; I. R., "Vesti iz Peterburga," *Rampa i žizn'* 46 (13 November 1911): 11-12; *Teatr i iskusstvo* 22 (1911): 320; Moody, "The Ancient Theatre," 32.

54. Čudovskij, "O Starinnom teatre," *Russkaja xudožestvennaja letopis'*, 58, 62.

55. Mgebrov, *Žizn' v teatre*, 2:105; *Studija* (St. Petersburg).

56. Stark, *Starinnyj teatr*, 40-41.

57. Christopher Moody has this to say about the production history of *Fuente Ovejuna* in Russia:

> The play was put on the Russian stage in 1876 at the Moscow Maly Theatre for the benefit of M. N. Ermolova, with the actress taking the leading part. But it had to be taken off in view of the inflammatory nature of the subject—a popular uprising. It was therefore an adventurous choice of play in 1911. It managed to pass the censor partly because in this production it was somewhat diluted and partly because the censor at the time was Baron Driezen.

Moody, "The Ancient Theatre," 33.

58. Stark, *Starinnyj teatr*, 46-47.

59. A. R. Kugel', *Teatr i iskusstvo* 48 (25–27 November 1911): 937.
60. Èm. Beskin, "*Fuente Ovejuna,*" *Rannee utro* 38 (16 February 1912): 5.
61. Čudovskij, "O Starinnom teatre," *Russkaja xudožestvennaja letopis'*, 58–59, 62.
62. Ljubov' Gurevič, "Peterburgskie teatry," *Russkie vedomosti* 273 (27 November 1911): 5; Mgebrov, *Žizn' v teatre*, 2:55.
63. Aleksandr Benois, "Xudožestvennye pis'ma: Starinnyj teatr," *Reč'* 345 (16 December 1911): 3.
64. Stark, *Starinnyj teatr*, 49–53.
65. Čudovskij, "O Starinnom teatre," *Russkaja xudožestvennaja letopis'*, 59. It was customary in the Spanish theatre to contemporize all costumes and to translate foreign attire into something basically Spanish. Costumes were often very expensive. The only time characters appeared in costumes that were not contemporary was in plays based on Spanish history or legend. In these cases an attempt was made to reproduce the spirit of the age in question. Rennert, *The Spanish Stage in the Time of Lope de Vega*, 104–7.
66. N. Karabanov, "Starinnyj teatr," *Teatr* 1025 (22 February 1912).
67. A. Izmajlov (Smolenskij), "U rampy: Starinnyj teatr-*Blagočestivaja marta i Velikij knjaz Moskovskij*," *Birževye vedomosti* 12659 (29 November 1911): 4.
68. Evgenij Pskovitinov, *Tiflisskij listok*, quoted in Stark, *Starinnyj teatr*, 52–53, translated in Moody, "The Ancient Theatre," 36–37.
69. Stark, *Starinnyj teatr*, 51–52.
70. The word "Saint" was removed from the title when the play was presented at the Ancient Theatre as a concession to the censor. The play was cut to half its original length so as not to bore the audience, which was unfamiliar with the material. Stark, 60–61.
71. Stark, *Starinnyj teatr*, 60–61, quoted in (and translated by) Moody, "The Ancient Theatre," p. 39.
72. Stark, *Starinnyj teatr*, 60–61.
73. Čudovskij, "O Starinnom teatre," *Russkaja xudožestvennaja letopis'*, 60.
74. Stark, *Starinnyj teatr*, 62–63.
75. Nikolaj Karabanov wrote that for the first evening's presentation of the Spanish cycle the theatre was less than half full. N. Karabanov, "Starinnyj teatr," *Teatr* 1025 (22 February 1912).
76. Evreinov, *Pro Scena Sua*, 142.
77. Čudovskij, "O Starinnom teatre," 58; Gurevič, "Peterburgskie teatry," *Russkie vedomosti*, 5; Kugel', "Teatral'nye zametki," *Teatr i iskusstvo*, 846–47.
78. Raz-ij, "Starinnyj teatr (K gastroljam v Moskve)," *Studija* 20 (18 February 1912): 6–7.
79. Moody, "Nikolai Nikolaevich Evreinov 1879–1953," 678–81.
80. N. N. Evreinov, "Ispytanie vremenem," in *Sto let Malomu teatru 1824–1924*, ed. A. R. Kugel' and V. Filippov (Moskva, 1924), 27.

81. Stark, *Starinnyj teatr,* 69.

82. P. A. Markov, *O teatre,* vol. 1, *Iz istorii russkogo i sovetskogo teatra* (Moskva: Iskusstvo, 1974), 289.

83. The Theatre of Russian Drama in Paris, organized under the auspices of the Society of Friends of Russian Art, was dedicated to the reconstruction of the Russian classics. A number of Russian émigrés were involved in this work, including: actors and actresses K. M. Dubravina, Ju. P. Zagrebel'skij, O. V. Karelina, Elizaveta Kedrova, B. N. Kuznecov, V. I. Motyleva, V. V. Pomostov and M. A. Tokarskaja; the composer N. N. Kurov; designer R. M. Dobužinskij; and the director E. N. Roščina-Insarova. This theatre, founded in 1938, lasted three seasons. Russian productions resumed in 1943 at the Theatre *"Yen" (Iena)* under the direction of Sergej Lifar', E. N. Roščina-Insarova, and N. N. Evreinov, with the generous patronage of Pavel Al'bertovič Jurševič and the administrative participation of B. N. Šupinskij. N. N. Evreinov, *Pamjatnik mimoletnomu. Iz Istorii èmigrantskogo teatra v Pariže* (Paris, 1953), 37-38; N. N. Evreinov, "Kak nado stavit' *Nedoroslja* D. Fonvizina," Issledovanie (1939) CGALI SSSR, fond no. 982, opis' no. 1. ed. xr. no. 39, pp. 33-35.

84. Evgenij A. Znosko-Borovskij, *Russkij teatr načala XX veka* (Prague: Plamja, 1925), 340-42.

85. Stark, *Starinnyj teatr,* 33.

86. George Kalbouss, "The Plays of Nikolaj Evreinov," *Russian Language Journal* 92 (1971): 24; Evreinov, *Pro Scena Sua,* 142; N. N. Evreinov, *The Beautiful Despot* ("The Last Act of a Drama"), in *Five Plays with One from the Ukrainian,* trans. C. E. Bechhofer (New York: E. P. Dutton and Co., 1916), 63-67.

Notes for Chapter 6

1. Evreinov, *Teatr kak takovoj,* 109-10.

2. The most popular journal of its day, the weekly *Satyricon* (former *Strekoza*) was founded in St. Petersburg on 3 April 1908. It stopped publishing in 1914. Taking its name from the famous work by Petronius (Titus Petronius Niger, d. AD 66) which presented a "kaleidoscopic, nightmarish montage of the dissipation in the epoch of Nero," the journal was designed to focus on contemporary social and political issues. Under the editorship of G. Kornfel'd, *Satyricon* modelled its humor on foreign journals—primarily English, French, and German. A number of the poets who were associated with *Satyricon* had connections with symbolist circles. Others affiliated with this journal would later work with Evreinov at the Crooked Mirror Theatre and elsewhere. Among them were N. A. Teffi, A. N. Benois, M. K. Dobužinskij, B. F. Gejer, A. Averčenko, P. Potemkin and M. A. Kuzmin. Lidija Alekseevna Evstigneeva, *Žurnal "Satirikon" i poèty-satirikoncy* (Moskva: Nauka, 1968), 5-6, 8-13, 24, 118, 398; M. Ja. Poljakov, ed., *Russkaja teatral'naja parodija XIX—načala XX veka* (Moskva: Iskusstvo, 1976), 825.

3. The Cabbage Party was composed of parodies and satirical pieces, burlesques and grotesques, individual musical and comic numbers and the like. Such occasions, which gave serious artists the chance to let their hair down, were originally closed but later opened to the public. The theatre used the paid admissions to aid the more needy among its actors. Stanislavski, *My Life in Art,* 450-52.

Notes for Chapter 6   263

4. A. G. Alekseev, *Ser'eznoe i smešnoe. Polveka v teatre i na èstrade* (Moskva: Iskusstvo, 1967), 3-4.

5. The Litejnyj Theatre was located at 51 Litejnyj Prospekt and the Intimnyj at 12 Krjukovoj canal. Materials from the Manuscript Division of the Leningrad State Theatrical Museum on the Petersburg theatres of small forms, "Otkrytoe zasedanie soveta sodejstvija posvjaščennoe teatru 'Krivoe zerkalo' (K 65-letiju so dnja osnovanija)," 30 marta 1973 goda, 5-7. The famous entrepreneur Kazanskij originally tried to open a theatre "Grand Guignol" on Litejnyj Prospekt (1909), modelled after the form sweeping Paris at that time. However, the enterprise was not a success and was replaced after one year by a theatre of small forms. Z. Xolmskaja, "Krivoe zerkalo," *Rabočij i teatr* 9 (September 1937): 53.

6. For further background on Western European cabaret *see* Lisa Appignanesi, *The Cabaret* (London: Studio Vist, 1976). *See also* Anthony Pearson, "The Cabaret Comes to Russia: 'Theatre of Small Forms' as Cultural Catalyst," *Theatre Quarterly* (Winter, 1980): 31-44, for brief discussions of the Bat, the Crooked Mirror, the Stray Dog (*Brodjačaja sobaka,* 1910-1915) and the Comedians' Halt (*Prival komediantov,* 1916-1919). Evreinov was directly involved with the last three.

7. Kugel', *List'ja s dereva. Vospominanija,* 196-97, 199.

8. Xolmskaja, 52, 56. The Theatrical Club was a group of artists and dramatists organized in 1908 and located on Litejnyj Prospekt. The directorate included Ju. M. Jur'ev, A. A. Pleščev, I. N. Potapenko, and A. R. Kugel' among others. Material from the Theatrical Museum, A. G. Avvakumov, 21.

9. N. N. Evreinov, "Slovo o Kugele," *V škole ostroumija. O teatre "Krivoe zerkalo,"* Materials from Central'nyj gosudarstvennyj arxiv literatury i iskusstva SSSR (CGALI SSSR), fond 982, opis' no. 1., ed. xr. no. 12, p. 31; materials from the Theatrical Museum, L. S. Ljubaševskij, 19.

10. "Teffi" was, as Prince D. S. Mirskij tells us in his highly opinioned *A History of Russian Literature,* the pseudonym of Mme. N. A. Bučinskaja, sister of the "exotic" poetess Mirra Loxvitskaja (1869-1905) and a writer of short stories (especially for the journal *Satyricon*) in "the good old traditions of Russian literary humor." Her genteel humor, based upon "the careful choice of suggestive detail," makes her, in Mirskij's estimation, a disciple of Čexov. Mirskij is far less generous with her fellow *Satyricon* contributor and Crooked Mirror writer Arkadij Averčenko who, he says, "is a pupil of the Anglo-American school of comic writing...full of crude buffoonery and extravagantly funny situations" (*see* Evreinov's parody of American humor and humorists in his comedic compendium *A Feast of Laughter*). He is, says Mirskij, "as international and plebeian as Teffi is refined and Russian." Averčenko was also editor of the satirical journal *New Satyricon (Novyj satirikon).* D. S. Mirsky, *A History of Russian Literature,* edited and abridged by Francis J. Whitefield (New York: Alfred A. Knopf, 1969), 406; Senelick, *Russian Dramatic Theory from Pushkin to the Symbolists,* 302 n.30.

11. Evreinov believed that the Strand failed because it embodied Mejerxol'd's belief that theatre is born of literature. Evreinov was fond of repeating this because he claimed that following the publication of his *Apology for Theatricality (Apologija teatral'nosti,* 1908) and *The Theatre as Such* (1912) Mejerxol'd reversed his position. Volkov, *Mejerxol'd,* 2:37-39; G. Kryžickij, "Vospominanija, 'Laboratorija smexa,' " *Teatr* 8 (August 1967): 110-11, 116; Kugel', *List'ja s dereva,* 198; Xolmskaja, "Krivoe zerkalo," 53; materials from the Leningrad State Theatrical Museum, K. A. Guzynin, 7.

12. Zolotnickij, *Zori teatral'nogo oktjabrja,* 158; Guzynin, 9-10; Xolmskaja, "Krivoe zerkalo," 56.
13. Materials from the Leningrad State Theatrical Museum, L. N. Semenova, 30.
14. Xolmskaja, "Krivoe zerkalo," 53-54; N. N. Evreinov, "Pervye šažki, šagi i šagice," in *V škole ostroumija.* O teatre "Krivoe zerkalo," OGALI SSSR, 72, 77-78.
15. Mixail N. Volkonskij (pseudonym Ančar Mancenilov) was the author of short stories, novels, and plays as well as editor of the journal *Cornfield (Niva)* His many literary and theatrical parodies include *Vampuka* and the equally popular *Ryčalov's Tour,* which was also written for the Crooked Mirror Theatre (it also played at the Free Theatre). Volkonskij had a complex and difficult relationship with the Crooked Mirror Theatre which eventually led to a final break between the two. P. P. Gnedič, *Kniga žizni. Vospominanija* (Leningrad, 1929), 245-46; M. Ja. Poljakov, "Kommentarij— Princessa Afrikanskaja," *Russkaja teatral'naja parodija...,* 803-6; Kryžickij, "Vospominanija. 'Laboratorija smexa,' " 111-12; Xolmskaja, "Krivoe zerkalo," 54; Kugel', *List'ja s dereva,* 198.
16. Kryžickij, "Vospominanija. 'Laboratorija smexa,'" 111-12; Christopher Moody, "The Crooked Mirror," *Melbourne Slavonic Studies* 7 (1972): 27-28.
17. Xolmskaja, "Krivoe zerkalo," 55. The production was directed by R. A. Ungern. Kryžickij, "Vospominanija. 'Laboratorija smexa,' " 112.
18. Moody, "The Crooked Mirror," 28.
19. Kryžickij, "Vospominanija. 'Laboratorija smexa,' " 113. Anthony Pearson writes: "In the four and a half months of its first Petersburg season the theatre's box office had taken in 80,000 roubles." Added to this was 76,000 roubles from a 71-performance summer tour of Moscow. In other words, the Crooked Mirror was already a going concern for what it was. Pearson, "The Cabaret Comes to Russia...," 39.
20. Evreinov suggests that R. A. Ungern, who was handling much of the direction in the early days at the Crooked Mirror Theatre, was something of a rolling stone. Kugel' and Xolmskaja were uncertain about his allegiance to their theatre and wanted a director in whom they could feel more confident. Evreinov, "Kak ja stal glavnym režisserom 'Krivogo zerkala,' " *V škole ostroumija,* 90.
21. *Čereposlov* or "That is to say, The Phrenologist" (*Sireč frenolog*) parodies the "antiscientific" profession of phrenology which pretends to determine the nature of an individual's psyche by examining the shape of his skull (*čerepa* in Russian). Poljakov, "Russkij teatr v krivom zerkale parodii," *Russkaja teatral'naja parodija...,* 30; D. Zolotnickij, *Zori teatral'nogo oktjabrja,* 158; Evreinov, "Kak ja stal glavnym režisserom 'Krivogo zerkala,' " *V škole ostroumija,* 102-3.
22. It was not their first meeting. They had met earlier to discuss the possibility of Kugel''s editing Evreinov's plays. Evreinov and F. F. Komissarževskij also had consulted with Kugel' about a letter which they wrote to *Theatre and Art* to protest an exact imitation of their production of *Čereposlov* by B. S. Nevolin at his summer theatre in Petersburg. Evreinov first met Xolmskaja along with Baron Driezen at the tenth anniversary jubilee for *Theatre and Art* in 1906. Evreinov, "Kak ja stal glavnym režisserom 'Krivogo zerkala,' " 109-11, 122.
23. Evreinov recalls a certain degree of intransigence from some of the members of the troupe, Xolmskaja included, on the matter of changing the existing format of individual

variety numbers. One singer, A. S. Abramjan, the original "*Vampuka,*" refused to recognize the value of a theatre of satire, which is what the Crooked Mirror became under Evreinov. She was constantly trying to show the public that she was not like the others, that she was a serious singer, and to this end performed in a manner which was not consistent with the style of the productions in which she appeared. Evreinov, "Kak ja stal glavnym režisserom 'Krivogo zerkala,' " 125-26, 133, 142.

24. Ibid., 123; Kryžickij, "Vospominanija. 'Laboratorija smexa,' " 113; Materials from the Leningrad State Theatrical Museum, A. G. Avvakumov, 123.

25. A list of the productions which premiered at the Crooked Mirror Theatre during Evreinov's tenure as artistic director appears in Appendix C. Vas. R-n, "V krivom zerkale," *Birževye vedomosti* 12634 (14 June 1911): 7.

26. In a letter to L. A. Fenin dated 22 September 1914, Evreinov wrote: "My health is slowly improving. I live in Kuokkala, Finland, where it is so quiet and peaceful far away from dear Aleksandr Rafailovič Kugel'." Evreinov was on friendly terms with Fenin, whom he called the "ideal comic actor" in "the European sense of the word," that is, he could play serious drama as well as grotesque, sing, and perform mime. Furthermore, Evreinov admired Fenin's "devilish aristocratism, not only on the stage of the theatre but also on the stage of life." He was one of a number of the self-dramatizing kindred spirits with whom Evreinov came into contact during his lifetime. It is therefore quite reasonable that he would speak so derisively about Kugel' to Fenin since "dear Aleskandr Rafailovič" was of a different breed entirely. CGALI SSSR fond no. 2026, opis' no. 1, ed. xr. no. 159, Pis'ma Evreinova, Nikolaja Nikolaeviča k Feninu Lvu Aleksandroviču (22 September 1914).

27. A list of productions directed by Evreinov at the Crooked Mirror Theatre appears in Appendix D.

28. M. K. Jarockaja, "Letopis' teatra 'Krivoe zerkalo.' " Sbornik vyskazyvanij pressi, teatral'nyx dejatelej o teatre, programmy spektaklej teatra, sostav truppy i dr. za period 1908-1918 gg.; materials from CGALI SSSR, fond. no. 2353, opis' no. 1, ed. xr. no. 62, pp. 89-93.

29. Cited in M. K. Jarockaja, "Letopis' teatra Krivoe zerkalo," Sbornik vyskazyvanij pressi, teatral'nyx dejatelej o teatre, programmy i spektaklej teatra, sostav truppy i dr. za period 1908-1918 gg., CGALI, fond no. 2353, opis' no. 1, ed. xr. no. 62, p. 94.

30. A. Dejč, "Vospominaja minuvšee," *Zvezda* 5 (1966): 176; Evreinov, "O satiričeskoj monodrame i ispol'zovanii eë na scene 'Krivogo zerkala,' " 12; A. R. Kugel', "Teatral'nye zametki," *Teatr i iskusstvo* 39 (25 September 1911): 726-28; Evstigneeva, *Žurnal "Satirikon" i poèty-satirikoncy,* 372; Kugel', *List'ja s dereva,* 207.

31. Evstigneeva, *Žurnal "Satirikon" i poèty-satirikoncy,* 375-76; Evreinov, "O satiričeskoj monodrame i ispol'zovannii eë na scene 'Krivogo zerkala,' " 17.

32. Christopher Collins employs the term "polydrama" to distinguish the multiple-perspective play from the single-perspective one. *Stage-Wings* does not qualify as polydrama in that the several different perspectives on the action belong to a single self. Christopher Collins, "Nikolai Evreinov as a Playwright," in *Life as Theater: Five Modern Plays,* xvii-xviii.

33. Moody, "The Crooked Mirror," 32-34; Kryžickij, "Vospominanija. 'Laboratorija smexa,' " 114; Kugel', *List'ja s dereva,* 200; materials from the Leningrad State Theatri-

cal Museum, L. S. Ljubaševskij, 17-18; V. Xovin, "Teatral'naja žizn': Krivoe zerkalo," *Voskresnaja večernjaja gazeta* 21 (14 October 1912):3; *Teatr* 1822 (29 February 1916): 19; Evstigneeva, *Žurnal "Satirikon" i poèty satirikoncy,* 372, 375.

34. B. F. Gejer, *Èvoljucija teatra,* in Poljakov, *Russkaja teatral'naja parodija,* 569-587.

35. N. N. Evreinov, "Koz'ma Prutkov-počitaemym ocom 'Krivogo zerkala,' " *Vozroždenie* 50 (1956): 103; N. N. Evreinov, "K poznaniju teatral'noj parodii," *V škole ostroumija,* 66; Moody, "Nikolai Nikolaevich Evreinov 1879-1953," 670-71; Marc Slonim, *The Epic of Russian Literature* (New York: Oxford University Press, 1969), 223-24; M. Ja. Poljakov, "Russkij teatr v krivom zerkale parodii" (Predislovie), *Russkaja teatral'naja parodija XIX – načala XX veka,* 28.

36. Kryžickij, "Vospominanija, 'Laboratorija smexa,' " 115-16.

37. Fanger, *The Creation of Nikolai Gogol,* 123.

38. M. Ja. Poljakov, "Kommentarij – *Kuxnja smexa,*" *Russkaja teatral'naja parodija...,* 811-12.

39. Ibid.; Zolotnickij, *Zori teatral'nogo oktjabrja,* 275-76. It is intriguing how close in spirit and his devices Evreinov is to the modern masters of self-conscious metafiction. In his book *Partial Magic,* Robert Alter compiles a list of authors working in this mode which I will, for the sake of convenience, simply reproduce here: Raymond Queneau, Samuel Beckett, Alain Robbe-Grillet, Michel Butor, Claude Mauriac, John Fowles, Robert Coover, John Barth, Thomas Pynchon, Donald Bartheleme, Kurt Vonnegut, Jorge Luis Borges, Julio Cortazar and Vladimir Nabokov. As to Evreinov's proposed membership in this modern fraternity, one need only mention Raymond Queneau's highly Evreinovian *Exercices de style.* In this ingenious little book, a single, purposely banal anecdote is retold ninety-nine times through a variety of styles and a continually shifting narrative viewpoint. Queneau's tale, like Evreinov's *A Feast of Laughter* (and not unlike Evreinov's reworking of Gogol''s *The Inspector General*), hangs on the narrowest of threads – one from which a coat button has come undone. Alter, *Partial Magic: The Novel as a Self-Conscious Genre,* 219, 221-22.

40. Included in the cast of *The Inspector General* were: Mayor – L. A. Fenin; Anna Andreevna – Z. V. Xolmskaja; Mar'ja Antonovna – M. K. Jarockaja; Ljapkin – Tjapkin – S. M. Antimonov; Laughter – E. A. Xovanskaja; Satire – T. X. Dejkarxanova; The Clerk from the Special Commission Delegated by the Directorate of the Crooked Mirror Theatre – V. A. Podgornyj. Zolotnickij, *Zori teatral'nogo oktjabrja,* 158; Kugel', *List'ja s dereva,* 203; A. R. Kugel', "Teatral'nye zametki," *Žizn' iskusstva* 36 (11 September 1923): 5-7; N. N. Evreinov, "Predislovie," *Dramatičeskie sočinenija,* (Petrograd: Academia, 1923), 3:7.

41. This is a subject to which I will return in the concluding chapter. There is yet another possible connecting link to be added to the Evreinov-Xlestakov-Harlequin chain: the name of Vladimir Nabokov. Nabokov, who wrote a brilliantly idiosyncratic critical study of Gogol' and who was, in the estimation of many, his literary heir, was for a time a neighbor of the Evreinovs in Paris. Although they had little real contact, Anna Evreinova credits her husband with influencing the work of his fellow Russian émigré, especially one of his later novels entitled, appropriately enough, *Look at the Harlequins!* (1974). Nabokov, like Evreinov, played the role of literary harlequin, creating a self-contained, self-referential crooked looking glass world in which the author as transforming presence becomes the main character in his art. Nabokov participated in a

curious affair, an evening in Berlin entitled *The Judgment of Evreinov*. This mock tribunal was convened by Evreinov's fellow artists following the success of his play *The Chief Thing*, to consider whether the author should be permitted to propagate the idea of life as theatre. Owing to some physical resemblance, Nabokov was called upon to impersonate Evreinov, thus, at least momentarily, the image of the one was superimposed upon the other. Interview with A. A. Kašina-Evreinova; Paris, France; June 1976.

42. The Nevolin incident. See note 22. Evreinov, *Pro Scena Sua*, 55-56.

43. N. N. Evreinov, "V gostjax u carja Nikolaja II-go," *V škole ostroumija*, fond no 982, ed. xr. no. 13, opis' no. 1, p. 27; Evreinov, "Predislovie," *Dramatičeskie sočinenija*, 3:7; *Teatr i iskusstvo* 20 (1909): 349; N. N. Evreinov, "Iskusstvo režissera," in *Al'manax-spravočnik Vsja Teatral'no-muzykal'naja Rossija,* ed. N. Davingof (Petrograd: Teatr južnyj, 1914-15), 55-59.

44. Zolotnickij, *Zori o teatral'nogo oktjabrja,* 159; N. N. Evreinov, "O nekotoryx xodjačikh terminax (K pereizdaniju *Teatr kak takovoj),*" *Žizn' iskusstva* 44 (5 November 1922): 6; Evreinov, "V gostjax u carja Nikolaja II-go," 40; N. N. Evreinov, "K pereocenke teatral'nosti (Okončanie)," *Žizn' iskusstva* 38 (25 September 1923): 11-12; Poljakov, "Kommentarij — *Revizor,*" *Russkaja teatral'naja parodija,* 809-11; interviews with A. A. Kašina-Evreinova: Leningrad, U.S.S.R., August 1975 and Paris, France, June 1976; Kott, "The Eating of 'The Government Inspector,' " *Theatre Quarterly,* 29; Gogol, *The Inspector General,* in *Nineteenth-Century Russian Plays,* 272; Laurence Senelick, *Gordon Craig's Moscow "Hamlet": A Reconstruction* (Westport; Greenwood Press, 1982) 181-82; N. N. Čuškin, ed. *Moskovskij xudožestvennyj teatr. Tom pervyj 1898-1917* (Moskva: Iskusstvo, 1955), 303; Znosko-Borovskij, *Russkij teatr načala XX veka,* 328.

45. N. N. Evreinov, *Revizor, Dramatičeskie sočinenija,* 3:11-12.

46. Ibid., 12-15.

47. This would seem to be a humorous swipe at Stanislavskij himself. "The master" describes in his autobiography how he spent the summer of 1906 in Finland wrestling with himself over the stagnation he felt had taken hold in his acting. He wrote: "After I arrived, I would spend my mornings on a cliff that overlooked the sea, taking stock of my artistic past. I wanted to find out where all my former joy in creation had vanished." Although Stanislavskij does not indicate having heard a nightingale at this moment, he, like our agricultural expert, brought away from his communion with nature a new sense of inner vision and understanding which started him on the path to the development of his famous system. The moment changed his life. Constantin Stanislavski, *My Life in Art,* 458.

48. It was, of course, the custom at MXAT to travel to the actual scene which the theatre would try to re-create in a future production. For their production of *Julius Caesar* (1903), for example, Stanislavskij dispatched Nemirovič-Dančenko and Simov to Rome to gather material. In the meantime an entire department was set up in the theatre to deal with questions relating to "locale, the social conditions of life, the customs, buildings, and usages of the time of Caesar." Stanislavski, *My Life in Art,* 408-9.

49. Evreinov, *Revizor,* 15-18.

50. The Munich Secession was a union of German and Austrian painters and theatre artists founded in 1892 by F. Shtuk and which counted Ernst von Wolzogen among its mem-

bers. The group was opposed to official academic art and supported such movements as impressionism. It lasted until 1910. Poljakov, "Kommentarij — *Revizor*," 810-11.

51. Evreinov, *Revizor;* 28.

52. Kugel', *List'ja s dereva,* 46.

53. The play, subtitled *An Episode from the Life of Annuška, N. N. Evreinov's Maid,* parodies the turn-of-the-century modishness of chansonette-starlets. N. N. Evreinov, *Škola ètualej, Dramatičeskaja sočinenija,* 77-78; Poljakov, "Kommentarij, *Škola ètualej,*" 811.

54. Evreinov *Škola ètualej,* 81.

55. Anaïs Nin, *The Diary of Anaïs Nin,* vol. 2 (1934-39), ed. Gunther Stuhlmann (New York: The Swallow Press and Harcourt, Brace and World, 1967), 172.

56. N. N. Evreinov, *The Unmasked Ball (The Theater of Eternal War)* in *Life as Theater: Five Modern Plays by Nikolai Evreinov,* trans. and ed. Christopher Collins (Ann Arbor: Ardis, 1973), 223.

57. È. B. Krasnjanskij, a Soviet director of satire, took this idea one step further, writing that "the naturalistic tendencies of the Art Theatre (i.e., MXAT) led to the absurd." È. Krasnjanskij, *Vstreči v puti. Stranicy vospominanij* (Moskva, 1967), 80; Evreinov, "Kak mne rabotalos' v Krivom zerkale," 102-4.

58. The play has also been said to parody two particular productions of Goethe's *Faust:* Fedor Komissarževskij's staging at Konstantin N. Nezlobin's (Aljab'ev) theatre in Moscow (September 1912) and Iosif M. Lapickij's production during this same period. Poljakov, "Kommentarij — Četvërtaja stena," *Russkaja teatral'naja parodija...,* 812.

59. N. N. Evreinov, *Četvertaja stena. Buffunada v dvux častjax,* in M. Ja. Poljakov, *Russkaja parodija XIX — načala XX veka,* 708.

60. Such attempts to cast a role with a person whose own life embodied specific similarities had precedent in Stanislavskij's work at MXAT. He cast an old peasant woman in his production of *The Power of Darkness* only to find that her presence was too realistic amidst the fictional life of the stage. Stanislavski, *My Life in Art,* 401-3.

61. Johann Peter Eckermann's (1791-1854), *Conversations with Goethe in the Last Years of His Life* (3 vols., 1836-48). Evreinov, *Četvertaja stena,* 697-98, 701.

62. The MXAT production of *Faust* was divided into two successive evenings. It was directed by Vladimir I. Nemirovič-Dančenko and designed by V. A. Serov, and logged 110 rehearsals and 83 performances, premiering 12-13 October 1910 and closing on 21 June 1925. Čuškin, ed. *Moskovskij xudožestvennyj teatr. Tom pervyj 1898-1917,* 303; Poljakov, "Kommentarij — *Četvertaja stena,*" 813; Evreinov, *Četvertaja stena,* 703.

63. Ibid., 708, 716-17.

64. Ibid., 719-20.

65. Ibid., 723.

66. N. N. Evreinov, "Predislovie," *V škole ostroumija,* 22; N. N. Evreinov, "Sekret smešnogo. Teorija komizma," *V škole ostroumija,* fond no. 982, opis' no. 1, ed. xr. no. 10, pp. 2, 5, 8-9.

67. Evreinov, "Trying on Deaths," *The Theatre in Life,* 283.

68. Henri Bergson, "Laughter," in *Comedy*, ed. Wylie Sypher (Garden City: Doubleday and Co., 1956), 62-64, 73, 97, 129-30, 148-49, 155, 169-70.

69. N. N. Evreinov, "Ob ostroumii i ego projavlenijax," CGALI SSSR, fond no. 982, opis' no. 1, ed. xr. no. 5, čast' 4, pp. 8-9.

70. Nikolai Nikolaevič Urvancov's *The Fate of Man (Sud'ba mužčiny)*, performed at the Crooked Mirror in 1915, offered a comic reversal of Ibsen's *A Doll House*. It depicted the women going off to work with their ministry briefcases, leaving the men to stay home like "domestic dolls," with nothing better to do than recline on divans and read French novels. In the play's last scene, it is the husband who walks out and slams the door behind him. The declared purpose of this parody was to warn of the role reversals which could be expected to take place under the influence of women's liberation.

71. N. N. Evreinov, "K poznaniju teatral'noj parodii," *V škole ostroumija*, 40-41.

72. N. N. Evreinov, "O smexe s prepjatstvijami. K poznaniju groteska i jumora visel'nikov," *V škole ostroumija*, 3-4, 6, 18-20, 22-23, 64.

73. Bergson, "Laughter," 81-82, 84, 87, 89-90, 92.

74. Evreinov, "Sekret smešnogo. Teorija komizma," *V škole ostroumija*, 19-20.

75. Russian formalism, as Victor Erlich writes in his study of the movement, originated in 1915-16, reached its peak in the early twenties and was suppressed about 1930. Dealing with the study of poetic and prose language, linguistic structure, style and technique, how language signifies via sound and rhythm, formalism was a precursor of structuralism and modern semiotics. Its most famous proponents included Roman Jakobson, Jan Mukařovsky, Boris Ejxenbaum, Viktor Šklovskij, Boris Tomaševskij, Viktor Žirmunskij, Viktor Vinogradov and Jurij Tynjanov. Erlich calls Tynjanov's *Gogol' i Dostoevskij. K teorii parodii* "among the finest achievements of twentieth-century criticism." Tynjanov's collection of essays, *Arxaisty i novatory* was among the most influential documents published by the formalist school. His *Voprosy izučenija jazyka i literatury*, co-authored with Roman Jakobson and published in the journal *Novyj Lef*, became a cornerstone of formalist thought regarding interdisciplinary study. In the twenties Tynjanov turned away from literary scholarship and toward the authorship of literary fiction. He is represented in this area by: *Kjuxlja* (Leningrad, 1925) on Wilhelm Küchelbecker, a minor poet and schoolboy friend of Puškin; *Smert' Vazir-Muxtara* (Leningrad, 1927); and *Puškin* (Leningrad, 1936), as well as by a number of historical tales ("Podporučik Kiže," "Voskovaja persona," etc.). Erlich, *Russian Formalism: History-Doctrine*, 7, 12, 15, 85, 134, 141, 141 n.1, 150 n.52; Mirsky, *A History of Russian Literature*, 106 n.3 and 513 n.9; Poljakov, "Russkij teatr v Krivom zerkale parodii," 7 n.2.

76. Bergson, "Laughter," 162; Evreinov, "K poznaniju teatral'noj parodii," 45-47.

77. Erlich, *Russian Formalism: History-Doctrine*, 90 n.21, 93, 121, 151 n.55, 194, 251, 258.

78. Bergson, "Laughter," 48.

79. Meyerhold, *Meyerhold on Theatre*, 43.

80. Evreinov, "K poznaniju teatral'noj parodii," 48-49.

81. Alter, *Partial Magic: The Novel as a Self-Conscious Genre*.

82. Zolotnickij, *Zori teatral'nogo oktjabrja*, 279-81; Anthony Pearson, "The Cabaret Comes to Russia: 'Theatre of Small Forms' as Cultural Catalyst," 43.

83. Kryžickij directed *The Monastic Gardener,* the last theatrical pantomime performed at the Crooked Mirror Theatre. It was more realistic in character than the satirical pre-Revolutionary models which had been something of a subspecialty of the theatre. Of the latter, the two most significant with respect to Evreinov were *A Columbine of Today* (1915, co-authored with Miss, co-directed with Naulov, music by Evreinov) and *The Eternal Dancer* (1916, co-authored with Miss, music by Evreinov). Each of these pantomimes depicts in various stages the life of Woman (*Dancer* is basically a parody of Leonid Andreev's *The Life of Man*), proceeding from her youthful innocence through her various love relationships until she comes to rest in the arms of her final suitor, Death. These were performed in front of flatly painted backdrops, producing a purposely naive and primitive impression. The music Evreinov wrote for *Columbine* was said to have been "very delicate, beautiful, and impassioned," combining "primitive one-hundred-year-old forms with the contemporary rhythms of the American tap-dance and the two-step." "Krivoe zerkalo," *Teatral'naja gazeta* 10 (6 March 1916): 7; *Teatr i iskusstvo* 39 (25 September 1911); M. K. Jarockaja, "Letopis' teatr 'Krivoe zerkalo,' " fond. no. 2353, opis' no. 1, ed. xr. no. 62, pp. 122, 288; N. N-v, *Teatr i iskusstvo* 47 (1915); Rumnev, *O pantomime, teatr, kino,* 1318; Kryžickij, "Vospominanija, 'Laboratorijia smexa,' " 117-20.

84. Asked some two years prior to his death whether he thought a theatre of parody could still exist, Kugel' said no, given the size and heterogeneity of the contemporary audience. Materials from the Leningrad State Theatrical Museum, A. G. Avvakumov, p. 25; O. N. Malozemova, p. 28; K. A. Guzynin, p. 11.

85. N. N. Xodotov, *Blizkoe-dalekoe* (Leningrad-Moskva: Iskusstvo, 1962), 221; Kugel', *List'ja s dereva,* 199; Kryžickij, "Vospominanija. 'Laboratorija smexa,'" 120; N. N. Evreinov, "Kak voznik teatr 'Krivoe zerkalo,' " *V škole ostroumija,* 8-9.

86. M. I. Jarockaja, "Letopis' teatra 'Krivoe zerkalo,' " fond no. 2353, opis' no. 1, ed. xr. no. 59.

87. Evreinov, "Kak mne rabotalos' v Krivom zerkale," 118.

88. Dejč, "Vospominaja minuvšee," 177-78.

89. Materials from the Leningrad State Theatrical Museum, L. S. Ljubaševskij, 17.

90. Evreinov, "Kak mne rabotalos' v 'Krivom zerkale,' " *V škole ostroumija,* 10-11, 63, 73-74, 84-85, 88-89.

91. L. S. Ljubaševskij, 14-15.

92. Evreinov, "Kak ja stal glavnym režisserom 'Krivogo zerkala,'" 127-28. Kugel', "Teatral'nye zametki," 5; Kryžickij, "Vospominanija. 'Laboratorija smexa,' " 113-14.

93. Kugel', "Teatral'nye zametki," 5-7; Evreinov, "Kak mne rabotalos' v 'Krivom zerkale,'" 117-18.

94. CGALI SSSR, fond no. 982, opis' no. 1. ed., xr. no. 136, Pis'ma (25 marta 1953 goda) Evreinova N. N. k Čexovskoe izdatel'stvo v N'ju-Jorke ob izdanii svoix memuarov "V škole ostroumija" i issledovanija *Istorija russkogo teatra.*

Notes for Chapter 7

1. Huntly Carter, *The New Spirit in the Russian Theatre 1917-28* (New York: Brentano's, 1929), 6-7, 16-17; Nikolai A. Gorchakov, *The Theater in Soviet Russia,* trans. Edgar

Lehrman (New York: Columbia University, 1957; repr. Freeport, New York: Books for Libraries Press, 1972), 108 and 117. Lunačarskij's statement compares ironically with that of World of Art member M. A. Vološin who wrote one year later that "the art of the future can arise only out of the new barbarism." Vološin had in mind the neoprimitivist trend in Russian painting then being pursued by such World of Art style painters as himself and K. F. Bogaevskij, as well as by N. S. Gončarova, M. F. Larionov, A. V. Ševčenko and D. D. Burljuk, among others. Vološin's aesthetic was not related to politics as was Lunačarskij's. M. Vološin, "Mysli o teatre," *Apollon* 5 (1909-10): 39, quoted in Bowlt, "The World of Art," 415, 432 n.37.

2. Carter, *The New Spirit in the Russian Theatre*, 30-31, 141; Rolland, *The People's Theatre. an Aesthetic Essay for a New Theatre* (1903), quoted in Platon Keržencev, *Tvorčeskij teatr. Puti socialističeskogo teatra* (Moskva, 1919), 48-49; Zolotnickij, *Zori teatral'nogo oktjabrja,* 289.

3. Sergej Radlov, *Stat'i o teatre 1918-1922* (Petrograd, 1923), 38-39, 41-45.

4. Konstantin Deržavin, "Massa kak takovaja," *Žizn' iskusstva* 607 (12 November 1920): 2.

5. N. N. Evreinov, "*Vzjatie Zimnego dvorca,*" *Žizn' iskusstva* 596-97 (30, 31 October 1920): 1.

6. Beware Camilla Gray's discussion of "The Storming of the Winter Palace" in *The Russian Experiment in Art 1863-1922* (London: Thames and Hudson, 1962; repr., New York: Harry N. Abrams, 1970). Not only does she leave out the name of Evreinov and other actual participants, but she credits the design to Natan Al'tman, Ivan Puni and his wife Ksenija Boguslavskaja, none of whom had anything to do with the production. In fact, by the time the production was staged, Puni and Boguslavskaja had already emigrated. Jurij Annenkov, the production's actual scenic designer points this out in his *Dnevnik moix vstreč* (1966), 127. Evreinov, Petrov and Annenkov had still to collaborate on Evreinov's *The Chief Thing* at Petrograd's Theatre of Free Comedy (20 February 1921). *The Storming of the Winter Palace,* which represents *theatre-in-life* in practice, pre-dates the premiere of *The Chief Thing,* Evreinov's definitive theoretical statement on this theme in dramatic form. However, evidence shows that Evreinov had written *The Chief Thing* prior to the summer of 1920, and it had been germinating in his mind for some time before that. Collins, "Nikolai Evreinov as a Playwright," in *Life as Theater...*, xviii; Jurij Annenkov, *Dnevnik moix vstreč. Cikl tragedii,* (New York: Inter-Language Literary Associates, 1966), 2:120, 122; N. Šubskij, "Na ploščadi Urickogo. Vpečatlenija moskviča" and "Inscenirovka *Vzjatie Zimnego dvorca* na ploščadi tov. Urickogo, 8-go nojabrja 1920 goda," Manuscript Division of the Leningrad State Theatrical Museum.

7. V. G. Samojlov, "Revoljucionnye prazdnestva," in *Teatral'noe dekoracionnoe iskusstvo v SSSR* (Leningrad, 1927), 188-89, 191, 193; Šubskij, "Na ploščadi Urickogo: Vpečatlenija moskviča." "K. D.," *Izvestija Petrogradskogo soveta* (untitled article) in Manuscript Division of the Leningrad State Theatrical Museum; L. Nikulin, "Baltika," *Zapiski sputnika* (Leningrad: Izdatel'stvo pisatelej, 1932), 183.

8. Gorchakov, *The Theater in Soviet Russia,* 150.

9. Nikulin, *Zapiski sputnika,* p. 85; Šubskij, "Na ploščadi Urickogo: Vpečatlenija moskviča;" "K. D.," *Izvestija Petrogradskogo soveta.*

10. Samojlov, "Revoljucionnye prazdnestva," 188-89, 193.

11. Information derived from production photographs, Annenkov's sketches of the set and

various written breakdowns of the scenario for the spectacle in the Manuscript Division of the Leningrad State Theatrical Museum. Supplementary material was drawn from the German artist-publicist Arthur Holitscher's eyewitness account from his post in a window of the former State Archives Department, quoted in Huntly Carter, *The New Spirit of the Russian Theatre 1917-1928*, 144-48. Holitscher wrote *Das Theatre im Revolutionaren Russland*.

12. Tamara Baikova Poggi, *Il "Teatro Antico" e Misterija-Buff* (Genoa: Letteraria Dellautrice, 1974), 2, 6.

13. Evreinov met with a good deal of criticism for "selling out" his former ideas and, in a sense, a former way of life and set of (anti-Soviet) values, when he decided to stage *The Storming of the Winter Palace*. Interview with A. A. Kašina-Evreinova; Leningrad, U.S.S.R.; August 1975.

14. Carter, *The New Spirit in the Russian Theatre 1917-28*, 144-45; Interview with Jurij Konstantinovič Gerasimov, Leningradskij gosudarstvennyj institut teatra, muzyki i kinematografii (LGITMiK), Leningrad, January 1976.

15. Interview with A. A. Kašina-Evreinova, Leningrad, U.S.S.R.

16. Christopher Moody, "Nikolai Nikolaevich Evreinov," 689-90.

17. Pis'mo Evreinova Nikolaja Nikolaeviča—Mejerxol'du Vsevolodu Èmil'eviču (31 March 1921), CGALI SSSR, fond no. 998, ed. xr. no. 1383.

18. Moody, "N. N. Evreinov," 686.

19. Interview with A. A. Kašina-Evreinova; Paris, France; June 1976.

20. CGALI SSSR, fond no. 982, opis' no. 1, ed. xr. nos. 79-83, pp. 92-93, 99, 101-2.

21. N. N. Evreinov, *Pamjatnik mimoletnomu (Iz Istorii èmigrantskogo teatra v Pariže)* (Paris, 1953), 45, 52-53; A. A. Kašina-Evreinova, "Predislovie," in N. N. Evreinov, "V škole ostroumija," 1.

22. "Pis'mo Evreinova N. N.—Dana H. W. L. (19 August 1946), CGALI SSSR, fond no. 982, opis' no. 1, ed. xr. no. 113.

23. Christopher Moody, "Introduction," in N. N. Evreinov, *Istorija russkogo teatra* (1955; repr. Letchworth, Herts, England: Bradda Books, 1972), xxvi.

Notes for Chapter 8

1. Kott, "The Eating of 'The Government Inspector,' " 24.

2. *The Chief Thing* was performed in Russian for the first time in Paris on 30 April 1935, under the auspices of "the Society of Russian Artists." Evreinov staged the production. Evreinov, *Pamjatnik mimoletnomu*, 32.

3. Interview with A. A. Kašina-Evreinova; Leningrad, U.S.S.R.: August 1975.

4. T. K. Dejxarxanova, "N. N. Evreinov," *Novoe russkoe slovo* (18 October, 1953). Dejxarxanova was an actress at the Crooked Mirror Theatre and the Bat.

5. Interview with A. A. Kašina-Evreinova; Leningrad, U.S.S.R.: August 1975.

6. Jurij Konstantinovič Gerasimov, "Krizis modernistskoj teatral'noj mysli v Rossii (1907-1917)," in *Teatr i dramaturgija*. Trudy Leningradskogo gosudarstvennogo instituta teatra, muzyki i kinematografii. Vypusk 4 (Leningrad, 1974), 241.

7. Simon Karlinsky. *The Sexual Labyrinth of Nikolai Gogol* (Cambridge: Harvard University Press, 1976), 135.

8. Fanger, *The Creation of Nikolai Gogol,* 64-65, 83, 258.

9. Ibid., 59, 61, 64.

10. Evreinov, *The Theatre in Life,* 199; E. T. A. Hoffmann, "Ritter Gluck," in *Tales of E. T. A. Hoffmann,* ed. and trans. Leonard J. Kent and Elizabeth C. Knight (Chicago: University of Chicago Press, 1969), 4.

11. Fanger quotes the late Roland Barthes as saying that irony "is nothing but the question posed to language by language." Roland Barthes, *Critique et vérité* (Paris: Editions du Seuil, 1966), 74-75, quoted in and translated by Fanger, *The Creation of Nikolai Gogol,* 121.

12. Fanger, *The Creation of Nikolai Gogol,* 67-68, 85, 88, 92, 102-3, 106, 114. In his discussion of formalist writer-theorist Viktor Šklovskij, Victor Erlich wrote: " 'Laying bare the device' throws into focus the tension between 'form' and 'materials' and thus performs with regard to literary craft a service similar to that performed by the poet's verbal play vis-à-vis the 'sign.' " Erlich, *Russian Formalism: History-Doctrine,* 194.

13. The Russian formalist concept of *skaz* (a tale or first-person narration), made famous by Boris Ejxenbaum in his essay "How Gogol's Overcoat is Made" ("Kak sdelana 'Šinel'' Gogolija"), *Poètika* (Petrograd, 1919), 151-65, is relevant here. Victor Erlich defines *skaz* "tentatively" as "a narrative manner which focuses on the personal 'tone' of the fictional narrator." Fanger defines it as "a monologue in the guise of narration: colloquial, individuated, free from the constraints of consistency in point of view, permeated with a paradoxical lyricism and an irony that ranges from blatant to enigmatic—but *written* and serving literary ends." Elsewhere he revises this definition somewhat to read: "mannered narration in which the speaker unwittingly vies with his story for attention and vivid manner overshadows ostensible matter." Although Evreinov's concerns were less literary in a strict sense than Gogol''s, and although he was not a formalist, his *skaz* voice was clearly heard both in his written and live performances as artist and work of art. Fanger, *The Creation of Nikolai Gogol,* 102-3, 177; Erlich, *Russian Formalism: History-Doctrine,* 75 n.29, 238.

14. Interview with A. A. Kašina-Evreinova; Leningrad, U.S.S.R.; August 1975.

15. Interview with A. A. Kašina-Evreinova; Leningrad, U.S.S.R.; August 1975.

Note for Appendix A

1. These lists were compiled from the following sources: Nikolaj Volkov, *Mejerxol'd,* vol. 1 (1874-1908) (Moskva-Leningrad, 1929), 260, 262; *Obozrenie teatrov* (for the years 1907-1909, 1915-1916).

Notes for Appendix B

1. I was unable to locate a cast list for this production.

2. *Teatr* 21 (23 March 1908): 12.

3. *Teatr* 213 (25 March 1908): 12-13.

4. *Teatr* 212 (23 March 1908): 12-13.

5. Ibid.
6. Christopher Moody lists Mgebrov in the role. Moody, "The Ancient Theatre," 33.
7. Moody lists Frenc in the role.
8. Moody lists Glinskaja in the role.
9. "Starinnyj teatr," *Teatr* 1023 (19-20 February 1912): 33.

Note for Appendix C

1. Appendixes C and D have been transcribed from Evreinov's memoirs, *In the School of Wit. About the "Crooked Mirror" Theatre and My Many Years of Work There as Dramatist and Chief Artistic Director (V škole ostroumija. O teatre "Krivoe zerkalo" i moej mnogoletnej rabote v nem, kak dramaturga i glavnogo režissera).* Evreinov explains in this work that he is depending on his memory in compiling the lists of productions that were staged by him and others during his tenure as artistic director of the theatre. This accounts for discrepancies between the two lists (e.g., productions that are listed in Appendix D as having been directed by Evreinov but which are not listed in Appendix C as having been staged at all at the Crooked Mirror during this period). Similarly, Evreinov has offered more complete descriptions of the productions listed in Appendix C than of those listed in Appendix D. Wherever possible, I have augmented Evreinov's descriptions in Appendix C with material from the following sources: M. K. Jarockaja, *Letopis' teatra "Krivoe zerkalo." Sbornik vyskadyvanij pressi, teatral'nyx dejatelej o teatre, programmy spektaklej teatra, sostav truppy i dr. za period 1908-1918gg;* Materials from CGALI SSSR, fond. no. 2353, opis' no. 1, ed. xr. no. 62, pp. 89-98, 101-2, 106-10; A. Dejč, "Vospominaja minuvšee," *Zvezda* 5 (1966): 176; "Krivoe zerkalo," *Teatral'naja gazeta* 10 (6 March 1916): 7; A. B., "Krivoe zerkalo," *Teatr i iskusstvo* 51 (19 December 1910): 988; Kryžickij, *Vospominanija.* "*Laboratorija smexa,*" 114.

Bibliography

Russian Language Sources

Books

Ajxenval'd, Julij. *Slova o slovax: kritičeskie stat'i*. Petrograd: Knigoizd byvš. M. V. Popova (?1923).
Alekseev, A. G. *Ser'eznoe i smešnoe*. Polveka v teatre i na èstrade. Moskva: Iskusstvo, 1967.
Alpers, B. *Teatr social'noj maski*. Leningrad-Moskva, 1931.
Al'tšuler, A. Ja., ed. *Vera Fedorovna Komissarževskaja. Pis'ma aktrisy, vospominanija o nej, materialy*. Leningrad-Moskva, 1964.
Anastas'ev, A. *MXAT v bor'be s formalizmom*. Moskva: Iskusstvo, 1953.
Annenkov, Jurij. *Dnevnik moix vstreč*. Vol. 2, *Cikl tragedij*. New York: Inter-Language Literary Assoicates, 1966.
Belenson, A. *Iskusstvennaja žizn'*. Petrograd, 1921.
Beljaev, Ju. *Teatr Lit.-xud. obščestva*. Illjustrirovannaja programma Malogo teatra. Vyp. 10, 1907.
Benois, Aleksandr. *Vozniknovenie "Mira iskusstva."* Leningrad, 1928.
Bjalik, B. A. *Gorkij v bor'be s teatral'noj reakciej*. Leningrad-Moskva: Iskusstvo, 1938.
Boguslavskij, A. O. and Diev, V. A. *Russkaja sovetskaja dramaturgija 1917-35. Osnovye problemy razvitija*. Moskva: Akademija nauk SSSR, 1963.
Bol'šaja sovetskaja ènciklopedija. 1954 ed., s.v. "Monodrama."
Brokgauze and Èfron. *Novyj ènciklopedičeskij slovar'*. Vol. 17. St. Petersburg.
Brukson, Ja. *Problema teatral'nosti* (Estestvennost' pered sudom marksizma). Petrograd: Tret'ja straža, 1923.
———. *Teatr Mejerxol'da*. Moskva, 1925.
Burlakov, N. S. *Valerij Brjusov*. Moskva, 1975.
Čukovskij, K. *Sovremenniki*. Portrety i ètudy. Moskva, 1962.
Čuškin, N. N. *Moskovskij xudožestvennyj teatr. Tom pervjy, 1898-1917*. Moskva: Iskusstvo, 1955.
Dejč, A. *Golos pamjati*. Moskva: Iskusstvo, 1966.
Driezen, N. V. *Sorok let teatra. Vospominanija 1875-1915*. St. Petersburg: Prometej, 1916.
Eventov, I. *Majakovskij v Petrograde-Leningrade*. Leningrad, 1963.
Evreinov, N. N. *Azazel i Dionis*. O proisxoždenii sceny v svjazi s začatkami dramy u semitov. Leningrad: Academia, 1924.
———. *Beardsley, Kritičeskij očerk*. St. Petersburg: Sovremennoe iskusstvo, 1912.
———. *Čto takoe teatr?* Petrograd: Svetozar, 1921.

———. *Dramatičeskie sočinenija*. Vol. 1. St. Petersburg: Izdatel'stvo avtora, 1908.
———. *Dramatičeskie sočinenija*. Vol. 2. St. Petersburg: Sovremennoe iskusstvo, 1914.
———. *Dramatičeskie sočinenija*. Vol. 3 (p'esy iz repertuara Krivogo zerkala). Petrograd: Academia, 1923.
———. *Istorija russkogo teatra,* 1955; repr. ed Introduction by Christopher Moody. Letchworth, Herts, England: Bradda Books, 1955.
———. *Istorija telesnyx nakazanij v Rossii*. St. Petersburg: V. K. Il'incik, 1924.
———. *K postanovke "Xil'perika."* St. Petersburg, 1913.
———. *Krepostnye aktery. Istoričeskij očerk.* St. Petersburg: Izdanie Direkcii Imperatorskix Teatrov, 1912.
———. *Kul'bin*. St. Petersburg: Obščestvo Intimnogo teatra, 1912.
———. ed. *Nagota na scene*. St. Petersburg: Novoe vremja, 1911.
———. *Nesterov. Očerk*. Petrograd: Tret'ja straža, 1922.
———. *O novoj maske*. (Avtobio-rekonstruktivnoj). Petrograd: Tret'ja straža, 1923.
———. *Original o portretistax* (K probleme subbektivizma v iskusstve). Moskva: Gosizdat, 1922.
———. *Pamjatnik mimoletnomu (Iz Istorii èmigrantskogo teatra v Parize)*. Paris, 1953.
———. *Pervobytnaja drama germancev (Iz pra-istorii teatra germano-skandinavskix narodov)*. Petrograd: Poljarnaja zvezda, 1922.
———. *Proisxoždenie dramy. Pervobytnaja tragedija i rol' kozla v istorii eë vozniknovenija. Fol'klorističeskij očerk.* St. Petersburg: Petropolis, 1921.
———. *Pro Scena Sua*. Petrograd: Prometej, 1914.
———. *Samoe glavnoe*. Petrograd: Gosudarstvennoe izdatel'stvo, 1921.
———. *Tajna Rasputina. O mifologičeskoj maske.* Leningrad: Byloe, 1924.
———. *Teatr dlja sebja*. 3 vols. Petrograd: Sovremennoe iskusstvo, 1915–17.
———. *Teatr kak takovoj*. St. Petersburg: Sovremennoe iskusstvo, 1912.
———. *Teatralizacija žizni* (Poèt, teatralizirujuščij žizn'). Moskva: Vremja, 1922.
———. *Teatral'nye novacii*. Petrograd: Tret'ja straža, 1922.
———. *Vvdenie v monodramu*. St. Petersburg: Sovremennoe iskusstvo, 1909.
Evstigneeva, Lidija Alekseevna. *Žurnal "Satirikon" i poèty-satirikoncy*. Moskva: Nauka, 1968.
Gnedič, P. P. *Kniga žizni*. Vospominanija. Leningrad, 1929.
Golovašenko, Ku. A., ed. *Teatr i dramaturgija*. Vypusk 4. Leningrad: LGITMiK, 1974.
Gusanova, D. *Mir iskusstva*. Leningrad-Moskva, 1934.
Il'inskij, I. *Sam o sebe*. Moskva, 1961.
Ispanskij teatr. Stat'i Baron N. V. Driezen, K. Miklaševskogo, N. Evreinova. St. Petersburg, 1912.
Istorija sovetskogo dramatičeskogo teatra. Ed. K. Rudnickij. Vol. 1: *1917–1920*. Moskva: Akademija nauk SSSR, 1966.
Ivanov, Vjačeslav. *Borozdy i meži. Opyty èstetičeskie i kritičeskie.* Moskva: Musaget, 1916.
Kamenskij, V. V. *Kniga o Evreinove*. Petrograd: Sovremennoe iskusstvo, 1917.
Kašina-Evreinova, A. A. *N. N. Evreinov v mirovom teatre XX veka*. Paris, 1964.
Kazanskij, B. V. *Metod teatra* (Analiz sistemy N. N. Evreinova). Leningrad: "Academia," 1925. [Includes extensive bibliography of pre-1925 sources by and about Evreinov.]
Keržencev, P. *Tvorčeskij teatr. Puti socialističeskogo teatra.* Moskva, 1919.
Kogan, D. *Sergej Jur'evič Sudejkin 1884–1946*. Moskva, 1974.
Komissarževskij, Fedor. *Teatral'nye preljudii*. Moskva: n.p., 1916.
Kozincev, G. *Glubokij èkran*. Moskva: Iskusstvo, 1971.
Krasnjanskij, È. *Vstreči v puti. Stranicy vospominanij.* Moskva, 1967.
Kryžickij, G. K. *Dorogi teatral'nye*. Vol. 2, *V predgrozovye gody*. Moskva: Vserossijskoe Teatral'noe Obščestvo, 1976.

———. *Filosofskij balagan.* Teatr naoborot. St. Petersburg, 1922.
———. *Režisserskie portrety.* Moskva-Leningrad: Teakinopečat', 1928.
———. *Strel'skaja.* Leningrad, 1970.
———. *Teatr duxa i ploti.* Odessa, 1921.
———. *Xristos ili Arlekin?* Leningrad, 1924.
Kugel', A. R. *List'ja s dereva. Vospominanija.* Leningrad: Vremja, 1926.
———. *Profili teatra.* Leningrad, 1929.
———. *Russkie dramaturgi.* Moskva, 1934.
———. *Teatral'nye portrety.* Ed. M. O. Jankovskij. Leningrad: Iskusstvo, 1967.
———. *Utverždenie teatra.* Moskva: Teatr i iskusstvo, 1923.
Kuzmin, M. *Uslovnost'. Stat'i ob iskusstve.* Petrograd, 1923.
Kuznecov, E. M., ed. *Istorija sovetskogo teatra.* Vol. 1, *1917–1921.* Gos. izdat. xudož. lit., 1933.
Levik, S. Ju. *Četvert' veka v opere.* Moskva: Iskusstvo, 1970.
Ljubaševskij, L. and Del', D. *Rasskazy o teatre i kino.* Leningrad-Moskva: Iskusstvo, 1964.
Lunačarskij, A. V. *Sobranie sočinenij.* Vol. 3. Moskva, 1964.
Mackin, A. *Portrety i nabljudenija.* Moskva, 1973.
Makovskij, S. *Na parnase serebrjannogo veka.* Munich, 1962.
Markov, P. A. *Novejšie teatral'nye tečenija (1898–1923). Opyt populjarnogo izloženija.* Moskva, 1924.
———. *O teatre.* 4 vols. Moskva: Iskusstvo, 1974.
———. *Teatral'naja ènciklopedija.* Vol. 2. *Glovackij-Keturakis.* Moskva: Sovetskaja ènciklopedija, 1963.
Mejerxol'd, Vsevolod. *O teatre.* St. Petersburg, 1913.
———. *Perepiska 1896–1939.* Moskva: Iskusstvo, 1976.
———. *Stat'i, pis'ma, reči, besedy.* Edited by A. V. Fevral'skij. Vols. 1 and 2. Moskva: Iskusstvo, 1968.
Mgebrov, A. A. *Žizn' v teatre.* 2 vols. Moskva-Leningrad: Academia, 1929–32.
Miklaševskij, K. *Gipertrofija iskusstva.* Petrograd, 1924.
Mokul'skij, S. S. *Istorija sovetskogo teatra.* Vol. 1, *1917–21.* Leningrad, 1933.
Nosova, V. *Komissarževskaja.* Moskva, 1964.
O Komissarževskoj. Zaboty i novoe. Moskva, 1965.
Petrov, N. *50 i 500.* Moskva: Vserossijskoe Teatral'noe Obščestvo, 1960.
Piotrovskij, Adrian. *Teatr, kino, žizn'.* Leningrad: Iskusstvo, 1969.
———. *Za sovetskij teatr!* Leningrad: Academia, 1925.
Pjast, V. *Vstreči.* Moskva: Federacija, 1929.
Poljakov, Mark Ja. *Russkaja teatral'naja parodija XIX – načala XX veka.* Moskva: Iskusstvo, 1976.
Prokof'ev, Vl. *V sporax o Stanislavskom.* Moskva: Iskusstvo, 1962.
Radlov, Sergej. *Stat'i o teatre 1918–1922.* Petrograd, 1923.
Red'ko, A. E. *Lit-xudožestvennye iskanija v konce XIX i načale XX vv.* Leningrad: Sejatel', 1924.
———. *Teatr i èvoljucija teatral'nyx form.* Moskva: M. and S. Sabašnikovyx, 1926.
Rumnev, A. *O pantomime, teatre i kino.* Moskva: Iskusstvo, 1964.
Sceničeskie načinanija Kružka Baronessy I. A. Budberg. Al'bom, 1913.
Ščepkina-Kupernik, T. L. *Teatr v moej žizni.* Leningrad-Moskva, 1948.
Skafer, V. *Sorok let na scene russkoj opery, vospominanija 1890–1930.* Leningrad, 1936.
Sokolova, Natalija. *Mir iskusstva.* Leningrad-Moskva, 1934.
Sovetskij teatr: Dokumenty i materialy 1917–1967. Edited by A. Z. Jufit. Vol. 1, *Russkij sovetskij teatr 1917–1921.* Leningrad: Iskusstvo, 1968.
Stanislavskij, Konstantin Sergeevič. *Žizn' i tvorčestvo K. S. Stanislavskogo. Letopis'.* Edited

by I. Vinogradskaja. Vol. 2, *1906-1915*. Moskva: Vserossijskoe teatral'noe obščestvo, 1971.
Stark, Edward. *Starinnyj teatr.* St. Petersburg: Tret'ja straža, 1922.
Tairov, A. Ja. *Zapiski režissera, stat'i, besedy, reči, pis'ma.* Moskva: Vserossijskoe Teatral'noe Obščestvo, 1970.
Teatr, kniga o novom teatre. Sbornik statej. St. Petersburg: Šipovnik, 1908.
Teatr literaturno-xudožestvennogo obščestva (Illjustrirovannye programmy sezona 1906-7). Vyp. 8.
Verigina, V. P. *Vospominanija.* Leningrad: Iskusstvo, 1974.
Vinogradskaja, I., ed. *Žizn' i tvorčestvo K. S. Stanislavskogo. Letopis'.* 8 vols. Vol. 2, *1906-1915,* edited by N. N. Čuškin. Moskva: Vserossijskoe Teatral'noe Obščestvo, 1971.
Volkonskij, Kn. Sergej. *Čelovek na scene.* St. Petersburg: Apollon, 1912.
———. *Otkliki teatra.* Petrograd, 1914.
Volkov, Nikolaj. *Mejerxol'd.* 2 vols. Moskva-Leningrad: Academia, 1929.
Vološin, M. *Liki tvorčestva.* St. Petersburg, 1914.
Vsevolodskij (Gerngross), V. *Istorija russkogo teatra.* Leningrad-Moskva, 1929.
Xodotov, N. N. *Blizkoe-Dalekoe.* Moskva-Leningrad: Iskusstvo, 1962.
Xudožestvennoe nasledstvo. I. Repin. Akademija nauka SSSR, 1948.
Zamjatin, Evgennyj. *Rasskaz o samom glavnom.* Petrograd, 1923.
Znosko-Borovskij, Evg. A. *Russkij teatr načala XX veka.* Prague: Plamja, 1925.
Zolotnickij, D. *Zori teatral'nogo oktjabrja.* Leningrad: Iskusstvo, 1976.

Articles and Chapters in Books

A. A. "V teatrax miniatjur." *Teatral'naja gazeta* 41 (9 October 1916): 7.
A. B. "Krivoe zerkalo." *Teatr i iskusstvo* 47 (21 November 1910): 892.
———. "Krivoe zerkalo." *Teatr i iskusstvo.* 51 (19 December 1910): 892.
A. L. "Po malen'kim teatram." *Vestnik teatra i iskusstva* (13 July 1922): 4.
A. M. "Teatr i muzyka: *Krivoe zerkalo.*" *Reč'* 292 (25 October 1913): 7.
A. P. "Èrmitaž: *Francesca da Rimini.*" *Russkoe slovo* (5 September 1908): 4.
———. "Monodrama g. Evreinova (Lekcija v Xudožestvennom kružke)." *Russkoe slovo* 292 (17 December 1908): 5.
Ajxenval'd, Ju. "Novye knigi: *Teatr dlja sebja. Čast' 1.*" *Utro Rossii* 334 (5 December 1915): 5.
———. "Novye knigi: *Teatr dlja sebja. Čast' 2.*" *Utro Rossii* 120 (20 April 1916): 5.
———. "Otricanie teatra." (Publičnaja lekcija, pročitannaja, pod zaglaviem "Literatura i teatra," v Moskve 16 marta 1913 g.). In *V sporax o teatre,* 9-38. Moskva: Knigoezdatel'stvo pisatelej, 1914.
Ančar. "Recenzija: *Kuxnja smexa.*" *Birževye vedomosti.* 13820 (24 October 1913): 5.
Antimonov, L. "*Teatr dlja sebja* (O knige N. N. Evreinova)." *Teatr i iskusstvo* 27 (22 November 1915): 884-85.
Apollon 7 (1912): 32.
Apollon 8 (1910): 35.
Arns, L. "Mesalliance v Vol'noj komedii." *Žizn' iskusstva* 814 (25 October 1921): 1.
———. "N. N. Evreinov (K 15-tiletiju ego literaturnoj i sceničeskoj dejatel'nosti)." *Žizn' iskusstva* 3 (17 January 1922): 2.
Arvatov, B. "Evreinov i my." *Èrmitaž* 13 (1922): 6.
———. "Teatr kak proizvodstvo." In *O teatre,* 113-22.
B. Ja. "Recenzija: *Čto takoe teatr.*" *Vestnik teatra i iskusstva* 8 (2 December 1921): 4.
B. T. "*Francesca da Rimini* na scene teatra Komissarževskoj (Beseda s N. N. Evreinovym)." *Rannee utro* 236 (30 August 1908): 4.

B., Vl. "Scena Žan D'ark (Malyj teatr)." *Rus'* 124 (6 May 1908): 5.
B. X. *Reč'* (13 November 1910).
Balmašev. Mix. "Odin iz četyrëx." *Teatr i žizn'* 2981 (24 October 1953).
Batjuškov, F. "Po povodu spektaklej Starinnogo teatra." *Studija* 11 (10 December 1911): 1-4.
Bazilevskij, Vas. "Peterburgskie ètjudy." *Rampa i žizn'* 48 (27 November 1911): 14.
———. "Peterburgskie ètjudy." *Rampa i žizn'* 50 (11 December 1911): 12-13.
———. "Peterburgskie ètjudy." *Rampa i žizn'* 51 (18 December 1911): 12-13.
Belenson, Aleksandr. "Samoe glavnoe o *Samom glavnom.*" *Žizn' iskusstva* 682-84 (24 March 1921): 1.
Beljaev, Ju. "Malen'kij fel'eton: *Takaja ženščina.*" *Novoe vremja* 11667 (4 September 1908): 2.
———. "Teatr i muzyka: *Krasivyj despot.*" *Novoe vremja* 11064 (31 December 1908): 5.
———. "Teatr i muzyka," *Novoe vremja* 10696 (24 December 1905): 5.
Benois, Aleksandr. "Xudožestvennye pis'ma: Starinnyj teatr." *Reč'* 345 (16 December 1911): 3.
———. "Xudožestvennye pis'ma: Dve vystavki." *Reč'* 280 (12 October 1912): 2.
———. "Xudožestvennye pis'ma: Reč' Arlekina." *Reč'* 45 (15 February 1913): 2.
Beskin, Èm. "*Fuente Ovejuna.*" *Rannee utro* 38 (16 February 1912): 5.
———. "Listki" (ob idejax Tairov, Mejerxol'd i Evreinov). *Teatral' naja gazeta* 15 (1917): 10-12.
———. "Moskovskie pis'ma." *Teatr i iskusstvo* 48 (25 November 1912): 945.
———. *Teatr i iskusstvo* 17 (28 April 1913): 380.
Bezpjatov, Evg. "Novye knigi o teatre." *Teatr i iskusstvo* 8 (24 February 1913): 183-84.
———. "Novye knigi o teatre." *Teatr i iskusstvo* 2 (1914): 35-36.
———. "Recenzija *Vvdenija v monodramu.*" In *Eżegodnik Imperatorskix teatrov,* 75-81. March 1909.
Bol'šaja sovetskaja ènciklopedija, 1932 ed. Either edited by O. Ju. Schmidt. S. V. or Evreinov.
Borozdin, I. "Srednevekovyj teatr. Po povodu moskovskix gastrolej S. Peterburgskogo Starinnogo teatra." *Vesy* 4 (1908): 96-98.
Bostunič Grigorij. "Teatralizacija žizni (Po povodu *Teatra dlja sebja* N. N. Evreinova)." *Južnaja Kopejka* 2233 (14 February 1917): 1.
Brodskaja, G. Ju. "Brjusov i teatr." *Literaturnoe nasledstvo* 85 (1976): 167-199.
Brodskij, Aleksandr. *Maski* 1 (1913).
Burljuk, David. "Privet N. N. Evreinovu." *Russkij golos,* 21 March 1926.
Burnašev, M. N. "Avtorskoe pravo režissera." *Teatr i iskusstvo* 22 (1909): 385-87.
Čadovec, Vsevolod. "Samoe glavnoe v *Samom glavnom.*" *Iskusstvo* (Kiev) 1 (31 March-7 April 1922): 6-7.
Ćekan, Viktorija. "Starinnyj teatr: Ispanskij cikl, Evreinov-Driezen." *Žizn' iskusstva* 21 (29 May 1922): 4.
Černyj, V. "Teatral'nyj fel'eton: Evreinovskaja nedelja." *Žizn' iskusstva* 27 (11 July 1922): 2.
Čudovskij, Valerian. "Krivoe zerkalo i monodrama." *Russkaja xudožestvennaja letopis'* 5 (March 1912): 75-76.
———. "O Starinnom teatre." *Russkaja xudožestvennaja letopis'* 4 (February 1912): 56-63.
Dejč, A. "Vospominaja minuvšee." *Zvezda* 5 (1966): 173-83.
Dejkarxanova, Tamara. "N. N. Evreinov." *Novoe russkoe slovo.* (18 October 1953).
de Miranda, Valerio. "K ispanskim postanovkam Starinnogo teatra." *Teatr i iskusstvo* 46 (13 November 1911): 883.
Deržavin. Konstantin. "Massa kak takovaja." *Žizn' iskusstva* 607 (12 November 1920): 2.
Derman, A. "Teatr vmesto žizni." *Russkoe bogatstvo* 11 (November 1913): 393-403.
Dmitriev, Viktor. "Èta zagadočnaja uslovnost'." *Literaturnaja gazeta* 14 (2 April 1975): 6.

280 Bibliography

Dol'. "Prem'era Krivogo Džimmi." *Teatr i muzyka* 10 (5 December 1922): 164–65.
Dolgov, N. "Po povodu 'istoričeskogo teatra.' " *Teatr i iskusstvo* 35 (2 September 1907): 567–68.
———. "Smert' ili vozroždenie." *Teatr i iskusstvo* 17 (28 April 1913): 380–82.
Dolinin, L. "Starinnyj teatr." *Rampa i žizn'* 11 (11 March 1912): 10.
Driezen, Baron N. V. "Počemu pojavilis' dva starinnyx teatra srazu (Beseda s Bar. N. V. Driezen)." *Rannee utro* 35 (12 February 1912): 5.
———. "Starinnyj teatr (Vospominanija)." *Stolica i usad'ba* 71 (1 December 1916): 8–12.
Èfros, Abram. "Otraženija: N. Evreinov." *Teatral'noe obozrenie* 2 (1921): 5–6.
Ejxenbaum, Boris. "Kak sdelana 'Šinel'" Gogolija." *Poètika* (Petrograd, 1919): 151–65.
Èrmitaz 8 (4–10 July 1922): 14.
"Ešče o Starinnom teatre," *Teatr* 55 (28 September 1807): 11–12.
Evreinov, N. N. "Apologet narkoza" (Predislovie). In *Respublika ljubvi*. Kniga stixov i prozy by Vladimir Ort. Petrograd, 1918.
———. "Čem ja objazan Sobinovu." In *Leonid Vitallevič Sobinov 1893–1923*. Ed. Vl. I. Nemirovič-Dančenko.
———. *Četvërtaja stena*. In *Russkaja teatral'naja parodija XIX–načala XX veka*. Ed. Mark Ja. Poljakov, 693–723. Moskva: Iskusstvo, 1976.
———. "Demon teatral'nosti: Leonid Andreev i problema teatral'nosti v žizni." *Žizn' iskusstva* 7 (14 February 1922): 2.
———. "Ego smert'." In *Skrjabin* by V. G. Karatygin. Petrograd. 1911.
———. "Iskusstvo režissera." In *Al'manax-spravočnik Vsja Teatral'no-muzykal'naja Rossija*. Edited by N. Davingof. Petrograd: Teatr južnyj, 1914–15.
———. "Ispanskij akter XVI–XVII vv." (Novaja redakcija stat'i promeščennoj). *Ežegodnik Imperatorskix teatrov*. Vypusk 6/7 (1909).
———. "Ispytanie vremenem." In *Sto let Malomu teatru 1824–1924*. Edited by A. R. Kugel' and V. Filippov. Moskva: Vserossijskoe Teatral'noe Obščestvo, 1924.
———. "K pereocenke teatral'nosti." *Žizn' iskusstva* 37 (18 September 1923): 8–9.
———. "K pereocenke teatral'nosti" (Okončanie). *Žizn' iskusstva* 38 (25 September 1923): 11–12.
———. "Koz'ma Prutkov—počitaemym ocom Krivogo Zerkala." *Vozroždenie* 50 (Paris, 1956).
———. "O nekotoryx xodjačix terminax (K pereizdaniju *Teatr kak takogo*)." *Žizn' iskusstva* 44 (5 November 1922): 6.
———. "O novom fenomen iskusstva." *Kino* 1 (1 May 1931): 7.
———. "Ob otricanii teatra. Polemika serdca." *Strelec* II (1914): 36–51.
———. Pis'mo N. I. Butkovskij. *Glagol* 2 (1978): 173–76.
———. *Predstavlenie ljubvi*. Monodrama v 3-x dejstvijax. In *Studija impressionistov*. St. Petersburg: Sovremennoe iskusstvo, 1909.
———. "Režisser G. Gagemana, perevod P. P. Nemvrodova." *Ežegodnik Imperatorskix teatrov*. Vypusk 3 (1910): 131–35.
———. "Režisser i dekorator." *Ežegodnik Imperatorskix teatrov*. Vypusk 1 (1909), 80–89.
———. "Satiričeskaja dominanta v tvorčestve Il'i Saca." In *Il'ja Sac*. Leningrad-Moskva, 1923.
———. "Starinnyj teatr: Ob aktere srednix vekov." *Teatr i iskusstvo* 50 (16 December 1907): 837–41.
———. "Tajna čërnoj polumaski." Razoblačenie. [Istorija proisxoždenija maski]. In *Arena*. Teatral'nyj al'manax. Ed. E. Kuznecova. St. Petersburg: Vremja, 1924.
———. "Teatr buduščego." *Zarja* (1 January 1930).

———. "Teatral'noe: Kotr-reklama moej lekcej (K segodnjašnej lekcii na temu *Teatr dlja sebja*)." *Birževye vedomosti* 15217 (19 December 1915): 6.
———. "Teatroterapija. Quasi-parodox N. Evreinova." *Žizn' iskusstva* 578–79 (9 and 10 October 1920): 1.
———. "Urok professionalam." *Teatr i iskusstvo* 51 (22 December 1913): 1054–58.
———. "Vzjatie Zimnego dvorca: Stat'ja glavnogo režissera postanovki." *Krasnyj milicioner* 14 (1920): 4–5.
———. "Vzjatie Zimnego dvorca." *Žizn' iskusstva* 596–97 (30 and 31 October 1920): 1.
———. "Začatki tragedii v drevnej Rusi (Kompendij podgotovljaemoj k pečati raboty "Pjaženaja kozla i načalo drevne-russkoj tragedii)." *Žizn' iskusstva* 697–99 (19–22 March 1921): 1.
Filippov. Vl. "Recenzija. *Čto takoe teatr*." *Kul'tura teatra* 1–2 (1922): 61–62.
Filisov, D. "Teatr i muzyka." *Naša gazeta* (24 February 1909): 6.
Filosofov, D. *Reč'* (October 1913).
———. "Teatral'nye zametki." *Reč'* (18 January 1913): 2.
G-ej, I. "Nočnye pljaskii Sologuba." *Večer* 271 (10 March 1909): 3.
"General'naja repeticija Starinnogo teatra." *Peterburgskaja gazeta* 317 (18 November 1911): 5.
Gerasimov. "Kievskaja drama. Konec zimnego sezona." *V mire iskusstv* 4 (15 March 1907): 18–20.
Gerasimov, Jurij K. "Krizis modernistskoj teatral'noj mysli v Rossii (1907–1917)." *Teatr i dramaturgija*. Trudy Leningradskogo gosudarstvennogo instituta teatra, muzyki i kinematografii. Part 4 (1974): 202–244.
———. "V. Ja. Brjusov i uslovnyj teatr." *Teatr i dramaturgija*. Trudy Leningradskogo gosudarstvennogo instituta teatra, muziki i kinematografii. Part 2 (1967): 253–273.
Glagolin, B. "Russkij argonavt." *Žurnal teatra Literaturno-xudožestvennogo obščestva* 1 (1909–10): 19–20.
Gorchakov, N. A. "Evreinov." *Grani* 20 (Frankfurt, 1953).
Grabar', Igor'. "Teatr i xudožniki." *Vesy* 4 (1908): 92–95.
Gri, Anton. *Večer* 291 (1 April 1909): 3.
Gris-chat. "Teatr kak takovoj (Po povodu knigi N. N. Evreinova)." *Sovremennyj bajan* 2 (February 1913).
Grošikov, Fedor. "Teatralizacija žizni." *Žizn' iskusstva* 430 (22 April 1920): 1.
Gurevič, Ljubov'. "Peterburgskie teatry." *Russkie vedomosti* 273 (27 November 1911): 5.
———. "Starinnyj teatr v S. Peterburge." *Russkie vedomosti* 293 (22 December 1907): 5.
I. O. *Obozrenie teatrov* (15 November 1911).
I. P. "Vesti iz Peterburga." *Rampa i žizn'* 46 (13 November 1911): 11–12.
"Impr." "Malyj teatr." *Teatr i iskusstvo* 19 (11 May 1908): 335.
Izmajlov (Smolenskij), A. "U rampy: Starinnyj teatr—*Blagočestivaja Marta* i *Velikij knjaz Moskovskij*." *Birževye vedomosti* 12659 (29 November 1911): 4.
Jakov, Tarle. "Toržestvo teatral'noj pravdy N. Evreinova." *Novyj mir* (28 March 1926): 6.
Janov. V. M. "Novye izdanija. *Teatra i iskusstva: Vojna. drama v 3-x dejstvijax N. Evreinova*." *Teatr i iskusstvo* (16 September 1907): 605–6.
Jašin, V. "Dnevnik peterburgskogo teatrala." *Teatr* 1222 (25 January 1913): 4–5.
Ju., Petr. "Krivoe zerkalo." *Teatr i iskusstvo* 27 (20 November 1911): 900–01.
———. "Krivoe zerkalo." *Teatr i iskusstvo* 43 (21 October 1912): 817.
———. "Krivoe zerkalo." *Teatr i iskusstvo* 51 (16 December 1912): 1009.
———. "Litejnyj teatr." *Teatr i iskusstvo* 46 (13 November 1911): 877.
Jur'ev, M. "*Teatr kak takovoj* (Po povodu knigi N. Evreinov)." *Rampa i žizn'* 11 (17 March 1913): 15–16.

Južnyj, P. *Teatr i iskusstvo* 43 (1912).
K. D. *Izvestija Petrogradskogo soveta* (untitled article). In Manuscript Division of the Leningrad State Theatrical Museum.
Kamyšnikov, L. "*Samoe glavnoe* N. N. Evreinova. Postanovka teatra Gil'da." *Russkoe slovo* (23 March 1926).
Karabanov, Nikolaj. "Starinnyj teatr." *Teatr* 1019 (15 February 1912): 5-6.
―――. "Starinnyj teatr." *Teatr* 1025 (22 February 1912).
―――. "Starinnyj teatr." *Teatr* 1029 (6 March 1912): 5.
Kašina-Evreinova, Anna. "Tret' veka ne rasstavajas'." *Novyj Žurnal (The New Review)* 140: 114-31.
"Kinematograf i inscenirovka 'Vzjatija Zimnego dvorca.'" *Petrogradskaja pravda* 248 (4 November 1920): 2.
Kleberg, L. "Sootnošenie sceny i zritel'nogo zala. K tipologii russkogo teatra načala XX veka." *Scando-Slavica* XX (1974): 27-38.
"Knižnik." "Recenzija: *Teatr dlja sebja*." *Obozrenie teatrov* 2866 (9 September 1915): 12-13.
Koval'skie, K. and O. "Xudožnik-idealist." *Novaja studija* 6 (12 October 1912): 9-10.
Kregetov, Sergej. "Nečto o dvux režisserax i o novoj nezlobinskoj postanovke." *Rampa i žizn'* 47 (18 November 1912): 5-7.
―――. "Opyt pervoj russkoj operetty." *Rampa i žizn'* 45 (10 November 1913): 17.
Kremlev, Anatolij. "Popytka restavracij srednevekogo teatra." *Teatr i iskusstvo* 7 (17 February 1908): 134-37.
―――. "Popytka restavracij srednevekogo teatra." [Conclusion.] *Teatr i iskusstvo* 8 (24 February 1908): 151-53.
"Krivoe zerkalo," *Birževye vedomosti* 13196 (15 October 1912): 7-8.
"Krivoe zerkalo. K predstojaščim gastroljam (Beseda s A. R. Kugelem)." *Rannee utro* 35 (12 February 1913): 5.
"Krivoe zerkalo." *Rannee utro* 37 (15 February 1912): 5.
"Krivoe zerkalo." *Rannee utro* 73 (29 March 1913): 5.
"Krivoe zerkalo." *Teatral'naja gazeta* 10 (6 March 1916): 7.
"Krivoj Džimmi. Beseda s N. N. Evreinovym." *Zrelišče* 4 (September 1922): 17-18.
Krušnin, Vsevolod. "Veselyj teatr." *Teatr i iskusstvo* 14 (5 April 1909): 255.
Kryžickij, G. "Vospominanija 'Laboratorija smexa.'" *Teatr* 8 (August 1967): 110-20.
Kugel', A. R. "*Fuente Ovejuna*." *Teatr i iskusstvo* 28 (25-27 November 1911): 937.
―――. "Recenzija: *Francesca da Rimini*." *Novaja Rus'* 52 (6 October 1908): 3-4.
―――. "Recenzija: *Van'ka-ključnik i paž Žan Sologuba*." *Novaja Rus'* 9 (10 January 1909): 5.
―――. "Spektakli Starinnogo teatra: *Tri volxva, Dejstvo o Teofile*." *Rus'* 330 (9 December, 1907): 5.
―――. "Teatral'nye zametki." *Teatr i iskusstvo* 50 (16 December 1907): 845-57.
―――. "Teatral'nye zametki." *Teatr i iskusstvo* 39 (25 September 1911): 726-28.
―――. "Teatral'nye zametki." *Teatr i iskusstvo* 51 (18 December 1911): 1007-10.
―――. "Teatral'nye zametki." *Žizn' iskusstva* 36 (11 September 1923): 5-7.
―――. "Zametki." [Problema teatral' nosti. O knige *Teatr kak takovoj*]. *Teatr i iskusstvo* 10 (10 March 1913).
"*Kuxnja smexa*." *Russkoe slovo* 245 (24 October 1913): 7.
L. K. "U N. N. Evreinova." *Teatral'naja Moskva* 33 (28 March-2 April 1922):
L. N. "Teatr i muzyka: Starinnyj teatr." *Reč'* 298 (18 December 1907): 5.
"*Kuxnja smexa*." *Russkoe slovo* 245 (24 October 1913): 7.
L. K. "U N. N. Evreinova." *Teatral'naja Moskva* 33 (28 March-2 April 1922):
L. N. "Teatr i muzyka: Starinnyj teatr." *Reč'* 298 (18 December 1907): 5.

"Lambda." "Novyj teatr: *Fundament sčast'ja*. Komedija v 3-x dejstvijax N. N. Evreinova." *Birževye vedomosti* 8647 (2 February 1905): 6.
Lebedev, N. "Teatr i muzyka. Krivoe zerkalo." *Reč'* 354 (24 December 1915): 5.
Lev, A. "Spektakl' iz proizvedenij N. N. Evreinova." *Žizn' iskusstva* 3 (17 January 1922): 3-4.
Levinson, Andrej. "Recenzija: Teatr dlja sebja. *Čast' pervaja*." *Severnye zapiski* 3 (March 1916): 220-21.
Literaturnaja ènciklopedija, 1930 ed. Edited by O. M. Beskin. S.v. "Evreinov, N. N."
"Lur." *Teatr i iskusstvo* 40 (3 October 1910): 732.
L'vov, Ja. "Starinnyj teatr." *Rampa i žizn'* 8 (19 February 1912): 13.
M. B. "*Beglaja*." *Den'* 304 (9 November 1913): 6.
M. V. *Den'* (19 May 1913).
Makovskij, Sergej. "Evreinov (K 75-letiju so dnja ego roždenija)." *Novoe russkoe slovo* (14 March 1954).
———. "Retrospektivnye mečtateli." *Stranicy xudožestvennoj kritiki*. St. Petersburg, 1909. Book 2, 114-41.
"Malen'kaja xronika." *Teatr i iskusstvo* 41 (14 October 1907): 673.
"Malen'kaja xronika." *Teatr i iskusstvo* 45 (11 November 1907): 735.
"Malyj teatr." *Teatr i iskusstvo* 35 (31 August 1908): 616-17.
Markov, K. P. "Iz Pariža. Toržestvo russkogo iskusstva N. N. Evreinov." *Naša žizn'*, 26 March 1929.
Markov, P. "Kritika: *Samoe glavnoe* Evreinova." *Teatral'noe obozrenie* 2 (1921): 6-7.
Martynov, F. "Xudožestvennoe tvorčestvo i problema uslovnosti." *Sovetskaja kul'tura* 15 (4 February 1965): 2-3.
Matveev, A. "V avangarde teatra N. N. Evreinov." *Russie Illustrée* (3 November 1934).
Mazurova, Aleksandra. "Teatr i žizn'." *Russkaja žizn'* (23-24 April 1949).
Mejerxol'd, Vsevolod, ed. *Ljubov' k trem apel'sinam. Žurnal Doktora Dapertutto* 4-5 (1914): 109.
———. "Recenzija. *Kniga o Evreinove*." *Birževye vedomosti* 16092 (10 February 1917): 5-6.
"Moskovskie pis'ma." *Teatr i iskusstvo* 17 (28 May 1913): 379-80.
Muratov, P. *Russkoe slovo* (27 March, 1908): 5.
N. "Krivoe zerkalo." *Teatr i iskusstvo* 43 (24 October 1910): 797.
N. D. N. "Teatr Krivoe zerkalo." *Zritel'* 7 (10 September 1916): 16.
N. N. "Krivoe zerkalo." *Teatr i iskusstvo* 1 (3 January 1916): 7.
———. *Teatr i iskusstvo* 47 (1915).
"N. N. Evreinov i ego p'esa. *Samoe glavnoe*." *Russkij golos*, (21 March 1926) Sunday Magazine, sec. 2.
"N. N. Evreinov (K ego vozvraščeniju v Peterburg)." *Žizn' iskusstva* 552 (9 September 1920): 1.
N. N. V. "O skandale v iskusstve." *Novoe vremja* 13052 (14 July 1912): 12.
N. V. "Naturalizm ili simvolizm." *Rampa* 4 (1909): 49-52.
"Ne-akter." "Otvet [Protiv stat'i N. N. Evreinovu]." *Teatr* 412 (26 February 1909): 5-6.
Nedolin, S. "Ob uslovnom teatre" *Južnoe slovo* 148 (13 February 1913): 3.
Nelidov, Anatolij. "Uslovnost' v teatre." *Teatr* 1350 (28 September 1913): 6-8.
Nevedomov, I. "S bol'noj golovy...(iz pisem v redakciju)." *Rampa* 10 (8 March 1909): 155.
Niks. "Teatr i muzyka: Dražajšee potešenie." *Russkoe slovo* 40 (9 February 1903): 4.
Nikulin, L. "Baltika." In *Zapiski sputnika*. Leningrad: Izdatel'stvo pisatelej, 1932.
Nilli, N. "O teatre buduščego (Mysli o teatre buduščego)." *Zapiski peredvižnego teatra* 20 (1919): 4-8.
"Novosti inostrannoj literatury i iskusstva." *Žizn' iskusstva* 17 (3 May 1922): 6.
"Novye knigi." *Voskresnaja večernjaja gazeta* 40 (17 February 1913): 3-4.

O. M. "U vozroditelja Starinnogo teatra." *Teatr* 212 (23 March 1908): 22-23.
Oblomov, Il'ja. "Jubilej N. N. Evreinova." *Vestnik teatra i iskusstva* 4 (13 January 1922): 4.
Obozrenie teatrov 203 (23 September 1907): 12.
Obozrenie teatrov 719 (4 May 1909).
Odesskie novosti (16 June 1910).
"Okolo rampy. Malyj teatr. *Orleanskaja deva.* s g. Glagolinym." *Birževye vedomosti* 10486 (5 May 1908): 3.
Osipov, I. "Malyj teatr: *Takaja ženščina* N. N. Evreinova i *Kazennaja kvartira* V. A. Ryškova." *Obozrenie teatrov* 509 (4 September 1908): 4-5.
Osipov. I. "Teatr Komissarževskoj: *Van'ka ključnik i paž Žan* F. Sologuba." *Obozrenie teatrov* 629 (10 January 1909): 5-6.
P. Ju. *Teatr i iskusstvo* 17 (17 April 1916): 343.
P-kov, P. "Slon za rojalem (Pervyj večer-grotesk N. N. Evreinova v Dome iskusstv)." *Žizn' iskusstva* 669-71 (5-8 February 1921): 1.
"Pazsejannost' 'aristokrata' (Bibliografičeskaja zametka)." *Rampa i žizn'* 17 (24 April 1916): 11.
"Peterburg." *Teatr* 1355 (5 October 1913): 11-12.
Pil'skij, Petr. "Kritičeskie stroki." *Solnce Rossii* 17 (April 1916): 9-13.
Piotrovskij, A. I. "Xronika Leningradskix prazdnestv 1919-22g." In *Massovye prazdnestva.* Leningrad, 1926.
Poljakov, Mark Ja. "Russkij teatr v krivom zerkale parodii." In *Russkaja teatral'naja parodija XIX – načala XX veka.* Ed. Mark Ja. Poljakov. Moskva: Iskusstvo, 1976.
"Poslednie novosti." *Teatr* 250 (24 and 25 August 1908): 12.
"Prodolženie spektaklej Starinnogo teatra. (Beseda s N. N. Evreinovym)." *Teatr* 257 (4 September 1908): 6.
"Prospekt spektaklej Starinnogo teatra (Pis'mo v redakciju iz M. N. Burnaševa, Bar, N. V. Driezen. N. N. Evreinova)." *Teatr i iskusstvo* 22 (3 June 1907): 359.
"Prospero." "Temy dnja [O režissere N. N. Evreinove]." *Teatr* 1477 (23 March 1914): 9-11.
R-n, Vas. "Okolo rampy: 'Veselye spektakli' v teatre Komissarževskoj." *Birževye vedomosti* 11073 (24 April 1909): 4-5.
———. "V Krivom zerkale." *Birževye vedomosti* 12634 (14 November 1911): 7.
Rabinovič, M. "Pis'mo iz Kieva." *Teatr i iskusstvo* 16 (18 April 1910): 337-39.
Raz-ij, S. "Starinnyj teatr (K gastroljam v Moskve)." *Studija* 20 (18 February 1912): 5-7.
———. "Starinnyj teatr (K gastroljam v Moskve)." *Studija* 23 (10 March 1912): 7-8.
"Razmax na Evreinova." *Zritel'* 91 (18 and 19 April 1917): 20-21.
"Recenzija na knigu Starka." *Kniga i revoljucija* 9-10 (1922): 94.
Red'ko, A. E. "Otkrovenija o žizni i teatre." *Russkie zapiski* 3 (March 1916): 285-97.
Rossov, N. "Uprek ne po adresu." *Teatr i iskusstvo* 5 (2 February 1914): 106-8.
Rostislavov, A. "Lekcija v 'Salone.' " *Teatr i iskusstvo* 8 (1909): 154-55.
Rostislavov, A. "O postanovkax Starinnogo teatra." *Teatr i iskusstvo* 51 (18 December 1911): 1002-3.
Ryndina, Lidija. "Ix bylo četvero. Pamjati bol'šogo režissera N. N. Evreinova." *Naše vremja* (3 October 1953).
S. S. M. "Teatr i muzyka: Dve novye p'esy K. N. Nezlobina." *Russkoe slovo* 263 (14 November 1912): 6.
"*Salome* ili *Carevne,* O." *Birževye vedomosti* 10785 (30 October 1908): 5.
Samojlov, B. G. "Revoljucionnye prazdnestva." In *Teatral'noe dekoracionnoe iskusstvo,* 185-94. Leningrad, 1927.
Saxnovskij, Vas. "K gastroljam Starinnogo teatra. Po povodu odnoj monografii *Starinnyj teatr* È. A. Stark." *Studija* 22 (2 March 1912): 5-6.
Ščerbakov, Sergej. "Teatral'noe segodnaja: Krivoj Džimmi." *Zrelišča* 1 (1922).

Šebuev, N. "Iz besedy s A. R. Kugelem." *Teatr* 710 (27 December 1910).
———. *Obozrenie teatrov* (23 December 1915).
———. "Palas teatr: *Beglaja*—russkaja operetta L. N. Urvancova s muzykoj N. N. Evreinova." *Obozrenie teatrov* 2258 (9 November 1913): 11-12.
———. "Vpečatlenija" [O *Nagote na scene*]. *Obozrenie teatrov* 1392 (7 May 1911): 6.
———. "Zametki. *Samoe glavnoe.*" *Teatral'noe obozrenie* 1 (1921): 14-15.
"Simvol very N. N. Evreinova." *Russkij golos,* 2 March 1926.
"Sinod i p'esa *Carevna.*" *Birževye vedomosti* 10786 (31 October 1908).
Šklovskij, Viktor. "Drama i massovye predstavlenija." *Žizn' iskusstva* Nos. 688-689-690 (1921).
———. "Tysjača sel'dej." *Žizn' iskusstva* 780-85 (19-24 July 1921): 2.
"Sluxi i vesti" (xronika). *Teatr i iskusstvo* 2 (13 January 1908): 26.
Smolenskij. "Okolo rampy. Teatr g-ži Komissarževskoj—*Francesca da Rimini* G. D'Annunzio." *Birževye vedomosti* 10743 (6 October 1908): 4.
Sologub, Fedor. "Mečtatel' o teatre." *Teatr i iskusstvo* 1 (3 January 1916): 11-15.
"Starinnyj teatr." *Birževye vedomosti* 10217 (23 November 1907): 4.
"Starinnyj teatr." *Obozrenie teatrov* 249 (13 November 1907): 13.
"Starinnyj teatr." *Rannee utro* 17 (7 December 1907): 4.
"Starinnyj teatr." *Teatr* 46 (19 September 1907): 1172.
"Starinnyj teatr." *Teatr* 139 (22 December 1907): 13-14.
"Starinnyj teatr." *Teatr* 1023 (19 and 20 February 1912): 33.
Stark, Edward. *"Francesca da Rimini." Teatr i iskusstvo* 17 (28 April 1913): 376-77.
———. "Krivoe zerkalo." *Teatr i iskusstvo* 43 (27 October 1913): 856.
———. "Otkrytie Starinnogo teatra." *Obozrenie teatrov* 274 (9 December 1907): 14.
———. "Toska po krasote." *Teatr i iskusstvo* (14 January 1907): 30-32.
———. "Vtoroj spektakl' Starinnogo teatra." *Obozrenie teatrov* 283 (18 December 1907): 13-14.
"Staryj drug." "U kolybeli teatra." *Teatr* 213 (25 March 1908): 15-18.
"Staryj drug." "Vtoraja *Francesca.*" *Teatr* 259 (6 September 1908): 3-7.
"Staryj vorobej." "Veselyj teatr." *Obozrenie teatrov* 686 (1 April 1909): 6-7.
"Staryj vorobej." "Veselyj teatr." *Obozrenie teatrov* 687 (2 April 1909): 6.
"Stoličnaja pečat' " Po povodu zapreščenija *Carevny.*" *Birževye vedomosti* 10783 (29 October 1908): 5.
Storicyn, Petr. "Teatr i muzyka: Svobodnyj teatr." *Petrogradskaja pravda* 143 (30 June 1922): 4.
Svetlov, V. "Teatral'noe èxo: Starinnyj teatr i ispanskie tancy." *Peterburgskaja gazeta* 320 (21 November 1911): 5.
Tal'nikov, D. "Recenzija: *Pro Scena Sua.*" *Sovremennyj mir* 10 (October 1914): 214-15.
Tamarin, N. "Dramatičeskaja studija N. N. Evreinova na Kursax g-ži Rigler-Voronskoj." *Teatr i iskusstvo* 18 (2 May 1910): 378.
———. "Dramatičeskij teatr V. F. Komissarževskoj." *Teatr i iskusstvo* 41 (21 October 1908): 704.
———. "K postanovki *Van'ki-ključnika i paža-Žana.*" *Teatr i iskusstvo* 3 (1909): 49.
Teatr (23 March 1903): 6.
Teatr 212 (23 March 1908): 12-13.
Teatr 213 (25 March 1908) 12-13.
Teatr 343 (3 December 1908): 7-8.
Teatr 1023 (19-20 February 1912): 33.
Teatr 1028 (6 March 1912): 32.
Teatr 1460 (23 and 24 February 1914): 30.

Teatr 1465 (1 March 1914): 17.
Teatr 1471 (16 and 17 March 1914): 37.
Teatr 1822 (29 February 1916): 19.
"Teatr Èrmitaz." *Rannee utro* 241 (5 September 1908): 4.
Teatr i iskusstvo 19 (1909): 333.
Teatr i iskusstvo 20 (1909): 349.
Teatr i iskusstvo 22 (1911): 320.
Teatr i iskusstvo 39 (25 September 1911).
Teatr i iskusstvo 47 (1915).
"Teatr i muzyka." *Izvestija* (Kazan') 101 (10 May 1923): 4.
"Teatr i muzyka." *Novoe vremja* 10373 (21 January 1905): 5.
"Teatr i muzyka." *Reč'* 219 (16 September 1907): 4.
"Teatr i muzyka." *Reč'* 289 (7 December 1907): 5.
"Teatr kak takovoj." *Reč'* 353 (24 December 1912): 4.
Teatr Literaturno-xudožestvennogo obščestva (Illjustrirovannye programmy sezona 1906-7). Vyp. 8: 65-72.
"Teatr Mozaika." *Birževye vedomosti* 12626 (9 November 1911): 4.
"Teatr Vol'noj komedii." *Žizn' iskusstva* 554 (11 and 12 September 1920): 2.
"Teatral." "Golubaja krov'." *Teatr* 1845 (1 and 2 May 1922): 4.
"Teatral'naja žizn'." *Žizn' iskusstva* 792-97 (2-7 August 1921): 5.
"Teatral'nye gorizonty Peterburga (Beseda s F. F. Komissarževskim)." *Teatr* 482 (21 September 1909): 7-8.
Teatral'nyj kur'er 18 (8 October 1918): 7.
Trell', Niks. "Malen'kij fel'eton: S nosom." *Žizn' iskusstva* 42 (24 October 1922): 3.
"U rampy: Starinnyj teatr." *Birževye vedomosti* 12524 (10 September 1911): 5.
V. A. "Teatr i muzyka: Starinnyj teatr." *Reč'* 329 (30 November 1911): 4-5.
V. W. "Russkaja drama v 1907 godu." *Novoe vremja* 11424 (1 January 1908): 5-6.
"V Starinnom teatre." *Peterburgskaja gazeta* 339 (10 December 1911): 5.
V-ij, N. "Naturalizm ili simvolizm." *Rampa* 4 (1909): 49-52.
Vas-ij, L. "Teatr i muzyka: Starinnyj teatr." *Reč'* 298 (18 December 1907): 5.
Vasil'evskij, L. "Peterburgskie pis'ma." *Studija* 8 (19 November 1911): 8-11.
———. "Peterburgskie pis'ma." *Studija* 10 (3 December 1911): 7-8.
———. "Peterburgskie pis'ma." *Studija* 12 (17 December 1911): 12-13.
———. "Teatr i muzyka. Malyj teatr." *Reč'* 211 (4 September 1908): 5.
———. "Veselyj teatr." *Reč'* 87 (1 April 1909): 5.
Vejkone, M. "Monodrama (Lekcija N. N. Evreinova v teatral'nom klube)." *Novaja Rus'* 53 (24 February 1909): 5.
———. *Reč'* (October 1910).
———. "Teatr Komissarževskoj." *Teatr i iskusstvo* 44 (2 November 1908): 764.
Veselovskij, Ju. "Otkrytie spektaklej Starinnogo teatra." *Russkie vedomosti* 71 (25 March 1908).
Voinov, V. "Xudožestvennye pis'ma iz Peterburga." *Studija* 10 (3 December 1911): 14-16.
Volkonskij, Kn. Sergej. "Evreinov v inostrannom repertuare." *Poslednye novosti* (20 April 1929).
———. "Teatr v žizni." *Dermières Nouvelles* (3 April 1930).
Vološin, M. A. "Arxaizm v russkoj živopisi." *Apollon* 1 (1909): 43.
Voronov, V. "Teatr i muzyka: Litejnyj teatr." *Reč'* 108 (21 April 1916): 5.
Voskresenskij, A. "Recenzija: *Teatr kak takovoj.*" *Den'* 94 (8 April 1913): 5.
Voskresnaja večernjaja gazeta 107 (2 March 1914): 4.
"Vostoržennyj filosof." *Zrelišča* (Sverdlovsk) 1 (November): 6.

Vysockij, N. "O monodrame." *Rampa i žizn'* (17 May 1909): 319.
Xolmskaja, Z. An Interview. *Teatr* 447 (1909).
———. "Krivoe zerkalo." *Raboč̌ij i teatr* 9 (September 1937): 52–56.
Xovin, V. "Teatral'naja žizn': Krivoe zerkalo." *Voskresnaja večernjaja gazeta* 21 (14 October 1912): 3.
"Xronika." *Kul'tura* 1 (January 1922): 13.
"Xronika." *Obozrenie teatrov* 253 (17 November 1907): 14.
"Xronika." *Obozrenie teatrov* 273 (8 December 1907): 12.
"Xronika." *Obozrenie teatrov* 306 (13 January 1908): 18.
"Xronika." *Teatr i iskusstvo* 29 (22 July 1907): 468.
"Xronika." *Teatr i iskusstvo* 39 (30 September 1907): 628.
"Xronika." *Teatr i iskusstvo* 41 (14 October 1907): 673.
"Xronika." *Teatr i iskusstvo* 45 (11 November 1907): 732.
"Xronika." *Teatr i iskusstvo* 2 (12 February 1908): 27.
"Xronika." *Teatr i iskusstvo* 32 (10 August 1908): 543.
"Xronika." *Teatr i iskusstvo* 7 (1909): 124.
"Xronika." *Teatr i iskusstvo* 20 (16 May 1910): 402.
"Xronika." *Teatr i iskusstvo* 36 (5 September 1910): 658.
"Xronika." *Teatr i iskusstvo* 10 (4 March 1912): 212.
"Xronika." *Vestnik teatra i iskusstvo* 14 (23 December 1921): 4.
"Xronika." *Žizn' iskusstva* 721–23 (20–22 April 1921): 1.
"Xronika." *Žizn' iskusstva* 742–45 (28–31 May 1921): 2.
"Xronika." *Žizn' iskusstva* 767–69 (2–5 July 1921): 2.
"Xronika." *Žizn' iskusstva* 30 (1–7 August 1922): 5.
"Zabytyj." "V lapax." Protiv raboty V. È. Mejerxol'da i N. N. Evreinova v teatre Komissarževskoj. *Teatr* 253 (31 August 1908): 7–8.
"Žakass." "Malen'kij fel'eton: Teatr vnutri vas." *Teatral'naja gazeta* 17 (April 1916): 13.
"Zametki o lekcii N. N. Evreinova 'Teorija monodramy.' " *Zolotoe runo* 4 (1909): 86–88.
Zin. L. "Èkscentričeskij teatr (Disput)." *Vestnik teatra i iskusstva* 10 (9 December 1921): 3.
Znosko-Borovskij, Evg. "Krivoe zerkalo." *Russkaja molva* 5 (13 December 1912): 5.
———. "Recenzija: *Nagota na scene*." *Russkaja xudožestvennaja letopis'* 11 (August 1911): 172–73.
Zolotoe runo 10 (1907): 76.
———. 11–12 (1907): 117.

Archival Sources

Materials from the Central State Archive of Literature and Art USSR (Central'nyj gosudarstvennyj arxiv literatury i iskusstva SSSR).

Fond Babenčikova, M. V. Pis'ma Evreinova, Nikolaja Nikolaeviča–Babenčikovu, Mixailu vasil'eviču. 3 pis'ma (Undated, 6 March 1908, 18 March 1908). Fond no. 2094. Opis' no. 1. ed. xr. no. 261.
Fond Babenčikova, M. V. Šutočnyj rukopisnyj žurnal *Babenčikov* s učastiem M. V. Babenčikova, N. N. Evreinova, S. Ju. Sudejkina i dr, 1913. Fond no. 2094. Opis' no. 1. ed. sr. no. 578.
Fond Evreinova, N. N. "Estestvennost' na scene," Metod xudožestvennoj rekonstrukcii teatral'nyx postanovok." Fond no. 982. Opis' no. 1. ed. xr. no. 30.
———. "K postanovke *Gore ot uma* A. S. Griboedova (1935)." Fond no. 982. Opis' no. 1. ed. xr. no. 38.

———. "Kak nado stavit' *Nedoroslja* D. Fonvizina." Issledovanie (1939). Fond no. 982. Opis' no. 1. ed. xr. no. 39.
———. "Lekcii o teatre (1917-1920)." Fond no. 982. Opis' no. 1. ed. xr. no. 44.
———. "O nagote." Lekcija (1929). Fond no. 982. Opis' no. 1. ed. xr. no. 48.
———. "Paradoks ob iskusstve" (1920-1930). Fond no. 982. Opis' no. 1. ed. xr. no. 49.
———. Proekt postanovki *Skazka o care Saltane* opery N. A. Rimskogo-Korsakova. Režisserskaja razrabotka spektaklja Russkoj opery v Pariže v Teatre Elisejskix polej. 4 September 1928.
———. "Simvolizm putešestvija v posvjatitel'nom rituale" (1930). Fond no. 982. Opis' no. 1. ed. xr. no. 50.
———. *Svoja sem'ja* Griboedova (K otkrytiju Teatra Russkoj dramy). Fond no. 982. Opis' no. 1. ed. xr. no. 42.
———. "Tajna Rasputina (Ob aktere, igravšem rol' boga)." Lekcija (1926). Fond no. 982. Opis' no. 1. ed. xr. no. 47.
———. *V škole ostroumija. O teatre Krivoe zerkalo i moej mnogoletnej rabote v nem, kak dramaturga i glavnogo režissera.* Fond no. 982. Opis' no. 1. ed. xr. nos. 4, 9, 10, 12, 13.
Information on émigré productions directed by N. N. Evreinov. Fond no. 982. Opis' no. 1. ed. xr. nos. 79-83, 92, 99, 101-2.
Letters from Wladimir Gaidarow to N. N. Evreinov. (3 May-18 November 1928). Fond no. 982. Opis' no. 1. ed. xr. no. 166.
Pis'mo Evreinova, N. N. k Dana, H. W. L. (19 August 1946). Fond no. 982. Opis' no. 1. ed. xr. no. 113.
Pis'mo Evreinova, Nikolaja Nikolaeviča k Borisu Nikolaeviču Rubinštejn, OGALI SSSR, f o n d
no. 982, ed. xr. no. 131, opis' no. 1.
Recenzii tvorčestva Evreinova. Fond no. 982. Opis' no. 1. ed. xr. no. 109.
Fond Fenin, L. A. Pis'ma Evreinova, Nikolaja Nikolaeviča — Feninu, L'vu Aleksandroviču. 2 pis'ma (22 September 1914, 18 September 1917). Fond no 2026. Opis' no. 1. ed. xr. no. 159.
Fond Gejrota A. A. Pis'ma Evreinova, Nikolaja Nikolaeviča k Gejrotu, Aleksandru Aleksandroviču. 2 pis'ma (7 September 1914, 6 November 1914). Fond no. 997. Opis' no. 1. ed. xr. no. 139.
Jarockaja, M. K. "Letopis' teatra Krivoe zerkalo." Sbornik vyskazyvanij pressi, teatral'nyx dejatelej o teatre, programy spektaklej teatra, sostav truppy i dr. za period s 1908g-1918g. Fond no. 2353. Opis' no. 1. ed. xr. nos. 59, 61, 62.
Fond Mejerxol'd, V. È. Pis'ma Evreinova, Nikolaja Nikolaeviča k Mejerxol'du Vsevolodu Èmil'eviču. 5 pisem (17 January 1912, 27 July 1917, 18 December 1920, 27 December 1920, 31 March 1921). Fond no. 998. ed. xr. no. 1383.
Programs for the Veselyj teatr N. Evreinova i F. Komissarževskogo v teatra V. F. Komissarževskoj. Fond no. 778. Opis' no. 2. ed. xr. no. 176.
Fond Rubinčik, Agnessa Davydovna. Pis'ma Rubinčik, A. D. ot Evreinova, N. N. 3 pis'ma (7 July 1924, 11 August 1924, 16 June 1924). Fond no. 848. Opis' no. 1. ed. xr. no. 1.

Materials from the Manuscript Division of the Leningrad State Theatrical Museum (Leningradskij gosudarstvennyj teatral'nyj muzej).

"Blokada Rossii," Teatr na Kamennom ostrove. 20 June 1920 (photo).
Drawings and photographs from productions at the Crooked Mirror Theatre: *The Fourth Wall* (6 drawings by Ju. Annenkov); *The Inspector General* (3 drawings by Verejskij); *Homo sapiens* (1 photo).

Evreinov, N. N. Bibliography on folklore for his work on the Russian folk ritual theatre.
———. Doklad na "Kursax muzykantov pedagogov" pri učastij v kačestve opponenta B. G. Karatygina (13 March 1921).
———. "O muzyke drevne-russkix kozloglasovanij."
"Gimn osvoboždennogo truda." Misterija-posvjaščennaja pervomu maja (photo).
Inscenirovka *Vzjatie Zimnego dvorca* na ploščadi tov. Urickogo, 8-go nojabrja 1920 goda.
3-'ja godovščina oktjabr'skoj revoljucii; Obščij scenarij; Plan postanovki Beloj ploščadki i Krasnoj ploščadki; Sxema scenarija.
"K mirovoj kommune"—Massovaja inscenirovka v čest' Vtorogo kongressa III internacionala. 19 July 1920 (model).
Otkrytoe zasedanie soveta sodejstvija posvjaščennoe teatru "Krivoe zerkalo" (K 65-letiju so dnja osnovanija). 30 March 1973. Reports by K. A. Guzynin, L. S. Ljubaševskij, A. G. Avvakumov, O. N. Malozemova, L. N. Semenova, A. I. Kaverzin.
Pantomima-balet *Fuente Ovejuna*. Libretto i postanovka N. V. Petrova. Xudožnik Ju. P. Annenkov. Ploščad Urickogo. 1 May 1921 (photo).
Papka s zamyslami N. N. Evreinova: "Russkij obrjadovyj teatr."
Photos from productions at the Ancient Theatre: *Blagočestivaja marta; Robin et Marion; Dejstvo o Teofile; Tri volxva; Čistilišče Patrikka; Fuente Ovejuna*.
Photos from *Vampuka*. The Crooked Mirror Theatre.
Photos of *Vzjatie Zimnego dvorca*.
Pis'ma (2) N. N. Evreinova k svoej sestre (20 April 1932, 31 May 1931).
Pis'mo (1) Evreinova, N. N. k Idel'son, E. L. (3 March 1932).
Press release regarding *Vzjatie Zimnego dvorca. Izvestija Petrogradskogo soveta*.
Programmes from the Crooked Mirror Theatre.
Spektakl' na otkrytom ploščadi-Nevskij prospekt pered Teatrom Komedii, Leningrad. 1 May 1921 (photo).
Šubskij, N. "Na ploščadi Urickogo: Vpečatlenija moskviča."
"Xronologičeskaja sxema Leningradskix prazdnestv."
Zasedanie soveta sodejstvija, posvjaščennoe artističeskomu Kabare "Brodjačaja sobaka." 10 April 1972. Reports by Ju. M. Pirjutko, V. G. Perm. "Brodjačaja sobaka i Prival komediantov (Opyt živopisno-plastičeskogo kompleksa)." Reports by Valentina Petrovna Verigina, Jadviga Janovna Karmina, Aleksandra Vasil'evna Smirnova, L. S. Il'poščenko.

Materials from the Manuscript Division of the Moscow State Central Theatrical Museum in the name of A. A. Baxrušin (Gosudarstvennyj central'nyj teatral'nyj muzej im. A. A. Baxrušina).

Evreinov, N. N. "Ja o sebe [Avtobiografija]." Pis'mo k G. V. Švarcu. Fond no. 96. No. postuplenija 192.153.
———. P'esy klasičeskogo i posle-klassičeskogo teatra kotoryx vstrečajutsja *Èsafot ili kazn'*. Dlja issledovanija N. N. Evreinova sobral G. V. Bospunič. Fond no. 96. No. postuplenija 192.160.
———. Programma lekcii "Tajna Rasputina." New York (31 October 1926). Fond no. 96. No. postuplenija 192.165.
———. Programma spektaklja *The Ship of Saints*. New York 1926–27. Fond no. 96. No. postuplenija 192.166.
———. *Ruslan i Ljudmilla*. Solnečnyj mif (O fol'klornom principe postanovki opery M. I. Glinki).
———. "Teatre i èšafot." (materialy zametki, vyrezki). Fond. no. 96. postuplenija 192.161–192.162.

———. "Teatr Lope de Vega." Lekcija, pročitannaja na Kafedre ispanskoj literatury pri Sorbonne (May 1935).

Materials from the Manuscript Division of the State Public Library in the name of M. E. Sal'tykov-Ščedrin (Gosudarstvennaja publičnaja biblioteka im. M. E. Sal'tykova-Ščedrina).

Pis'ma (2) Evreinova, N. N. k Driezenu, Bar, N. V.

Materials from the Russian Archives, Columbia University

Evreinov, N. N. *Otkrovenie iskusstva.* The Russian Archives. Columbia University. EVR. A. A. 26-1.K-6.6.22.

English and Other Non-Russian Sources

Books

Abel, Lionel. *Metatheatre: A New View of Dramatic Form.* New York: Hill and Wang, 1963.
Alter, Robert. *Partial Magic: The Novel as a Self-Conscious Genre.* Berkeley: University of California Press, 1975.
Appignanesi, Lisa. *Cabaret.* London: Studio Vist, 1976.
Aronson, Arnold. *The History and Theory of Environmental Scenography.* Ann Arbor: UMI Research Press, 1981.
Artaud, Antonin. *The Theatre and Its Double.* Trans. Mary Caroline Richard. New York: Grove Press, 1958.
Bakshy, Alexander. *The Path of the Modern Russian Stage and Other Essays.* London: Cecil Palmer and Hayward, 1916.
———. *The Theatre Unbound.* London: Cecil Palmer, 1923.
Balakian, Anna. *The Symbolist Movement: A Critical Appraisal.* New York: Random House, 1967.
Beardsley, Aubrey. *The Collected Drawings of Aubrey Beardsley.* Ed. Bruce S. Harris. New York: Crown Publishers, 1967.
Beaumont, Cyril W. *The History of Harlequin.* New York: Benjamin Blom, 1926.
Beeson, Nora Beate. "Vsevolod Meyerhold and the Experimental Pre-Revolutionary Theater in Russia (1900 to 1917)." Ph.D. diss., Columbia University, 1960.
Bergson, Henri. *Creative Evolution.* Trans. by Arthur Mitchell. New York: Henry Holt and Co., 1911.
———. *The World of Dreams.* Trans. by Wade Baskin. New York: The Philosophical Library, 1958.
Braun, Edward, trans. and ed. *Meyerhold on Theatre.* New York: Hill and Wang, 1969.
———. *The Theatre of Meyerhold. Revolution on the Modern Stage.* New York: Drama Book Specialists, 1979.
Brockett, Oscar G., and Findlay, Robert R. *Century of Innovation: A History of European and American Theatre and Drama Since 1870.* Englewood Cliffs: Prentice-Hall, 1973.
Browning, Oscar. *Peter the Great.* London: Hutchinson and Co., 1898.
Brustein, Robert. *The Theatre of Revolt.* Boston: Little, Brown and Company, 1964.
Burns, Elizabeth. *Theatricality: A Study of Convention in the Theatre and in Social Life.* New York: Harper and Row Publishers, 1972.
Cambon, Glauco, ed. *Pirandello: A Collection of Critical Essays.* Englewood Cliffs, N. J.: Prentice-Hall, 1967.

Cannac, Genia. *Nicolas Evreinoff en France.* Paris: Bibliotheque Théâtrale, 1978.
Carnicke, Sharon Marie. "The Theatrical Instinct." Ph.D. diss., Columbia University, 1979.
Carter, Huntly. *The New Spirit in the Russian Theatre 1917-28.* London: Brentano's, 1921.
Clark, Barrett H. *European Theories of the Drama.* New York: Crown, 1957.
———, and Freedley, George, eds. *A History of Modern Drama.* New York and London: D. Appleton-Century Company, 1947.
Clough, Rosa Trillo. *Futurism: The Study of a Modern Movement.* New York, 1961.
Craig, Edward Gordon. *On the Art of the Theatre.* London: William Heinemann, 1911.
———. *The Theatre Advancing.* Boston: Little, Brown and Co., 1919.
———. *Towards a New Theatre.* London: J. M. Dent, 1913.
Dana, H. W. L. *Handbook on Soviet Drama.* New York: The American Russian Institute, 1938.
de Grunwald, Constantin. *Peter the Great.* Trans. Viola Garvin. New York: The Macmillan Company, 1956.
Domenico, Vittorini. *The Drama of Luigi Pirandello.* Philadelphia: University of Pennsylvania Press, 1935; repr. New York: Dover Publications, 1957.
Dostoyevsky, Fyodor. *Crime and Punishment.* Trans. Sidney Monas. New York: A Signet Classic from New American Library, 1968.
Eisenstein, Sergei M. *Immoral Memories: An Autobiography* (Advance Uncorrected Proof). Trans. Boston: Houghton Mifflin Company, 1983.
Ellmann, Richard, ed. *Oscar Wilde: A Collection of Critical Essays.* Englewood Cliffs, N.J.: Prentice-Hall, 1969.
Erlich, Victor. *The Double Image: Concepts of the Poet in Slavic Literatures.* Baltimore: The Johns Hopkins Press, 1964.
———. *Russian Formalism: History-Doctrine.* New Haven: Yale University Press, 1981.
Esslin, Martin. *The Theatre of the Absurd.* 2d ed. Garden City, N.Y.: Doubleday and Co. (Anchor Books), 1969.
Evreinov, Nikolaj. *Le Théâtre en Russe Sovietique.* Texte francais de Madeleine Eristov. Les Publications Techniques et Artistiques, 1946.
———. *Life as Theater: Five Modern Plays.* Trans. and ed. Christopher Collins. Ann Arbor: Ardis Publishers, 1973.
———. *The Theatre in Life.* Trans. and ed. Alexander I. Nazaroff. London: George G. Harrap and Co., 1927.
Fuchs, Georg. *Revolution in the Theatre: Conclusions Concerning the Munich Artists' Theatre.* Condensed and adapted from the German by Constance Connor Kuhn. Ithaca, N.Y.: Cornell University Press, 1959.
Füllöp-Miller, René and Gregor, Joseph. *The Russian Theatre.* 2d ed. Trans. Paul England. New York and London: Benjamin Blom, 1968.
Gassner, John. *Masters of the Drama.* 3d ed. New York: Dover, 1954.
Gorchakov, Nikolai A. *The Theater in Soviet Russia.* Trans. Edgar Lehrman. New York: Columbia University Press, 1957; repr. Freeport, New York: Books for Libraries Press, 1972.
Gorchakov, N. M. *The Vakhtangov School of Stage Art.* Trans. G. Ivanov-Mumjev. Moscow: Foreign Languages Publishing House, 1959.
Gorelik, Mordecai. *New Theatres for Old.* New York: Samuel French, 1948.
Gray, Camilla. *The Russian Experiment in Art 1863-1922.* London: Thames and Hudson, 1962; repr. New York: Harry N. Abrams, 1970.
Greene, Naomi. *Antonin Artaud: Poet without Words.* New York: Simon and Schuster, 1970.
Harrison, Fraser, ed. *The Yellow Book: An Anthology.* New York: St. Martin's Press, 1974.

Hoffmann, E. T. A. *Tales of E. T. A. Hoffmann.* Ed. and trans. Leonard J. Kent and Elizabeth C. Knight. Chicago: University of Chicago Press, 1969.
Hoover, Marjorie L. *Meyerhold: The Art of Conscious Theater.* Amherst, Mass.: University of Massachusetts Press, 1974.
Houghton, Norris. *Moscow Rehearsals.* New York: Harcourt, Brace, 1936.
———. *Return Engagement: A Postscript to Moscow Rehearsals.* New York: Holt, Rinehart, Winston, 1962.
Kalbouss, George. "The Plays of Fjodor Sologub." Ph.D. diss., New York University, 1968.
Karlinsky, Simon. *The Sexual Labyrinth of Nikolai Gogol.* Cambridge: Harvard University Press, 1976.
Kent, Leonard J., ed and trans., and Garnett, Constance, trans. *The Collected Tales and Plays of Nikolai Gogol.* New York: Farrar, Straus and Giroux (Octagon Books), 1978.
Kern, Gary, and Christopher Collins, eds. *The Serapion Brothers: A Critical Anthology of Stories.* Ann Arbor: Ardis, 1975.
Kirby, E. T., ed. *Total Theatre: A Critical Anthology.* New York: E. P. Dutton and Co., 1969.
Kirby, Michael. *Futurist Performance.* New York: E. P. Dutton and Co., 1971.
Knapp, Bettina L. *Antonin Artaud: Man of Vision.* New York: Avon Books, 1971.
Kuhlke, William Lonnie. "Vakhtangov's Legacy." Ph.D. diss., State University of Iowa, 1965.
Leyda, Jay, and Zina Voynow. *Eisenstein at Work.* New York: Pantheon Books/The Museum of Modern Art, 1982.
Markov, Vladimir and Sparks, Merrill, eds. *Modern Russian Poetry.* New York: The Bobbs-Merrill Company, 1966.
Markov, Vladimir. *Russian Futurism: A History.* London: MacGibbon and Kee, 1968.
Marroquin, Francisco. *La Pantella y el Telon.* Madrid, 175-195.
Marshall, Herbert. *The Pictorial History of the Russian Theatre.* New York: Crown Publishers, 1977.
Maslenikov, Oleg A. *The Frenzied Poets: Andrey Biely and the Russian Symbolists.* Berkeley: University of California Press, 1952.
Matthaei, Renate. *Luigi Pirandello.* Trans. Simon and Erika Young. New York: Frederick Ungar Publishing Co., 1973.
Miłosz, Czesław. *The History of Polish Literature.* London: The Macmillan Company, 1969.
Mirsky, D. S. *A History of Russian Literature.* New York: Alfred A. Knopf, 1949.
Moestrup, Jorn. *The Structural Patterns of Pirandello's Work.* Odense University Press, 1972.
Nassaar, Christopher S. *Into the Demon Universe: A Literary Exploration of Oscar Wilde.* New Haven, Conn.: Yale University Press, 1974.
Nemirovitch-Dantchenko, Vladimir. *My Life in the Russian Theatre.* Boston: Little, Brown and Co., 1936.
Nicoll, Allardyce. *British Drama.* London: George G. Harrap and Co., 1962.
———. *The Development of the Theatre.* New York: Harcourt, Brace, 1937.
———. *Masks, Mimes and Miracles.* London: Harrap and Co., 1931.
———. *World Drama from Aeschylus to Anouilh.* New York: Harcourt, Brace and Co., 1949.
———. *The World of Harlequin: A Critical Study of the Commedia dell'arte.* London: Cambridge University Press, 1963.
Nietzsche, Friedrich. *Beyond Good and Evil.* Trans. Marianne Cowan. Chicago: Henry Ragnery Co., 1955; Gateway edition, 1966.

Niklaus, Thelma. *Harlequin Phoenix or The Rise and Fall of a Bergamask Rogue.* London: The Bodley Head, 1956.
Nin, Anaïs. *The Diary of Anaïs Nin.* ed. Gunther Stuhlmann. Vol. 2 (1934–1939). New York: A Harvest Book, the Swallow Press and Harcourt Brace and World, 1967.
Oliva, Lawrence J., ed. *Peter the Great.* Englewood Cliffs, N.J.: Prentice-Hall, 1970.
Pearson, Hesketh. *The Life of Oscar Wilde.* London: Methuen and Co., 1946.
Philippe, Michel. *Présentation de N. Evreinoff.* Paris: Education et Théâtre, 1954.
Pirandello, Luigi. *Naked Masks.* Ed. Eric Bentley. New York: E. P. Dutton and Co., 1952.
Poggi, Tamara Baikova. *Il "Teatro Antico" e Misterija-Buff.* Genoa: Letteraria dell'autrice, 1974.
Proffer, Ellendea, ed. *Evreinov: A Pictorial Biography.* Ann Arbor: Ardis, 1981.
Proffer, Carl and Ellendea, eds. *The Silver Age of Russian Culture.* Ann Arbor: Ardis, 1971.
Putnam, Peter Brock. *Peter, the Revolutionary Tsar.* New York: Harper and Row Publishers, 1973.
Raeff, Marc, ed. *Peter the Great: Reformer or Revolutionary.* Lexington, Mass: D. C. Heath and Co., 1963.
Ragusa, Olga. *Luigi Pirandello.* New York: Columbia University Press, 1968.
Rank, Otto. *The Double: A Psychoanalytic Study.* Trans. and ed. by Harry Tucker, Jr. Chapel Hill, N.C.: University of North Carolina Press, 1971.
Reeve, Franklin. *Alexander Blok: Between Image and Idea.* New York: Columbia University Press, 1962.
Rennert, Hugo Albert. *The Life of Lope de Vega (1562–1635).* New York, 1937.
———. *The Spanish Stage in the Time of Lope de Vega, with an Alphabetical List of Spanish Actors and Actresses, 1560–1680.* New York: The Hispanic Society of America, 1909; repr. New York: Dover Publications, 1963.
Rice, Martin P. *Valery Briusov and the Rise of Russian Symbolism.* Ann Arbor: Ardis Publishers, 1975.
Roberts, Spencer E. *Soviet Historical Drama.* The Hague: Martinus Nijhoff, 1965.
Rudnitsky, Konstantin. *Meyerhold: The Director.* Trans. George Petrov. Ann Arbor: Ardis, 1981.
San Juan, Epifanio, Jr. *The Art of Oscar Wilde.* Princeton: Princeton University Press, 1967.
Sayler, Oliver M. *The Russian Theatre under the Revolution.* Boston: Little, Brown and Co., 1920.
Schmidt, Paul, ed. *Meyerhold at Work.* Austin: University of Texas Press, 1980.
Sellin, Eric. *The Dramatic Concepts of Antonin Artaud.* Chicago and London: The University of Chicago Press, 1968.
Senelick, Laurence. *Gordon Craig's Moscow Hamlet: A Reconstruction.* Westport: Greenwood Press, 1982.
———, trans. and ed. *Russian Dramatic Theory from Pushkin to the Symbolists: An Anthology.* Austin: University of Texas Press, 1981.
Shattuck, Roger, and Simon Watson Taylor, eds. *Selected Works of Alfred Jarry.* New York: Grove Press, 1965.
Simonov, Ruben. *Stanislavsky's Protegé: Eugene Vakhtangov.* Translated and adapted by Miriam Goldina. New York: Drama Book Specialists Publications, 1969.
Slonim, Marc. *The Epic of Russian Literature.* New York: Oxford University Press, 1969.
———. *From Chekhov to the Revolution.* New York: Oxford, 1962.
———. *Russian Theater: From the Empire to the Soviets.* New York: Collier Books, 1962.
Stanislavski, Constantin. *My Life in Art.* Trans. J. J. Robbins. New York: Theatre Arts Books, 1952.

Stuart, Donald Clive. *The Development of Dramatic Art.* New York: Dover, 1960.
Swierczewski, Eugenyusz. *Yevreinow.* Warszawa, 1925.
Symons, James M. *Meyerhold's Theatre of the Grotesque.* Coral Gables: University of Miami Press, 1971.
Tairov, Alexander. *Notes of a Director.* Trans. William Kuhlke. Coral Gables, Florida: University of Miami Press, 1969.
Taschian, Norair Noric. "Nikolaj Evreinov: Theorist of the Russian Theater." Ph.D. diss., University of California, 1974.
van Gyseghem, Andre. *Theatre in Soviet Russia.* London: Faber and Faber Ltd., 1943.
Varneke, Boris V. *History of the Russian Theatre, Seventeenth through Nineteenth Century.* Trans. Boris Brasol. New York: The Macmillan Company, 1951.
Weisbaden, N. "Une résurrection du théâtre médiéval a Saint-Pétersburg en 1907-08." In *Mélanges Cohen,* 271-76. Paris, 1950.
West, James. *Russian Symbolism: A Study of Vyacheslav Ivanov and the Russian Symbolist Aesthetic.* London: Methuen and Co., 1970.
Wiener, Leo. *The Contemporary Drama of Russia.* Boston: Little, Brown and Co., 1924.
Wilde, Oscar. *Complete Works of Oscar Wilde.* 3d ed. Introduction by Vyvyan Holland. London: Collins, 1973.
Woodcock, George. *The Paradox of Oxcar Wilde.* New York: The Macmillan Company, 1950.
Znosko-Borovskij, Evgennyj A. *Evreinoff.* Paris: l'Oeuvre, 1924.

Articles, Chapters in Books, Essays, Plays in Anthologies

Abensour, Gérard, ed. *Nicolas Evreinov: L'Apôtre Russe de la Théâtralité.* Paris: Institute d'études slaves, 1981. An entire journal of articles devoted to Evreinov, commemorating the centennial of his birth.
"All of Us are Actors." *The New York Sun,* 14 April 1927.
"All the World in Make-up." *The Philadelphia Record,* 4 June 1927.
Anderson, John. "The Play." *New York Evening Post,* 23 March 1926.
Annenkov, Yuri. "Merry Sanitorium." Translated by Lynn Ball. *The Drama Review* 19 (December 1975): 110-12.
Appia, Adolphe. "The Work of Living Art." In *The Work of Living Art and Man is the Measure of All Things.* Trans. H. D. Albright. Coral Gables, Florida: University of Miami Press, 1960.
Artaud, Antonin; Blin, Roger; and others. "Antonin Artaud's *Les Cenci.*" Translated by Victoria Nes Kirby, Nancy E. Nes, and Aileen Robbins. *The Drama Review* 16 (June 1972): 90-145.
Atkinson, J. Brooks. "Even Drama Grows." *The New York Times,* 28 March 1926.
Baehr, Stephen L. "The Masonic Component in Eighteenth-Century Russian Literature." In *Russian Literature in the Age of Catherine the Great,* ed. A. G. Cross, 121-39. Oxford: Meeuws, 1976.
Balmont, Konstantin. "Elementary Words on Symbolist Poetry (excerpts)." Trans. Samuel Cioran. In *The Silver Age of Russian Culture,* an anthology edited by Carl and Ellendea Proffer, 20-31. Ann Arbor: Ardis Publishers, 1975.
Bennett, Arnold. "Books and Persons." *The Evening Standard* (London), 11 August 1927.
Bentley, Eric. "Il Tragico Imperatore." *Tulane Drama Review* 10 (Spring 1966): 60-75.
Bergson, Henri. "Laughter." In *Comedy,* 61-190. Introduction and appendix by Wylie Sypher. Garden City, N.Y.: Doubleday Anchor Books, 1956.

Bernstein, Herman. "Nicolas Evreinoff and *The Chief Thing.*" In *The Chief Thing* (Theatre Guild edition), xiii–xvii. Garden City, N.Y.: Doubleday, Page and Company, 1926.

Blok, Alexander. *The Puppet Show.* In *An Anthology of Russian Plays.* Vol. 2 (1890–1960), ed. and trans. F. D. Reeve. New York: Random House, 1963.

Bowlt, John E. "The World of Art." In *The Silver Age of Russian Culture,* 397–432. See Balmont, Konstantin.

Brock, H. I. "Play-acting Viewed as a Fundamental Human Instinct." *The New York Times Book Review* (15 May 1927): 11.

Bryusov, Valery. "K. D. Balmont, LET'S BE LIKE THE SUN. A BOOK OF SYMBOLS." Trans. Rodney Patterson. In *The Silver Age of Russian Culture,* 20–31. See Balmont, Konstantin.

———. "On Art." Trans. Michael F. Tomasini. *Russian Literature Triquarterly* 11 (Winter 1975): 201–10.

———. "Verities." Trans. Rodney Patterson. *Russian Literature Triquarterly* 11 (Winter 1975): 196–200.

Burlyuk, D.; Kruchenykh, Alexander; Mayakovsky, V.; and Khlebnikov, Viktor. "A Slap in the Face of Public Taste." Trans. Helen Segall. *Russian Literature Triquarterly* 12 (Spring 1975): 179.

Coleman, Robert. *"The Chief Thing* at the Guild." *New York City Mirror,* 27 March 1926.

Collins, Christopher. "Nikolai Evreinov as a Playwright." *Russian Literature Triquarterly* 2 (Winter 1972): 373–98 [This was later published as Collins's introduction to his translation of five Evreinov plays *Life as Theater: Five Modern Plays.*]

Copeau, Jacques. "Un essai de rénovation dramatique." *La Nouvelle revue française* (1913): 337–53.

D'Amico, Silvio. "Tutto il mondo fa l'istrione." *Dramma sacro e profano* (Rome, 1924).

Dana, H. W. L. *The Harvard Crimson,* 1 December 1925.

Deák, František. "Russian Mass Spectacles." *The Drama Review* 10 (June 1975): 7–22.

———. "Two Manifestos: The Influence of Italian Futurism in Russia." *The Drama Review* 19 (December 1975): 88–94.

Dostoyevsky, Fyodor. "Notes from Underground." In *Notes from Underground, White Nights, The Dream of a Ridiculous Man and Selections from The House of the Dead.* Trans. Andrew R. MacAndrew. New York: A Signet Classic from New American Library, 1961.

Drama Review, The. (Russian Issue) 17 (March 1973).

Durant, Will. "Henri Bergson." In *The Story of Philosophy.* New York: Simon and Schuster, 1926, 336–350.

Evreinov, Nikolai. *The Beautiful Despot (The Last Act of a Drama).* In *Five Russian Plays with One from the Ukrainian.* Trans. C. E. Bechhofer. New York: E. P. Dutton and Co., 1916.

———. *The Inspector General,* translated and with an introduction by Laurence Senelick. *Performing Arts Journal* (to be published in 1984).

———. Preface to *The Chief Thing* (Theatre Guild edition), vii–xii. Trans. Herman Bernstein. Garden City, N.Y.: Doubleday, Page and Company, 1926.

———. *Styopik and Manya.* In *Theatre Wagon: Plays of Place and Any Place,* ed. Margaret and Fletcher Collins, Jr., 261–73. Charlottesville: University Press of Virginia, 1973.

Gabriel, Gilbert W. *"The Chief Thing* at the Guild." *New York City Evening Sun,* 23 March 1926.

Gerould, Daniel. "Sologub and the Theatre." *The Drama Review* 21 (December 1977): 79–84.

———. "Andrei Bely: Russian Symbolist." *Performing Arts Journal* 3, 2 (Fall 1978): 25–29.

———. "Valerii Briusov: Russian Symbolist." *Performing Arts Journal* 3, 3 (Winter, 1979): 85-99.
Gogol, Nikolai. *The Inspector General.* In *Nineteenth-Century Russian Plays.* Ed. and trans. F. D. Reeve, 231-314. New York: W. W. Norton and Company, 1961.
Golub, Spencer. "Mysteries of the Self: The Visionary Theatre of Nikolai Evreinov." *Theatre History Studies* 2 (May 1982): 15-35.
———. "Nikolai Evreinov (1879-1953)." In *The Modern Encyclopedia of Russian and Soviet Literatures.* Gulf Breeze, Florida: Academic International Press, projected 1984.
Gordon, Mel. "Radlov's Theatre of Popular Comedy." *The Drama Review* 19 (December 1975): 113-16.
Green, Michael. "Mikhail Kuzmin and the Theater." *Russian Literature Triquarterly* 7 (Fall 1973): 243-66.
———. "The Russian Symbolist Theatre: Some Connections." *Pacific Coast Philology* 12:5-14.
Hammond, Percy. "The Theaters." *New York Herald Tribune,* 23 March 1926.
Hayward, Max, and Labedz, Leopold, eds. *Literature and Revolution in Soviet Russia 1917-62: a Symposium.* London: Oxford University Press, 1963; repr. Westport, Conn.: Greenwood Press, 1976.
Herman, William. "Pirandello and Possibility." *Tulane Drama Review* 10 (Spring 1966): 91-111.
Hildebrand, Olle. "Harlekin Frälsaren. Teater och verklighet i Nikolaj Evreinovs dramatik." *Uppsala Slavic Papers No. 1.* Stockholm: Almqvist and Wiksell, 1978.
Ivanov, Vyacheslav. "The Theatre of the Future." Trans. Stephen Graham. *English Review* 10 (March 1912): 634-650.
Ivanov, Vyacheslav. "Thoughts on Symbolism." Trans. Samuel Cioran. In *The Silver Age of Russian Culture,* 32-39. See Balmont, Konstantin.
K. A. L. "*The Chief Thing* Opens at the Theatre Guild." *Graphic* (New York City), 23 March 1926.
Kalbouss, George. "From Mystery to Fantasy: An Attempt to Categorize the Plays of the Russian Symbolists." *Canadian-American Slavic Studies* 8 (Winter 1974): 488-500.
Kalbouss, George. "The Plays of Nikolai Evreinov." *Russian Language Journal* (Michigan State, East Lansing) 92 (1971): 23-33.
Kott, Jan. "The Eating of 'The Government Inspector.' " *Theatre Quarterly* 17 (March-May 1975): 21-29.
Kozintsov, Georgy, Kryzhitsky, Georgy, Trauberg, Leonid, and Yutkevich, Sergei. "Eccentrism." *The Drama Review* 19 (December 1975): 95-109.
Metcalfe. "A Bit of Russian." *The Wall Street Journal* (New York City), 27 March 1926.
Mickiewicz, Denis. "*Apollo* and Modernist Poetics." In *The Silver Age of Russian Culture,* 360-95. See Balmont, Konstantin.
Moody, Christopher. "The Ancient Theatre in St. Petersburg and Moscow 1907-8 and 1911-12." *New Zealand Slavonic Journal* 2:33-54.
———. "The Crooked Mirror." *Melbourne Slavonic Studies* 7 (1972).
———. "Nikolai Nikolaevich Evreinov 1879-1953." *Russian Literature Triquarterly* 13 (Fall 1975): 659-95.
"N. Evreinoff et son rôle dans le Théâtre du XXe Siecle" (commemorative pamphlet).
Nathan, George Jean. "The Week in the Theater." *Journal* (Louisville, Kentucky), 4 April 1926.
New York Evening Post, 27 March 1926.
Nietzsche, Friedrich, "The Birth of Tragedy." In *The Birth of Tragedy and The Genealogy of Morals.* Trans. Francis Golffing. Garden City, N.Y.: Doubleday and Co. (Anchor Books), 1956.

Osborn, E. W. "Theatres." *New York City Evening World*, 27 March 1926.
Palmer, John. "La Comedie Du Bonheur." *Saturday Review* (12 March 1927).
"Paris Stage, The: A Fantasy by Evreinoff." *The Times* (Paris), 23 November 1926.
Pearson, Anthony G. "The Cabaret Comes to Russia: 'Theatre of Small Forms' as Cultural Catalyst." *Theatre Quarterly* (Winter 1950), 31-44.
———. " 'Crooked Jimmy' and 'Limping Joe': Russian Theatrical Satire in the 1920's." *Theatre Research International* (May 1979).
Pirandello, Luigi. "On Humor." Trans. Teresa Novel. *Tulane Drama Review* 10 (Spring 1966): 46-59.
Poggi, Tamara Baikova "La *Francesca da Rimini* per la regia dell'ideatore di un nuovo tipodi monodramma" (1971): 51-62.
———. "Ludwig Tieck, on anello di congiunzione tra Nikolaj Evreinov e Luigi Pirandello." 2 (1981): 132-48.
Radlov, Sergei. "On the Pure Elements of the Actor's Art." Trans. Lynn Ball. *The Drama Review* 19 (December 1975): 117-23.
Rozanov, V. V. "On Symbolists and Decadents." Trans. Joel Stern. *Russian Literature Triquarterly* 8 (Winter 1974): 281-92.
Sayler, Oliver M. *Footlight and Lamplight*. Vol. 3. 15 (5 May 1927).
Seeley, Evelyn. "Radio-Futurism-Nothing but Colored Space—Is Born into World of Art in Fourth Dimension Show." *New York Telegram,* 23 March 1929.
Segel, Harold B. "Fin de Siècle Cabaret." *Performing Arts Journal* 2 (Spring 1977): 41-57.
Senelick, Laurence, ed. *Russian Satiric Comedy* (Includes Evreinov's *The Fourth Wall*). New York: Performing Arts Journal Publications, 1983.
Souvenir de Nicolas Evreinoff. Paris, 1959.
Squarzina, Luigi. "Directing Parandello Today." An interview by Gino Rizzo, *Tulane Drama Review* 10 (Spring 1966): 76-85.
———. "Notes for *Each in His Own Way*." Trans. Joseph Williman. *Tulane Drama Review* 10 (Spring 1966): 87-90.
Turkevich, Ludmilla B. "Andreev and the Mask." *Russian Literature Triquarterly* 7 (Fall 1973): 267-84.
Uttal, Lillian. "Happiness Troupe on Broadway." *New York Telegraph*, 11 April 1926.
Vreeland, Frank. "Footlight Reflections." *New York City Evening Sun*, 27 March 1926.
———. "The Happiness Boys." *New York City Evening Telegram and Mail,* 23 March 1926.
Weiss, Auréliu. "The Remorseless Rush of Time." Ed. and trans. Simone Sanzenbach. *Tulane Drama Review* 10 (Spring 1966): 30-45.
Wilde, Percival. *Contemporary One-Act Plays from Nine Countries*. Boston: Little, Brown, 1936.
Woodward, J. B. "From Brjusov to Ajkhenval'd: Attitudes to the Russian Theatre 1902-1914." *Canadian Slavonic Papers,* 7 (1965): 173-188.

Index

À rebours (Huysmans), 25
Abramjan, A.S., 149, 152, 156, 264 n.23
Absurdism, 46-47
Acmeism, 2
Adamsspiel (author unknown), 111
Aestheticism, xvii, 3-4, 10-11. *See also* Ancient Theatre, The; Evreinov, Nikolaj Nikolaevič
African, The (Meyerbeer), 152
Ajxenval'd, Julij, 8, 55-57
Al'berg, Ida, 110
Alchemy, 14, 75, 76
Alter, Robert, 33, 182, 266 n.39
Al'tman, Natan I., 271 n.6
Ancient Theatre, The, xix, 20-22, 32, 37-38, 45, 58, 69, 154, 207, 258 nn.8 and 10; and aestheticism, 138; Aristotelian basis of, 254 n.27; cast lists of productions at, 223-26; critical and popular response to, 113-22, 128-35, as cultural indicator, xix, 108-9, 139-40; founding of, 107; free composition (stylization) and *uslovnpost'*, 122-23, 126, 130; influence on Evreinov's career, 120-21, 139-43; influence on Mejerxol'd, 137-38; inheritance from the World of Art, 139; and the mass spectacle *(The Storming of the Winter Palace)*, 139, 200-1; staff of and advisors to, 127-28. *See also* Archeological reconstruction (Naturalism); Artistic reconstruction; Reconstructing the spectator; Retrospectivsm (cultural)
—the Medieval Cycle: 127; *Amusing Farces about a Tub and about a Cuckold's Hat* (Dabondance), 113, 120; descriptions of performances and critical response to, 113-22; *The Fair on the Day of St. Denis*, (Evreinov), 111; *Le Jeu de Robin et Marion* (Adam de la Halle), 112, 118-21, 176-77; *Le Miracle de Theofile* (Rutebeuf), 112, 115-17, 120; preparations for, 110-13; *Present-day Brothers* (author unknown), 112, 117-18; primitivism and naiveté of, 28-29, 117-18, 120, 133-34; *The Three Magi* (Prologue by Evreinov), 110, 112-115, 121, 201, 258 n.20
—the Spanish Cycle: background information on Spanish Theatre, 260 n.50, 260 n.51, 261 n.65; descriptions of performances, 128-36; *Fuente Ovejuna* (Lope de Vega), 126, 128-31, 132-33, 197, 260 n.57; *El Gran Ducque da Moscovia* (Lope de Vega), 134-35; *Marta la Piadosa* (Tirso de Molina), 132-34; preparations for, 126-29; public's response to, 261 n.75; *El Purgatorio de San Patricio* (Calderón de la Barca), 135-36, 261 n.70
Andreev, Leonid N., 6, 57, 158-59, 213; *Anathema*, 158; *The Black Masks*, 158; *He Who Gets Slapped*, 158; *The Life of Man*, 158, 251 n.11, 270 n.82; *The Sabine Women*, 159
Andreeva, Marija F., 73, 256 n.45
Aničkov, E.V., 7, 109-11, 113
Annenkov, Jurij P., 65, 184; designer at the Crooked Mirror Theatre and the Theatre of Free Comedy, 256 n.45, 271 n.6; designer for *The Storming of the Winter Palace*, 197-99, 271 nn.6 and 11; Evreinov portraitist, 30-31, 249 n.49
Annenskij, Innokentij F., 244 n.24
Antimonov, Sergej I., 149, 156, 167, 183
Apollo, 7, 241 n.1, 244 n.22, 244 n.31
Arabaznin, K.I., 137
Arbatov (Arxilov), Nikolaj N., 109
Archeological reconstruction, 123-24, 130
Aristocratism, 3, 5, 137. *See also* Evreinov, Nikolaj Nikolaevič
Aristophanes, 217
L'art et la nature (Cherbuliez), 54
Artaud, Antonin, xix, 63-64, 142, 214, 220, 254 n.27

Artistic reconstruction (Evreinovian methodology): developed at the Ancient Theatre, 122-25, 136-37, 196, 213; employed in his émigré career, 139-40, 202-3; referred to in plays at the Crooked Mirror Theatre, 172
Atheism, 5. *See also* Evreinov, Nikolaj Nikolaevič
Autumn Violins (Surčučev), 157
Averčenko, Arkadij, 262 n.23, 263 n.10
Avvakumov, A.G., 184-85, 251 n.17
Axmatova (Gorenko), Anna A., 1, 241 n.1, 243 n.17
Azov, Vladimir A., 148, 161, 178

Bain, Alexander, 179
Bakshy, Alexander, 46
Bakst, Leon (Lev) S., 3, 128, 242 n.7
Baliev, Nikita F., 145-46
Bal'mont, Konstantin D., 6, 29
Barabanov, Nikolaj F. (Z.F. Ikar), 149, 151, 153, 156
Barthes, Roland, 273 n.10
"Bat, The," 127, 145-46, 263 n.6
Baudelaire, Charles-Pierre, 4
Beardsley, Aubrey, 4, 47; Evreinov's monograph on, 23-25, 258 n.9
Beckett, Samuel, 266 n.39; *Endgame*, 47; *Waiting for Godot*, 64
Belenson, Alexandr, 175
Belinskij, Vissarion G., 106
La Belle Élène (Offenbach), 202
Belyj, Andrej (Boris N. Bugaev), 4, 7, 242 n.9, 243 n.16
Benois, Aleksandr N.: critic, essayist and journal contributor, 7, 57, 131-32, 262 n.2; designer at the Ancient Theatre, 110-11, 258 n.89; member of World of Art group, 3-4, 242 n.10
Bernhardt, Sarah, 9, 47, 76
Bilibin I. Ja.: designer at the Ancient Theatre, 110, 112, 116, 128, 136; designer for the Strand, 148; member of the World of Art group, 242 n.9
Blok, Aleksandr A., 6, 112, 117, 243 n.17; *The Fairground Booth*, 2, 241 n.4, 244 n.31
Bobyšov, Mixail P., 31, 42, 248 n.26, 249 n.49
Bogaevskij, K.F., 257 n.2
Boguslavskaja, Ksenija, 271 n.6
Borozdin, I., 117
Bowlt, John E., 242 n.10
Brecht, Bertolt, 214
Brjusov, Valerij Ja., 4-5, 7-8, 242 n.9
Bronze Horseman, The (Puškin), 5
Brothers Karamazov, The (Dostoevskij), 172
Bulgakov, Mixail A., 214
Bunin, Ivan A., 6

Burljuk, David D., 31, 33, 249 n.49, 270 n.1
Burnašev, M.N., 108, 112-13, 127
Butkovskaja, N.I., 110, 127-135, 137, 258 n.9
Bygone Years, 5

"Cabbage parties," 146, 262 n.3
Čadovec, Vsevolod, 74
Čajkovskij, Petr I., 19
Calderón de la Barca, 131, 180; *La Devocion de la cruz*, 127, 243 n.16, 260 n.47; *La vida es sueña*, 126
Camus, Albert, 47
Carter, Huntly, 191-92
Čekan, Viktorija Vl., 127
Cervantes, Miguel de, 126, 266 n.39; *Don Quixote*, 33-34, 59-60
Čexov, Anton Pavlovič: *The Cherry Orchard*, 58; *Ivanov*, 158
Chambers, V. Ju., 110, 113, 136, 148
Chapman, Pierre, 111
Collins, Christopher, 265 n.32
Columbine's Scarf (Schnitzler/Donani), 245 n.37
Comedians' Halt, The, 2, 263 n.6
Commedia dell'arte: "the love comedy"— betrayal theme in, 12, 26, 60; masks of, 3, 13-15, 43, 255 n.36; metaphor in and influence on Evreinov's work, 11-14, 69, 72-73, 198-99; revival in pre-revolutionary St. Petersburg, 1-3, 5-6, 15, 194. *See also:* Evreinov, Nikolaj Nikolaevič, Harlequin as alter-ego for, influences on; Harlequin, harlequinade and masquerade
Commission for Old Petersburg, The, 5
Conversations with Goethe (Kommisarževskij), 171-72
Craig, Gordon, xvii, 7, 9-10, 163, 213; acting, actors and the *Über-marionette*, 6, 9-10, 245 n.39; *Hamlet* at the Moscow Art Theatre, 10, 163, 167
Crime and Punishment (Dostoevskij), 61-62
"Crisis in the theatre, The," 6
Crisis in the Theatre, The, 8
Crooked Jimmy, The, 182-83, 203
Crooked Mirror, The (Izmajlov), 147
Crooked Mirror Theatre, The, xix, 22, 29, 126, 137, 203, 213; critical and popular response to, 153-54, 187, 264 n.19; its demise, 183-85; Evreinov's influence on and successes at, 185-86, 264 n.20; founding of, company and staff in the early years, 146-50; influence on Evreinov, 46, 69, 120-21, 142-43, 207-8. Productions and performances: "Ceremonial conferences," 158-60; *Chanteuse* (Ikar), 151; *Days of Our Lives* (Andreev parody), 148; *Duncan* (Ikar), 151; *The Enchanted and Disenchanted Forest*

(Geben), 151, 177; *The Fate of Man* (N. Urvancov), 269 n.70; final productions, 184-85; *In the Stage-Wings of the Soul* (Evreinov), *See* Evreinov, Nikolaj Nikolaevič, Plays and Performances; *Jacques Nuar or Henri Zaverni* (Urvancov), 149, 177, 183; *Love Through the Centuries* (Teffi), 148; *Love's Delights* (Urvancov), 150, 177; *Maud Allen* (Ikar), 151; *The Monastic Gardener,* 269 n.82; parodied forms, 177-78; *A Play About Mr. Ivanov* (Vencel-Benedikt), 150; premieres during Evreinov's artistic directorship of (Evreinov's list), 227-235, 274 n.1; *Prima Ballerina* (Ikar), 151; productions staged by Evreinov at (Evreinov's list), 237-40; *Ryčalov's Tour* (Volkonskij-Mancenilov), 149, 168, 183-84, 255 n.37, 256 n.45, 264 n.15; *Salome's Funeral,* 148; *Sarah Bernhardt* (Ikar), 151; *Vampuka* (Volkonskij/Èrenberg), 149, 151-54, 183-84, 264 n.15
Cubism, 2
Čudovskij, Valerian A., 128, 130, 135-36
Čukovskij, Komej I., 196
Čulkov, Georgij I., 7
"Cults of the body and of silence," 245 n.37

Dalcroze, Emile Jacques, 10; eurhythmics, 9, 127, 166
Danton's Death (Büchner), 62
Darskij, M.E., 107, 137
Darwin, Charles, 54
Davydov, Vladimir N. (Ivan N. Gorelov), 137
Davydova (née Gravel), Julia Ivanovna, 74, 256 n.46
de Vogüé, Melchoir, 216
Deák, František, 251 n.7
Dejč, Aleksandr I., 187
Der Ring (Wagner), 202
Deržavin, Konstantin N., 195, 198
Die Entführung aus dem Serail (Mozart), 203
Djagilev, Sergej (Serge) P., 4, 132, 242 nn.10 and 11
Dobužinskij, Mstislav V.: designer at the Ancient Theatre, 21, 110-11, 112, 119, 128, 136; designer for the Strand, 148; Evreinov portraitist, 31-32, 249 n.49; journal contributor, 262 n.2; member of the World of Art group, 242 n.9
Doctor Dapertutto, *See* Mejerxol'd, Vsevolod E.
Dogrose, 7
Doll House, A (Ibsen), 269 n.70
Don Juan (Moliere), 123, 124
Driezen, Baron Nikolaj V., 7, 110; censor, 129, 260 n.57; co-foudner and producer of the Ancient Theatre, 5, 107-9, 124, 127; director at the Ancient Theatre, 112-13, 118; relationship with Evreinov, 108, 110, 137, 264 n.22
Dullin, Charles, 74
Duncanb, Isadora, 9, 169
Duse, Eleanora, 9

Eckermann, Johann Peter, 171, 268 n.61
Èfros, Nikolaj E., 172
Egoism and Individualism, 3-4, 46-47
Ejxenbaum, Boris M., 269, n.75, 273 n.12
Èrenberg, Špis, 128
Èrenberg, Vladimir G., 151, 184
Erik XIV (Strindberg), 168
Erlich, Victor, 181, 269 n.75, 273 nn.11 and 12
Esslin, Martin, 47
Eurhythmics: *See* Dalcroze, Emile Jacques
Evening of the Paper Ladies, The, 2
Evreinov, Nikolaj Nikolaevič, xvii-xix, 5, 7-8, 244 n.31; on actors, acting, and the actor-audience relationship, 12-13, 36-38, 115, 125-27; on aestheticism, xvii, 11, 18-19, 22-23, 25, 145, 213, 220; on amateurism and dilettantism, 17-18, 58-59; on aristocraticism, xvii, 10-11, 18, 24-25, 31-32, 57-58, 201, 220, 265 n.26; atheism of, 20, 28-29, 43, 65-67, 218; on decadence ("talented scandal"), sensuality, and the Demonic Woman, 18, 22-24, 25-27, 39, 43, 56-57; on directors' rights, 162-63; education of, 19-22, 50-51; emigré career of, xvii-xix, 139-40, 204-8, 262 n.83; and expressionism, 46, 74-75, 252 n.24; and formalist narrative, 273 n.12; and the grotesque, primitivism, 201-2, 210-11; irony and ironic detachment of, 13-14, 32, 39, 60, 164-65, 189-90, 212, 217-18; and the mass spectacle, 194, 195-203; on nudity as an aesthetic value, 25-26, 248 nn.26 and 27; originality of, xvii, 14-15, 18; on origins and essences, 13, 20-21, 29, 45, 189-90, 210, 249 n.38; and paradox, xvii-xviii, 12, 18, 43, 214-15, 217-18; 174-82, 213; "playing the audience" (audience consciousness) in the works of, 12-13, 48, 51, 247 n.18; subjectivism of, 10-11, 24, 44, 46-47, 60, 213; on theatre as ritual, curative and salvation, 49-50, 53-54, 59-60, 67, 73-74, 220, 284 n.29; on theatre as pre-aesthetic instict (the will to theatre), 12-13, 54-55, 55-57; as visionary artist, xvii-xviii, 43-44, 69-70, 77, 164-65, 212. *See also* Ancient Theatre, The; *Commedia dell'arte;* Crooked Mirror Theatre, The; Grotesque, The; Harlequin, etc.; Metatheatre; Monodrama; Theatre-in-life, The;

Theatricality; Transformation
—Influences: Henri Bergson, 23, 30, 44, 48-49, 72, 175-77, 179-81; *commedia dell'arte*, 11-13, 17-19, 21-22, 43-45, 47-48, 69, 163, 211-12, 216, 218; Isadora Duncan, 9, 27, 43, 68; Freemasonry, 74-77, 206; Friedrich Nietzsche, 20, 23, 218; parents, 18, 21-22; Arthur Schopenhauer, 40; symbolism, 29, 38-39, 47-49, 53
—Plays and Performances: 112-13; *The Beautiful Despot*, 22-23, 26-27; *The Chief Thing (The Main Thing)*, xix, 12, 23, 26, 30, 40, 49-50, 61, 63-77, 142, 158, 189, 205-7, 209, 218, 256 n.45, 266 n.41, 271 n.6, 272 n.2; *A Columbine of Today*, 20, 26, 183, 256 n.45, 269 n.82; *The Eternal Dancer*, 270 n.82; *A Feast of Laughter*, 159-62, 178, 256 n.45, 263 n.10; *The Foundation of Happiness*, 22, 26, 38-39, 107, 178; *The Fourth Wall*, 170-74, 178; *Grandmother*, 22; *Idols, Pagan Gods*, 20; *In the Stage-Wings of the Soul (The Theatre of the Soul)*, 41-45, 46-48; 67, 77, 156-57, 162, 183, 184, 201, 207, 218, 248 n.26, 251 n.17, 252 n.24, 253 n.7, 256 n.45, 265 n.32; *The Inspector General*, 161-68, 170, 184, 266 n.40; *Karagez*, 177; *A Merry Death*, 20, 26, 45, 47-51, 69, 76-77, 142, 154-55, 252 n.28, 256 n.45; *The Power of Goblets*, 20; *Plutus* (adapted from Aristophanes), 22; *The Presentation of Love*, 12, 26, 39-42, 157, 251 n.11; *The Rehearsal*, 20; *The School of the Stars*, 168-69, 184, 256 n.45; 268 n.53; *The Ship of the Righteous*, xviii-xix, 27, 206; *Stepik and Manjuročka*, 21-22; *The Storming of the Winter Palace*, See Storming of the Winter Palace, The; *Such a Woman (A Catarrh of the Soul)*, 22, 26, 183, 256 n.45; *The Theatre of Eternal War (The Unmasked Ball)*, xix, 21, 26, 169, 206, 219; *The Unalterable Betrayal*, 26; *War*, 22
—The problem of identity: Harlequin as alter-ego for, 13-14, 18, 19-20, 24, 27, 29, 31-32, 33-34, 35, 57-58, 63, 215, 266 n.41; the Harlequin-Christ, 63-65, 69-70, 72, 77, 209-10, 218-20; identity crisis of, 11, 27, 212, 213-14; as theoretical personality (persona/mask/self-dramatizer), xvii-xix, 17-18, 22-23, 27, 30, 33-34, 212, 220
—Relationships: with Baron Driezen, 137; with Vsevolod Mejerxol'd, xvii, 23, 126, 163, 168, 203-4, 207, 210, 213, 249 n.49, 251 n.11, 253 n.13, 260 n.47; with Konstantin Stanislavskij, 207, 213, 252 n.18, 267 n.47
—Theoretical and Historical Works: *Apology for Theatricality*, 35-36, 253 n.13, 263 n.11; *Azazel and Dionysus*, 62-63, 202; *Beardsley, See* Beardsley, Aubrey; *Histoire du Théâtre Russe*, 206-7, 254 n.30; "In the Commission of Experts" (in *The Theatre for Oneself, Part III*), 217-18, 249 n.49; *In the School of Wit*, 189, 204; *Introduction to Monodrama*, 35-37, 39, 61, 250 n.4, 255 n.36; *Memorial to the Transient*, 204; *Nesterov, See* Nesterov, Mixail V.; *On the New Mask*, 140; *The Origin of Drama*, 202; *The Original on the Portraitists*, 30-34; *The Primordial Drama of the Germanic Peoples*, 202; *Pro Scena Sua*, 253 n.7, 258 n.11, 260 n.50; *The Revelation of Art*, 207; *Rops, See* Rops, Felicien; *The Secret of Rasputin*, 60; *Serf Actors*, 202; *The Theatre and the Scaffold*, 61-63, 213, 254 n.26, 254 n.29; *The Theatre as Such*, 53-55, 57, 168, 217, 253 n.13, 263 n.11; *Theatre for Oneself, Parts I-III*, 12, 32, 46, 54-55, 57-61, 139, 156; *Theatrical Innovations*, 257 n.6

Evreinova, Anna A. Kasina-, xvii, 202, 210; on husband's beliefs, 211, 218, 254 n.27, 266 n.41; on husband's character, 21, 25; on husband's Freemasonry, 75; on marital relationshp with husband, 252 n.22

Fall of the Theatre, The, 8
Fanger, Donald, 159, 216, 218, 249 n.51, 273 nn.10 and 12
Faust (Gounod), 169-70
Fenin, Lev A., 149, 152, 153, 156, 265 n.26
Fichte, Johann Gottlieb, 45
Filosofov, Dmitrij V., 4, 159, 242 n.10
Fokine, Mixail M., 110, 120, 155, 206
Foregger, Nikolaj M., 150, 184
Formalism, 6, 8; Evreinov as formalist, xvii; Russian formalists, 269 n.75
Francesca da Rimini (D'Annunzio), 37
Freemasonry, *See* Evreinov, Nikolaj Nikolaevič
Fregoli, Leopold, 255 n.36
Freud, Sigmund, 45, 46, 175-76, 179, 252 n.27, 253 n.7
Fuchs, Georg, 245 n.40; the re-theatricalization of the theatre, 6
Futurism, 1-2

Ganako, 9
Gautier, Theophile, 54

Geben, Lev, 148
Gejer, Boris F., 157, 177-78, 184, 262 n.2;
  Aeolian Harps (co-written with Evreinov),
  157-58; *Aqua Vitae,* 157-58; *Dream,* 157;
  Evolution of the Theatre, 158-59, 178, 183;
  Reminiscences, 157-58
George Dandin (Moliere), 180
Gerasimov, Jurij K., 65, 75
German modernist journals, 4
German Romanticism, 1, 4
Gippius, Zinajda N., 159, 242 n.9, 243 n.17
Glazunov, Aleksandr K., 22, 50, 110, 128
Gnedič, Petr P., 151-52
Goethe, Johann von, 53; *Egmont,* 62; *Faust, Part I,* 62, 268 nn.58 and 62; *Götz von Berlichingen,* 62
Gogol' (-Janovskij), Nikolaj V., 159, 215-20, 249 n.51, 255 n.41, 273 n.12; comparison with Evreinov, 215-20; *The Inspector General,* 11, 147-48, 161-69, 215-16; *Marriage,* 158; *Mirgorod,* 216; *Nevskij Prospekt,* 198; *The Nose,* 50, 186; *The Portrait,* 30-31; and *pošlost,* 255 n.37
Golden Age of Russian Theatre, The, xvii, 213
Golden Fleece, The, 6
Golovin, Aleksandr Ja., 241, 242 n.9
Gorchakov, Nikolaj A., 197
Gorkij, Maxim (Aleksej M. Peškov), 206
Gornfeld, A., 7
Gorodeckij, Sergej M., 33, 112
Gozzi, Carlo, 1, 243 n.17
Grabař, Igor È., 121
Gray, Camilla, 271 n.6
Grillparzer, Franz, 56
Guardainfantes, 129-30
Gurevič, Ljubov' Ja., 115, 117-19, 130-31

Habladores, Los (Cervantes), 130-31
Harlequin, harlequinade and masquerade, 1-3, 17-18; origin of "Harlequin," 64-66
Hartmann, Nicolai, 70-71
Hasty Turk, The (Prutkov), 159
Hegel, Georg Friedrich, 72
Heine, Heinrich, 4
Hoffmann, E.T.A., 1-2, 217, 241 n.4, 243 n.17, 255 n.36
Hofmannsthal, Hugo von, 166
Holitscher, Arthur, 271 n.11
Humperdinck, Engelbert, 166-67
Huysmans, Joris-Karl, 4, 25
Hypnosis, 2; art's power over the reader/viewer as a form of, 4, 20, 29, 68, 163

Impressionism, 2
In Favor of a World Commune, 194-96
In Life's Clutches (Hansum), 253 n.18

Inferno, The (Dante), 255 n.31
Intruder, The (Maeterlinck), 48
Ivanov, Vjačeslav I., 6-7, 27, 108, 243 n.16, 244 n.24, 244 n.31, 260 n.47
Izmajlov, A.A., 134, 147

Jakobson, Roman O., 269 n.75
Jakovlev, Mixail N., 155
Jarry, Alfred, xi, 19; *Caesar Antichrist* and *Ubu Roi,* 65
Javorskaja, L.B., 113
Judgment of Evreinov, The, 266 n.41

Kačalov (Šverubovič), Vasilij I., 163, 172
Kalin, Grigorij, 3
Kalmakov, N.K., 128, 249 n.49
Kamenev (Rosenfeld), Lev Borisovič, 203
Kameneva, Olga D., 203
Kamenskij, Vasilij V., 19, 249 n.49; *Book on Evreinov,* 246 n.7, 249 n.45; *The Theatricalization of Life* (Evreinov's book on), 30, 32
Karabanov, N., 117, 134, 261 n.75
Kazanskij, Boris Vasil'evič, xvii-xix, 3-4, 30, 54
Kerenskij, Aleksandr F., 199-201
Keržencev (Lebedev), Platon M., 194
Komissarževskaja, Vera F., 27, 139, 154-55
—Komissarževskaja, The Dramatic Theatre of Vera F., xix, 17, 149-50, 154-55, 250 n.4; Evreinov succeeds Mejerxol'd as artistic director at, 23, 126; Evreinov's productions at, 24, 37-38; Mejerxol'd's productions at, 122-23
Komissarževskij, Fedor F., 154-55, 264 n.22, 268 n.58
Kornfel'd, G., 262 n.2
Kott, Jan, 34, 163, 209
Krasnjanskij, Èmmanuil B., 268 n.57
Kremlev, Anatolij, 113, 117-18
Kryžickij, Georgij K., 122, 124, 183, 185, 188, 269 n.82; *Christ or Harlequin?,* 65; relationship with Evreinov, 259 n.42
Küchelbecker, Wilhelm K., 269 n.75
Kugel', Aleksandr Rafailovič (Homo novus): champion of actors' rights, 10, 161-63, 246 n.41; co-founder of and co-producer at the Crooked Mirror Theatre, 146-51, 270 n.83; critical comments on the Ancient Theatre, 113, 116-17, 121, 130, 137-38, 263 n.8; editor of *Theatre and Art,* 107, 242 n.7; relationship with Evreinov, 11, 110, 137-38, 154-56, 160, 174-75, 187-89, 204, 264 n.22, 265 n.26; takes credit for Evreinov's ideas, 44-45, 158, 161-63; works on *The Storming of the Winter Palace,* 197-98
Kul'bin, Nikolaj I., 31-33

Index

Kuzmin, Mixail A., 8, 22, 246 n.43, 262 n.2; compared with Evreinov, 244 n.31

Lansere, Evgenij E., 3, 110-111, 128, 136
Lapickij, Iosif M., 268 n.58
Legacy of Centuries, The (Zasodinskij), 54
"Laughter" (Bergson), 176
Lenin (Uljanov), Vladimir I., 191, 199-200, 214
Leoncavallo, Ruggero, 20
Lermontov, Mixail Ju., 214
Lifar', Sergej, 262 n.83
Light-mindedness, xvii, 10-11, 18, 31, 57, 140-43, 188-89, 214-15
Linder, Max, 167
Ljubaševskij, L.S., 188
Ljubimov, Jurij P., 214
Lope de Vega, 131. See also Ancient Theatre, The; *Fuente Ovejuna*
Louis XIV, 5
Loti, Cosme, 135
Loxvitskij, Mirra, 263 n.10
Lukin, F.M., 149, 152, 157
Lunačarskij, Anatolij V., 7, 21, 191-92, 203-4, 243 n.16, 270 n.1
Lunačarskij, Mixail, V., 21

Maeterlinck, Maurice, 245 n.40; *Sister Beatrice*, 122
Majakovskij, Vladimir V., 31, 33, 206, 214, 219 n.49
Majzel, Professor, 198
Makovskij, Sergej K., 5, 244 n.22; coins term "retrospective dreamers," 32
Manon (Massanet), 203
Marie Tudor (Hugo), 62
Marionetteness, 10
Markov, E.A., 168
Marquis de Sade, The, 4
Mass spectacles, 191-96, 201-2
Mefistofele (Boito), 71
Mejerxol'd, Vsevolod È. (Karl Theodor Kasimir Mejerxol'd), 7-8, 9-10, 127-28, 179, 182, 220, 244 n.31, 245 n.40; on the *balagan* and *commedia dell'arte*, 3, 10, 108, 242 n.6, 243 n.17, 245 n.37; *Doctor Dapertutto* and *The Journal of Doctor Dapertutto*, 2, 15, 241 n.4, 243 n.17, 255 n.36; and reconstructivism, 6, 122-25, 243 n.16, 260 n.47. See also Evreinov, Nikolaj Nikolaevič, relationship with V.È. Mejerxol'd; Strand, The
Mephistopheles, 18, 25, 171-72
Merežkovskij, Dmitrij S., 159
Merry Theatre for Grown-up Children, The, xix, 29, 46, 154-55, 213. Productions: *Beautiful Galatea* (Zuppe), 155; *Čereposlov* (Prutkov), 155, 158, 264 n.21-22; *Caesar*

and Cleopatra (Shaw), 155; *Diabolical Masquerade, The* (A.N. Tolstoj), 155; *Divertissement*, 155
Metafictional authors, 266 n.39
Metatheatre (Lionel Abel), 60; instances of, 60
Meyerbeer, Giacomo, 151-52; *Robert the Devil*, 151-52
Mgebrov, Aleksandr A., 17, 127, 131, 135
Miklaševskij, Konstantin M., 58, 110, 127-28, 130, 132-34, 137
Minor, The (Fonvizin), 146
Mišeev, N.I., 198
Moissy, Alexander, 9
Monodrama: and autoeroticism, 60; as form and approach, 9, 38, 39-40, 46-47, 77, 140-43, 148, 218; mass spectacle and Ancient Theatre productions as examples of, 197, 201-2; origins of, 250 n.2; philosophical monodrama, 217; theory of, 7-8, 11-12, 22-23, 35, 39-40, 45, 155, 187-88, 211-14. See also Evreinov, Nikolaj Nikolaevič, Plays and Performances; Gejer, Boris F.
Moody, Christopher, 129, 246 n.7, 247 n.20, 255 n.37, 258 n.14, 260 n.50, 260 n.57
Moscow Art Theatre, The, 136-37, 268 n.62; Evreinov's *The Fourth Wall* as parody of, 170-72; naturalistic-realistic production style of, 35, 125, 169, 267 n.47, 268 nn.57 and 60. See also Evreinov, Nikolaj Nikolaevič, Relationship with Stanislavskij; Nemirovič-Dančenko, Vladimir I.; Stanislavskij, Konstantin Sergeevič
Movšenson, Aleksandr G., 198
Munich Secession, The, 167, 267 n.50
Muratov, P., 121
Musaget, 7, 244 n.22
Museum of Old Petersburg, The, 5
Mystery of Freed Labor, The, 195

Nabokov (Sirin), Vladimir V., 266 n.39; *Look at the Harlequins!*, 266 n.41
Napoleon (Bonaparte), 24, 61
Narcissus, 46, 48, 50, 164, 215; Evreinov as, 18
Naturalism, 6, 8, 41, 124-26, 137. See also Moscow Art Theatre, The, naturalistic-realistic production style of
Nelidov, Anatolij, 8
Nelidov, V.A., 150
Nemirovič-Dančenko, Vladimir I., 7, 109, 267 n.47, 258 n.62
Neo-Raphaelism, 2
Nesterov, Mixail V., 59; Evreinov's monograph on and as influence on Evreinov, 27-30
Nevolin, B.S., 264 n.22
Nietzsche, Friedrich, 7, 20, 23, 59, 250 n.2
Nikolaj I, 168

Nikolaj II, 145, 168
Nilli, N., 74
Nin, Anaïs, 169
Notes from Underground (Dostoevskij), 61
Novalis, 70
Novrok, A.P., 3
Nuvel', Val'mer F., 3

Oedipus Rex (Sophocles), 37
"Old Friend," 116, 120-21
Ol'denburgskij, Prince, 151
Oval Portrait, The (Poe), 30-31
Ostrovskij, Aleksandr N.: *Diary of a Scoundrel*, 71; *Enough Stupidity in Every Wise Man*, 20; *The Forest*, 158; *The Storm*, 158

Pascal, Blaise, 179
Pearson, Anthony, 263 n.6, 264 n.19
Petr I (the Great), 5, 191
Petrov, D.K., 6, 128
Petrov, Nikolaj V., 73, 194, 196, 198, 256 n.45, 271 n.6
Philosopher's Stone, The, 14, 77, 207
Piotrovskij, Adrian I., 74, 194
Pirandello, Luigi, xix-xx, 34, 72, 74, 142; *Enrico IV*, 22, 60; comparison between Pirandellian and Evreinovian conventions, xvii, 22-23, 164
Plastique, 9-10, 11, 127, 130, 172, 248 n.27
Poggi, Tamara Baikova, 200-1
Polydrama, 157, 265 n.32
Portrait, The (Strug): See Gogol', Nikolai V.
Potapenko, Ignatij N., 147, 263 n.8
Princess Turandot (Gozzi), 163, 168
Potemkin, P., 262 n.2
Prometheus Bound (Aeschylus), 62
Prutkov, Koz'ma, 155, 158-59
Pugačev, Emiljan I., 193
Puni, Ivan, 378 n.6
Puškin, Aleksandr S., 214, 269 n.75; *Tales of Belkin*, 37

Queneau, Raymong, *Exercises de style*, 266 n.39
Quo Vadis? (Sinkiewicz/ Evreinov), 49, 69, 72, 145, 158, 255 n.37

Rabelais, François, 50-51
Radlov, Sergej, 194-95, 243 n.17
Rafalovič, S., 7, 158
Rajx, Zinajda N., 210
Ratov, S.M., 107
Raxmanova, S.A., 184, 251 n.17
Razin, Stepan (Sten'ka), 192
Razumnij, Mixail, 203, 205
Read, Mayne, 19

Realiora, 7, 181
Realism and Rational Positivism, 2, 27-29, 212-13
Reconstructing the spectator (Evreinovian methodology): and the creation of a present-tense theatrical event, 27, 109, 124, 138; developed at the Ancient Theatre, 13, 122-23
Reconstructivism (Theatrical), 5-6, 11. *See also* Ancient Theatre, The; Artistic reconstruction; Reconstructing the spectator
Reinhardt, Max, 9, 37, 129, 166-67, 195, 213
Remizov, Aleksej M., 6
Rennert, Hugo, 259 n.50
Repin, Il'ja E., 31, 33, 249 n.49
Rerix, Nikolaj K., 3, 110-11, 112, 128-29, 136, 257 n.2
Retrospective dreamer, 53, 209. *See also* Makovskij, Sergej
Retropsectivism (Cultural), 3, 5-6, 257 n.2
Ribot, Théodule Armand, 45, 54
Rigler-Voronkova, M.A., 110, 248 n.27
Rimskij-Korsakov, Nikolaj A., 22, 50, 206, 244 n.31
Ring and the Book, The (Browning), 37
Rjabušinskij, N.P., 6
Roi s'amuse, Le (Hugo), 62
Rolland, Romain, 193-94, 198
Rops, Felician, 43; Evreinov's monograph on and influence on Evreinov, 25-27, 258 n.9
Roščina-Insarova, E.N., 262 n.83
Ruslan and Ljudmilla (Puškin), 148
Russian Icons, 5

Sac, Il'ja A.:at the Ancient Theatre, 109-10, 112, 119, 128, 135; at the Crooked Mirror Theatre, 155-56, 178; Evreinov's article on, 247 n.18
St. Petersburg: as mythical setting, 5-6
Salome (The Tsar's Daughter, Wilde), 24, 179, 258 n.9; Salome as character, 43, 62, 68
Satirical journals, 145
Saketti, L.A., 109-10, 128-29
Sanin (Šenberg), Aleksandr A., 110-12, 118, 201
Sartre, Jean-Paul, 45-46
Satyricon, 145, 160, 262 n.2
Scales, The, 6
Scapegoat, The, 62-63
Ščerbakov, S.S., 178, 184-85
Schiller, Friedrich, 62; *The Maid of Orleans*, 37; *The Robbers*, 20
Scorpion, 7, 244 n.22
Ščuko, V.A., 110, 112, 128, 136
Sekiev, N., 151
Senigov, G.I., 20

Serapion Brothers, The, 2, 241 n.3
Serov, Valentin A., 19, 242 n.9, 268 n.62
Servadšidze, Prince A.K., 31, 128, 258 n.9
Shakespeare, William, 58, 62, 131; *As You Like It*, 71; *Julius Caesar*, 58n, 267 n.47; *Macbeth*, 180; *Othello*, 180; *Twelfth Night*, 66
Shtuk, F., 267 n.50
Siposkij, V.V., 6
Sišmarev, V.F., 110-11
Skalon, Nikolaj, 3
skaz, 273 n.12
Šklovskij, Viktor B., 269 n.75, 273 n.11
Šljapin, I.A., 6
Smirnov, Nikolaj G., 178, 184-85
Smyšljaev, Valentin S., 169
Snow Queen, The (Andersen), 147-48
Sobinov, Leonid Vitalievič, 20
Society of Russian Artists, The, 205
Sologub, Fedor (Fedor Kuzmič Teternikov), 6-7, 137, 213, 243 n.17; *Theatre of One Will*, 7-8
Solov'ev, Vladimir N., 6, 194, 243 n.17
Solov'ev, Vladimir S., 158
Somov, Konstantin A., 3-4
Sorin, Salevij A., 31-32, 249 n.49
Spencer, Herbert, 54
Stanislavskij (Alekseev), Konstantin Sergeevič, xvii, 7, 36, 58, 109, 220, 268 n.60; approach to acting 50; satirized by Evreinov, 45-47, 68-69, 163, 165-66, 168-69, 173; work with Gordon Craig, 9-10, 163. *See also* Evreinov, Nikolaj Nikolaevič, relationship with Stanislavskij; Moscow Art Theatre, The
Stark (Zigfrid), Edward A., 109, 138; eyewitness accounts of Ancient Theatre productions, 113, 116-17, 118-22, 129, 132-35
Storming of the Winter Palace, The (Evreinov), 191, 202-3, 251 n.7, 271 n.6, 272 n.13; and artistic reconstruction, 13, 196; Evreinov's reasons for staging, 200-2; performance of, 197-202; preparations for, 197-98; sources of information on, 271 n.11
Strand, The, 148, 263 n.11. Productions: *Honor and Revenge* (Sollogub), 148; *Last of Usher, The* (adapted from Poe), 148; *Monument* (Andreev), 159; *Petruška* (Potemkin), 148; *Prologue* (Averčenko), 148. *See also* Mejerxol'd, Vsevolod È.
Stray Dog, The, 263 n.6
Strindberg, August, 6
Studio of the Impressionists, The 32, 39
Stylization, 6
Subjectivism, 3-4. *See also* Evreinov, Nikolaj Nikolaevič, subjectivism of
Sudejkin, Sergei Ju., 75

Surrealism, 2
Suvorin, Aleksej S., 22
Symbolism, 26, 212-13; congregate action as goal of, 7, 108; French and Belgian, 4; myth-creation as goal of, 7; Russian, 4, 6, 53, 213, 244 n.22; the search for essences of, 2-3, 5-6. *See also* Evreinov, Nikolaj Nikolaevič, Influences on

Tairov, Aleksandr Ja., 149, 163, 206, 253 n.13
Teffi, Nedežda A. (N.A. Bučinskij), 148, 262 n.2, 263 n.10
Temkin, Dimitrij I., 197
Tertullian, 63
Theatrarch, 76, 247 n.13
Theatre: as event, xvii-xviii, 12-13, 22-23, 27, 125; as illusion, xvii-xviii; as shared mystery and communion, 13, 201
Theatre: A Book on the New Theatre, 7, 158
Theatre and Art, 22, 107
Theatre Guild, The: Production of *The Chief Thing*, 74, 255 n.38, 256 n.43
Theatre in life, The, 14, 29-30, 53-54, 211-12, 271 n.6; in Evreinov's dramaturgy, 49-50, 68, 72-73; and Evreinov's monodrama, 46; and Evreinov's work at the Ancient Theatre, 126, 139-43; in *The Storming of the Winter Palace*, 197, 201, 271 n.6
Theatre of Five Fingers, The, 19
Theatre of Quest, The, 8
Theatres of pre-revolutionary St. Petersburg (list of), 221-22
Theatre of Russian Drama, The (Paris), 262 n.83
Theatre of small forms, The, 145-47, 213
Theatre "Yen" (Paris), 262 n.83
Theatricality, 32-33, 124, 126, 187-88, 209; as essence of theatre, 58; Evreinov's contribution to theatre, 212-13, 253 n.13, 233 n.18; as pre-aesthetic instinct in Evreinov's work, 53-57; in relation to naturalness, 108; and the Spanish theatre of the golden age, 126; and *The Storming of the Winter Palace*, 196, 201
Tieck, Johann Ludwig, 70, 217
Tigler, N., 59
Tirso de Molina, 131
Tixonov, V.A., 147
Tjutčev, Fedor I., 245 n.37
Tolstoj, Count Aleksej K., 158, 206
Tolstoj, Count Lev Nikolaevič, 28; *The Power of Darkness*, 268 n.60
Transformation, 3-5, 43, 53; theatre as transformation and imaginative play, 18-20, 29-30, 40, 53-56, 58, 210, 217-18; transcendance through transformation, 48-49, 70; as school of acting, 65
Traxterev, I.S., 209

Tristan und Isolde (Wagner), 123
Trockij (Bronštejn), Lev D., 203, 205
Trubnikov, A.M., 113
Tynjanov, Jurij N., 180-82, 269 n.75

Ul'janov, Nikolaj P., 241 n.4
Unfortunate Betrayal, The (Potapenko), 147
Ungern, Rodol'f A., 264 n.20
Urvancov, Nikolaj N., 149-50, 184
Uslovnost', 8, 107-8, 148, 179, 196, 214

Varlix, Jugo, 197
Vaxtangov, Evgenij B., 163
Vejkone, M., 156
Vencel, N.M., 112
Verigina, Valentina P., 241 n.4
Verlaine, Paul, 4
Viv'en, Leonid S., 258
Vol'kenstein, Vladimir M., 180
Volkonskij, Mixail N. (Ančar Mancenilov), 264 n.15
Volkonskij, Prince Sergej M., 9-10, 127
Volkov, Nikolaj D., 9
Vološin, Maximilian A., 257 n.2, 270 n.1
Vrangel', N.N., 113
Vsevolodskij (Gemgross) Vsevolod N., 125
Vvedenskij, Arsenij, 20

Walpole, Horace, 66-67
Wandering Comedians, The, 205
Weininger, Otto, 70
Whirpool, The (Vladykin), 20
Wilde, Oscar, 1, 23-24, 29-30, 54, 241 n.2; comparisons to Evreinov, xvii, 56; *The Importance of Being Earnest,* 66; *Lady Windemere's Fan,* 241 n.2; *The Picture of Dorian Gray,* 30, 56; *Salome, see Salome (The Tsar's Daughter)*
Woe from Wit (Griboedov), 37, 71
Wolzogen, Ernst von, 3, 146, 267 n.50
World of Art (group), The, 3-5, 8-9, 53, 122, 136-37, 242 n.9, 241 n.31, 378 n.1; designers from, 5, 257 n.2
The World of Art (journal), 4, 242 n.10
Wundt, Wilhelm, 45; *Fantasy as the Basis of Art,* 59

Xlestakov, Ivan A., 11, 15, 166, 215; Evreinov as a Xlestakov, 18, 34, 162, 219, 266 n.41
Xodotov, Nokolaj, N., 185
Xolmskaja (Timofeeva), Zinajda V., 183-84, 264 nn.20 and 22; as actress at the Crooked Mirror Theatre, 149, 156, 264 n.23; and the founding of the Crooked Mirror Theatre, 146-50, 242 n.7; and productions at the Crooked Mirror Theatre, 153-54, 161-62

Yellow Book, The, 2, 23
Yom Kippur, 62

Žemčužnikov brothers (Aleksandr M., Aleksej M., Vladimir M.), 158
Zinov'evaja-Anibal, Lydija D., 243 n.16
Znosko-Borovskij, Evgenij A., 140, 164
Zolotnickij, David I., 65, 155, 161, 183
Zoščenko, Mixail M., 206

JUN

S

QI